Also by Esther Wojcicki

Moonshots in Education (coauthor)

How to Raise Successful People

SIMPLE LESSONS FOR RADICAL RESULTS

———

Esther Wojcicki

Esther Wojcicki (signature)

Houghton Mifflin Harcourt
Boston   New York

hmhco.com

Library of Congress Cataloging-in-Publication Data is available.
ISBN 9781328974860
ISBN 9780358120582 (international edition)

Book design by Chloe Foster

Printed in the United States of America
DOC 10 9 8 7 6 5 4 3 2
4500764743

To my husband, Stan, my three daughters, Susan, Janet, and Anne,
my ten grandchildren, and all other members of my family,
a wish for TRICK in their lives and in the world.

Contents

KINDNESS

How to Raise Successful People

Foreword

AS THE THREE "WOJ" offspring, we thought it was only fitting that her children do the foreword on what it was truly like to be raised the Woj Way. Woj, of course, is the affectionate nickname coined by our mother's students decades ago — it stuck — and her method focuses on trust, respect, independence, collaboration, and kindness (TRICK), the universal values she explores in the coming pages.

Life has brought all kinds of surprises, from our careers at Google, YouTube, 23andMe, and the UCSF Medical Center, to the challenges of parenting our own children, a total of nine among the three of us. As we have ridden the ups and downs that come with any life, we owe much of our ability to thrive to the way our parents raised us.

When our mother told us she was writing this book, we dug up stashes of our journals from grade school through college. Our mother, forever the journalist, thought it was a great idea for us to keep journals for every trip, especially when we moved to France in 1980. While there are many fun stories of fights and bad behavior, there are also some key themes: independence, financial responsibility, actionability, open-mindedness, fearlessness, and an appreciation for life.

One of our greatest joys today is the feeling of independence. Our parents taught us to believe in ourselves and our ability to make decisions. They trusted us and gave us responsibility at an early age. We had the freedom to walk to school on our own, bike around the neighborhood, and hang out with our friends. We gained confidence that our parents reinforced by being respectful of our opinions and ideas. We don't remember ever having our ideas or thoughts dismissed because we were children. At every age, our parents listened and acted like it was a two-way street for learning. We learned to advocate for ourselves, to listen, and to realize when we might be wrong.

In tenth grade, Anne had an eye-opening discussion at our temple about relationships between parents and children. The parent she was partnered with talked about how it was the child's job to listen. She explained that in our family we argued, but that our parents always listened to us; they never just said, "No, because I'm the parent." She later wrote in her journal how grateful she was to have parents who didn't rule because of authority. We rarely fought. We argued, but we didn't fight. As a result, we are extraordinarily grateful to them for the early independence we experienced.

Hand in hand with independence is financial freedom. Financial freedom does not mean being rich; it means being careful with money and planning for those items or aspects in life deemed essential. Our parents are fiercely disciplined with spending and saving. Both grew up as children of immigrants and reminded us often of how people waste money on unnecessary items and then suffer by not being able to afford what they need. The importance of this came as daily lessons. We would go out to dinner but never ordered drinks or appetizers. Before we went grocery shopping, we always cut our coupons and went through the newspaper ads. Once, our mother brought home the extra airplane food from her recent trip and served it to Anne as dinner — her childhood friends have never forgotten!

When we were in grade school, our mother showed us a compound interest chart, and we became determined to save at least a couple thousand dollars every year. We got credit cards and checkbooks before we could drive because our mom wanted to teach us the discipline of paying off our credit card monthly and balancing our checkbooks. We were also encouraged to start our own little businesses as kids. We sold so many lemons from our neighbor's abundant tree for years that the neighbors called us the "lemon girls." Susan had a business selling "spice ropes" (spices on a braid to hang in a kitchen) and made hundreds of dollars as a sixth-grader. It was her idea, but our mom bought the supplies and supported her going out to sell them. We sold hundreds of Girl Scout cookies door to door. And when we were really bored, we would package up our old toys and try to sell them to the neighbors, who actually bought them — sometimes.

As a family, travel and education were our top priorities, and everything else got minimal financial resources. (Note: Our father has been wearing the same pair of sandals for sixty years.) When we traveled, we stayed in the cheapest hotel, and always with a coupon. Spending money was all about making intentional choices. We were never wealthy, but our spending decisions allowed us the financial freedom to have the experiences we wanted in life.

Our mother is a master at never procrastinating or whining. If something can get done today, she's getting it done! She taught us all how to do the laundry, clean the house, vacuum, make phone calls, and exercise — all at the same time and in under an hour. We have never met anyone as efficient as our mother. She taught us how painless it is to just get something done versus procrastinating, how much better the weekend can be when homework is finished on Friday versus having it hang over your head all weekend and then finally doing it on Sunday.

While most of our mom's philosophy was about building skills, she would occasionally resort to bribery. One example Susan remembers years later is her bad habit of biting her nails. Our mom promised her a bunny if she stopped. After six weeks of Susan not biting (Mom said this was the period of time necessary to break a bad habit), Mom bought her a pet rat since the storekeeper convinced her that a rat was a better pet than a bunny. In fact, she bought three pet rats: Snowball, Midnight, and Twinkle.

Our mom is a people person. She truly enjoys being around all different types of people and gives off a very warm, approachable air because she is open-minded about learning new things at all times. She is a natural entrepreneur, constantly open to change and innovation. It was not a coincidence or "good luck" that she was successfully able to incorporate technology into her lesson plans and classrooms as Silicon Valley was burgeoning; she loves to innovate. She is constantly learning from her students, and this is, in part, why they trust and respect her — because she believes (and thrives herself) in their visions for change. Adults can be reluctant to change routines, making it difficult for them to engage with teenagers. But our mom — herself a "senior citizen"! — is completely the opposite, and that's why students flock to her. They know she will respect them and encourage their ideas, no matter how crazy. Sometimes it appears that she prefers the crazier ideas! We are often astounded that our mom, who is in her seventies is energized (yes, not tired!) after a late night (almost midnight) with teenagers working on the school newspaper.

One of her best traits in being a teacher and parent is trying to really understand the student as a person and working within the student's interests to be self-motivated rather than forcing them to do something. If one of us would come home and say we didn't like a subject, she would ask why. She would try to understand what was happening: Did we need the help of a tutor? Or did we have an issue with a teacher or other students? She would then try to come up with a solution that fit our needs and would help us solve the problem. Similarly, she worked to understand our passions over the years. She supported Anne's interest in ice-skating, Janet's focus in African studies, and Susan's efforts with art projects. She inspired us with books, interesting articles, talks, and classes. She always let her students pick the topics for their newspaper and argue their own points of view. When we talk about parenting, she reminds us that we can't force a child to do something: we need to motivate them to want to do it themselves.

We would also like to emphasize our mom's fearlessness, particularly in the pursuit of justice. She is the first person in the room to call out the emperor who is wearing no clothes. She is not afraid to state her mind, defend the underdog, or challenge the status quo. This is a natural fit in the context of journalism and freedom of the press. Janet remembers being in line at a store where the clerk was trying to sell us something below par, and of course we had to ask for the manager or invoke the threat of "reporting them to the California Bureau of Consumer Affairs." Our mother's mantra was always "If you don't speak up, speak out, or complain, then the exact same thing is going to happen to someone else." Another of Janet's memories: our mom challenging the pediatrician who wanted to prescribe antibiotics. "Does she really need them?" our mom would ask. "Can I look at her ear too?" Convention, authority, and power were not to be feared. On the flip side, it was not always fun to have a mother who would freely speak her mind to teachers, parents of friends, boyfriends, etc. After all these years of having her as a parent, it's impossible to think of a situation in which our mom would feel uncomfortable or be unwilling to state her honest opinion. She is not even shy about giving the secretary of education her candid appraisal of the education system. This type of approach to the world fosters an environment in which young people gain the strength and endurance to follow dreams and passions, without giving up or being intimidated. We believe that a large part of our drive and determination comes from an early modeling of our mother's unwillingness to give up or give in.

Lastly, and most memorably, our mother taught us to love life. She is silly. She makes jokes. She has few formalities and breaks stereotypes. She absolutely loves to have a good time. She first ran into our father (literally) when she was sliding down some stairs in a cardboard box in her dorm at Berkeley. She has gotten us kicked out of restaurants for her (not her kids') bad behavior! At the age of seventy-five, she discovered Forever 21 and decided it was the best clothing store ever for herself. Ten years ago she called Anne from NYC with a dozen of her high school journalism students in tow, saying, "Anne! We found a bargain on stretch limos, and we are riding around NYC with our heads out the sunroof! What club should we go to? We want to dance!" Our mother celebrates adventure and exploration. Her students love her because she balances her ability to execute and be serious with her openness and creativity. She is serious about teaching journalism but she has no problem with her students riding exercise bicycles during class while they listen. As we were writing this, we just saw our mother post pictures of herself dressed like a hot dog at Target. We may not wear Forever 21, but we certainly have learned how to have a positive attitude and find happiness every day because of her.

We three sisters are the original output of our mom's philosophy, but after us came many thousands of students in her journalism program. All around the world we meet people who stop us to say, "You know, your mom really changed my life. She believed in me." She doesn't just influence people while they are in her class. She influences them for life.

As proud daughters, we just want to say, Thank you, Mom, for raising us the Woj Way!

—Susan, Janet, and Anne Wojcicki

Introduction

THERE ARE NO NOBEL Prizes for parenting or education, but there should be. They are the two most important things we do in our society. How we raise and educate our children determines not only the people they become but the society we create.

Every parent has hopes and dreams for their children. They want them to be healthy, happy, successful. They also have universal fears: Will their child be safe? Will she find purpose and fulfillment? Will he make his way in a world that feels increasingly driven, competitive, and even at times hostile? I remember how all of those unspoken and largely unconscious worries crowded into the small birthing room as I held my first daughter.

I lay in the hospital bed cradling Susan on my chest. The nurse had wrapped her in a pink blanket and put a tiny yellow knit hat on her head. Stan, my husband, sat by my side. We were both exhausted but elated, and in that moment, everything was clear: I loved my daughter from the second I saw her, and I felt a primal desire to protect her, to give her the best life possible, to do whatever it took to help her succeed.

But soon the questions and doubts started to creep in. I couldn't figure out how to hold Susan, and I didn't know how to change a diaper. I'd stopped teaching only three weeks earlier, which didn't give me much time to prepare. And I never really understood exactly *how* I was supposed to prepare in the first place. The ob-gyn told me to take it easy for at least six weeks after the birth. My friends and colleagues gave me all kinds of conflicting advice. They told me labor was going to be long and hard, that nursing was too difficult and restrictive, that bottles and Similac were better. I read a few books on nutrition for adults (there weren't any titles specific to children at that time), and I bought a crib, some clothing, and a small plastic bathtub. And then suddenly Susan was there in my arms, with her big blue eyes and peach-fuzz hair, staring up at me as if I knew exactly what to do.

I was just on the verge of being discharged when I really started to worry. This was 1968. Back then you got three days in American hospitals after your baby was born. Now most hospitals discharge you after two days. I don't know how mothers today do it.

"Can I stay for another day?" I pleaded with the nurse, half embarrassed, half desperate. "I have no idea how to take care of my baby."

The next morning the nurse gave me a crash course in infant care, including, thankfully, how to change a diaper. This was the era of cloth diapers and safety pins. I was warned by the nurse to make sure that the pins were closed properly or they could stick the baby. Whenever Susan cried, the first thing I did was check the pins.

Even though it wasn't popular at the time, I was determined to breastfeed, so the nurse showed me how to position the baby's head and use my forearm for support. The baby had to "latch on" and only then could I be sure that she was getting milk. It was not as simple as I had hoped, and sometimes poor Susan got sprayed. The plan was that she should keep to a four-hour schedule and I agreed to follow that as best I could.

"Make sure you hug your baby" was the last piece of advice the nurse gave me. Then Stan and I were on our own.

Like all parents, I saw my daughter as hope — hope for a better life, hope for the future, hope that she might change the world for the better. We all want children who are happy, empowered, and passionate. We all want to raise kids who lead successful and meaningful lives. That's what I felt the moment Susan was born, and later on when we welcomed our other two daughters, Janet and Anne. It's this same wish that unites people from all different countries and cultures. Thanks to my long and somewhat unusual teaching career, I now attend conferences around the world. Whether I'm meeting with the secretary of education in Argentina, thought leaders from China, or concerned parents from India, what everyone wants to know is how to help our children live good lives — to be both happy and successful, to use their talents to make the world a better place.

No one seems to have a definitive answer. Parenting experts focus on important aspects of child-rearing like sleeping, eating, bonding, or discipline, but the advice they offer is mostly narrow and prescriptive. What we really need isn't just limited information about the care and feeding of children, as important as that may be. What we most need to know is how to give our kids the values and skills to succeed as adults. We also have to face the massive cultural shifts over the past few years — especially technological changes and how those changes impact our parenting. How will our children succeed in the age of robots and artificial intelligence? How will they thrive in the tech revolution? These anxieties are familiar to parents the world over. All of us are overwhelmed by the pace of change and the desire for our children to keep up. We know that our families and schools need to adapt to these changes, but we don't know how, and we don't know how we hold on to the values that are most important to us and to raising children who thrive.

As a young mother, I felt the same way — some of the challenges may have been different, but they were just as daunting. I took what little guidance and advice I could find, but for the most part I decided to trust myself. It may have been my training as an investigative journalist or my distrust of authority that had come from my childhood, but I was determined to find out the truth on my own. I had my own ideas about what kids needed, and I stuck to them, no matter what other people thought. The result was — to many people's eyes — idiosyncratic at best, or just plain odd. I spoke to my daughters as if they were adults from day one. Most mothers naturally turn to baby talk — a higher-pitched voice, simpler words. Not me. I trusted them and they trusted me. I never put them in danger but I also never stood in the way of them experiencing life or taking calculated risks. When we lived in Geneva, I sent Susan and Janet to the store next door to buy bread, on their own, when they were ages five and four. I respected their individuality from the beginning. My theory was that the most important years were zero to five and I was going to teach them as much as I could early on. What I wanted more than anything was to make them first into independent children and then into empowered, independent adults. I figured that if they could think on their own and make sound decisions, they could face any challenges that came their way. I had no idea at the time that research would validate the choices I had made. I was following my gut and my values, and what I saw worked in the classroom as a teacher.

It's rather strange to be a "famous" parent and to have your family profiled on the cover of magazines. I certainly don't claim all the credit for their successes as adults, but all three have turned out to be accomplished, caring, capable people. Susan is the CEO of YouTube, Janet is a professor of pediatrics at the University of California–San Francisco, and Anne is the co-founder and CEO of 23andMe. They rose to the top of ultracompetitive, male-dominated professions, and they did so by following their passions and thinking for themselves. Watching my daughters navigate the world with grit and integrity has been one of the greatest rewards of my life. I'm especially impressed by how they compete and cooperate, focusing not on being the only woman in the room, but on finding solutions to the problems we face.

Meanwhile, as a journalism teacher to high school students for more than thirty-six years, I have been doing something similar. Every semester, I have approximately sixty-five students, ranging from sophomores to seniors, and from day one I treat them like professional journalists. They work in groups and write on deadline. I provide support and guidance when students need it, but I've found that project-based, collaborative learning is the best way to prepare them for the challenges they'll face as journalists and as adults. I've watched thousands of students excel through my teaching methods, and Facebook helps me stay in touch with them — even my students from the 1980s. They have had amazing successes and become incredible people. I've had the privilege of teaching so many young people, including my first editor in chief of the student newspaper, Craig Vaughan, now a child psychologist with the Stanford Children's Hospital; Gady Epstein, the media editor at the *Economist*; Jeremy Lin, a Harvard graduate and point guard for the Atlanta

Hawks; Jennifer Linden, a professor of neuroscience at University College London; Marc Berman, a California State Assemblyman from the district that includes Palo Alto; and James Franco, the award-winning actor, writer, and director. I have had hundreds of students tell me that my belief in them and the values I taught them in my classroom made a profound difference in how they saw themselves and who they would become.

As my daughters rose to prominence in the tech and health sectors, and as my journalism program gained national and international recognition, people started to notice that I was doing something different. They saw how my parenting approach and educational method could offer solutions to the problems we face in the twenty-first century, and they wanted to know more. Parents constantly ask me for advice — okay, sometimes beg for the strategies I used with my daughters that they might apply to their own parenting. Teachers do the same, wondering how I escaped being a disciplinarian and instead found a way to guide students who are genuinely passionate about the work they're doing. Without really intending to, I found I'd started a debate about how we should be raising our kids and how to make education both relevant and useful. What I'm offering, and what has struck a chord with so many people across the world, is an antidote to our parenting and teaching problems, a way to fight against the anxiety, discipline problems, power struggles, peer pressure, and fear of technology that cloud our judgment and harm our children.

One of the biggest mistakes we make as parents is to assume personal responsibility for our children's emotions. As Dr. Janesta Noland, a respected pediatrician in Silicon Valley, argues, "Parents are so compelled to hold their child's happiness . . . they feel like they are responsible for it, and that they control it." We'll do anything to prevent our children from struggling or suffering, which means that they never have to deal with hardships or adversity. As a result, they lack independence and grit, and they're fearful of the world around them instead of empowered to innovate and create. Another big mistake: We teach them to focus almost exclusively on themselves and their own performance — because they must have a perfect grade point average, must be selected by a top-tier college, must find an impressive job. They are so busy focusing on themselves that they rarely have time to consider how they might help and serve others. Kindness and gratitude are often overlooked, even though these are the qualities that research shows will make us most happy in life.

There is also dysfunction in the classroom. Schools and universities are still teaching in the style of the twentieth century, essentially preparing students to follow instructions for a world that no longer exists. The lecture model, based on the assumption that the teacher knows everything and that the role of the student is to listen quietly, take notes, and take a test, is still dominant worldwide, despite the fact that technology now allows us to find information on our own — in an instant, with the library we all have in our pockets, the cell phone. Students learn *about* required subjects instead of learning *through* interest-based learning or experience. Curriculums are geared toward statewide exams and assessments rather than project-based learning that teaches real-world skills and allows students to find their passion. And tests and exams are the last things that promote passion and engagement, which research shows are the foundation of effective education and happiness in life. Above all, this outmoded system teaches us to obey — not to innovate or think independently. When it's time to graduate, we celebrate the end of learning! We should be celebrating the mastery of skills that will allow us all to continue to educate ourselves throughout life.

Is it any wonder, given how we're teaching and parenting, that kids end up depressed and anxious, completely unprepared to face the normal challenges of life? According to the National Institute of Mental Health, an estimated 31.9 percent of thirteen- to eighteen-year-olds in the United States suffer from anxiety disorders, and when researchers looked at mental health problems that occurred during 2016, they found that roughly two million teenagers experienced at least one major depressive episode. A 2016 study from Brazil reported that almost 40 percent of adolescent girls and more than 20 percent of adolescent boys suffered from common mental disorders such as anxiety and depression. In India, a study showed that one-third of high school students displayed clinical symptoms of anxiety. A survey conducted by the Norwegian Institute of Public Health found that among participants between the ages of fourteen and fifteen, more than 50 percent reported regularly feeling "sad or unhappy," and almost half reported feeling "restless." This epidemic is universal, and it should be a call to action for us all.[1]

There is a better way. We've made parenting into an incredibly complicated, unintuitive endeavor, filled with fear and self-doubt. We're stressed out because we've become slaves to our children's happiness. We're worried that they won't make it in this highly competitive world that we live in. We get upset when they don't get into a prestigious preschool, or when they don't yet know the alphabet but all the other kids their age seem to know it. We are the ones who are creating this frantic, overly competitive world for our kids. In truth, parenting is really quite simple — as long as we rediscover the basic principles that allow children to thrive in homes, in schools, and in life. Through my decades of experience as a mother, grandmother, and educator, I've identified five fundamental values that help us all become capable, successful people. To make it easy to remember in all walks of life, I call these values "TRICK":

TRUST, RESPECT, INDEPENDENCE,
COLLABORATION, AND KINDNESS

TRUST: We are in a crisis of trust the world over. Parents are afraid, and that makes our children afraid — to be who they are, to take risks, to stand up against injustice. Trust has to start with us. When we're confident in the choices we make as parents, we can then trust our children to take important and necessary steps toward empowerment and independence.

RESPECT: The most fundamental respect we can show our children is toward their autonomy and individuality. Every child has a gift, and is a gift to the world, and it's our responsibility as parents to nurture that gift, whatever it may be. This is the exact opposite of telling kids who to be, what profession to pursue, what their life should look like: it's supporting them as they identify and pursue their own goals.

INDEPENDENCE: Independence relies upon a strong foundation of trust and respect. Children who learn self-control and responsibility early in life are much better equipped to face the challenges of adulthood, and also have the skills to innovate and think creatively. Truly independent kids are capable of coping with adversity, setbacks, and boredom, all unavoidable aspects of life. They feel in control even when things around them are in chaos.

COLLABORATION: Collaboration means working together as a family, in a classroom, or at a workplace. For parents, it means encouraging children to contribute to discussions, decisions, and even discipline. In the twentieth century, when rule-following was one of the most important skills, parents were in total control. In the twenty-first century, dictating no longer works. We shouldn't be telling our children what to do, but asking for their ideas and working together to find solutions.

KINDNESS: It is strange but true that we tend to treat those who are closest to us without the kindness and consideration that we extend to strangers. Parents love their children, but they are so familiar with them, they often take basic kindness for granted. And they don't always model kindness as a behavior for the world as a whole. Real kindness involves gratitude and forgiveness, service toward others, and an awareness of the world outside yourself. It's important to show our kids that the most exciting and rewarding thing you can do is to make someone else's life better.

TRICK is essential to functional families, and it's also the solution to the challenges we face in education. The most effective classrooms are founded on trust and respect, encourage independent thought, and include project-based collaborative learning that mimics work in the real world. Educational leaders are finally starting to realize that rote memorization and lecturing are completely inappropriate for teaching the skills of the twenty-first century. I've spent over three decades perfecting my own "blended learning" model, a style of teaching that gives kids some control over their education and emphasizes the responsible use of technology. Teachers across the country are now emulating my methods, and I routinely travel throughout Europe, Asia, and Latin America, speaking to educational leaders and helping to implement new governmental policies based on the core values of TRICK.

Businesses, too, are recognizing the power of TRICK and starting to adopt these values in their company culture. TRICK is not just how we raise happy and successful children; it is also how we bring out the best in people at any age. Companies seek employees with grit, creativity, independent thinking skills, and the ability to collaborate and adapt to a constantly changing world. When the Educational Testing Service conducted an analysis of the Occupational Information Network, a large employment database maintained by the U.S. Department of Labor, they found that today's jobs require five key skills that stem from the TRICK values: problem-solving, fluid intelligence, teamwork, achievement/innovation, and communication. Flexible thinking, problem-solving, and innovation all arise from a strong sense of independence, which itself is built upon trust and respect. Teamwork and communication aren't possible without the kindness and collaborative spirit required to consider other people's opinions and ideas. This is why a global hotel chain is now using TRICK to train and empower their employees. This is why the founders of the Gap, the worldwide clothing retailer, recently met with my daughter Anne and me, hoping to learn how to create more successful business leaders like her. And this is why so many major companies — like the top global consulting firm Deloitte; Mercado

Libre, Latin America's most popular e-commerce platform; Panera Bread, the bakery and café chain; and even Walmart and McDonald's — are now embracing TRICK-like philosophies and encouraging independence, collaboration, and innovation among their workers.

When I spoke at the Conscious Capitalism conference in 2017 to a room packed with business leaders, the audience was so excited by TRICK that no one wanted to leave. I talked with CEOs such as John Mackey of Whole Foods and Daniel Bane of Trader Joe's, both of whom lead successful grocery chains known for employee empowerment. Amit Hooda, the CEO of Heavenly Organics, an environmentally friendly food manufacturer, Jeffrey Westphal of Vertex, the tax software provider, and many others told me they wanted to help spread my philosophy across the world. TRICK values permeated every discussion at this conference, because we need to empower the people we work with, and collaborate to make a real difference. The leaders I met with talked about training their employees for the twenty-first century through hands-on, project-based learning, just like what I've been doing in my classroom at Palo Alto High School.

The ultimate goal of TRICK is creating self-responsible people in a self-responsible world. This is what we're doing as parents, teachers, and employers — not just raising children or managing classrooms and boardrooms, but building the foundation of the future of humankind. We're evolving human consciousness, and we're doing it faster than ever before.

This book is about how to raise successful people. It doesn't offer yet another parenting fad or a precise recipe for putting your child to bed — it shows parents how to use a universal philosophy of human behavior to confront the problems we face today and prepare our children for the many unknown challenges that lie ahead. It doesn't offer a new curriculum for the classroom, but rather a new way to teach the curriculum, a new approach to teaching (in school and at home) that leads to empowerment and independence and always builds from a foundation of trust and respect. In the chapters that follow, I present the core principles that will help you to create a home (or classroom) that will allow you and your children to thrive.

What I did as a parent is no different than what parents have done throughout human history when they were forced to trust themselves, value their children's independence, and approach parenting as a community collaboration. The ultimate proof is that my methods have been scientifically validated to work across the world, and also by parents' own powerful, collective experience. They have been used in my classes for the past thirty-six years and with my own children starting fifty years ago. TRICK really does work for everyone, no matter the age, culture, or circumstances. And it's never too late to start. You can correct early parenting mistakes and missteps, improving both your life and the life of your child. Best of all, embracing TRICK will make you the kind of parent you want to be, and will help you raise the kind of child you want to be around — a child who also wants to be around you. The kind of child that others want, need, and value, and the kind of child who will confront the challenges we face as communities, as countries, and as a world.

It is a joy and a privilege to share stories and principles that arise from TRICK with you in the pages ahead. I hope they will guide you back to a deep trust in yourself and in your child, and be memorable so you can use them to guide yourself. You are the parent your child needs, and with your trust and respect, your child will become exactly the person they are meant to be.

1

The Childhood You Wish You'd Had

WE ALL TEND TO PARENT the way we were parented, but when I became a mother, the one thing I knew for sure was that I didn't want to repeat the mistakes of my parents. Every one of us has trauma and challenges from childhood that influence the way we relate to our children, and if we don't understand that trauma, if we don't carefully assess what went wrong, we're destined to repeat it. Failing to examine our unconscious patterns and programming undermines our best efforts to raise a family based on TRICK. As you'll see from my story, I wasn't raised with these fundamental values. I had to learn them the hard way. By sharing my experiences as a child and my parents' approach to parenting, I hope I'll inspire you to explore your own story, so you can understand the role model you witnessed and how it was or was not based on TRICK.

The story of the parent I became begins in a tenement building on New York's Lower East Side. I lived there in a small one-bedroom apartment with my parents, Russian Jewish immigrants who came to this country with nothing. My mother, Rebecca, was from Krasnoyarsk, Siberia, a place that seemed impossibly cold and remote to me as a young girl. She told me it snowed so much there that her entire house would be buried. They had to dig tunnels to get out. She was strikingly beautiful — people tell me that whenever they see her pictures — and she had an accent no one could place, some combination of Yiddish and Russian that I picked up but lost when I started school. My father, Philip, was an artist who specialized in watercolor and charcoal drawings, and was even awarded a scholarship at Rensselaer Polytechnic Institute. Sadly, he couldn't accept it because he had to support my mother and me. He and his family had fled the pogroms in the Chernivtsi region of the Ukraine, walking all the way to Vienna, where they could apply for papers to the United States. For years, I disbelieved the story of them walking so far. He used to tell me how they put all their possessions in a wooden cart and pulled it until their hands bled. It seemed an absurd exaggeration — until I read about the Syrian refugee crisis and how those people walked for hundreds of miles to escape the war. I still regret that I never thanked my father for what he did.

We were always on the verge of financial ruin. Beyond art, my father had few skills — we weren't exactly living the American Dream. So when he ran out of the odd jobs that kept us afloat, he heard the "Go west, young man" call of the day and decided to seek his fortune in California. It seemed like the land of sun, fun, and opportunity. It seemed like we could make a whole new life there. Unfortunately, it didn't turn out as he'd planned.

I still don't know why my parents picked Sunland-Tujunga, an agricultural community at the northeastern corner of the San Fernando Valley. The San Gabriels towered in the distance, and the streets were wide and made of dirt. A few years later, my brother and I started a business by freeing cars that got stuck in the sand. It happened often, and I was thrilled to earn a dollar each time. Grapevines were everywhere, as were gray stones that came tumbling from the foothills. We lived in a small house built of those same stones, and just behind us was the Tujunga Canyon Wash, a tributary of the Los Angeles River, where rattlesnakes hid between the giant boulders along the bank.

My father tried a variety of commercial art jobs in California, and even attempted to work in the entertainment industry, without success. Finally, he was forced to take a job as a gravestone cutter, one he kept for the rest of his life. You can still see hundreds of the gravestones he made in cemeteries all over Los Angeles — the only artistic legacy he ever had. The work was grueling and the pay low, and at night he would come home, slam the door, and proceed to stomp around the small house, saying nothing. It always scared me. I learned to stay away from him. If I didn't, I'd be caught in the middle of a firestorm. "Spare the rod, spoil the child" is something he said to me often, and he meant it. My mother did her best to protect me from his outbursts, and sometimes even bought me my favorite foods — green Jell-O and canned apricots — rare treats that became our little secret. At night I'd sit in my room and listen to them fight. Always, always about money.

The most difficult part of my life was dealing with the Orthodox tradition that deemed men the most important members of the family. And not only the family: men were the most important members of society. The whole community was focused on men. Kaddish, the prayer for the dead, can only be read by men; the Torah, our sacred books of the Bible, can only be held and read by men. Essentially, if you want to talk to God, you have to be a man. I guess that's why Orthodox men awake every morning and thank God they weren't born women.

I spent my Saturdays in a small synagogue where I sat upstairs with the women and children. It was always warm, yet the women wore long sleeves and hair coverings as the religion required — conservative, definitely not comfortable. I liked it there because I got to whisper to the other kids while the men prayed beneath us. They seemed to exist in a different world, one I knew I could never enter.

Women in the Orthodox Jewish tradition have one clearly defined role: mother of the family. That means women don't need an education. They only need to know how to take care of the children and their husband, and how to maintain a household. As I grew up, I realized that all the women around me were in subservient positions. My mother always had to listen to my father. The women at the synagogue dutifully obeyed their husbands. My grandfather on my father's side, Benjamin, who had been a rabbi, controlled the whole family. The goal for me was to marry a rich Jewish man when I was eighteen and have lots of children. The fact that I had different goals caused a rift in my relationship with my grandfather that lasted until his death.

The importance of men was dramatically illustrated to me when my brother Lee was born on May 23, 1945, three days before my fifth birthday. My parents brought him home on my birthday, and I could hardly contain my excitement when my father opened the door and led my mother inside. He was holding a basket, and inside was my new little brother. I thought of him as my own special gift. I ran forward, wanting to see him up close, but my father caught me by the shoulder and pushed me back. "Don't get too close to the baby," he scolded. "You could make him sick." I stopped in my tracks, more confused than hurt. My mother stood there, silent. Then my father told me something that still shocks me to this day. "Your brother Lee is a boy," he said plainly, "and in our family boys are more important." He delivered this news as if he had no understanding of how it might affect me. Even now, it's hard for me to imagine someone saying that to a young child. At first I didn't really understand what he meant — that now I would be second in line — but I knew it wouldn't be good. Prior to Lee's birth, I had been the darling of the family, the only child and the center of attention, even if that attention was sometimes negative. But I quickly learned how this would play out. Lee's needs were prioritized over mine. He got dozens of toys when I got none. He got new clothing instead of hand-me-downs from our cousins in New York. He could eat all he wanted at dinner, while I was reprimanded for taking too much food.

Looking back, I realize I wasn't bothered as much as you might expect. Part of what helped me cope was the constant love of my mother; she was patient, never critical, and she made me feel important despite what my father had said. I also genuinely liked Lee. He was a very cute baby and it was fun to play with him. He was like a life-sized doll for me, and I enjoyed helping my mother and feeling like a useful member of the family. As I got older, I was expected to do almost everything on my own because resources were limited and all the attention was focused on Lee. But even this was a blessing in disguise, because I became unintentionally empowered from so much independence. I learned how to do the laundry, wash the dishes, clean the house, cook meals for Lee, run errands, make the beds, and sweep the floors and carpets (we didn't have a vacuum). I grew up thinking I could do anything. Meanwhile, Lee grew up thinking he always needed help and support. He was pampered to the point of paralysis, an unintentional consequence of all that devotion.

My independence wasn't appreciated at school, however. There learning happened through force and strict obedience. I'd always been somewhat of a contrary student, and was sometimes even paddled by the principal. Corporal punishment is still lawful in public schools in nineteen U.S. states, and in all private schools except those in New Jersey and Iowa (people don't know this, but they should) — I was just one of many kids who suffered because of this inhumane policy. Often, the teachers didn't seem to have any idea what to do with me. When I was in second grade, my teacher threw me under her desk when she found me helping other students instead of staring into space once I'd finished my assignment. She got even angrier when I waved to my classmates from under the desk. I was given an "Unsatisfactory" in "Deportment," the only grade my father cared about. As you can probably guess, he wasn't happy with me.

The public library was my sanctuary. I loved to put on my roller skates, zoom over to the tiny Sunland-Tujunga library branch, and sit down with a tall stack of books. Reading helped me to think for myself, and it offered me glimpses into other worlds, those that were very different from my own. One summer I even won a prize for reading more books than any other student in the city. I also sold more Girl Scout cookies than any other girl in Sunland-Tujunga. I had no lessons, afterschool classes, or special performances, but the public school loaned me a violin and I dutifully practiced every night in my bedroom. Music was and still is a great passion for me. By fifth grade, I was good enough to be in the school orchestra, and I was fortunate to play all four years of high school. Even back then I seemed to understand that music makes it easier to be poor.

In 1948 my parents had another son, David, which put even more financial stress on the family. He was a beautiful baby, with bright blond hair and translucent blue eyes. I remember him being very curious, and that he cried a lot. My mother was overwhelmed by taking care of three children and couldn't always meet David's needs. I did my best to help her. I played with him, and carried him around the house and backyard. I showed him my favorite pepper tree near the creek and told him in a few years I'd teach him how to climb it.

One day, when David was sixteen months old, he was playing on the kitchen floor and came across a bottle of aspirin. He thought it was a toy and started shaking it. Out came dozens of pills (back then Bayer did not have safety caps), and he swallowed all of them before my mother realized what had happened. She called the doctor's office and was told by the nurse to put David to bed and check on him in a few hours (we had only one car, which was with my dad at work). I suspect this nurse didn't offer a better answer because we couldn't pay full rate at the clinic. My mother did just as she was told. A few hours later David woke up vomiting.

We then took him to the county hospital, where they pumped his stomach and released him. He got worse. We took him back. They told us there were "no beds available" (code for "no proof of payment"). So we took him to Huntington Memorial, where they also claimed they had no beds, and then to another hospital, St. Luke's, at which point he was in such bad shape that the doctors agreed to treat him. But it was too late: David died there that night. When I think of my childhood, the most powerful emotion I have is the pain of this loss, how it covered our house like a black cloud, how my parents never really recovered, especially my mother. David's death affected me like no other event in my childhood. Except one.

A few months after David's death, my brother, Lee, who was five at the time, fainted and collapsed on the living room floor. My mother picked him up and shook him, but he didn't wake up. Within minutes, I started to feel faint too. At that point my mother was smart enough to run out of the house, but she told me to stay put. "Lie down on the bed and I'll come and get you," she said, rushing Lee outside. I was woozy and disoriented, but I refused to listen to her. Already my skepticism was taking over. I held on to the walls for support, and once I was out of the house I lay down on the gravel in our front yard and started to come to. I saw my mother sitting with Lee on the concrete strip of our driveway. He had also woken up. But we still had no idea what was happening. My mother called a neighbor, and after a few more hours it was determined that our faulty wall heater had filled the building with carbon monoxide. Lee was the smallest and most vulnerable, so he fainted first. I would have been next, and had I stayed there on the bed like I'd been told, I wouldn't have survived.

That incident, together with the tragedy of David's death, set me on a course that deeply influenced the rest of my life. It solidified my decision to think for myself no matter what. I would always ask what was sensible, even if it sounded wrong, even if I had to challenge my parents or my teachers. I felt I needed to do it. If I didn't, I could be injured or even killed — that's how serious it was to me. I didn't blame my mother for being obedient. It wasn't her fault that David died, or that she didn't think to get us all out of the house in a moment of clear danger. Yet in a way it was her fault, or at least that's how I saw it as a child. She was a victim of poverty, and she was an immigrant with little education. She'd never been taught how to think things through, and she blindly trusted authority because of the tradition she was brought up in, just like many people at that time. But listening and obeying and not thinking critically led to the greatest loss a parent can endure. I decided I wanted to live a different kind of life. I wanted a life where girls and boys were treated equally. I wanted a life in which I could make smart decisions and didn't always have to worry about money. I wanted out of the world I'd been born into, and I resolved to do it by thinking for myself.

I did get out, eight years later. I won a full scholarship to UC Berkeley — I wouldn't have been able to afford college otherwise, as my father had cut me off financially. I was supposed to get married to a wealthy Jewish man, not go to school. In August of 1959 I got on a Greyhound bus to Berkeley with my two suitcases and never looked back. During my sophomore year, I met my future husband, Stan, an experimental physicist. I was sliding down a flight of stairs in a giant cardboard box — just another Monday night in the Sherman Hall co-op — and happened to land on his feet. We fell in love. I realized he also had a certain skepticism toward the world. He grew up in Krakow during World War II, right next to the train tracks that transported Jews to Auschwitz. The Nazis occupied part of his family's apartment, forcing them into two small rooms. He and his brother and mother survived only because they were Catholic. His father worked in the Polish government in exile in London. After the war, Stan escaped to Sweden, along with his mother and brother, by hiding under the coal storage bins of a cargo ship. In a tragic turn of events, his father was told there was not enough room on the ship and to come on the next one. There was no next one. He was arrested on the dock by the newly established Communist authorities. He was kept as a political prisoner until 1955 when Stalin died. Not surprisingly, Stan had a strong distrust of authority and government, and he was also deeply skeptical of historical documents, something I hadn't even considered. He knew from experience how governments change history to reflect the views of the winners. It makes sense that he dedicated his life to studying neutrinos, the smallest of the elementary particles, and challenging Einstein's theories. He was seeking the origins of the universe, trying, somehow, to make sense of the world.

After we got married, Stan received a National Science Foundation Fellowship and we spent a few years living in Geneva and Paris. I first enrolled at the University of Geneva in the School of International Relations and then at the Sorbonne in Paris. I loved living in Geneva and Paris and loved learning and speaking French. Then we moved back to Berkeley, and a year later to Palo Alto when Stan was offered an assistant professorship in physics at Stanford. We didn't expect to stay long because it was a non-tenured job, but in 1967 he was offered a tenure track position. We were thrilled. In 1968, we became parents. Neither of us really knew what we were in for. It was incredible to become a mother, of course, but it was so much harder than I thought. Stan focused on being the provider and giving the family stability and structure. His work as a Stanford professor was extremely demanding. He was always under pressure to "publish or perish," and he worked constantly. He also traveled all over the world for academic conferences and presentations. His passion was high-energy particle physics, which meant visiting research laboratories in Brookhaven, New York, the Fermi Lab in Chicago, and CERN (European Organization for Nuclear Research) in Geneva. We still have a world map on the wall in our family room that has a pushpin for every place Stan has visited. There are hundreds of pushpins. When he was home, he was a good father — but he was rarely home. Though I was frustrated, and sometimes I wished I had more support, I learned to accept it.

It was up to me to raise our three daughters. I got a lot of medical help from my doctors at Kaiser in Redwood City, California, but they didn't offer parenting advice. The advice from my friends didn't really meet my needs. None of the books I read made any sense until I found Dr. Spock, the parenting guru of the 1960s, and his iconic book, *Dr. Spock's Baby and Child Care*. His message resonated with me from the start. He told me and thousands of other new mothers: "You know more than you think you do . . . You want to be the best parent you can be, but it is not always clear what is best. Everywhere you turn there are experts telling you what to do. The problem is, they don't often agree with each other. The world is different from how it was twenty years ago, and the old answers may not work anymore." I read that passage and felt as if he was speaking directly to me. The old answers didn't work for me. The religion and culture I grew up in didn't value me as a human being. Experts and authority figures didn't have my best interests at heart. I was the only one who knew what was right for my daughters, what was right for me.

Many mothers read Dr. Spock, but few of them raised their children the way I raised mine. I found my own path, mainly by rebelling against my own childhood. I was scared of falling into patterns from the past. I knew that if I wasn't careful, I could expose my daughters to the behaviors and values that caused me so much suffering as a child. I did want to recreate the strong emotional and physical attachment to my children that I had with my mother, but that's where the similarities ended. Somehow I realized that if I wanted to do things differently, I would have to consciously address my own childhood. I didn't read about it. Dr. Spock didn't teach me that, nor did anyone else. It just seemed to make sense. In order to change, I couldn't be on autopilot, parenting the way I'd been shown. I would need to be reflective instead of reactive. I would need a lot of patience, and a lot of resolve.

It turns out that my intuitive understanding is explained by the field of attachment research. Attachment was first described by John Bowlby, a British scientist whose research from the 1950s forged a new understanding of human relationships. Bowlby's theory of attachment suggests that the way we interacted with our parents when we were young will help determine our interpersonal relationships as adults, dramatically influencing the way we relate to other people, and most importantly to our partner and our own children.

In the 1970s, L. Alan Sroufe, a psychologist and researcher at the University of Minnesota, began collecting data for the Minnesota Longitudinal Study of Parents and Children. Sroufe was inspired by Bowlby's work and wanted to know if early attachment patterns could predict behavior in adult life. The results of this ongoing study suggest that early attachment does indeed influence our behavior as adults, especially in the categories of self-reliance, emotional regulation, and social competence. Sroufe and colleagues found that "attachment experiences provide certain core attitudinal, motivational, and emotional components that are a platform for entering the world of peers and coping with the challenges that arise."[2] In other words, your early experiences with attachment give you a sort of compass for navigating your life. Take self-reliance, for instance. Sroufe's study showed that nursery school children with anxious and avoidant attachment patterns were more dependent on their teachers. Another analysis of the same longitudinal study found that securely attached children were rated more sociable by their grade school teachers, had more friends at age sixteen, and were better able to resolve conflicts in their romantic relationships as adults.[3]

These findings affirm what we all know is true: Childhood experiences deeply affect us as adults. But here's where it gets really interesting. Another psychological researcher, Mary Main, wondered whether these patterns could change over the course of our lives, and if so, how. In order to find out, she and her colleagues developed a questionnaire called the "Adult Attachment Interview." During this research interview, an adult subject would discuss his or her childhood experiences with a researcher, answering questions like "Which parent did you feel closer to and why?" "When you were upset as a child, what did you do, and what would happen?" and "How do you think your overall early experiences have affected your adult personality?" The results of these surveys were groundbreaking. Main found that adults are actually able to change and revise their attachment patterns throughout life. We can move from insecure to secure attachment. But how? Positive relationships with people other than our parents (which introduce us to other forms of attachment) were found to be helpful, but equally important was conscious reflection on one's childhood. Main's analysis showed that those participants who had coherent narratives about what had happened to them as children, who spoke thoughtfully about their parents and what they themselves struggled with, were associated with secure attachment — regardless of whether they'd experienced difficulty, trauma, or loss as children. Those subjects whose narratives were less coherent, dismissive, or contradictory were associated with anxious or insecure attachment that had persisted into adulthood.

I think all of us know this instinctively. We tend to parent the same way we were parented, primarily because this is the one model we have. The family values we learn as children can influence us so deeply that we may not always be able to feel or understand the extent of that influence. We often find ourselves saying things or doing things that our parents did and wondering how our parents got into our head or under our skin. In some families there are cycles of violence and intergenerational abuse, with people seemingly trapped within the same dysfunctional patterns for generations. One study found that one third of abused children went on to be neglectful or abusive parents themselves.

The first thing every parent should do, then, is reflect on their experiences. It sounds simple, but we often fail to do it. As the psychiatrist and UCLA researcher Daniel J. Siegel writes in *Mindsight*, "The best predictor of a child's security of attachment is not what happened to his parents as children, but rather how his parents made sense of those childhood experiences." Siegel, Main, and others have discussed how this experience of making sense of your life results in "earned secure attachment." We all have the ability to "earn" security through conscious self-reflection, which we can then pass on to our children.

I wish I would have known all this earlier. I wish someone would have told me *how* to reflect, what questions to ask, what answers I should be looking for. Somehow I figured it out on my own. For one thing, I had the laboratory of experience. Whatever I was doing was working: my girls were happy, thriving, capable. But there were so many challenges I couldn't have predicted.

What I realized, through a lot of conscious effort, is that parenting gives us perhaps the most profound opportunity to grow as human beings. As Dr. Siegel cautions in *Parenting from the Inside Out*:

"When parents don't take responsibility for their own unfinished business, they miss an opportunity not only to become better parents but also to continue their own development." In other words, if you don't act as your own therapist, and interrogate your own childhood, you won't be the best parent you can be. A parental perspective allows you to understand the challenges your parents faced that you might not have recognized as a child. A child's perspective is myopic, and it's impossible for us as children to understand all the factors that influence our parents' behavior.

Our childhood memories can also be distorted. As an adult I went back to that stone house in Sunland. In my memory it was a big house with a backyard that stretched all the way to the foothills. But when I saw it again, I was shocked by how small it was. I couldn't believe that all five of us lived there. The backyard was a narrow lot that stretched only to the next row of small one-story houses. The tragic events that happened there were so profoundly important to my life and my understanding of myself that I'd made a massive house in my mind, when in reality there stood only a modest stone home for a family of modest means. Seeing the house helped me to recognize how much my parents must have struggled. I saw my father as partly a victim of his circumstances, like so many other imperfect parents. He had a life of physical labor combined with anger at a world that never supported him. He gave up his dreams of being an artist for us. He came from a culture that shaped his authoritarian behavior. Understanding all of this allowed me to forgive him. I had succeeded in spite of the ideas he had for my life, and deep down I knew forgiving him would allow me to move on.

Parenting is how culture gets transmitted to the next generation.

It's your chance to pass on your core principles and values, and to use all of your wisdom and insight in order to improve someone else's life. It's also your chance to affect eternity. I'm reminded of one of my favorite quotes about the art of teaching: "Teachers affect eternity; they can never tell where their influence stops." The same is true for parenting. You never know how your parenting will impact future generations.

I think the most important question we need to ask ourselves is whether the principles and values we're handing down to our children are ethical, and whether they're beliefs we want to perpetuate in society. We are all part of a community, part of a country, part of the earth. Are you teaching your children the things you want to see them teach their own children? Will this improve their lives, the culture, the world?

Even after I left the Orthodox tradition, I still experienced gender discrimination — as a reporter, I couldn't get into the San Francisco Press Club because they only accepted men. I couldn't get a credit card in my name in the 1970s. It was easy for me to want a different path for my daughters, a path where they could be who they wanted to be, a path where they were not subservient to their husbands, where they had a voice and a passion in life. I wanted my daughters to have some control early on, and I was determined to develop their decision-making skills. I was always asking, "Do you want grapes or an apple?" "Do you want to do an art project or play outside?" I helped them become skillful decision-makers from a very young age, and now, some forty years later, I'm in awe as I watch them make some of the most complicated and important decisions in health-care and media. So how does this relate to you, the reader? The primary goal of this book is helping you understand, think about, and implement effective parenting strategies that will positively affect you, your children, your family, our society, and future generations.

I knew it wasn't going to be easy to get there — family culture can be hard to change or revise — but I wanted to try. One empowered, purpose-driven child positively affects you, your family, your community, and the whole world. It's a powerful ripple effect, and it starts in the home.

TRICK QUESTIONNAIRE

I may have figured out a lot on my own, but I'm the first to admit that parenting would have been much easier with some guidance. So that's what I'd like to offer you here — guidance. Below you'll find a set of questions to help you think about your own experiences and how they align with the values that lead to lifelong success. You'll also look at your partner's values, and the values held by your community, both of which deeply influence the way you parent. This kind of reflection can help you at any stage of parenting, whether you're expecting your first child, confronting problems with a rebellious teenager, or working to repair a relationship with an adult child. It can also help if you are a teacher, grandparent, or other caregiver responsible for the well-being of children. We all need Trust, Respect, Independence, Collaboration, and Kindness, and we all need to be conscious of these important values in order to practice them.

Please use these questions as you make your way through the coming chapters. My hope is that in answering them, you'll discover which aspects of your childhood to keep, and which to leave behind. You may wish to reflect on these, write them down in a journal, or discuss them with your partner or a trusted friend.

1. YOUR FAMILY. How were the TRICK values either encouraged or discouraged in your family? What could be improved or revised?

    TRUST — Was your home a trusting environment? Did you trust your parents as a child? Did they trust you? How was trust shown or demonstrated in your family? Was there ever a breach of trust? If so, how was it resolved? How could you improve upon what you learned about trust as a child? What kind of a trusting environment do you want to create for your child? What are some little things you can do to help develop trust with your children? Make a list.

    RESPECT — Did you feel respected as a child? Were your ideas and opinions taken into consideration? Did you feel like an important member of the family? Did you ever feel disrespected? If so, were you able to regain respect? How? How could you improve upon what you learned about respect as a child? What are some small things you can do to help show your children you respect them? It can be as simple as letting them wear whatever they want to a special occasion or letting them help create the menu for a dinner party. Make a list for yourself.

    INDEPENDENCE — Did you feel a strong sense of independence as a child, or were you dependent on your parents for daily activities like meals, cleaning, and homework? What steps did your parents take to encourage your independence? How could you improve upon what you learned about independence as a child? What can you do to help promote your child's independence?

    COLLABORATION — Was there a collaborative environment in your household? How did your parents encourage collaboration? Did you feel as if your family functioned as a team, or that there was usually one person in control? How could you improve upon what you learned about collaboration as a child? What are some small things you can do to encourage collaboration? What about having your children work on a communal project of their choice?

KINDNESS — How was kindness shown in your household? Were you taught to appreciate and be grateful for what you had? Were you raised with a sense of service toward others in your community? How could you improve upon what you learned about kindness as a child?

2. YOUR CULTURE

Your community, culture, and religion also have a deep impact on the way you raise your child.

What are the assumptions about child-rearing in your community and religion (if applicable)?

What do you agree with? What don't you agree with?

Which practices are evolving or in need of challenging? For example, so-called snowplow parenting means you eliminate all obstacles for your child, never exposing them to any kind of risk. How could you introduce experiences that teach kids independence and grit? What about your culture might be holding them back?

Which beliefs and practices align with the TRICK values? Which ones don't?

3. YOUR PARTNER'S FAMILY AND CULTURE

If you're parenting with a partner, you should answer these questions together to determine how you will function as a parenting team. I suggest you have a discussion (not an argument) about the pros and cons of different approaches to parenting — and you should do this earlier rather than later. What are the best aspects of how you were raised? What ideas and practices from your partner might help your child succeed? Can you come up with a philosophy that combines the strengths of each approach? Stan and I had no idea what kind of parents we would become. It turns out that we had very different parenting styles, which isn't surprising given that he grew up in a very different culture, with his father in exile in London. He and his mother and brother were in the countryside in Poland, hoping to avoid the bombing. So when we started to parent, Stan had somewhat strict Polish ideas of how to make our daughters behave. Spanking was considered okay in Polish culture. But I, having experienced hitting as a child, did not think it was acceptable or helpful. I know it is hard to resist hitting or spanking, because even with my positive attitude, I sometimes had problems resisting the urge. But I wanted to have an emotional connection with the kids. I wanted to treat them kindly. (I won the debate partly because Stan was away so often — victory by default.) Differences in parenting styles is one of the main contributors to relationship stress and can even result in divorce. Seek to understand one another's values and their grounding in each other's childhood and culture. TRICK is not a culturally specific approach to parenting. These are universal values that exist in all cultures and increasingly are being seen as the basis for health, happiness, and success in the world of today — and tomorrow.

A FINAL WORD: ACCEPT YOURSELF — NO ONE CAN BE PERFECT

Parents are human: despite all your thinking and planning, you *will* make mistakes. I made tons of them. I punished the wrong child for something the other one did, or I got mad for no reason, or I used the wrong shampoo and it got in their eyes. On a cross-country campervan trip from Palo Alto to Chicago, Anne had what looked like bites all over her legs and body and I kept spraying her with Off, thinking she'd been bit by mosquitoes. I did this for days before I realized she had chicken pox!

We moved our family to Geneva, Switzerland, when my daughter Anne was an infant and Janet was only three. Janet had a really hard time adjusting to her new sister — she used to ask me if we were going to take Anne back to the hospital. "I am done playing with her, Mommy," she would tell me. She was also confronted with a new culture (Swiss) and a new language (French). What she needed most at that time was security, and yet her world had changed in an instant. I underestimated how much of a challenge this would be for her, and for all of us. Yet, like all families, we made the best choice we could at the time, and who's to say this experience didn't help her build grit and independence?

My grown daughters still joke about what Stan and I did wrong as parents. Anne should have had more tennis lessons, Susan should have had more art classes, and Janet should have had more piano lessons. They always tell me we should have gotten them another dog. (Okay, these are the jokes of happy, successful adults. I made more serious mistakes too, believe me.)

Our goal is not to create a stress-free and hardship-free environment for our children. The painful and difficult experiences are often how we grow. Our goal is not to take these challenges and the growth that results from them away from our children — the fatal flaw of helicopter parenting — but to help our children face these challenges and learn from them. We don't need to be perfect, but we do need to make sure our children can use the TRICK values to persist even in the face of difficulty.

There is no perfect parent, spouse, or child. We all try our best. What you want to do is use the TRICK values consistently and not give up. Don't beat yourself up when you make mistakes. The first person you need to forgive is yourself. Life can be complicated and difficult. If you do something counterproductive as a parent, recognize it and try to avoid it in the future. You may make the same mistake again. And again. It takes time to learn as parents as much as it takes time for our children to learn. Focus on creating intimate relationships with your children, and raising them with the values of TRICK so that you'll be proud of the people they become. We all want to raise good humans.

We each have a story. We all have experienced trauma and in many cases tragedy. I resolved to do the best I could to not recreate my childhood, but I also understood that my children would face difficulties no matter what I did. It wasn't my job to be perfect or make their lives perfect, but to do my own reflection and spare them any unnecessary suffering. As we explore the values in this book, I encourage you to keep questioning and examining your own experiences. Think about what could be improved, and how. And then be willing to change: for yourself, your children, and the world.

TRUST

2

Trust Yourself, Trust Your Child

BEING A PARENT IS HARD. Being a grandparent is no joke either.

It was early morning in San Francisco, and the traffic was fierce. I was on grandparenting duty for the week while my daughter Janet was working on children's nutrition in Rwanda and Kenya. My first task was to drive my grandkids to school, which sounds simple enough, except for the Bay Area traffic. And the fact that they went to schools on opposite sides of the city. And the fact that I'd no sooner dropped off one child before I found out that I had to drive back to my grandson's school to deliver homework he'd accidentally left in his room.

By ten a.m., I was done with driving, but then it was time to walk the dog, administer antibiotics to the two family cats, who'd come down with some kind of infection right before Janet left, and then clean up from breakfast. I wondered again how Janet managed to juggle this on a daily basis. The traffic alone was enough to unravel me. This is why most people in the Bay Area meditate — we would all be facing road rage charges without it.

My kids used to walk to school by themselves, but times have changed.

The next day, Saturday, was more chaos, but of a different kind. I was helping my daughter Susan in addition to taking care of Janet's kids. Susan asked me to take her daughters to Target for school supplies. Janet's son needed a haircut.

It was about time. He looked like a shaggy dog.

The traffic was a little better in suburban Los Altos, but with all the errands in front of us, I decided that this particular Saturday would be a great opportunity to transform a day of chauffeuring into a day of learning.

Why not show the kids I trusted them? Less driving. More trust. More fun for the kids. It would be a win-win.

I brought my grandson (age twelve) to the hair salon and let him handle the appointment on his own. He knew exactly what kind of haircut he wanted, and he'd been going to the same salon on and off for a year. Then I drove my other two granddaughters (both age eight) to Target. On the way, we went over the list of school supplies they needed, which they saved on their phones. The plan was for them to meet by the registers in an hour and contact me. I would come in and pay with my credit card, but it was up to them to make sure they gathered everything on the list. If they needed me, they could call. But I was sure my granddaughters would be fine. I'd been shopping with them dozens of times. I'd taught them how to conduct themselves in stores, use a shopping cart, stay together, and find what they needed. I'd taught my own daughters the same skills. They'd learned how to shop early on at Patterson's Dime Store on California Avenue, about a mile from our house in Palo Alto. They'd bike there on their own and agonize — for hours — over which tiny toy or piece of candy to buy with their allowance. They had to make sure their purchases were under a dollar, which involved careful math and difficult decisions. They would come home so proud of themselves, beaming and carrying their little paper bags filled with goodies. Maybe I'm just a teacher at heart, but I always saw shopping as an opportunity to empower kids, and also to have some fun. Why not help them learn the skills for life as early as possible? And why get stressed about the errands you have to run when you can make each trip into a little adventure?

I watched my granddaughters pass through Target's sliding-glass doors, feeling as proud as I did of my own daughters years ago. I drove back to the hair salon. My grandson was waiting for me, as planned, with his long hair transformed from an unkempt mess into a short cut that made him look like a dashing young man. Back on the road, we listened to Beyoncé on the radio, and in the back of my mind, I was thinking about what we were all going to have for dinner. We'd just about reached Target when my cell phone rang.

It was Susan. I told her about my grandson's fancy new haircut, and she asked where the girls were.

"They're shopping at Target," I said.

"You left them alone? How could you have done that?"

I was surprised by her alarm. She was talking about Target as if it were a dangerous place where kids should never be left unsupervised.

"It's Target," I said. "It's a well-run store."

"But, Mom —"

"And the girls know how to shop by themselves. They're going to text me when they're done."

Susan was polite — *controlled* might be a better word — but she was mad. I pulled into the parking lot and saw my granddaughters waiting inside. Turning off the engine, I told Susan that they were fine.

"You shouldn't have left them there," she said. "It isn't safe."

"Well," I said, walking toward the entrance with my grandson, "they seem pretty safe to me."

In the end, it all worked out. Susan was stressed for a few minutes — really stressed — but I called her while we were at the checkout to confirm that the kids were safe and had done a great job selecting their school supplies. My granddaughters loved it, by the way. They'd had a lot of fun shopping on their own and felt empowered. Susan had a bit of a breakthrough too: Kids were more capable than she realized.

I'm not suggesting that everyone immediately drop their children off unsupervised at stores around the world — but the question of where our children are safe, and where they aren't, is an important one. As is just how much we can trust them to handle on their own. Those back-to-school shopping lists (the source of stress to parents everywhere) are a great place to start.

THE CRISIS OF TRUST

All parents need to understand this: The digital age and the ease of transmitting information has resulted in a crisis of trust, and it's affecting the way we live and the way we parent. We don't trust ourselves and our own instincts, we have a hard time trusting our partners and our children, and many of us live in fear of our neighbors and fellow citizens. But living without trust is miserable. It makes us dysfunctional. We become so fearful and anxious — and what do we do? We pass this fear and anxiety on to our children. They grow up nervous and afraid, just like us, and we wonder why more and more kids are incapable of transitioning to adult life. If you think this is an issue that only affects families, you're wrong. The global erosion of trust is bad for mental health, relationships, business, and foreign relations, and it's especially bad for democracy.

Distrust has seeped into every sphere of our lives. The 2018 Edelman "Trust Barometer," a measure of the general public's average trust in institutions, found that the United States dropped nine points in the Global Trust Scale, the steepest decline in trust ever measured in this country. Italy dropped by five points, and Ireland, South Africa, Japan, and Russia were ranked last in terms of public trust. The same thing is happening in our neighborhoods. A recent Pew Research report found that just 52 percent of Americans agree that they trust all or most of their neighbors. Even more disturbing, only 19 percent of millennials agree that most people can be trusted — a lower percentage than all other segments of the population.

Here in Palo Alto — arguably one of America's safer communities — I rarely see kids playing in the street or walking to school. Back when my daughters were young, there were kids everywhere. We had a street sign that read SLOW — CHILDREN AT PLAY to alert drivers. Those signs are gone now. Kids stay in their backyards or, more often, inside in front of their phones. When it comes to children, we don't trust our neighbors, and we definitely don't trust daycare centers. That's why parenting blogs are filled with posts like "Can You Trust Your Babysitter?" and "Ten Things Your Daycare Center Doesn't Want You to Know." We have to install cameras in order to monitor the situation. We even do the same with dog daycare!

The effects in schools are just as troubling. Teachers are not allowed to be in a room alone with a student. We're told never to hug students. I almost got into trouble at Palo Alto High School for giving a ride to a student — until I proved that the kid in question was my grandson who had come to visit my class for the day. We don't trust teachers to do their jobs. That's why we burden them with statewide exams. No one seems to have faith that teachers are teaching what they're supposed to, so when a child does poorly on an exam, the assumption is that the teacher is at fault, not the outdated curriculum or lack of resources. Parents don't feel they can trust anyone at the school — administrators, teachers, or even other students and their parents. Almost 50 percent of teachers leave the profession after five years. They cite lack of trust and respect as the main reasons for leaving. In many states we have a major teacher shortage, which only appears to be getting worse.

Now, I'm exposed to the twenty-four/seven news cycle like everyone else. I hear stories that frighten me all the time, and I understand why parents are frightened too. It's normal to be afraid, especially in a world with so much distrust, so much uncertainty. Just the other day, I ran into a former student with her two-month-old baby, and as we were talking, she mentioned how concerned she was about having a child in this unsafe world. This was in Palo Alto, for heaven's sake. We are all extrapolating from what we read online. We're reading too many scary things, watching too many scary news clips. Having lived in France and Switzerland, and because I travel all over the world to give talks, I sense that Americans are more fearful than most people. So it's important for us to really look at the statistics and challenge our assumptions about just how dangerous our lives are. In Steven Pinker's eye-opening book *Enlightenment Now: The Case for Reason, Science, Humanism, and Progress,* he tackles these assumptions head-on. Of our fears that the world is getting less safe, less predictable, less hospitable, he claims:

> Contrary to the impression that you might get from the newspapers — that we're living in a time of epidemics and war and crime — the curves show that humanity has been getting better, that we're living longer, we are fighting fewer wars, and fewer people are being killed in the wars. Our rate of homicide is down. Violence against women is down. More children are going to school, girls included. More of the world is literate. We have more leisure time than our ancestors did. Diseases are being decimated. Famines are becoming rarer, so virtually anything that you could measure that you'd want to call human well-being has improved over the last two centuries, but also over the last couple of decades.[4]

Our own institutions reflect this too. Data from the FBI and the Bureau of Justice Statistics shows that violent and property crimes have fallen since 1990, though most Americans — six in ten — believe that crime rates are increasing each year. The Office of Juvenile Justice and Delinquency Prevention states that between 1999 and 2013, both the rate of missing children and the number of missing children reported to the police have decreased. The National Crime Information Center's Missing Person and Unidentified Person reports show that the number of missing children under the age of eighteen fell from 33,706 in 2016 to 32,121 in 2017. Furthermore, the National Center for Missing and Exploited Children confirms that family abductions and runaway cases are much more common than stranger abductions, the most feared kind.

What Steven Pinker argues over hundreds of pages, and what all the data shows, is that there is a clear downtrend in violence over time. Yes, I know we're saturated with school shootings and the trials of serial child molesters and myriad news stories that can terrify you as a parent. In the media business, bad news sells better than good news, and every shooting can become a huge story in the echo chamber of social media. It can be really hard to accept that the world's safer than ever when we hear anecdote after scary anecdote. But it's the truth. We all need to take a collective deep breath. Here are some simple statements that you should read and repeat to yourself:

The majority of people are trustworthy.

The last thing you want to teach your child is that people, in general, can't be trusted, or to overprotect them to the point where they lack the independence necessary to thrive on their own. And don't we want our children to have an open-minded attitude toward the world, not to be closed off to life's possibilities?

We have to start somewhere. We have to combat all this fear and reestablish trust in ourselves and the world around us. The solution starts in the home, and that means it starts with you.

TRUST YOURSELF

A culture of trust in your family paves the way for all the subsequent values we're going to explore. As I've said, we might not all be able to trust our parental conditioning — that is, we might not want to repeat everything about the way we were parented. But if you (and your partner) do the work of sorting through your past, and if you honor the core human values represented by TRICK, you can trust your instincts when it comes to parenting.

And you must. Why? Because you're the one who truly knows what works for your family. You might find, as I did, that the parenting philosophy in your culture isn't a good fit. Nor is what your pediatrician tells you to do, or what everyone in your neighborhood is doing. You are the foremost expert on your family, which means that *you* know better than any other parenting experts, including me. I'm writing a parenting book, but I don't know you, and I don't know your children. Only you can determine how best to apply these universal principles. My goal here is to give you guidelines — not prescriptive advice — and permission to trust your own expertise, because if you don't trust yourself, you won't be able to instill trust in your children.

Still, I know how hard all of this is. Socially, it can be challenging if you don't follow the rules and do what everyone around you is doing, even when your kids don't fit in with those rules. Even when problems arise. We're afraid our children might fail, and their failures will be our fault. We're racked with anxiety about not knowing what we're doing, but we're certain that whatever we choose, we'll screw everything up.

The culture has trained us to think we need to consult a specialist for every problem or challenge. When it comes to kids, there are ADD and ADHD specialists, autism specialists, psychologists, psychiatrists, and multiple types of doctors. Some families have tutors for each child, each grade level, each subject. All of this specialization and expertise undermines our ability to think for ourselves as parents and to make the best choices for our children. Somehow we're convinced that all of these other people know better than we do.

But that's not true.

You have to trust that you know what's best for your child and your family.

WALK THE TALK

My grandson Ethan still wasn't talking at two and a half years old. He walked and slept through the night and knew his favorite foods, but he didn't want to talk. It can be nerve-racking for parents when a child lags behind the normal developmental curve, and it's important to investigate and ask questions. And yet it's a simple fact that some children acquire skills later than others. Some of us adults do as well. In most cases it means nothing about our intelligence or abilities — it's just the way it is. That's how my daughter Janet thought about it — at least at first. But as time went on, we wondered when Ethan would start talking, and we got a little worried. So Janet took him to the pediatrician, who recommended a specialist, saying it was nothing to worry about, that lots of kids need speech therapy. And that's what we did. Ethan cooperated, sort of, but he still wasn't talking after several sessions.

His parents took matters into their own hands. They read him books every night, every weekend, after every nap. They bought him a tape recorder, a pair of big headphones, and some children's books on tape (and even recorded a number of stories themselves). Ethan absolutely loved those stories. He'd sit in the family room with his headphones, just listening at first. He loved riding in the car and taking walks — always wearing his headphones. We reassured ourselves that there's no timetable for development except in parenting books — and kids don't read those books.

I learned that Albert Einstein didn't talk until he was three.

Ethan was in good company.

It was more than three months of therapy before Ethan finally started talking, and when he did, instead of speaking in single words, he spoke in complete sentences. He had always been obsessed with elevators, and one of the first things he said to me was "I want to ride in the elevator." He listened to his taped stories for years after, and still loves audiobooks. Now he's a voracious reader, a leader in his class, and on the debate team.

Sometimes you question your abilities because your child is not developing as you'd like. One thing I failed to do was teach proper table manners when my children were little. I kept postponing the lesson. When was the right time to teach manners? I didn't have a clue. Well, it turns out they learn good manners (or bad manners) from the start. There is no such thing as "baby manners" or "kid manners," and if you allow them to behave poorly at the beginning, they will think that is the way to behave at the table. Breaking a bad habit is more difficult than establishing good ones at the beginning. I wish I'd known how important it is to teach basic manners early on — it took me a long time to correct this mistake.

Our dinners back in the seventies were complete chaos and constant whining — enough to drive me crazy! Restaurants were the worst, especially when we lived in Switzerland and France. I'd look at the other tables and the perfectly well-behaved kids and think, *What have I done?* The Swiss and French didn't take any crap from their children. Those kids sat patiently waiting between courses. They certainly didn't seem to be struggling as I was. A few years later, at an Italian restaurant in Mountain View, my daughters started flinging peas at each other. One pea shot off Stan's forehead, and I made the mistake of laughing — because it was hilarious — and we were promptly kicked out. We've avoided that restaurant for years. My girls did learn their manners eventually, and I came to realize that their behavior wasn't a reason not to trust myself as a parent. It was a sign that there were still lessons to be learned.

Here's another challenge: How many of us grew up in an environment full of trust? Not many. I sure didn't. As I said, my father was in total control of the family, and my mother and I lived in fear of crossing him. A lot of us have a hard time building trust, and can be more susceptible to anger, frustration, and depression. It sometimes seems like it's impossible to trust ourselves, let alone our children.

If this sounds familiar, I suggest that you write down all the negative things your parents said, all the breaches of trust you experienced, all the pain and anger. Then analyze each one. It's not going to be easy, but it's going to help you. Ask yourself: Was what your parent said actually true, or was it a comment that came from a lot of anger that had nothing to do with you? Were you at fault for the mistakes in your childhood, or were you simply part of a dysfunctional family system, through no fault of your own? Why did breaches of trust happen? Is it because your parents were raised in an environment short on trust? As adults, we have the ability to look back and see how flawed some of our parents' statements were and to perceive how we got caught up in the emotional shortcomings of other people. Just doing this work of unpacking painful memories helps you to see the past more clearly and to have faith in yourself as a parent.

It helps to make a list of things you do well. It sounds simple, but writing this down can quickly increase your confidence. Everyone does something great — absolutely everyone. I use this exercise with my students at the start of the semester. They interview each other and are tasked with finding out something special about the other person, something at which they excel. At first the kids are shy — both the subjects and the interviewers. Some of them are convinced they don't do anything well, which is a pretty tragic reflection of the experiences they've had at school and at home. But if the interviewers persist, and if they get creative with their questions, they can uncover all kinds of special talents: juggling, dog walking, being a good sister, listening.

These conversations build trust in our classroom and help students feel good about themselves and their ability to succeed. It can be so helpful for parents to find people who trust in their abilities, just as my students trust in each other. Who supports you and understands that you're doing the best for your family? Surround yourself with people who will build your confidence, even when things go wrong, as they inevitably will.

No matter what challenges we face as parents, we can all see the evidence before our eyes. Look at your children. Observe them. Talk to them. Are they happy? Are they thriving? We are subjected to so many influences — especially other people's opinions — that we forget to simply look at our families and see what's working and what's not. If something isn't working, you can change it. Assess the situation honestly without blaming yourself or becoming insecure. All parents struggle. But struggle doesn't mean we should lose faith: It means we need to believe in ourselves even more.

BUILD TRUST IN YOUR CHILD

All you need is one person, just one person who trusts and believes in you, and then you feel you can do anything. Unfortunately, a lot of children don't have even one person. Michael Wang, a former student of mine, was one of these kids. He was an editor in chief of the *Campanile*, Palo Alto High's newspaper, in 2013, and his struggles represent those of so many of my students at Paly, and students across the country and world. For Michael, the pressures and expectations started early.

"I had very strict parents," Michael says. "They would tell me if I didn't do well in school, I'd be homeless."

His elementary school teachers weren't very supportive either. Michael now knows he gave off the impression of being tired and upset, but it was extremely difficult for him to wake up at seven a.m., and he always felt like his brain didn't work. He would stare at a piece of paper, knowing he couldn't read it, couldn't discern what it meant, and he resigned himself to failure. People misinterpreting his behavior and motivations was a common theme in his life.

"I would get admonished," he says, "by peers and educators telling me if I followed the rules and paid attention, of course I'd do better. It was almost part of my core being, to be this thing that was trodden on; everything I did turned into some kind of moral shortcoming."

By the time he made it to my class, Michael described himself as "completely burned out like a pile of ash." The school newspaper was the only thing he derived any meaning from, and still he could barely muster the will to show up. But he did. I got to know him as a really bright but disconnected kid: he'd come into class and have no idea what he wanted to do, no idea what he wanted to write about. He was six feet tall, a big kid, and you stick out when you're that tall and unsure of yourself.

I've seen so many students like this. They're afraid but also re-bellious. They're not cooperative. They're difficult, even aggressive, and that's because every single one of them feels bad about him-self. They have such low self-esteem that they fight back, but that's from trying to prove to themselves that they're better than everyone thinks.

During one of our production nights for the school newspaper, Michael was struggling with his music theory homework. "I was ex-hausted, trying to figure out this assignment," he says, "and I was half-assing it. A few sanctimonious peers took it upon themselves to share some wisdom I'd obviously never heard before: Suck it up, study harder."

Other students teased him for struggling, and he thought to him-self, as he often did, *That's right, I can't do it.*

I saw what was happening, walked up to these kids, and said, "He's taking longer because he's smart." Michael was a talented writer — he just needed more time to focus on his work. And I knew deep down he wanted to get it right, not just rush through it.

That was the first time an adult had said that his abilities and intelligence were seen and respected. "To hear outside confirmation that someone believed in me," Michael says, "even in the presence of other students who didn't — it was awesome. It helped me not to crumble."

That day was a turning point for Michael. In truth, he was smart — he just had an attitude problem. For the first time, he started to trust himself, and he called upon this newfound confidence throughout his undergraduate years whenever he encountered obstacles or someone who told him he'd never make it. He went on to earn his degree in neuroscience at Johns Hopkins, where he's now a neuro-psychiatric researcher. He'd found his one person to believe in him by accident, and that made all the difference.

Parents and teachers have to know that one word, sentence, or phrase can build a kid up, can save his life — or shatter his confidence. We forget how important we are in the lives of our children, how much control we have in shaping their confidence and self-image. And it all starts with trust, with believing your child is capable, even through setbacks and surprises and all the complications that come with growing up.

Trusting is empowering in the classroom and in the world at large — and this process starts earlier than you think. Infants who are securely attached to their parents — that is, infants who feel they can trust and depend on their parents — avoid many of the behavioral, social, and psychological problems that can arise later. Your child's fundamental sense of security in the world is based on you being a trusting caregiver.

This is why children are so highly attuned to their environments. They're wired to figure out whom they can trust, to identify the person who will respond to them and meet their needs. Studies show that four-year-olds can accurately identify trustworthy adults and later seek them out. I see this in my four-year-old granddaughter, Ava, all the time. When I walk in the door, she smiles at me, but sometimes she runs away and hides. She knows me, but she's constantly sizing me up to see whether I can be trusted.

Remember, trust is mutual. The degree to which your children can trust you will be reflected in their own ability to trust. When children don't have a sense of trust and security in the world, they experience all kinds of difficulties. Studies show that children rated as less trustworthy by their teachers exhibit higher levels of aggression and lower levels of "prosocial behavior" such as collaborating and sharing. Distrust in children has also been associated with their social withdrawal and loneliness.

If we don't feel trusted when we're kids, or if there isn't anyone close to us we can trust, we don't get over that. We grow up thinking we're not trustworthy, and we accept that as a character trait. Our relationships are turned upside down. We become what we think we are, and we suffer for it.

So how do we go about building trust in our children? We think of trust as handing our teenager the car keys, or letting our twelve-year-old stay home alone for the first time. But we underestimate the power of children — especially infants. Trust needs to start when they're born. We usually don't think of building trust in babies, but we should. They're smarter and much more perceptive than we think. Your child is watching you from day one.

Trust me on this. Your baby is observing your every move. They're learning how to get what they need from you. They know exactly what they're doing. Every time you fumble with a diaper, they see it. They know how to make you smile. They know how to make you cry. They may be dependent on us for everything, but they're a lot more intelligent than we give them credit for. You do need to respond to their needs, especially early on, so that they feel you and their environment are trustworthy, but this is also a fantastic time to start teaching your child some of the most important lessons in life.

So, let's talk about sleep.

And trust.

And how as parents you can use trust to solve those ever-persistent sleep problems.

Sleeping was really important for my girls when they were infants, and it was important to my husband and me — we knew we wouldn't survive years of not sleeping. We're not vampires! It is important for all parents and it has become an international problem. There are entire books devoted to getting your child to sleep. I saw sleeping as fundamentally about trust, and I saw it as a teachable skill. From day one, babies are learning about the world, their circadian rhythms are adjusting, and, though my daughters seemed to have their clocks set for the wrong continent, they needed to learn their most important infant skill: how to put themselves to sleep. It never occurred to me that they would have trouble sleeping beyond the first six weeks. Why wouldn't they be able to sleep? It's one of the three things they could do from birth: eat, poop, and sleep. They grow when they sleep; their brains develop when they sleep. Sleep is a natural state for babies and toddlers. I trusted they innately knew how, and if they needed some reassurance, I was there to help.

We didn't have a lot of money when the girls were young. Susan had a crib and a small bed that I created out of a wicker laundry basket with a nice little mattress (Susan still uses the same basket today, though not for sleeping). The point was to keep them safe and nearby. They slept in their own cribs and in their own rooms from the beginning (except when we were in our small apartment in Geneva and there weren't enough rooms — then Anne slept near us in a little box fitted with blankets). We were fortunate not to have to deal with colic or illness — these parents do have to be more responsive than usual to keep their child safe. Still, I think what I did will work in the majority of cases. I simply placed them on their stomachs, patted their backs, sat with them a few minutes, and let them fall asleep on their own. If they were restless and started to whimper or cry, I'd make sure they weren't hungry or didn't need to be changed, and then I reassured them with a soft pat on the back and they went back to sleep. Of course, now we know that the safest sleeping position for infants is on their back, in which case parents can pat the child's stomach. Babies have short sleep cycles and tend to wake up and cry or whimper, but they can often put themselves back to sleep. I was always there to comfort my daughters, but it wasn't always necessary to pick them up. I trusted they could get to sleep on their own, and they did. By the time they were three months old, they were sleeping most of the night. And as toddlers, they slept for twelve hours, from seven p.m. to seven a.m. Their sleep habits were such a gift to Stan and me. All parents need some time to be together.

I intuitively knew to trust my daughters, but I realize it can be hard for parents to project a strong sense of trust that then empowers their children. What they often project is fear. They think their child will be afraid to sleep by himself, that he needs his parents, that he can't do it on his own. How do you think a child learns to become afraid of sleeping? From exactly this kind of thinking on the parents' part.

I'm not out to blame anyone. I just want to explain how our ideas affect our children. Many parents are operating from their own insecurities or doubts: Doesn't their child need them? And if he doesn't, what kind of parents are they? You'll hear this message loud and clear from me throughout this book: You want your child to *want* to be with you, not to *need* to be with you. The first place this tension arises is with sleep. Your children can and will sleep on their own if you believe they can do it, and if you teach them how. Their beds can be a sanctuary instead of a scary place. Kids learn to self-soothe — when given the opportunity — by sucking their thumb or using pacifiers, or playing with toys. My daughters always had stuffed animals in their beds. Sometimes I'd wake up and find Susan talking to her teddy bear. Janet used to sing in bed. They all felt comfortable. We'd built a relationship of trust, and they learned that they could entertain themselves and meet a lot of their own needs — which meant that Stan and I got to sleep! A win-win.

As kids grow, they can be given more and more opportunities to build their own trustworthiness. Remember, the choices you make with your child will dictate the culture of your family. You always want to ask whether you're actively building trust or shutting your child down. For young children, each little achievement builds their trust and belief in themselves. They tie their own shoes, and it works! They put on their own clothes, and it works! They walk to school, and that works too! They can see the tangible results of their efforts. You can't trust a small child to make intelligent choices, but you can guide him in considering options and picking the best one. If I gave my nine-year-old grandson a lollipop and told him not to eat it, I know he still would. But if I explained why he shouldn't eat it, that sugar isn't healthy — that it might even give him cavities — and that eating before dinner will spoil his appetite, he'd be able to learn how to make better choices. Okay, he might still eat the lollipop, but if we worked on these kinds of decisions over time, he'd eventually build the skills for living a healthy life. And then I could trust him to take care of himself.

Each age brings its own instances of trust. Feeding is another opportunity. I gave my daughters as much finger food as possible, as soon as they were ready for solid food. It allowed them to learn to feed themselves. I still remember how they would "clean up" when they were done eating, which meant throwing the food they didn't want on the floor. The floor was a mess, but my daughters were also capable of feeding themselves and determining when they were full. A little later on, when they were around five years old, I could ask whether they were hungry, and I believed their answer. I did bring all kinds of snacks with me in case they misjudged their hunger. I was famous for carrying little yogurts whenever we left the house. When the girls were hungry, even little warm yogurts were welcome. And if we were on a long car ride and they didn't want to eat, I'd explain that we wouldn't stop at another restaurant for several hours and then let them determine what to do. I trusted them with their food decisions.

For teenagers, parents can build trust in a series of steps. For instance, here's how I would build trust with shopping, one of my favorite educational activities: 1) the parent does everything (selecting and buying the items needed); 2) trust your child to go with you to the store and make most of the purchasing decisions (giving kids a specific budget is a wonderful way to teach financial responsibility); 3) now your child is capable of gathering the items on her own, and you can meet afterward at the registers — on time — and make the final purchases together; 4) once you've built a foundation of trust and you've taught your child how to be responsible with money, give them your credit card and let them shop on their own (many major credit cards allow you to add a minor as an authorized user). Of course, make sure to check the charges and teach them to verify the credit card statement at the end of the month as well.

You can also gauge your teenager's trustworthiness by testing whether they make good on their word. They said they'd be home by eight p.m. Were they? If they were late, did they call? If they prove themselves trustworthy, keep increasing their freedoms and responsibilities. If they still need to learn to come home on time, have a conversation about what went wrong and troubleshoot together for the next time. Some kids just have a hard time being on time. Don't give up. Give them more opportunities to learn. Time management is a skill that many adults lack. That's why we have so many self-help books on time management. It's one of the most important skills for success in life.

If children aren't empowered with trust, if they don't feel trustworthy, they'll have a very difficult time becoming independent. The main problem is that they don't learn to trust and respect themselves. When we are fearful and hover over our children, they become afraid too. Yet children need to take risks. Kids really do copy what we model for them. I'm afraid of heights, but I wanted to make sure my kids weren't, so I was careful not to show my fear to them. I let them climb all kinds of playground equipment — but I stayed back. My daughters, though, were completely fearless.

Here is another simple mantra for you: Children need to take risks. You might need to repeat this to yourself on multiple occasions. Too many parents instinctually resist the idea.

TRUST IN ACTION

You'll be surprised what's possible. For sixteen years, I brought groups of fifty-two students on field trips to New York. The point was to visit editors at the nation's top publications and learn more about journalism in the real world. We met with staff at the *New York Times*, the *Wall Street Journal*, *Vanity Fair*, and *Sports Illustrated*, as well as with David Remnick, editor of *The New Yorker*, and other leading journalists such as Anderson Cooper. Every year was different, and every year was amazing. The kids loved it; I loved it, and it became legendary in Palo Alto. Everyone wanted to go on the New York trip. One of my motivations was to give students some freedom, to allow them to discover New York City, one of our country's most amazing cities, and to convince them that they were capable of a lot more than they thought. This was the most valuable lesson I could teach before they finished high school and left for college — belief in themselves to navigate a big city. I also wanted them to enjoy themselves, and I don't think anyone on any of those trips ever complained about not having enough fun.

In the mornings, we'd visit the publications and speak with editors, and the kids would navigate the subways with me — when I wasn't lost myself. I didn't know where I was going half the time, and it was empowering for the kids to lead me. They were much better at reading maps (in the 1990s) and using their phones (from 2000 on) than I was. They also saw me get lost and figure my way out of that. Getting lost is not a problem, provided you don't get stressed. I never did, even one day when I got on the train with half of my kids and watched the other half of the group zipping by in the opposite direction. There were a few frustrating minutes, but they used their cell phones and made their way to our destination despite the unintended detour. In all those years I never lost a kid. I did lose one chaperone who almost missed her flight back to San Francisco, but not a single child.

In the afternoons, they were free to explore the city in groups of four. I figured I'd taught them how to navigate and they'd be fine on their own. I was right. I also gave my students some control when it came to planning our excursions. They could decide what we would do in the evenings. Sadly, most high schools today do not allow any field trips that include even a little unchaperoned travel — kids may need to learn how to navigate a big city, but they won't learn that through school.

BROKEN TRUST

Whatever you do as a parent, your child will end up violating your trust at some point. That's part of life and part of the learning process. One student told me he was helping a friend who "had a bad day." At first I thought, *Oh, that's nice of him.* Then I found out that he was at the shopping center across from the high school and had spent his afternoon not helping a friend, and not participating in my class, but eating cookies!

Well, I had to confront him. When he came back the next day, I told him I knew he'd been at the store. I also told him that the first thing he had to do was buy me a cookie! I use humor for many situations like this, whenever the infraction is not deeply serious. It was important to call him out, however, and important to give him even a lighthearted assignment. Kids should take an active step to repair the trust they've broken. It helps them to understand the impact of what they've done. But I'm not mean about it. Having a sense of humor keeps me from rupturing a relationship. Yes, I do get upset, and there is a penalty — trusting doesn't mean not holding kids accountable — but the punishment isn't to revoke trust. It's to enforce trust *even more*.

I always say that lack of trust and respect causes the problem, and these values are also the solution. Use trust to get trust. Instead of getting mad and cutting off a relationship when trust is broken, repair it. Look at those marriages that could be saved if people talked to each other. Students want my trust — even when they've screwed up. My actions told this particular student that he was important to me, though I was disappointed in his recent behavior. I gave him the chance to rectify things so I could continue believing in him. And something amazing happened: He never screwed up again.

This goes for more serious infractions, too. I once discovered that several of my students were storing their beer in the darkroom and drinking it on school property. They would spend hours in there — I thought they were developing photos. But one day I overheard a conversation and then realized what was really going on. After observing the situation for a few days, I called them all into my office. It was a pretty tense discussion. I could tell they were scared.

I didn't yell at them, but I told them in no uncertain terms how disappointed I was in them, how they had violated my trust, and how they'd put the entire newspaper at risk. Unfortunately, if there is a serious violation like alcohol or drug consumption on campus, bullying, or any kind of sexual harassment, then it is out of my hands. I'm required to report it to the administration. That is true in most schools in the country. So I turned the kids in, and they were suspended from school for a week (the suspension was also noted on their transcripts). I didn't publish any of their stories in that week's edition of the paper.

Fortunately, none of them ever did it again. They were regretful and upset by what they'd done. And they understood why I had to turn them in, because we'd talked about it, and I'd explained my side of the situation. Like so many things when it comes to teenagers, it was just poor judgment on their behalf. I forgave them, they learned their lesson, and we were all able to restore the trust that is so important in my classroom.

Another inevitable truth of parenting is that at some point, despite your best efforts, your children might lose their trust in you. This happened to me — briefly — and has become one of our most famous family stories. The problem was that we had three teenage daughters who wanted to drive at the same time. Not easy for a family on a budget. Susan inherited our 1963 Volvo — with stick shift on the floor! — that we'd bought while living in Europe and shipped to California. I figured Volvos were the safest cars on the road and perfect for the beginning drivers in our family: anyone in an accident with a Volvo would lose. They're built like tanks — all steel, no plastic. By the time we gifted that car to Susan, it had more than 300,000 miles on it but was still going strong. When she took her driver's test, the DMV employee looked terrified! She passed with flying colors, probably because he wanted to get out of that ancient Volvo.

Susan was taken care of, but I still had to figure out what to do about Janet and Anne. We couldn't afford two more cars. But then I stumbled on a bargain: another trusty Volvo, this one a four-door sedan in that muted shade of brown that screams the 1970s. I love bargains, and I love Volvos. So I bought it and came up with a creative solution that I laugh about to this day. First, I gave the car to

Janet, who was a freshman at Stanford. She wanted to keep it with her at school, but I wisely said that there were parking problems on campus and it was expensive, and so she should leave the car at home. She agreed. But since the car was often sitting there, I decided to also "give it" to Anne, who was still in high school. Both girls thought it was "their car." A little white lie.

I know it sounds kind of crazy, but it worked for over a year. And then one day they found out that they'd each been "given" the car. As you can probably guess, they weren't happy with me. Actually, that's an understatement. They were furious. I apologized profusely and tried to explain myself. Eventually they listened. I told them I understood that they felt betrayed, and explained that my motivation had been to give them both the gift they wanted. In the end, they forgave me, partly because I agreed to buy another old car, but also because I listened to them. Listening makes such a huge difference. Plus, we could all laugh about it. Eventually. Even today they bring up this story. At least now they acknowledge my creativity: I'm never beyond being creative. Whenever I give Anne a gift, she always asks if it's really for her or if I've given it to Janet too!

By the time your kids get out into the work world, their ability to trust themselves, their ideas, and their coworkers will be a huge asset. Fearless kids have the best chance of succeeding — especially if they're innovators. I remember the early days of Google when Larry Page and Sergey Brin, the company's co-founders, agreed to rent the ground floor and garage of Susan's house as their first office space. They were two young computer scientists with a great idea, and they needed somewhere to work. Susan needed help paying her mortgage. It seemed like a perfect arrangement, and Larry and Sergey were obviously up to something super interesting, but Susan had no clue that they'd be there *all the time,* hunched over dozens of computers in the garage. Cables ran up and down the hallway, which I tripped on every time I visited. There was even a computer perched on the bathroom sink!

Having them in the house was exciting, but it also had some drawbacks. One was that they were hungry at night (not surprising because they never stopped working), and the closest food was in Susan's refrigerator — not part of their rental. When you're starving at two a.m., you just "borrow" the food and then plan to replenish it the next day. But when Susan came down in the morning for breakfast, her food was gone. Eventually she gave them her refrigerator when she bought herself a new one. That solved the problem — as long as they remembered to keep it stocked. Now there's food available twenty-four/seven for Google's employees, and that may be inspired by all those all-nighters at Susan's house.

Larry and Sergey were smart enough to understand that they had to focus on their product — Google — and that was more than a full-time job. Once they started hiring people, they were incredibly selective, and then were willing to delegate and give their workers massive responsibilities. This is how startups work: Employees have multiple jobs because there aren't enough people to fill each role. It's exhilarating but also exhausting. Their business model was about hiring the smartest and best people they could find and then trusting them to do the job. Of course that process was often chaotic, full of mistakes and missteps, and required that they have faith in their team. They were creating something new — these were uncharted waters. They completely rejected the idea that success was about perfection and tidiness and certainty, and that mind-set made all the difference.

When Larry and Sergey first moved in, Susan was working at Intel. She took a chance and joined Google as its sixteenth employee, and was immediately given large responsibilities, including marketing Google and creating several key consumer products such as Google Images and Google Books. Larry and Sergey were focused on the search engine and making the world's information searchable and useful to all of us. Their goal was not to make money; it was to make the best search engine, which was no small task. Susan was accustomed to having faith in herself and taking on big challenges, and she loved the atmosphere of freedom and trust, despite all the chaos. This company ethos powered some of Google's most renowned policies, including the 20 percent time policy, which was based on trust and respect for an employee's interests. Employees were given 20 percent of their time to work on individual projects that in some way related to Google's goals. They could choose anything they were passionate about. Gmail, for example, came out of a 20 percent project, as did a lot of other innovative programs and concepts. It was a perfect example of the role of trust in innovation. Google is consistently voted the number one place to work. And the company continues to show us that work can be a place to trust and respect each other in the process.

Don't we want to extend this same kind of trust to our children? Of course we want to train our children to work in an environment where they are trusted and respected, not monitored all the time. If we do, if our children have the trust and confidence to thrive on the cutting edge, they'll be the ones that companies like Google seek out. And they'll be the ones to have the next big breakthrough.

In 1998, I flew halfway around the world to Johannesburg, South Africa, to visit my daughter Janet. At that time Johannesburg was considered one of the most dangerous cities in the world outside of any active war zone due to the high crime rate. Janet had arrived there a year earlier and was teaching social anthropology at the University of Witwatersrand. She did not seem to be bothered by that statistic, but I was. Typical mother behavior. What kind of parent would want her child to willingly live in a high-risk, dangerous environment? I certainly didn't. Honestly, I was terrified. Before Janet left California, I tried to be logical. "Why Johannesburg? Why now? Isn't there somewhere else you could go, somewhere a little safer?" But I knew I couldn't stop her. And if I did try to fight her decision, I was sure I would lose.

On my second day there, she asked if I wanted to stay at home or go to work with her. Never one to turn down an adventure, I agreed to accompany her to the clinic in Soweto, or South Western Township, part of Johannesburg (1.8 million people) that was created during the apartheid years to separate and house the African population. Janet, true to form, failed to tell me much about Soweto, an area that both Nelson Mandela and Desmond Tutu had once called home.

We made our way in Janet's red Volkswagen through the streets of Johannesburg, onto the highway, and then into Soweto. Soweto is a heterogeneous area comprised of middle-class neighborhoods with larger homes and informal settlements with homes made out of corrugated iron that do not have running water or electricity. Janet explained to me that the population she was serving were sex workers and HIV-infected women. Poverty was rampant in certain parts of Soweto, and some women were forced by the lack of employment opportunities to exchange sex for money, which had contributed to the ongoing HIV epidemic. Janet had been brought in to study the epidemic and to do something about it. That sounded noble to me, of course, but it also sounded dangerous. I kept thinking: *What has Janet gotten herself into?*

Janet had always been passionate about African culture. At Stanford, she participated in a semester abroad program in Kenya, and she went on to receive a master's in African studies at UCLA. And then she went to Johannesburg to teach at the University of Witwatersrand. She'd found her calling, a way to use her unique talents and passions, and as scared as I was for her safety, I didn't want to stand in her way.

We parked in front of the clinic. For a second I hesitated. But Janet motioned to me and started toward the door. She looked so confident, so capable, in this place so very different from where she'd grown up. She was in her element. I still didn't quite understand it, but I wanted to support her, and I wanted to know more.

Inside the clinic was a big waiting room filled with women, some in traditional African dress — brightly patterned skirts and wraps — sitting on chairs and on the floor. Dozens of children were there too. In the center was a big table made out of a door propped on cinder blocks. Janet greeted the women in English and Zulu and introduced me, the new guest, as her mother. The women sprang to their feet, started talking excitedly, and many of them hugged me. They were so kind, so enthusiastic. We later learned that bringing your mother to meet your friends is the very highest honor in the culture. And it was worth celebrating. Many of the women rushed back to their houses and prepared dishes with what little food they had. Soon the repurposed table in the clinic was filled with traditional South African food — vegetable stews, roasted squash, beans, and yellow rice. The food was delicious, and I was overwhelmed by how much these women had celebrated my daughter and me. The experience was more powerful than any Mother's Day I'd ever had. And while we were enjoying our meal inside the clinic, the men were outside, washing Janet's car. Again, to honor me, her mother!

I came away with a tremendous appreciation for the people of Soweto, and also such respect and pride for my daughter. I'd taught her to be fearless and to live with purpose, and there she was, contributing to the world, making it better each day.

Now, I'm not saying that Janet's work didn't make me nervous. It did, and it still does, but who am I to tell her what to do? My anxiety has to do with my fear, not hers. And I've learned over the years that I can't and shouldn't project my fear onto my daughters, despite how they always seem to be testing my resolve. When Susan lived in India after college, she got extremely ill and was fortunate enough to have taken Septra, a powerful antibiotic, with her. Thankfully it did the trick. She didn't tell me until she got home, but just hearing about it gave me nightmares. People can die from the kind of gastro-intestinal infection that she had. Later, Janet was bitten on the butt by a rabid dog in Kenya (on her first trip to Africa)! Again, she didn't tell me. She couldn't. She was in a remote region and there were no cell phones. I found out only later that she'd done the whole rabies protocol on her own, and I was impressed that she'd known how to take care of herself. Similarly, my daughter Anne once told me she was taking "a tour" through Russia from Istanbul on the Trans-Siberian Express. Later I found out she was on a tour of one — that is, she did it all by herself. At one point I hadn't heard from her in months, and I got desperate. I knew she was visiting Krasnoyarsk, my mother's hometown in Siberia, so I decided to track her down. I hadn't spoken Russian in years, but you'd be surprised what you're capable of when you think your child might be in danger. I called every single hotel in Krasnoyarsk — and I found her.

When she answered the phone she was shocked and she said, "Mom! How did you find me?" I told her, "It wasn't easy, but I persisted." She wasn't very happy to hear from me, and of course she was fine. My daughters' travels were really a test of my trusting them to be independent and follow their dreams, and it had worked — even if it was hard on me. When their lives were different from the ones I'd imagined for them, I couldn't stop them. I gave up trying to ever control them: we weren't connected by some magic string. I could only support them in what they wanted to do. Sure, I was nervous a lot of the time. But I believed in them and we all got through it.

As parents we have to take ourselves in hand and trust that we taught our children to make good decisions. We have to trust the basic goodness of people and the basic goodness of the world. And sometimes, our children can be our greatest teachers.

RESPECT

3

Your Child Is Not Your Clone

LET THEM LEAD

My first grandson, Jacob, didn't want to walk. When he was eighteen months old, the whole family would watch in anticipation as he scooted around the living room on his butt, waiting, just waiting for him to prop himself up and take that first step. It was cute but concerned us. Susan, his mother, was really worried. So was I. But the doctor assured us there was nothing wrong with Jacob's legs. He was a healthy, normal toddler — except for the walking part. He seemed satisfied, scooting on the carpet to grab his toy truck or a stray Lego. It was as if he'd decided he would skip walking altogether. He couldn't understand what all the fuss was about.

Jacob's greatest love at that time was basketball. I used to visit him several times a week, and the main thing he wanted me to do was hold him up so he could throw a basketball into the hoop at the nearby park or into any hoop in anyone's driveway that he spotted from his stroller. I helped Jacob make baskets for hours on end. So did his parents. He would squeal in delight as the ball wound around the rim and then dropped through the basket. To him, it was the greatest thing on earth. So one day I took him to Gymboree, a gym for children, so he could crawl around and play—and be around a lot of basketballs.

The second we walked through the door, Jacob spotted a group of kids playing basketball. He lit up watching every move as they dribbled the ball and darted from side to side. One kid scored a three-point shot. After a brief celebration, the game was over. The basketball sat at center court. I swear to you Jacob got up and *ran* to the ball. He didn't walk: he ran! I watched him bend over and hoist the ball to his chest, triumphant. He'd known how to walk and stand the whole time. He just hadn't found a good reason to do it.

When we got back to Susan's house, I said, "Guess what? Jacob walks."

"What?" she said, turning off the tap and looking at me as if I were crazy.

"He walks and he runs," I told her.

Well, it wasn't exactly a magical transformation. The minute he got home, he was back to scooting on his butt. It took a few more days for him to realize that walking was a faster way to get to a basketball hoop. It also meant he could hold the ball at the same time—a very important skill. But once he understood the clear advantage of walking, he was completely hooked. And the rest of us relaxed.

I'm going to say this more than once: Parents need to calm down. Your kids will walk. They will talk. They will learn to use the bathroom. They'll do it in their own time. No one asks how old you were when you were toilet trained. Or when you gave up your pacifier. This is never cocktail conversation. My grandson was adhering to his own schedule, and he's turned out to be incredibly smart.

Respect is a complicated topic. First, there is respect for your child as an autonomous person. Respecting the timeline of a child's development isn't only about walking and talking. Patience — sometimes lots of it — is needed there. Development is also about turning into the person we're meant to be. And this process requires a deeper layer of respect: accepting a child for who he is and letting his life unfold accordingly. Kids need to be allowed to take the lead. That means *you* follow *them*. Children know who they are. Your job is to honor and respect that.

It pays to start early. Letting kids take the lead when they're young is important training for parents. It gives us the skills we need to deal with more, should I say, *advanced* tasks once they're older. Finding out who you are can be a messy and inefficient process. When kids are leading, they take all kinds of detours. Few find their passion right away. Honestly, most kids go through a period where they don't know what the heck they're doing — but I promise you eventually they'll figure it out.

Anne was the daughter who showed me the value of patience in parenting. She got her degree in biology from Yale, came back home to Palo Alto, and decided to become a professional babysitter. Yep, that's right: a babysitter. "Really?" I said. "After you worked so hard at college? What about biology?" The next thing I knew, she'd posted a handwritten advertisement at our local swim and tennis club, and shortly after that she was working for two families she adored. A month went by, then two. I was trying to give her time to figure out what she really wanted. Recent college graduates need to decompress and get their bearings. I wasn't one of those parents who had been forcing my daughter to interview for jobs during her entire senior year. Her college education was *her* experience. Still, I realized this might be a time when she could use a little advice.

One morning I said, "Anne, there's a job fair in Santa Clara. Don't you think you should go?" I figured it might show her what else was out there. Well, she went, but only as a favor to me. She came back and said the whole thing had been boring.

"You didn't meet anyone interesting?" I asked. It turns out she *had* met someone interesting, an investor who wanted to bring her to New York for an interview. What Anne was excited about, however, wasn't so much the prospect of her first major job out of college but the free trip to New York. Of course, I wanted her to go. The company put her up in the Helmsley Hotel on Forty-Second Street, and on the first night she called me from what sounded like the middle of a terrible rainstorm. "There's a phone in the shower!" she said, and proceeded to describe the hotel's amenities.

Her interview went well, and after a week the company offered her a job in their biotech investment fund. Stan and I were thrilled. What a great opportunity for Anne. It seemed like the perfect start to a fascinating career. For a moment I thought my work was finished.

"I don't know," Anne kept saying. "I like these families I'm babysitting for." At this point I was about ready to have a heart attack. I thought to myself: *There's no way this brilliant girl is going to be a babysitter for the next thirty years.* But I forced myself to say nothing. I knew I had to be patient, and to respect her choices, even if I disagreed with them.

Anne thought about her decision for a couple days, and then turned the offer down.

Okay, at this point I wanted an explanation. She kept saying she loved the kids she was babysitting, but I kept pointing out that she'd been offered a dream job. I wished *I* could have taken that job. But it wasn't what she wanted. So I had to calm down. And I did. I bought her a T-shirt that said BEST BABYSITTER, which she was. At least she was doing something productive.

After a few weeks, and likely after picking up on some ideas from her friends and from Stan and me, Anne started wondering if she'd made the wrong choice. "It might be fun to live in New York," I said. "It sounds like a good job."

Two weeks later, she called them back.

"We've been waiting for you," they told her — but they needed her to do one final interview, this time in Palo Alto. Always the California girl, Anne wore shorts and flip-flops. Imagine going to an interview in shorts and flip-flops not even knowing who'd be interviewing you! This was pre-Google, and she hadn't done her research. But we had to let her make her own decisions (and mistakes). How else would she learn?

The person who came to meet her was none other than Marcus Wallenberg himself, the prominent Swedish investor. It turned out to be a great interview despite Anne's choice of wardrobe, and that's how she started working in the Investor AB biotech fund for the Wallenberg family, an experience she loved and that led her to a career on Wall Street.

It all worked out well for Anne, but some children need a bit more guidance. Nowadays, many college graduates have no idea what they want to do, so they come home and sit there. Not a good plan. How do you know when to let them find their way and when to intervene? Here's my policy: They have to be doing *something*. Not doing anything is the problem. And "something" does not mean playing video games, unless your child is serious about becoming a gaming programmer. What we want is for our children to contribute to society in some way. They should earn a paycheck, or have an internship.

And there should be a limit on free rent. You want to give them time to land on their feet, but after six months or so, they should be paying to live in your home, even if it's at an insider's price. This is also a part of respect: holding your children to standards. Respectful parenting is supportive *and* demanding.

As a student at Berkeley, I had the unglamorous job of cleaning houses. It paid well, and it provided a good service to my customers. I also had the glamorous job of being a runway model for Roos Atkins, an upscale department store in San Francisco, and a catalogue model. That paid very well. In addition, I worked as a playground supervisor at the local Berkeley public schools. In some way, each of those jobs contributed to the world we live in. I wasn't sitting around waiting for a handout. I was a responsible member of society, and I was learning how to be an adult.

Susan had a temporary summer job filing and answering the phone at Palo Alto Sanitation, where she was in close communication with all the garbage trucks in Palo Alto. It was her responsibility to make sure they followed the route and got washed after they were finished each morning. Not a high-prestige job, but very useful and important. And it came with perks. I remember one day she called me excitedly to tell me that the workers had picked up a really nice red couch, and did I want it for the school. Of course I did. It was promptly delivered and became the most popular lounging spot in the media center. That red couch helped a lot of students write a lot of articles.

Beyond temporary jobs, seeing the world is the best education kids can have. It gives them great ideas. They can travel with a friend, volunteer in a foreign country, spend a few months learning another language, or work with a foundation they believe in. I serve as an advisor on Roadtrip Nation, where kids can travel around the United States and meet people from all walks of life. I'm also on the advisory board of Global Citizen Year, a gap-year program that helps connect kids with their passion. I always say to my students, "Take your pick, but do something!" And I have the same advice for parents: Be open-minded and let your child lead the way.

SEEING OURSELVES IN OUR CHILDREN

Sixteen-year-old Greg was a genius in graphic design. I first saw his drawings in the 1990s, when he was a student in my journalism program, and I knew he was something special. He'd draw the most beautiful landscapes and complex architectural designs, and he loved making page layouts for the school newspaper. At that time, graphic design was still being done on paper, but I had a hunch that computer-based design would be big in the future, so I suggested Greg use a computer to draw. Why not add technology to his art? He loved the idea and ran with it.

The problem was that Greg's father was a physician and his mother was a medical researcher. The very last thing they wanted their son to become was some creative type, let alone a graphic designer. He was supposed to be a doctor, a lawyer, or — best of all — a scientist. His parents demanded he take an overwhelming load of AP science courses, so he spent most of his time studying and fighting for a little time to practice the art he loved. Greg did well academically because he was very smart — but he was miserable. Everyone could see it. By the time he got to his senior year, he was really depressed.

One day, about halfway through the fall semester, Greg's mother called me to discuss his grades. I invited both parents to talk after school. I was concerned about Greg and wanted to help. The parents told me that science was very important to them, and I respected their accomplishments. I could see why they wanted their son to follow in their footsteps. Here's the thing: The vision that parents have for their child's life is important. They sacrifice a lot for their children. I gave up my career for a decade to raise my daughters, and Stan worked day and night to support us (and because he was so passionate about physics). Our opinions and ideas matter. But sometimes a child has a different dream, a different path to follow.

Greg's parents and I brainstormed different strategies for using journalism to inspire him when it came to science. "How about having him write some articles about research at Stanford?" his mother suggested. They were laser-focused on making him "interested" in science. "I'll see what I can do," I told them, but at the same time I knew Greg already had different interests. Ones his parents refused to acknowledge.

I did suggest that Greg write some articles about scientific topics, which he did without much enthusiasm, but he kept drawing . . . all the time. He had notebooks and notebooks full. Drawing was inborn, part of his DNA. I was reminded of my father and what a great artist he was, but also how poor we were. Greg's parents were right to be concerned about what his life would be like if he chose a creative path. But their child simply didn't want to be a scientist.

I've seen this situation so often in my thirty-six years of teaching. Parents tend to define their goals for their children solely in terms of their own interests and experience — and they do this because they desperately want their children to succeed. I get it. It's coming from a good place. Parents also tend to project their fears and anxieties onto their children, especially when it comes to less familiar career and life choices. Better to do something safe, they think, than forge a new path. I see parents of elementary school kids who program their children into afterschool activities that the parent wants, not the child. What the child wants is to come home, hang out with friends, and play outside. In other words, to be a child. Later on, parents of high school kids are upset because their kids are "distant." Well, they're distant because they don't want to be told what to do all the time. They want to follow their passions and live their own lives. And instead they feel disrespected and misunderstood.

None of this got me anywhere with Greg's parents. The mother started calling me every week to "check in." She kept saying, "See what you can do to change his mind." Then his parents decided he needed a therapist. Greg went to the sessions, but nothing changed. He kept rebelling in his own polite way. He did his schoolwork for those science classes, but at the same time he dedicated himself to graphic design. He refused to fight with his parents, but he also refused to do what they told him. His whole existence was fixated on not becoming a physicist.

My policy is always to support students while also meeting the needs of the parents. It is tough. I told Greg, "I know we have to deal with your parents. Don't worry, I'll help you." And I did. I told him the only thing he had to worry about in my class was becoming who he wanted to be. In all of my years as a teacher, I've learned it's usually the parents who have a fit when they don't get what they want — not the kids.

My class became his passion, the antidote to the drudgery of his AP science classes. He spent hours creating graphic designs for the newspaper; he created an exceptional graphic for the back of our T-shirts; he helped redesign the pages so they looked professional.

He was always checking out magazines for new ideas. I subscribe to about twenty magazines and when I am done, they all end up in my classroom — even today.

Some twenty years later, Greg is a well-known graphic artist and web designer who runs a successful company in Los Angeles. He took a few physics classes in college to appease his parents but ultimately pursued his dream.

Another student, Lisa, wasn't as lucky. She was a beautiful girl, outgoing and social, a student body president and a born leader in my journalism program. Her dream was to be a teacher, but her parents wanted something more prestigious for her: medicine. And because she was a good daughter who wanted to please her mom and dad, she did what they asked. She completed pre-med studies at an Ivy League college and got into a prestigious medical school. She did well, graduated, and got married, in that order. Everyone expected her to go into pediatrics because she loved kids, but she decided to "postpone" practicing. That postponement has lasted twenty years. She never went into medicine. She decided she didn't want to be a doctor, no matter what — and she quit.

Lisa is now in her fifties. She took up valuable space in medical school, spent years studying something she never wanted to study, and did it all only to please her parents. What she ultimately wanted was to be a stay-at-home mother, and that's what she is today. She's happy. Finally.

The lesson in all of this: Children will listen to you — they want your approval and love — but if they want to be happy, they're going to have to listen to themselves.

Another one of my students was in constant war with her father about having to wear a headscarf at school. The family had moved to Palo Alto from Cairo, and though they were looking for a new life, the father was convinced that his daughter should conform to their religious norms. Most immigrant parents want their children to maintain the culture of the country of origin, for understandable reasons. Tradition is important. It's what sustains and defines us. But at the same time, these parents want their children to "become American." For a child, this is pretty confusing.

The parents are also confused. They make great sacrifices to give their child a better life, but they can also have a hard time respecting the culture of the new world. I remember my grandparents struggled with seeing me growing up as an American. They lived next door to us in Sunland-Tujunga and expected me to be like a religious Jewish girl from Chernivtsi, Ukraine. There was always tension about what I was doing and saying when I was a teenager. I definitely didn't act like I'd been raised in Ukraine. There were two things that shocked them: one was my height. I am five-ten and come from a family where the women were about five-two and the men were five-seven. Sunday family conversation always included someone asking, "Has Esther grown this week again?" much to my horror as a self-conscious teen. I always worried that they had picked up the wrong baby in the hospital until my brother, Lee, grew to be six-two. My wanting to be a journalist was just as shocking. Girls were never journalists. "That's a career reserved for smart men," they told me, and at that time the journalistic world would have agreed with them. In so many cultures, children are assumed to be some mirror of the parent or grandparent, reflecting all the same values and choices — even physical characteristics, and when this doesn't happen, relationships break down.

My student from Cairo didn't come to me right away, but when I found her crying in the computer lab, I suggested she talk to her father honestly about her struggles. She tried that. It worked for a few weeks, but then her father told her she had to wear the headscarf. They continued to fight. Her father said that unless she conformed, she'd be thrown out of the house.

She was so desperate that she went to look at homeless shelters and asked her friends if she could live with them. Can you imagine a sixteen-year-old girl moving into a homeless shelter — on her own? She did end up moving in with a friend. And while she was out of the house, things got a little better. Thank goodness for the friend who took her in. But the problem was that she missed her family and they missed her. She was a teenager. She needed them. After a few months, the father said she could come back home, but only if she wore the headscarf, so she agreed. What an ordeal for all of them. This student was put in a position of having to choose between following what she thought was right and being part of her family. And her father, who wanted the best for her, failed to realize that sometimes moving to a different country means adapting to a different culture. Here's the hardest lesson for parents: You can't win a battle like this. You might say, "Until you are eighteen, you have to do it my way!" But your child knows she will turn eighteen, and she has every right to her opinions. Don't win a battle while losing a war.

We tend to see our child as an extension of ourselves. This is one of the primary reasons that we have kids — to live out our goals and dreams forever, to create replicas of ourselves so that all the wisdom we've gained won't be lost. Isn't that one of the first things you hear about a baby, that little Johnny looks just like his dad? Parents are always looking for signs of how their child is similar to them in looks and in personality, or like someone else in the family. It certainly doesn't help when a child looks exactly like her parent or behaves in the exact same way. It can be really confusing. Some people even think that a deceased relative has been reborn in the body of the new child. Sometimes it feels like our fates are sealed the day we're born. I recently met a man who told me that there were ten generations of doctors in his family, back several centuries. He was proud of this lineage, and he should be, but I wonder about the children who didn't want to follow that path.

Psychologists might call this the "ego" in parenting. "*I'm* the mother. This is *my* daughter." Naming kids after their parents or grandparents is a common symptom of parental ego: We think of that child as a replacement. Sometimes we try to measure our self-worth according to what our children achieve, the type of car they drive, or how much money they make. I call this the pet show — parading a child around to boost your own ego. "Look at what my kid can do, and he's only two years old!" I've seen videos of kids who can translate up to five languages by the time they are five, or kids who have memorized the times tables by age six. Who is happy about this? Clearly, it's the super-proud parent. I'm not so sure about the child. And have you ever wondered why some parents have trouble teaching their own children? It's because they see themselves — and all their insecurities and imperfections — in their children. When the child doesn't understand something right away, or god forbid fails, the parent is instantly angry and frustrated, the exact opposite of a good teacher.

If you think about it, this assumption that our children will follow in our footsteps is pretty problematic in the twenty-first century. It's so much harder to prepare for a career — because we don't know what the jobs will be. Ten years ago, who would have thought we'd have synthetic biology or 3D printing? Even seemingly stable professions like medicine are changing. Doctors now use electronic records, or they rely on robotics for surgery, and they take notes with Google Glass during consultations. In the near future, your x-rays might be more accurately read by robots. So maybe it isn't wise to encourage your child to become an accountant, even if it's been a great profession for you. Maybe accounting is a dying field. As Thomas Friedman says, this is the century of self-learning and passion. I think it's time we define "success" as "passion." And we all know kids don't develop passion through force.

Attempting to clone your kids in your own image, the failure to see and respect your children for who they are, can be a serious problem. As a teacher, I can see that kids are getting more depressed and desperate every year. According to the Department of Health and Human Services, roughly three million teens between the ages twelve and seventeen had at least one major depressive episode in 2016. There are a lot of reasons for this, ranging from the insecurity that comes from social media to an unmanageable load of high school classes to the pressure to get into the school of their dreams — or is it the school of their parents' dreams?

When the stress is too much to handle, kids can even be pushed to suicide. The CDC found that in 2016, suicide was the second leading cause of death for both ten- to fourteen-year-olds and fifteen- to twenty-four-year-olds. The overall trend is disturbing: Between 1999 and 2016, total suicides increased by 28 percent. Here in Palo Alto, we've had a string of teen suicides that shook our community to the core. Both local high schools, Gunn and Palo Alto, have taken serious steps to reduce the pressure on students. The former Palo Alto High principal Kim Diorio started a successful program with the help of Denise Pope, a Stanford education professor. The objective is to take the parental and societal pressure off kids so they can be themselves, focus on what is important to them, and realize that getting a B is not the end of the world. But how many other schools in the United States and across the world have adopted similar programs? How many kids are stressed and depressed? How many feel overwhelmed and misunderstood? The answer: lots.

Depression and suicide are complicated topics, I know. There are all kinds of risk factors. But at their core, aren't they really about kids feeling trapped, feeling forced into lives that aren't their own? And in some cases seeing no way out? When a researcher at Yale surveyed adolescents in affluent communities like Palo Alto, trying to discern the kinds of pressures they were under that might lead to suicide in extreme cases, she found two main causes of distress. The first was "pressure to succeed at multiple academic and extracurricular pursuits." This we know. But the second cause was isolation from parents. That's what happens when kids are not respected for their ideas, passions, or preferences. They learn to fear or resent their parents, which shuts down all communication. They are pushed away when they most need support.

Being respected for who we are is so fundamental that if someone — anyone — can show kids a little respect, they can be rescued, even when all seems lost. When I think about how important it is to find and nurture a kid's passion, to really understand him, I think of Caleb, a tall, handsome African American student in my freshman

English class. He smiled a lot, but there was a sadness in his eyes. This particular class had fifteen boys and three girls, all of whom were the lowest-performing English students in the school (below two or more grade levels in reading). I'd volunteered to teach the class. There weren't a lot of other teachers chomping at the bit to take on this challenge. But I wanted to help. I also wanted to know if my methods would work with non-performing kids. These students were struggling with all sorts of personal problems, and the traditional education system had done next to nothing to empower or encourage them.

As a teacher, I expect to have a few difficult students each semester, and Caleb was one of them. He didn't want to work. I could see he was depressed, even though he didn't display the common signs of depression. He had spent the first eight years of his schooling getting into trouble, and he figured this year would be no different. He had no goals. Well, he did have one goal: to disrupt the class. He got attention that way. A few weeks after school started, it became clear that Caleb was lost and unmotivated.

One day I stopped him after class. "Caleb, it looks like you'd prefer being somewhere else other than school," I said. "Is that true?"

"Yeah," he said. "I hate school."

"Really? Hate it?"

"Yeah. I really hate it."

We kept talking, and it came out that he lived in a small two-room apartment in East Palo Alto. His mom and sister were in the living room, and he was in the bedroom. It was hard for him to be in school with kids who had parents with so much money. His mom worked as a housecleaner, and the family struggled to pay the bills. "It isn't fun to hear what everyone is doing on the weekend, how much money they have," he said, looking pretty downtrodden. You can tell when a kid is depressed. Just look at their eyes. There's a dullness there, a lack of light. Caleb figured his chances of living past twenty-five were nil. He told me, "Black boys die early."

"Not all black boys die early," I said, "and you are going to be one who survives."

I decided to find out what he was interested in — everyone is interested in something. Turns out he was interested in shoes, of all things. Why? Shoes had status in his community, and they were something he could afford. People with certain kinds of shoes were considered "cool."

My next step was to encourage him to become an expert on shoes and how to buy them. I asked him to search for the kinds of shoes he wanted and compare the prices. Which shoes were the best and why? Which site offered the best price? I had him share his information with his friends. He liked that, too. Whenever kids can be experts in something, they feel good about themselves. They can be experts in Minecraft or in insects or whatever they want. It doesn't matter. They just need to be experts.

It sounds so simple, and hardly life-changing. But two things had happened: He now had a subject that he "owned," and he had one teacher who believed in him. Caleb started showing up on time, because he wanted to. His face changed. He smiled and wanted to talk to me all the time. And he did his work.

Caleb and I are still in touch. I take him to lunch sometimes. He's a sophomore now at a nearby community college with plans to be an electrician with his own company. What happened with Caleb can happen with all kids: we can rescue kids, through kindness and caring, through finding out about their passions and through having some trust and respect. Every student has potential, every student is worth rescuing.

WHEN RESPECT IS A CHALLENGE

Parenting presents so many challenges to the simple mandate to respect your kids. Take birth order, for instance. Raising one child is hard, but two is harder. And three or more means managing a daily circus. You only have two hands, and if there are three kids, what does the third kid hold on to? Every child is special and wants something different. Every child needs to differentiate themselves from their siblings, and every child needs to challenge their parents, especially as they grow older.

Birth order plays a major role in kids' development and how they choose to challenge you. With my daughters, I dealt with three individuals at three stages of development who all wanted different things. The firstborn child has the distinction of being the first, and the youngest child is the baby. But what about the middle child? If they're a different sex, he or she has that distinction, but if not, well, it isn't easy, but it's possible.

All of my daughters wanted to be held, have my attention, and, most important, be my "favorite." I remember one of their best-loved questions, always at inopportune times, such as at six thirty a.m.: "Mommy, am I your favorite?" You don't want that question at six thirty a.m. My answer was always this: Half asleep, I would hold up my hand and ask them, "Okay, which finger is my favorite? If I have to cut one off, which one should I cut off today?" That would do it. They would stop asking. Until the next week.

That explanation didn't stop Janet, the middle child, from wanting to be number one all the time. Younger siblings have two choices to attract attention: compete with their siblings, or rebel and be as different as possible. Janet chose the first. She always wanted to beat Susan, the firstborn, and she almost always did. She wanted to swim faster, run faster, read faster, talk faster, get more hugs, and be snuggled more. She did math early and started kindergarten at age four. It was amazing to see. She kept trying to be taller than Susan, though to her chagrin that didn't work. When Anne came along, Janet not only wanted to be as good as or better than Susan, but she also wanted to be as cute as Anne. She did a pretty good job, but it was hard to compete with Anne, who distinguished herself by being the ultimate charmer. You could see that in her even when she was only one year old. Smart kid. Being cute was the way to get what she wanted.

Birthday parties were tricky. I solved the problem by giving Janet birthday presents on Susan's birthday and doing the same thing for Susan on Janet's birthday. They agreed it was a great idea. Everyone got presents once Anne joined the family. A great boon for all.

Thousands of studies have looked at the effects of birth order, and most of them confirm what we know instinctively. People say that firstborns are more likely to conform. It's partly because they are outnumbered by two parents. But it's also because they have advantages over their younger siblings, so they can win parents' attention the easy way: just do what Mom and Dad want. According to Dr. Kevin Leman, a psychologist and author of *The Birth Order Book* and *The Firstborn Advantage,* firstborns are also held to higher standards. Well, you can see that didn't work in my family. Janet held herself up to the highest standards, and she succeeded. Leman says the middle child tends to be the "family peace-keeper" and is usually more agreeable and loyal. Maybe for some families. But I would never call Janet a peacekeeper. She was always up for something exciting and fun. If anything, she was the challenger, the inspirer, the creative spark. And in general, younger siblings are more likely "born to rebel," as the title of Frank Sulloway's book on the subject puts it.

What's buried in the research but rarely explicitly stated are the expectations we have for our children. If firstborns tend to be first at everything, that's probably because parents *expect* the first child to be first at everything. In our family, I expected *both* Susan and Janet to be good at what they wanted to do, and if they weren't good at it, they tried again. It was okay to make mistakes and start over. In fact, it was encouraged. After all, that's how children learn. And kids rise to your expectations. I had high standards for Susan, but I didn't exclude Janet from those standards. I expected both of them to meet my expectations, and when Anne was born, I had the same high expectations for her.

It bears repeating: Respect includes setting high standards. You don't respect your children's abilities if you coddle them. But you also don't respect your children if you force them to excel in activities that have no personal meaning for them. Enforcing high standards only works when kids can bring some passion to what they're doing. You want them to be successful in whatever *they* pick, not what *you* pick. That's one of the main problems: the parents are picking. Of course you can guide your children, but you should never force them. Otherwise there's a good chance they'll end up depressed and resentful. I watch Susan guide her five children; it isn't easy, because they have very different interests, but she respects that and encourages excellence in whatever they choose. Jacob loves music, so Susan supported his passion for the piano; Amelia is a gifted athlete, so Susan supported her joining the soccer team. Each child has the ability to choose, but the expectation is that they'll all perform at the highest possible level.

Sometimes your child might lose respect for you — but it can be repaired. It's harder when they're older, but it's still possible. One of the hardest things to do as a parent is to respect your child's privacy. And all kids need privacy — even infants. I asked my daughter Janet numerous times to clean her room when she was thirteen. She didn't listen, so one day I got fed up and decided I'd do it myself. Guess what I found underneath the bed? Her diary. I'm sorry to confess that I gave in to temptation and read it. It was fascinating to learn what she was doing and thinking, but I immediately knew that I'd violated her privacy. I felt horrible.

Some parents would probably have replaced the diary exactly as they found it and kept the incident a secret. But that didn't feel right to me. The only thing I could do was turn myself in. When Janet came home from school the next day, I confessed. I sheepishly gave the journal back to her. She screamed at me. She slammed her door and wouldn't let me anywhere near her room, but I kept apologizing. I explained to her that I'd lost my patience and done something I knew was wrong. I told her I was ashamed. Sometimes you have to help your children understand both sides of the story and the emotions you yourself are experiencing. I promised Janet I would never disrespect her privacy again. And she was kind enough to forgive me. Your children will see you make mistakes. They will learn more from how you respond to your own mistakes than from the mistake itself.

I can remember another time when my daughters did not want

me to come to a party where there were other parents. "You'll talk too much, Mom, and dominate," they said. My feelings were hurt, of course. But I thought to myself, *I don't want to invade their space if they don't want me there.* And they were probably right: I would dominate the conversation. So I didn't go and didn't hold a grudge. It was fine. I respected them, and it seemed as though we'd turned a corner. The next time there was a party, I was invited. I tried my best not to talk too much (a bit hard for me). What I think happened is that they wanted to feel in control, and when I agreed not to go, even just once, I reassured them that they were in control of their social lives. Saying it is not enough. Actions speak louder than words. That one party opened the door to my inclusion the next time, and I like to think I learned something they'd been trying to teach me.

I confess I had some learning to do when it came to my own grandchildren. I assumed that grandparents were like parents — a mistake a lot of people make — and that I could have as much control as I did with my daughters. Wrong. I was one of the worst about buying toys, clothes, candy. Just a relentless stream of gifts for my grandchildren, because I loved them. It turns out these gifts weren't always welcome. Susan looks at me suspiciously when I enter with a box or bag full of toys for the kids. "They don't need any more stuff, Mom," she tells me. "Okay," I say, "how about letting them play with the toys for an hour?" And I try to cut back, I really do. But I struggle.

I got into a habit of buying my granddaughter Sophie special sugar cookies that came not in a regular box but inside a plastic teddy bear. If you pushed a lever, a cookie came out. They were simple cookies but the packaging made them irresistible. What could I do? I kept buying them. But one morning Anne complained that Sophie had cried through the night: "She wanted *you*," she told me.

She was crying for me, but not because she wanted me. She wanted those cookies. Lesson learned. I was an overly enthusiastic grandmother who needed to be toned down. My daughters took care of that! *They* are the parents. I have to respect their ideas and wishes. They have their own families now.

TEACHING RESPECT MEANS LIVING IT

Sure, you should respect your child, and it would be great if that child also respects you. But have you ever thought about how you live in the world, how you show respect to the people around you, and what you're really modeling for your children? Everything — and I mean everything — is a learning opportunity. Kids don't miss a beat. They see (and feel) the respect that you show your spouse, other family members, neighbors, and friends. They hear how you talk about your boss and colleagues at work. They see how you respect yourself. And they pattern their own behavior and values from every single one of these.

Teaching respect means living it. Every day. It means respecting all the people in your life. If you model it, your kids will follow. Most of the time. They might need a little coaching. Whenever my girls misbehaved, I'd have them write me an apology and reflect on how they could improve (I guess I'm in good company, because Ruth Bader Ginsburg reportedly assigned essays when her children misbehaved). I'd have them apologize for anything they had done that was problematic. It could be fighting with their sister, being late for something, failing to do a job around the house. Writing is thinking, and thinking prompts change.

I've spent the past thirty-six years running my classroom as if it were the staff of a professional newspaper. That's how my program works. I don't give my students exercises that simulate a newspaper — they're tasked with all the real-world responsibilities, and they experience the real-world consequences. The student publications are self-supporting. That means the students go out and sell advertising to pay the publication costs. At the beginning of the semester, the whole class goes to downtown Palo Alto with contracts in hand and a copy of the newspaper to get advertising for the year. The students come up with the story ideas — not me. Some of those ideas are questionable, to say the least. But during our story idea session, led by the kids, the terrible ideas disappear on their own. The students always figure it out themselves. It happens naturally in the process of thinking it through and hearing other people's feedback.

Next, the editors make critical decisions about which students write which stories, and some of those stories are very sensitive. In the past we have written about poor teacher performance, student depression, students' attitudes toward sex, and irregularities on the school board, just to name a few. The most recent topics were about gun control and the Parkland, Florida, shooting as well as the resignation of our school principal.

What I've found over the years is that to meet deadlines and work under pressure, we have to have an atmosphere of respect. Journalism requires a lot of criticism and a lot of revision. I push the students to go far. Not only that, they push themselves and each other. They know I have their backs, so I don't mince words. When it comes to an editorial or feature article, I'll flat out say, "This ending needs some work. Do you want me to help you, or do you want to think about it yourself?" and we'll discuss how to make it better. You want to be sensitive to people who've worked hard. You want to respect them and their efforts. But I don't believe in everybody getting first place, and my students know it. I'll share which stories I think are the best for each issue and explain why. They do the same, and their opinion actually matters more. It is their newspaper or magazine, not mine. I am only the advisor. All of my students understand that I'm trying to make them more effective. I'm preparing them for the workplace, where they'll get criticism whether they want it or not. When they have a job and someone critiques their work, they'll be able to say, "Yes, I've experienced this before. I know what I need to improve, and I know I can improve."

Or it's the students who do the critiquing. My student editors are responsible for leading discussions about their fellow students' work. They have to manage a class of sixty kids, all of whom are reading and critiquing one another's articles. Imagine what amazing lessons they are learning, the most important of which is how to treat others with respect. My admonition at the beginning of the school year is "Be respectful if you expect the class to respect you. Never say mean things to anyone, and don't embarrass anyone in front of the class." I remind them that if they lose the respect of the class, getting it back is almost impossible. I don't let the editors yell at the class or say things like "Shut up." It's counterproductive. It shows lack of respect and creates a negative working environment. The kids get it right away. I don't have to belabor the point. They are all working toward the common goal: an outstanding newspaper. Have you ever seen groups of teens beg to stay at school late at night? That's what happens when they own the product and are obsessed with perfection. They realize the power of passion in life's work.

In 2016, we had an important election for new school board members. The *Campanile,* Palo Alto High School's newspaper, always makes recommendations about which candidates to vote for, and those recommendations are taken very seriously by the local community. In talking with my students, I realized we completely disagreed about which candidates to support. We all made our cases, arguing for what experience and expertise these people would bring to the school board. I respected their opinion, and they respected mine — but it's their newspaper. In the end, they won. The paper came out with the students' recommendations, and that article influenced the election.

Student teachers taught me another lesson about respect. For decades, I was a mentor for teachers earning their degrees at Stanford and the College of Notre Dame. I could usually size them up within the first two weeks as to whether they'd have a hard time learning to be an effective teacher. The main thing I looked for was their ability to connect with and respect the kids, to like the kids, and to laugh at themselves. If they strove for perfection through grades and punitive measures, it was going to be tough. Strict teachers expended a lot of energy getting angry at the kids for not following instructions, while they followed to a T their own guidebook on how to maintain control in the classroom. A former marine sergeant who couldn't communicate very well had a difficult time. While he had a lot to offer and was a smart teacher, kids hated his class and always wanted to transfer out. On the other hand, teachers who had high standards that were reachable through revision and mastery did very well.

What I try to do with everyone — students, student teachers, my daughters, and grandchildren — is respect them so that they can respect themselves. Amazing things happen when you have self-respect. Self-respect gives you the confidence to take risks and become independent. Without self-respect, you're afraid. You're obsessed with what other people think instead of following your own moral compass and your own passions. The number one regret people have on their deathbed is not pursuing their dreams and instead living a life someone else expected of them. Nobody wants this for their child.

I remember watching Anne ice-skating when she was only three years old. Stan and I couldn't skate to save our lives — Stan couldn't even walk on the ice without falling. But there was Anne, twirling and spinning around the rink, this tiny little girl who would grow up to be on a synchronized ice-skating team and play ice hockey in college and face all challenges with the fearlessness she displayed on the ice, doing something she loved — becoming who she was meant to be. The same thing happens with students. Sammy, the son of Mexican immigrants and a student beloved by the whole journalism program for his exceptional graphics, transformed before my eyes. He used the self-respect and confidence he gained in my program and through an advanced academic research program in which students pick their own topic to study for a year with the support of a community mentor to become an expert in graphic design, and went on to study it at San Francisco State University. He is the first person in his family to attend college.

As the poet Kahlil Gibran wrote: "Your children are not your children. / They are the sons and daughters of Life's longing for itself. / They come through you but not from you. / And though they are with you yet they belong not to you." Respect is what we want to give our children, but sometimes we are held back by our own insecurities. As parents, this is one of the most difficult obstacles to overcome, but we're all capable of treating our children respectfully if we keep the basics in mind. Honor their wishes and interests, which may be different from our own. Challenge them to be their best at whatever activities they choose. And above all, give them love and support so they gain the confidence they need to pursue their own path.

INDEPENDENCE

4

Don't Do Anything
for Your Children That They Can
Do for Themselves

IN THE FALL OF 2014, I found myself on a brightly lit stage in Puebla, Mexico. Seated next to me was Amy Chua, author of *Battle Hymn of the Tiger Mother* and a vocal proponent of tiger parenting, a form of strict child-rearing common in China and other Asian countries. We'd been invited to debate each other at the Ciudad de las Ideas Festival, an annual gathering of some of the world's brightest minds in education, public policy, and technology. The auditorium was filled with more than seven thousand people eager to hear how we'd raised our daughters.

It was a bit strange to be on a stage at such a large venue, but my innovative teaching philosophy and my daughters' success in Silicon Valley had gained me some recognition. I was voted California Teacher of the Year in 2002, and I helped to form GoogleEdu, a teacher and student resource platform. For years I consulted at the U.S. Department of Education, the Hewlett Foundation, and *Time* Magazine Education. I also cared deeply about empowering kids and was speaking out more and more about changes that needed to be made in the classroom and in the home.

I was concerned after reading Amy Chua's book, which was a bestseller. The stories she shared about her daughters troubled me. She represented a growing trend in parenting that I thought was, well, really wrong. I'm sure some parents were reading her book and disagreeing with it, but I suspect many of them thought they ought to be tigers themselves. Chua is well known for her controlling, top-down, demanding style. Essentially, her philosophy is that the parent knows best and it's their responsibility not only to guide their children but to *enforce* the kind of behavior that leads to success. A few examples: She forbade playdates because they were distracting and useless. She decided which activities her daughters would pursue, regardless of their preferences or interests. It wasn't good enough for her daughters to get an A– or to be number two in the class. They had to get As *and* be number one ("in every subject except gym and drama"). Doesn't sound like much fun, does it?

Once, while Chua was trying to teach her three-year-old daughter, Lulu, how to play the piano, Lulu only wanted to smash her fists on the keys. Of course she did: she was three! Chua grew frustrated and swung open the back door. It was a cold winter day. She gave her daughter the option of obeying her mother or going outside. The three-year-old considered her options and decided that being outside was less unpleasant.

I have to say, I admire this little girl's spirit. And I do admire Chua's serious devotion to her daughters. Obviously, she wouldn't have gone to these lengths if she didn't care deeply about them, just as I cared about mine. The question, though, was how much agency her daughters had in their own lives — in other words, independence.

It's true that they did have tremendous success at a young age. One of them even performed as a soloist at Carnegie Hall, which is quite an honor, but how happy did this make the child? Or was it more about Chua's happiness? The fact that Lulu rebelled, at one point growing so enraged over a dinner in Russia that she said she hated her life and threw a glass onto the ground, shattering it, shows that she felt trapped in an existence that wasn't her own.

Chua's views are not isolated. They are shared by many other parents. Every year in December, I receive gift cards, expensive presents from Bloomingdale's and Neiman Marcus, and delicious homemade foods from my students' parents. I'm grateful for these gifts, and I'm grateful for what they represent: serious appreciation for teachers. The issue, though, is that we differ in our ideas of what teachers are supposed to do. These parents are accustomed to a controlling educational environment, while I'm all about independence.

In the media coverage of our debate, I was labeled a "panda mother." Of course, the press needed a parallel to "tiger mother," but to me the metaphor doesn't fit. Pandas are famous for sleeping and eating, and not much else. They are called "lazy," which, of course, is silly, but that's the popular image. My parenting is not lazy, not hands-free. But I do believe strongly in independence. Parents should encourage their children to be independent and self-starting. Other variations on Chua's style include "snowplow parenting," the most evocative term, in my opinion, because it means clearing all obstacles, all challenges the child might encounter. Most of us by now have heard of helicopter parenting, sometimes called overparenting, which the author Julie Lythcott-Haims explores in depth in her best-selling book, *How to Raise an Adult*. She cites her years of experience as a dean of admissions at Stanford, increasingly working with college students who were "somehow not quite fully formed as humans. They seemed to be scanning the sidelines for Mom and Dad. Under-constructed. Existentially impotent."

Her diagnosis? These parents were so involved in their children's lives that the kids couldn't function on their own. This was due to a whole host of reasons, including a growing culture of fear, media misrepresentations of threats against children, decreasing family size, and the so-called self-esteem movement. It can go pretty far. Parents have been known to rent apartments in the cities where their children are enrolled as college students or even to accompany them on job interviews. I wish I were kidding.

When I spoke with Lythcott-Haims about this unfortunate trend in parenting, she emphasized, and I agree, that overinvolvement in a child's life usually comes from a good place. Parents want their kids to succeed, so it's very painful for them to see children fail. *What's the harm in stepping in,* they think, *and making sure my child doesn't struggle?* Well, there's a lot of harm. As Lythcott-Haims told me, "It renders kids useless. They're veal-like humans. Accomplished, lovely to look at, but they don't know how to think things through as adults." She makes a strong case in her book for how overprotective parenting has led to anxiety, depression, and an alarming inability to deal with adult life.

As a teacher, I've seen kids become less empowered, less inde-pendent, and more afraid each year. They're scared to take a stand, scared to be wrong, scared to investigate controversial stories, and especially scared to fail. Their main source of motivation seems to be fear: the fear of disappointing their (usually overprotective) parents. They've been taught that perfect grades and the perfect college are all that matters. Some kids in Beginning Journalism are horrified to have their names attached to their articles. Why? They're worried about what other people might think. They are not empowered. And they do not possess the skills to make it in the twenty-first century. Confronting this crisis in parenting was one of my main motivations for writing this book.

But back to the "debate." It didn't turn out to be much of one. Chua talked for the first fifteen of our thirty allotted minutes. She reflected on her own childhood, recalling how she was whacked on the hand with chopsticks if she uttered a single word in English at home, and how if she scored a 99 out of 100, her mother would focus on the one missed point to make sure the next score was perfect. Here's a glimpse of Chua's father from her book: "In eighth grade, I won second place in a history contest and brought my family to the awards ceremony. Somebody else had won the Kiwanis prize for the best all-around student. Afterward, my father said to me: 'Never, ever disgrace me like that again.'" Chua claimed in the book and onstage that her parents' methods worked, and that she has a wonderful relationship with them. I have no doubt that she learned a lot growing up in this kind of unforgiving environment. My question is whether it was worth repeating.

She also spent a fair amount of time defending how she'd applied these same techniques to her own daughters. At one point Chua admitted, "Parenting is the hardest thing I've ever done." For her, the experience was an extraordinary struggle. She'd felt torn between two cultures and seemed to be convinced that she had to control her daughters or risk losing them to the mediocrity that came with American privilege. "If you're not a policeperson in your own house," I told Chua, "then you don't end up having such a hard time parenting." You see, I had the opposite experience. I told the audience that parenting was fun for me, that it doesn't have to be such a gruel-ing battle. Of course, that doesn't mean that parenting was without challenges, but I genuinely enjoyed it.

My main issue with Chua's method: It failed to instill a sense of independence or passion in her daughters. Her girls didn't really know what they were passionate about; they were too busy fol-lowing directions. All instructions came from Chua, which meant her daughters weren't required to think independently. But in my household, we prized independent thinking above all else. The last thing I wanted were kids who couldn't function without my mak-ing all their decisions. Our goals had nothing to do with our daugh-ters being number one in the class, which would mean that they had conformed and followed all the rules. I wanted them to find joy doing the things *they* cared about. I wanted them to confront problems in society and find innovative solutions. I wanted them to have warm and loving relationships with the people in their lives, including their parents.

Nobody is happy living a life that's dictated by someone else. If there's one thing I've learned as a mother and teacher, it's that kids of all ages need their independence.

So the question becomes: How?

THE BASICS OF BUILDING INDEPENDENCE

"My mother was determined to make us independent," Richard Branson wrote in his memoir *Losing My Virginity*. "When I was four years old, she stopped the car a few miles from our house and made me find my own way home across the fields." Four? Okay, this might not be the most appropriate way to teach a lesson, but Branson's mom was right about the importance of independence.

I felt the same way as a young mother. Perhaps this was a result of having been brought up in the 1950s when women had no rights . . . literally none. My mother had no money and no power. She always did what my father wanted. That's one of the reasons she didn't question the advice of the doctor who refused to treat my brother David. She never dared to challenge anyone who wielded power over her. The assumption was that I would live the same way.

But I rebelled — I learned how to sew my own clothes instead of waiting for hand-me-downs; I wrote articles for three cents a word as a teenager, dreaming of someday becoming a journalist, which I was told was a man's profession; I became a model to pay my way through college (those long, skinny legs came in handy after all). But in one way I did conform to the vision my parents had for me: I married young.

The night before my wedding, my mother-in-law showed me how to take care of my future husband's needs. "Here is how to make his bed," she told me, folding the top sheet with a kind of precision I had never seen and was pretty sure I couldn't replicate. Then we moved over to the dresser, where she showed me how to organize his clothing. And his breakfast order? I got that, too: scrambled eggs and poppy seed sweet rolls, with strong coffee. I am not making this up. There I was, about to become a wife and inheriting a caretaker role from a highly educated woman with a PhD, a pioneer in her own right.

I wanted a different kind of life for my daughters. That didn't mean they weren't going to be wives and mothers too; it just meant they weren't going to be held back because they'd been taught to be subservient. Their options wouldn't be limited because they were dependent on anyone, especially their parents. Independence, I decided, was going to start on day one. And I do mean from day one — from the very start, when they're babies and you think they need you hovering the most. That's when independence begins.

Let's revisit sleep: the single biggest source of confusion for parents of young children. Back in Chapter 2, I told you sleep was the first lesson in trust. It's also the first lesson in independence. Sleep is your child's first chance to self-soothe, to take care of her needs *on her own*. That last part is critical.

In Pamela Druckerman's international bestseller *Bringing Up Bébé*, she talks about the French "pause," the tradition in French parenting culture of waiting just a second before comforting a baby who wakes up in the night. Instead of immediately rushing in, French parents are told to pause, giving a child the chance to learn how to sleep on her own. Even newborns are thought of having responsibilities to the family. They have to learn how to sleep so the parents can sleep.

I didn't know anything about the "pause," but it turns out it's remarkably similar to what I did with my daughters. They spent some of their early years in France and Switzerland, so perhaps I was subconsciously influenced by those cultures.

New research supports what the French seem to understand intuitively: A 2017 study published in *Pediatrics* found that at four and nine months of age, babies who slept independently (in their own rooms) slept longer and had increased "sleep consolidation" (longer stretches of sleep).[5] Unfortunately, many of us never got this memo.

Dr. Janesta Noland, a well-known pediatrician based in Menlo

Park, California, says she commonly sees children at eight, nine, and ten months old who wake up throughout the night. There are even one-, two-, and three-year-olds who don't sleep through the night. Why? Because they haven't been taught. "Sometimes as parents we're frightened to give our kids the opportunity to learn," she says. "We feel like we're harming them, and that we're not supporting them in the way they need to be supported." Dr. Noland told me that at around three to four months of age, babies develop a kind of cognition that tells them they are an individual. "Suddenly they understand they're separate," she says, "and you want to get your baby out of your bed, and hopefully out of your room, before they learn this." According to Druckerman, the French have a similar theory about babies at four months of age: If they haven't learned to sleep by themselves at that point, it's going to be very difficult to teach them. They've learned that making a fuss means you'll rush in. Some babies (especially those with colic) can be more difficult. But the majority of children will benefit immensely from learning early on how to sleep through the night. And most important, it will put them firmly on the track to independence.

If you do have an older child who isn't sleeping through the night, the first thing I recommend is to talk to her. Explain that sleep is how kids grow. She may not understand completely, but communication is an important first step. It also helps to set an age-appropriate routine and follow it. Reading books (especially books about sleep) and singing songs are great rituals before bed — they're fun, and they make kids relaxed. Finally, and this is most important, do not rush in if they wake up in the middle of the night. Practice the "pause."

If sleep is about stepping back, then temper tantrums are about laying down the law. You know what temper tantrums are about? Control. That's right, a child wanting control over himself and his environment, which is a necessary step toward independence. What the child can't control as a toddler are his emotions. That's where the wailing and thrashing come in. But with time and a little patience, he can learn how to ask for something without falling to pieces.

Okay, so there are occasions when you probably should give your kids what they want without much discussion, as long as what they want has some value. If a child screamed because she wanted to go to the library, I'd tolerate that because I want to encourage a love of reading (though we would work on the screaming part). Once, we were at Disneyland when my girls decided they wanted to go on the "It's a Small World" water ride. *All afternoon.* Did you know that ride is only fifteen minutes long? We must have cycled through it a dozen times. It took days to get that song out of my head, yet my girls loved it, and I thought the song had a powerful message: it's a small world, and we're all alike. To me, they were learning an important lesson. I did have one rule that was non-negotiable, despite the anger it could cause: No public tantrums allowed, especially if they wanted something that I didn't consider important. One day we were at Macy's when Janet saw a toy she wanted, and she was going to have that toy or else. It was me against her. She had the wildest temper tantrum you've ever seen. She screamed like I had stuck a pin into her, and I had to march her out of the store and far away before she gave up. I'm not suggesting that parents can avoid this! But if you stick to a firm rule about it, eventually even the most willful child will learn.

Temper tantrums usually start around age two, when children are beginning to do things on their own. It can be putting on their shoes, brushing their hair, or dressing themselves. If you should dare to help them, watch out! They can easily fly into a tantrum and insist on starting all over and doing it *by themselves*. My advice? *Give them a chance.* It takes more time, it can be really, really frustrating, and they might end up with their shirt on backwards or their shoes on the wrong feet. I can't tell you how many times I let my daughters out of the house looking completely crazy, but I wanted them to feel they'd completed a task on their own. This is so important for instilling independence. You might not have time for this every day, but make a plan to occasionally give them the time they need. I suggest letting your child dress herself and do other simple tasks at least 20 percent of the time. Remember, it's a good sign that she wants to be independent.

For those really difficult tantrums, the kind where you find yourself dragging a thrashing child through Macy's, you have to reason with them. Children can be irrational. Really irrational. Sometimes logic doesn't work, especially with very young kids. But they need to learn to control themselves in order to learn independence. I encouraged my daughters to "use their words." I'd tell them, "I know you're sad and that you want something, but as long as you're having a tantrum, I can't help you." Young children are still human beings (with developing brains). "Tell Mommy what you want," I'd say, more than once. With time, kids learn to talk about their emotions. The one thing I knew for sure was that I couldn't give in. Otherwise they'd learn that acting out got a response from me, and then I'd really be in trouble. Parents: Watch out for this. Set clear boundaries. That cute little kid in the stroller knows exactly what he's doing! This is how children come to control *us* — but only if we let them.

On a more positive note, consider that your child feels safe enough with you to have a tantrum. Just think about it. They would never have a tantrum with someone they don't know or don't feel comfortable with. They wait until you come home to do it because they trust you. This is the road to independence, though it may be noisy and unpleasant. Don't take it personally.

And at times there's wisdom in a child's resistance. We lived in Switzerland from 1973–74, and both Janet and Susan attended the United Nations School in Geneva. (Susan was five at the time, and Janet was three.) They were both very independent and smart, but Janet was also determined to do everything Susan did. She even started talking at about the same time as Susan; she was that determined!

When it came to entering school, she did not like being assigned to a younger group. The UN school disagreed. If you were three, you were in the three-year-olds' class. But that didn't deter Janet.

Without permission, Janet moved herself to the five-year-olds' class. I still have no idea how she pulled this off. Janet was in that grade level for six weeks before the teachers figured out she wasn't in the right class, and this was only because someone overheard her saying she was three.

They moved her back with the three-year-olds. Janet was not happy. Never one to take an insult without a battle, she decided to quit school rather than be humiliated with those younger students. And she did. No matter what we said or did, she refused to go back. Eventually, we enrolled her in an all-French school. She was placed in her appropriate age group and wasn't thrilled about that but at least it was in French, which gave her a challenge.

By the time we got back to California the following year, she decided she was old enough to go to school. But the public school didn't take four-year-olds, so we enrolled her in the Ford Country Day School (a private school). She was right, and she excelled. She loved everything about reading, and by the end of first grade, she had nearly completed the math curriculum through grade five.

Janet showed me that children often know what's best for them. It's up to us as parents to listen — within reason. Yes, you need to step in when they want something dangerous or irrational: when a child wants to jump in a pool but can't swim, or if your daughter is having a crying fit because her ice cream is too cold. But if what they want is rational but inconvenient, consider striking a deal: "I'd love to let you go down the slide again, but we promised to meet Grandma for lunch and we don't want to be late. Let's make a plan to come back to the park tomorrow." And if they really want to take on a challenge or follow some passion that excites them, I say give them a chance.

When kids move past the toddler years, parents have to negotiate how to give the child control and where to lay down the law as they pursue new interests. For me, giving control was predicated on a foundation of safety. That was my first focus as a mother. We have a pool in our side yard — we're lucky to live in California — and I was always worried when the girls were young, even though the pool is fenced. So I decided they should learn how to swim as soon as possible, and I mean really swim, not just splash around. I wanted them to be able to jump in at one end of the pool, swim to the other end, and get out without assistance. I didn't think I needed to hire a teacher or take them to swimming lessons. I bought a book called *Teaching an Infant to Swim*. The black-and-white pictures made it look pretty easy. I learned that children hold their breath naturally, and that their attitude toward swimming, like so many things, is informed by their parents. We started with putting their heads underwater, then the doggie paddle, and then swimming the crawl. They weren't perfect, of course, but they were strong in the water. All of my daughters learned how to swim by the time they were two years old. Janet could swim at thirteen months (kids learn at different ages and rates, and parents should always take this into account and make safety their first priority).

Sometimes I'd take them to the Stanford Campus Recreation Association (SCRA), a faculty swim and tennis club, to meet friends. One April afternoon when Janet was about fifteen months, we were taking advantage of one of the first warm days in spring, and she was running around the pool area with Susan, who was then three. The next thing I knew, Janet jumped into the pool. I wasn't worried because she knew how to swim — I'd taught her myself — but an older gentleman sitting nearby sprang from his chair and leapt into the pool to "save" her. You should have seen Janet's face. She was shocked. It was great that he was so proactive, but Janet wanted to swim on her own. The man apologized to her — to a fifteen-month-old! — and swam off. After that, I made sure I told whomever was watching that Janet could swim.

Water safety was non-negotiable, but when it came to other activities, I put my girls in charge, for the most part. This is where I really differ from the tiger and helicopter parents. The last thing I want to do is force a kid into something he hates for hours on end. While we want to encourage children to try new things and not give up when they find an activity difficult, we still have to respect their feelings. We have to remember why our children have activities in the first place: to promote their interests and engagement in life and to develop their character. When it came to my daughters, any activity was okay — as long as they were doing *something*.

Though music was important to my husband and me, it never worked out for our girls. They took lessons in piano and violin for a while, but they didn't enjoy them. I pointed out that violins were portable, but that didn't work, and neither did cutting down from two lessons per week to one. Anne wanted to ice-skate. Janet liked swimming, and Susan liked tennis. So I let them choose their activities. The most important thing for me was that they pursue something they liked.

Appreciating *differences* is essential. My grandson Jacob is a talented musician and composer. During his senior year of high school, he staged an amazing musical at Menlo School called *Ones and Zeros*. He wrote the music and script and served as director and actor. But that doesn't mean that his siblings are the same. Jacob's sister Amelia doesn't play any instruments but for years took dance. Their brother Leon is great at chess, and he's a Lego master and plays golf. The youngest two, Emma and Ava, love ballet. There is so much to do in this world.

Another important point: Sticking with something is important, but parents need to allow for evolving interests. If the activity starts to feel like a chore, take a break and reevaluate. If they still want to quit, then I would let them look around for something else. Amelia is an incredible dancer who won national competitions for years. She used to train for hours a night and traveled around the country with her team. But last year she decided to focus on soccer instead. Her parents encouraged her to finish out the year — it was important to teach her not to quit mid-midseason. (This is one of many ways in which activities build character.) But they also asked her what she honestly preferred. Once she finished the dance season, she quit. A more controlling parent might have made her continue, arguing that she'd invested so much time and energy (and so much of the parents' money). Maybe she'd even become a professional dancer. But if that happened, whose life would she be living? How independent would she be, and would she be happy?

LAY OFF (IF AT ALL POSSIBLE)

For decades, fourth-graders in the state of California have participated in the California Mission Project. It's part of a social studies unit that teaches students about the history of the state. The assignment is simple: build a mission out of sugar cubes. Sounds like a fun project that can help bring history to life, right?

Wrong.

You should see some of these missions. They're elaborately engineered works of art. Arched corridors, bell towers, slanted tile roofs. But guess who's making them? It's not the students. It's usually the dads. Parents these days are highly competitive and controlling — it's hard to believe how much they feel they need to interfere. Some teachers have stopped the project altogether because they know the kids aren't making the missions, and why have a project for the parents? Other teachers warn the parents in advance that the kids should do the work. That seems an effective way to go — up to a point. A lot of parents cooperate, but there's still the occasional mission that belongs in a museum. We all know who did that one. When my daughters were in fourth grade, they made their own missions. It never occurred to me to help until I took their projects to class and saw the competition. Anne's mission looked like it had suffered an earthquake. She got points in my book for historical realism.

I always thought their homework was just that: *their* homework. They each had big desks in their rooms, and in the afternoons I knew they were there, doing homework. They did it without being prompted. It was part of the routine. Of course, there were no distractions like phones or tablets. But they liked doing their homework and keeping up in class. If they didn't do it, it was *their* problem. Though I did help on request, and it was usually fun for both of us. When it came to projects, I didn't concern myself with other parents who were stepping in way more than I did. I'd tell my daughters, "I believe in you, you can do this project well enough, and I'll like it no matter what." If they wanted my assistance, I would agree to help, but only if *they* directed *me*. I refused to do it for them.

In talking with my friend Maye Musk, a nutritionist and successful model and the mother of Elon Musk, I learned that we were on the same page. She never checked her kids' homework. She couldn't. She was working five jobs to make ends meet. When their assignments required a parent's approval, she had them practice her signature so they could sign for her. "I didn't have time," she told me, "and it was their work."

That's what kids need: not constantly being controlled or overprotected, but allowed to take responsibility for their own lives.

For parents, that means giving kids responsibility — early and often. To say it another way, this means *laying off*. You have to offer guidance and instruction, but they can do a lot more — and at a much younger age — than you think. When Susan was eighteen months old, she was my official helper. There were no baby monitors back then, and we lived in a big house. Her responsibility was to *be* the baby monitor. When Janet cried, Susan called out, "Mommy, Janet is crying!" Susan couldn't speak clearly, but that didn't matter. She was in charge, and she was very proud of herself. And she felt like an important member of the family. She also helped fold diapers. She thought it was a game. Well, I made it into a game. While she wasn't that great at folding diapers, it was good enough for me. I just wanted her to be proud of the job she'd done. After all, they were just diapers. I suggest all children have a job that's theirs and theirs alone. They'll build skills toward independence and also learn how to help out around the house — a critical lesson for both girls and boys.

Later Susan took on the role of "Janet's teacher." She gave Janet toys, showed her how the rattles worked, and made sure Janet always had something to do. A few years later in Geneva, it was pretty funny to watch Susan try to feed Anne mashed banana. Most of the food ended up on Anne's face, but Susan was happy to contribute to the family, even in a small way.

Washing dishes was another important chore in our house. All my daughters stood on a little stool at the sink and washed the dishes after dinner. They didn't wash everything perfectly — but it did teach responsibility to the family. My grandkids carry on this tradition today. Ava, who's just four years old, will pull up a stool and help her brother Leon with the dishes. My daughters were also expected to make their beds every morning. Ha! A bed made by a kid can look like she's still asleep in it. But I didn't fight them. As long as they did it, I was okay with it.

When we went grocery shopping, I'd ask the girls to get two pounds of apples and put them in the cart. Today there are those child-sized shopping carts for kids. But they didn't exist back then; my daughters had to deal with the big carts! They had to measure two pounds, and they had to know how to pick good apples, which I'd taught them. They knew the budget, too. And when we went over our budget, they helped me figure out which items to put back.

I made a point of giving them certain freedoms, even when they were young. One thing I let them control was decorating their own rooms (at least to some extent). They got to decide what they wanted their rooms to look like, and then they had to live with it. In those days, wall-to-wall carpeting was in. We went to the carpet store and they got to choose. At age six, Susan chose to decorate her room with hot pink shag carpet. And she had to live with it. (Susan always loved the rug; I was the one who failed to appreciate its beauty.) Years later, when Susan bought her own home, she'd had some experience with interior design (and I'm thankful she opted for more versatile neutral tones). Janet, not to be left out of this decorating opportunity, picked royal blue for her rug. I liked that better, but it was her room so that is all that mattered. When Anne was six, she too got to pick her carpet: lime green shag.

To be clear: I'm not talking about giving kids responsibilities they don't understand or aren't capable of, nor am I talking about letting kids play in the street if it isn't safe, or walk to the store if the neighborhood is dangerous. I also wouldn't leave a small child alone with an older child unless that child was a teenager. This kind of premature independence can be counterproductive if not traumatizing. But sometimes we can take it way too far. In Maryland, a ten-year-old and six-year-old brother and sister were taken into custody as they were walking unsupervised a few blocks from their home. A mother in Chicago reports being "mom-shamed" after a neighbor called the police because her eight-year-old daughter was walking the dog on her own. A recent op-ed in the *New York Times* tells the story of a mother who was arrested for leaving her four-year-old son alone in a car for five minutes (it was a cool day, the windows were cracked, the doors child-locked, and the alarm turned on). She went into a store to quickly buy something, and a passerby called 911. Thankfully, there has been some pushback. In May of 2018, Utah passed a "free-range kids" bill that allows children to enjoy previously illegal activities — like walking to school or playing outside alone. The state decided to redefine "neglect" so that it didn't include what a lot of people think are just basic freedoms for kids.

For me, independence has scaffolding and support. Chores and responsibilities require teaching and allow imperfect results. Freedom to roam the neighborhood (if it is indeed safe) comes with the obligation to call and check in. My daughters used to call me from the pay phone at the local pool. They had to stand on their tippy-toes to reach. It's a lot easier now with cell phones. Children should always have access to emergency numbers — they can be posted on the wall, but it's better if the child memorizes important numbers as well as your address. They should know emergency procedures in general, not only for when they're alone, but for when they're with their parents (what if something happens to you?). Don't forget your neighbors; they can be a wonderful source of extra support as your child is building independence. If you're leaving your child alone for the first time, make sure they have your cell number. Give them suggestions of what to do and tell them when you will be back. Structure it for them. In time, they will learn how to take care of themselves, but at first they need some guidance. Remember, kids are adults in training.

Something else you need to understand: When kids start to take control, a little chaos ensues. I'm reminded of this every time I enter the Media Arts Center during production week for our school newspaper. The building itself looks like it belongs on a college campus, but here it is, at a public high school in Palo Alto. It opened in 2015. All the journalism teachers in the program are eternally grateful to the school board and the citizens of Palo Alto for supporting its construction. Before the Media Arts Center was built, I spent thirty years in a portable classroom with erratically functioning air conditioning and scuffed linoleum flooring. For those who don't know, a portable is like a trailer. Well, it isn't like a trailer. It *is* a trailer. The school rolls them onto campus, hooks them up to electricity, and calls them classrooms.

On a typical production day, the madness begins at around three thirty p.m. That's when the kids start filing in, if they haven't been there all day already or half the previous night. They're lounging in beanbag chairs with their laptops or huddling around a computer in the lab, discovering errors that were supposed to have been corrected, complaining about how the color looks on the SpotLight page, or worrying about the ad that didn't come in on time. Many types of music are blaring, but these teenagers are concentrating in a way that can be impossible for adults to understand. There's also food: lots of food. I make sure they have snacks all afternoon (I love Costco!), and our dinners are provided by teams of parents. Sometimes we have In-N-Out burgers. Other nights it can be anything from Indian food to Egyptian food to homemade spaghetti and lasagna. We've had legendary meals over the years, including all-organic dinners brought and served by Steve Jobs and Laurene Powell Jobs, whose daughter, Lisa, was in the program in the mid-1990s.

It looks (and sounds) chaotic, but it's productive. I'm proud to report that in thirty-six years, there has never been a paper that failed to be published — not once. Okay, there were a few times where the paper came out a day late because the students missed the deadline, in which case they had to raise additional funds to cover the printer's five-hundred-dollar late fee, but it always comes out, and it always looks good. Almost always. One night more than twenty-five years ago, a student thought it would be funny to draw horns and a mustache on a school board member pictured in that week's paper. It was a joke, and he planned to take it off before the paper was published. Well, he forgot. I remember looking at the copies and thinking, *Oh my god! What are we going to do?* I drove to Target and bought one hundred black Sharpies. The kids sat there all afternoon and night, blocking out every single horn and mustache on all 2,500 copies. It wasn't funny at the time, but now I can see the humor.

The horns incident brings me to one of the most important aspects of my philosophy for both parents and teachers: the mastery system. The mastery system is based on how learning actually works, something a surprising number of parents and teachers don't understand. Here's the deal: Failure is part of learning. If you do something perfectly the first time, *there is no learning*. Mistakes are encouraged. Remember the motto of Silicon Valley? Fail fast, fail often, fail forward. Kids are *supposed* to screw up when they're kids so they screw up less as adults. Home and school are environments that should support learning, which means allowing for failure. But too many kids are afraid that if they do poorly on one math quiz, they'll never get into college. If they don't get elected class president, their parents will be disappointed. So many kids are suffering from the conflict of wanting to do something on their own and wanting to get it right. When does it end? How much perfection do we need? How long do we want to delay the actual process of learning? How can our kids function, let alone become independent, if they're completely afraid to fail?

Mastery means doing something as many times as it takes to get it right. Mastery doesn't happen automatically. It's a process. Being a teacher of writing taught me this. In the eighties and nineties, when I was developing my methods, one of the supposed characteristics of a good teacher — in addition to being in total control of the class — was that your class was so hard that many students failed. Your performance was based on the number of students you failed each semester. This sounds unbelievable today, but it was true.

I couldn't abide by this. It went against my gut and sense of decency. Kids who got an F on the first paper found it impossible to recover. And they were de-motivated to improve since they were starting out so far behind. I gave my students an opportunity to revise their work as many times as they wanted — imagine that! Their final grade was based on the final product. It was the learning and the hard work that I wanted to reward, not getting it right the first time. "Writer's block" completely disappeared. Students weren't afraid to make mistakes, so they could write without as much struggle. The English department accused me of being too easy, saying that my students weren't learning enough. But when time came for testing, my students performed in the ninetieth percentile on the state exams.

I realized along the way that it was important for the kids to know that I made mistakes too. After all, we never stop learning. If I'm confusing when I teach something, I'll apologize, say I messed up, and start over. Sometimes my students challenge me on my revisions or my thoughts on which articles to include in the newspaper, and I'll admit that I was wrong. Over the years, I've had the kids try all kinds of new software that didn't work out. Oops. So what? I can't tell you how helpful it is to demonstrate that you don't have all the answers. Kids tend to put teachers and parents on a pedestal, assuming we're perfect, that we never screw up. They're much better off once they learn the truth: Nobody's perfect, and everyone can learn.

Yes, we all make mistakes, especially kids, but you know what? Kids often come up with the best solutions — even better than yours. A few years ago my whole family — including all nine grandkids — went on a vacation to an absolutely beautiful resort in Napa Valley called Carneros. There were all kinds of activities for the kids. The only problem was that the kids were constantly on their phones. All parents know what it feels like to show your children something special only to have them glued to a device. It can drive you mad.

Some of my family members thought the best option was to confiscate the phones. That's what Rio de Janeiro and the whole country of France decided to do in their schools. In 2017, the French government announced that phones would be banned in all elementary and middle school classrooms. Though I agree with studies that show phones should be banned in elementary schools, I don't believe in confiscation for older kids, because technology provides a perfect way to teach them self-control. If we try to ban something, it only makes people want it more. Remember Prohibition?

I decided to talk to my grandkids. "Why don't you come up with a plan for how we should regulate these phones?" I said. You should have seen them light up when I suggested that *they* make the decision. They huddled together, talked about it, fought about it, and finally came up with a plan. Do you want to know what they decided? To ban phones all day long, from nine a.m. to nine p.m.! Can you believe that? It was way more restrictive than I would have proposed, and we all followed the choice they made for themselves.

Tech is one of the things parents ask me about the most. They're right to be concerned. A 2017 study found that both depressive symptoms and the rate of suicide increased in parallel with adolescents' screen time.[6] It's a crisis, and it's something we all have to learn to control. To that end, I hope it helps to share my Ten Commandments for Tech:

1. Set up a plan *with* your kids, not *for* your kids.
2. No phones during meals, whether in your house or someone else's. A 2018 study found that subjects who used their phones during dinner felt more distracted and experienced less enjoyment.[7]
3. No phones after bedtime. Children need to sleep, and phones are a distraction. Explain the critical importance of sleep for their brain development, and remind them that they grow when they sleep.
4. Use your discretion with small children. Younger kids, starting at age four, should be taught to use cell phones in case of an emergency. Show them how to call for help — they're smart and capable of learning. Starting in the third grade, children can be taught appropriate cell phone use for school assignments and at home.
5. Children should come up with their own cell phone policies for

family vacations, weekend events, or any kind of social activity where they need to be present. Be sure they also choose a penalty for disobeying their own policy (losing a certain amount of time on a device is a good way to teach them how to stick to the rules).

6. Parental controls can be important for young children. But after eight years of age, kids can learn self-control. If they violate your trust or your agreement, the parental control switches back on.

7. Parents should model how they expect their kids to behave around technology. I have seen parents on their cell phones nonstop, and they call that "family time." That is *not* family time.

8. Discuss with your kids what pictures are appropriate to take and what audio is appropriate to record. Sometimes kids lack common sense. Explain that whatever you do online (in written form or any type of media) leaves a digital footprint that you should be proud to share with the world.

9. Explain cyberbullying and help them understand its negative impact not only on others but on them. You never know what kids think or consider funny. Teaching children what defines humor is hard, but it's important. My rule: Laugh with your friends, not at them.

10. Teach kids not to give out personal identification information.

THE FRUITS OF INDEPENDENCE

Back in the eighties, my daughters were known in our Tolman Drive neighborhood as the lemon girls. One day they noticed our neighbor's lemon tree, and she nicely agreed to their plan of using it to start a business. They came up with a price (fifty cents per lemon), and sold their goods door-to-door. They even sold lemons back to the neighbor with the lemon tree. Once they filled up their piggy banks, they'd spend their earnings at their favorite dime store, Patterson's on California Avenue.

I guess being an entrepreneur runs in the family, because my granddaughter Mia has a successful business making and selling slime. Yes, slime. It's exactly what you think it is. Gooey, stringy, a total mess. But kids love it, especially when it has sparkles and rainbow colors. Mia was talented at designing new types of slime and got the bright idea to market it at age nine. My grandson Leon started working at a local arcade in Los Altos called Area 151 when he was thirteen years old. It was his idea to get a job there, not his parents'. Leon sells tokens to the customers, teaches them how to play the games, and even resets and repairs some of the machines. His latest obsession is bitcoins. Trust me, he is a self-made expert on cryptocurrency.

All of these projects came from a spark of curiosity, which itself arises from independent thinking. Do you want to know the single hardest assignment for my students? Coming up with their own topics. They find basic free-writing almost impossible. They complain that they don't know what's interesting. The main thing they want to know is if their "interesting idea" will earn an A. I tell them any idea is an A idea as long as they are interested in it, because if they're not, why would anyone else want to read it?

Lack of curiosity and the inability to free-write were such widespread issues in the 1990s, when I was an instructional supervisor for English, that I instituted a department-wide policy of daily free-writing for every student at Palo Alto High. I waited for the back-to-school sale at Target and bought two thousand notebooks. I don't think they expected a customer like me. They didn't have a limit at that time (they do now!), but they were surprised that I wanted to buy that many and asked if I was a reseller. "No," I said. "I'm a teacher and I'm buying these for all the kids at the high school." Once they heard that, they couldn't have been more helpful.

For the first few weeks, you'd have thought I was asking them to solve a difficult math problem. All I wanted them to do was free-write about any topic for the first ten minutes of the class. How hard could that be? Really hard, it turns out. Sometimes I brought up topics from the newspaper. "Look what happened yesterday," I'd say. "What do you think about this story?" They didn't even know what those stories were. But suddenly they were paying attention, taking an interest in the world around them, and forming their own opinions. They learned to love those notebooks, and writing every day became a welcome ritual that increased confidence and fluency. This exercise was the beginning of their independent thinking.

Students often don't know *why* they're learning something. Asking *why* is so important to kids and they deserve a better answer than "because it will be on the test." By the time kids reach middle school, they give up asking and focus on getting a good grade. To increase curiosity, it is important to address the "why" questions. Why are we reading *Hamlet*? Why are we solving quadratic equations? When teachers answer these questions, it prompts kids to think more deeply about the implications of what they're learning.

Parents can elicit curiosity in their children through similar methods. We don't need to have the right answers all the time, but we need to encourage kids to ask the right questions. If we don't know the answer, we can say, "Let's find out. Do some research on Google, and we can go from there." My grandson Noah is always asking about the stars, the planets, and the world around him, difficult questions like "What are black holes?" and "What does it mean to have a sound barrier?" Those are for my husband, the physicist. Noah asks questions about math, too — complex, philosophical questions. Again, those questions are for my husband, or, better yet, for Noah's father, Sergey.

When we support curiosity, what we're really developing is a child's imagination. Which brings me to creativity, a wonderful by-product of independence and curiosity. Unfortunately, when it comes to creativity and innovation, our kids are suffering. In one study, a test based on NASA's recruiting process for engineers and rocket scientists was used to measure creativity and innovative thinking in small children. At age five, 98 percent of the kids had genius-level imaginative abilities. But at age ten, only 30 percent of the children fell into that category. Want to guess how many adults maintain their creative thinking skills after making it through our educational system? Just 2 percent. No wonder Elon Musk says, "I hated going to school when I was a kid. It was torture." He hated it so much, in fact, that when it came to educating his sons, he decided to start his own school. It's called the Ad Astra School, and — you guessed it — the focus is on self-motivated learning, problem-solving, and an entrepreneurial mind-set. There's even a class on the ethics of artificial intelligence. Musk's solution is unique to his family; other families are pursuing their own solutions, including homeschooling, which has grown in popularity over the past few decades. Why? Because the parents had negative experiences in school themselves and are looking for a better alternative for their children.

Eddy Zhong, CEO of Leangap, a unique incubator for teen start-ups, sold his first tech company for $1.2 million at age sixteen and had a similar experience as a student. He claims that schools make kids less intelligent and less creative. As he says in his TED Talk, "The fact is, there are way too many people out there right now who are obsessed with telling kids to go to college, to find a good job, to be successful. There are not enough who are telling kids to explore more possibilities, to become entrepreneurs . . . No one has ever changed the world by doing what the world has told them to do."

Here's what you can do as a parent, even if your child's creativity isn't being encouraged at school: I used to set up all kinds of art supplies for my daughters on the kitchen table. There would be markers, colored paper, books, Play-Doh, yarn for braiding, and other arts and crafts. When they came home from school, they got to make whatever they wanted. I was always on the lookout for toys that they could assemble and design themselves. The YouTube Kids app now has instructional videos for any kind of creative project you can think of. My granddaughter Emma drew some pretty incredible pictures of animals — she probably could have sold them at age seven. How did she learn to do that? Following a YouTube video. There's also no shortage of videos on scientific experiments for kids, like the optical illusions that my grandson Leon loves. Dan Russell, a computer scientist in charge of search quality and user happiness at Google, was upset with his young daughter for spending too much time online — until he realized that she had taught herself five languages!

Projects like these allow kids to imagine and experiment and, most important, play. Creativity flows from a sense of play, and it's one of the easiest things to teach your child. Here's a tip: *Let them be.* They will create their own imaginary worlds without any help from you. Think of a child on a beach and all the wonderful games and adventures he creates on his own — collecting shells and rocks, building sandcastles, skipping stones, splashing in the waves. This is what makes kids happiest (and builds the right skills). Following the rules is not play, ever, unless you're pretending to be a policeman. And don't forget to play *with* them. One of my grandkids recently rated me the "craziest person" in my family because I get down to their level. I have been known to crawl under the table with the kids and bark with the dogs and have a sincere conversation with the cats. Sergey has the same playful spirit and for that reason was voted second craziest in the family. Steve Jobs had a similar attitude toward life, and even told his daughter, Lisa, that schools kill creativity. I remember him in our cramped classroom, camped out on the beige corduroy beanbag chair. He'd talk to the students, play on the computers, and, well, hang out. He never stopped playing and exploring, and we all know what came of his incredible imagination.

MAKE YOURSELF OBSOLETE

Now, I know this will sound crazy to some people, but here's my ultimate goal as a teacher and parent: to make myself obsolete. That's right. I want kids to be so independent that they no longer need me. Traditional education made the teacher into a "sage on the stage." The teacher knows all; the child's role is to listen. That is not my goal or my style. Well, maybe I was more of a teacher when they were young, but even then my goal was to point them toward ideas of their own. Passively receiving instructions or watching someone else performing are the worst ways to learn. As John Dewey, the famous educational psychologist, claimed at the beginning of the twentieth century, "Learning is doing." Dewey's ideas make a lot of sense. If you can't experience something, you can't fully understand it. *And you can't do it independently.* That's why I made myself a "guide on the side." My philosophy is not to have them ignore or not appreciate me; it's that they feel empowered to do everything themselves. That doesn't mean I don't want to be part of their lives, or that they don't love or respect me. It means that I want them to be so empowered that they feel comfortable acting independently. I help, I facilitate. But I'm not in charge, and I do not take over.

So what does this look like? My editors in chief run my classes. They take roll, open the class, set the tone, and determine the structure of the day. Why not? These are tasks they can do without me, and it gives them agency. They sit in five chairs at the head of the class and lead the discussions. They decide which stories to include, which to cut, which last-minute revisions need to be made. The students are always shocked when they realize this is how I conduct my classes.

I remember my very first editors in chief. The whole concept was new, for my students but also for me. One of the first stories the students wrote back in 1991 was about the alarming increase in teen pregnancies, an issue that mattered to them. In fact, one of the articles they wrote discussed how students need to learn to use protection. It felt a little daring for all of us, but we also knew it was important.

This was just after the 1988 Supreme Court *Hazelwood v.*

Kuhlmeier decision that limited the First Amendment rights of student journalists. Basically, anything they wanted to publish in the school newspaper could legally be censored by the principal or paper advisor. I thought this kind of censorship was absurd and un-American. So I disregarded the ruling, and so did the state of California. I was thankful when the state senate voted in an anti-*Hazelwood* education law that invalidated the decision (though *Hazelwood* is still the law in 36 states). Why shouldn't students have the same rights as all citizens? How else will they develop a voice to make a contribution to society?

Those articles about sexual activity had a major impact on school policy. As a result of that series, the Palo Alto School District decided to start a new course for all district students called Skills for Living. This course is still a requirement some thirty years later. The primary focus is how to protect yourself from sexually transmitted diseases and unwanted pregnancies, though it also teaches other important life skills, such as cooking and managing finances.

All because these students were free to write about what mattered.

Once students are engaged and empowered, there's no limit to what they can achieve. One of the most amazing things about seeing my daughters grow up is how they've turned into passionate, creative revolutionaries. Their goals are to make the world a better place for all people, all nations, all economic groups. Susan saw YouTube as a life-changing platform, which is why she convinced Google to buy it and worked hard to become its CEO. Her vision is to democratize video, to give people all over the world the chance to share their lives, their work, their opinions and ideas and products and services. The goal is to give everyone a voice. YouTube believes that the world is a better place when we listen, share, and build community through stories. This message is equally important in education, and I've been honored to collaborate with Susan on bringing YouTube into the classroom.

Meanwhile, Janet is on a radical mission to eradicate obesity in children and adults, and her number one target is the soda industry. She travels all over the world, to some of the most marginalized and needy communities, spreading this message about the dangers of sugar. She focuses on the health of pregnant women, infants, toddlers, and children, as well as the negative impact of sugar on the future population. To date, she has published more than a hundred research papers on various health-related topics ranging from the effects of obesity on breastfeeding to chronic disease in Alaska Native villages.

And then there's Anne, who left the man's world of Wall Street to forge her path in the medical world with 23andMe. Her focus is on empowering consumers to get the information they need about their health so they can make intelligent choices. One of her mottos is "No one cares more about your body than you." It was a major effort to convince the American Association of Physicians and the FDA of her mission, but she worked with them and showed them the power of giving each patient information about their risks for chronic diseases like Parkinson's, Alzheimer's, and breast cancer. Her idea is that once we are armed with this information, we can make lifestyle choices to dramatically reduce those risks. 23andMe is completely changing the landscape of patient knowledge and empowerment. It's a groundbreaking concept, and she's just getting started.

The thing is, we need creative, independent thinkers and revolutionaries now more than ever. Our kids will face so many challenges. They'll need to experiment and take risks and think for themselves just to survive. But they won't be able to do any of this if we control and overprotect them. We owe our kids their freedom so they can thrive in the most unpredictable century we've ever faced.

5

Give Your Child Grit

GADY EPSTEIN WOULDN'T TAKE no for an answer. His older brother, Amir, had been in my class, and Gady wanted to join too. The problem was, he couldn't fit Beginning Journalism into his schedule, but that didn't stop him from wanting to take it *now*. He was just fourteen, but he was so inquisitive and energetic. And persistent. I liked him right away.

We agreed to do an independent study, just the two of us, during his free period. It was great for him and fun for me. I love working with independent students because I really get to know them and their interests. Gady would find me at lunch and ask for feedback on a new paragraph he'd written. He was a fast runner who could spot me from the other side of the campus. I was impressed with his dedication.

From day one, he loved writing and reporting. He also loved reading the paper — I brought in sets of newspapers to class, local papers and sometimes the *New York Times*. Gady would always come to our meetings with ideas for articles — lots of ideas. And he was willing to revise as many times as necessary until he got it right.

As an eleventh-grader, Gady joined the Advanced Journalism

class. He did a great job working with the team, and in the spring of that year he decided to run for one of five editor in chief positions. It seemed logical because of his passion and hard work. He was really talented. I guess I assumed he would be elected. So did Gady. The election process, completely in the hands of the journalism students, includes a vote by the current editors, and while Gady was rated highly by his peers in his writing and leadership skills, he ended up losing the election.

This happens no matter how talented the student is. Gady was clearly upset, and so was I, but I have to honor the students' opinions.

For a couple weeks I was a bit worried about Gady. He was really bummed. After all, he wanted to be a journalist. But then one day he said, "I'm still going to work to make the *Campanile* the best it can be." "Okay," I said, impressed but still cautious. Teenagers change their minds all the time. But Gady did exactly what he said he would. He dove into the work with so much purpose that he became the go-to person on the staff. Everyone consulted with him. He wrote the best articles and assisted everyone who asked for help. Along with his classmate, Oliver Weisberg, he even mounted a sting operation at a local video store that was selling pornography to minors. As a result of the article they wrote, the police raided the store and shut it down for good.

The fall of his senior year, Gady decided to apply to Harvard. He didn't have a 4.0, and no, he hadn't been elected editor in chief, but he decided to try. I was honored to write his recommendation, in which I shared the story of the editor race and his subsequent behavior and passion as a team player. I described how Gady excelled despite this setback, and what a great writer he was. I guess my enthusiasm came through, because Harvard called me to talk about

Gady. I was stunned. I had never been called by the admissions office before. I explained how Gady performed at the highest level no matter the obstacles.

Harvard liked the sound of this — a lot. Gady got in without the fancy title, even without the 4.0 grade point average. He was accepted because they were more impressed by his character and his determination.

I have many stories about the editor in chief elections, which have become a litmus test for how children deal with loss and adversity. Every year, I tell my students about Gady Epstein. His is a story about how to cope with losing, how not to be defeated, even if you didn't win, and most important, how not to lose sight of your goals no matter what. It is a lesson for all of us, because we face disappointments constantly. Your reaction to those disappointments is what matters, and your reaction is something you can control. In fact, it's the only thing you can control.

Gady went off to Harvard, where he majored in international relations and followed his dream of becoming a journalist. After making his way through several jobs in the industry, including at the *Baltimore Sun* and *Forbes*, where he served as the Beijing bureau chief, he is now the *Economist*'s media editor.

Gady Epstein is not an isolated case. There are always students like him in my classes, and it's what keeps me excited about teaching after all these years. Driven by a meaningful goal, Gady pursued his devotion to journalism. What he had was a vision, and grit.

Grit is a popular buzzword in parenting and education. It means sticking with something no matter how hard it is or how much adversity you must face to achieve it. That's my definition. In her best-selling 2014 book *Grit: The Power of Passion and Perseverance*, the psychologist and researcher Angela Duckworth studied West Point cadets, inner-city Chicago high school students, salespeople, and contestants in the Scripps National Spelling Bee. As she searched for what made people in all walks of life successful over time, Duckworth found that "no matter the domain, the highly successful had a kind of ferocious determination that played out in two ways. First, these exemplars were unusually resilient and hardworking. Second, they knew in a very, very deep way what it was they wanted. They not only had determination, they had direction. It was this combination of passion and perseverance that made high achievers special. In a word, they had grit." More recently, other researchers have argued that grit is a combination of conscientiousness and perseverance, two traits long studied in the field of personality psychology. I agree that conscientiousness and perseverance are integral to grit, but when I think about grit, I also think about self-control, delayed gratification, patience, and courage, all aspects of grit that we'll explore in the coming pages. Duckworth's theory reflects my own: the most powerful kind of grit is coupled with passion.

Sometimes that passion or drive is automatic. Think of immigrants, like my own parents and so many others, who are known for having tremendous drive. The idea behind "immigrant grit" is that those who fought to leave their countries and remake their lives are by definition determined and focused. Amy Chua was worried about her daughters losing the edge that helped shape her own success. In *Battle Hymn of the Tiger Mother*, she writes of third-generation immigrants:

> This generation will be born into the great comforts of the upper middle class . . . They will have wealthy friends who get paid

for B-pluses. They may or may not attend private schools, but in either case they will expect expensive, brand-name clothes. Finally and most problematically, they will feel that they have individual rights guaranteed by the U.S. Constitution and therefore be much more likely to disobey their parents and ignore career advice. In short, all factors point to this generation being headed straight for decline.

Okay, maybe these kids aren't "headed straight for decline," but their lives aren't automatically filled with experiences that build grit. It's a variation on the old saying "shirtsleeves to shirtsleeves in three generations," referring to farmer's sons who made it to college and white-collar work, and whose children obediently followed suit, until the grandchildren, raised in too much comfort, lacking motivation, reverted back to manual labor. And there's some evidence showing that third-generation children of immigrants can lag behind previous generations and recent immigrants. One study of 10,795 adolescents found that children born outside the United States had higher academic achievement and school engagement than children born in the United States to both foreign-born and native-born parents.[8] Not surprising. There's a certain passion to make it here in America that dissipates over time. Shifts in the business sector show similar trends. Looking to the tech industry, we know that in 2016, immigrants in the United States founded or co-founded half of the billion-dollar startups. A 2017 study by the Center for American Entrepreneurship found that of the top thirty-five companies in the Fortune 500, 57 percent were founded or co-founded by an immigrant or the child of an immigrant. Sergey Brin is an immigrant. So is Elon Musk. And don't forget Albert Einstein. Sure, there are many variables to consider, but the inborn grit of immigrants and the success it leads to cannot be ignored.

Adversity itself can build a kind of automatic grit. Either you succumb to your circumstances or you fight tooth and nail to overcome them. In this case, grit is essentially your will to survive. Studies in "post-traumatic growth" have shown that children who suffered severe illnesses in their early years are more positive and resilient as adults. There's no shortage of examples that prove this point. Look at Oprah Winfrey. She survived childhood sexual abuse and inner-city poverty only to become a multi-billionaire media mogul widely considered one of the most powerful women in the world. Or Sonia Sotomayor. She developed Type 1 diabetes at seven years old and had to give herself insulin injections. Her father, an alcoholic with a third-grade education, died when she was nine. Her way out was education, just as it had been for me, and in 2009 she became the first Latina Supreme Court justice.

In the summer of 2018, the whole world was gripped as news broke of a Thai soccer team that was trapped in the Tham Luang cave due to flash floods. One of the soccer team members, fourteen-year-old Adul Sam-on, a stateless scholarship student whose parents sent him from Myanmar to Thailand in the hopes that he'd find a better life, played an instrumental role in the rescue because he could speak English with the British cave divers. His whole life up to that point had been an exercise in grit: He came from an impoverished, illiterate family, immigrated to Thailand, left his parents to live with a pastor and his wife so he could attend school, and against all odds flourished there, becoming the top student and winning numerous athletic awards. Is there any question that all the adversity he faced made him tough, resilient, and incredibly courageous?

I'm inspired by all of these people, perhaps because I see a hint of my own journey in theirs. As my daughter Anne says, I'm a believer. I had a real fighter mentality growing up. A lot of bad things happened in my life, but I taught my daughters that you can either let them control you, or you can make the rest of your life great.

I'm not arguing for imposing trauma or suffering on children. Obviously, adversity can have tremendous negative effects — physical and psychological — that can last well into adulthood. But I do want to point out that overcoming hardships can make us stronger, that sometimes it happens automatically, and that kids in difficult situations often end up building grit, resilience, patience, and other vital life skills.

But what about the rest of us? How do children raised in comfortable households develop grit? Are you praising your child's effort over his talent? Are you teaching him that setbacks are a necessary part of learning?

The answer: Probably not. Overprotective helicopter parenting has resulted in children who don't know how to do anything for themselves, let alone overcome fears and challenges and failures. They cry when they don't get the snack or toy they want. This is not a tragedy, but they can make you feel like it is. They're used to their parents giving in, and in some cases, catering to their every whim. They're not asked to do anything uncomfortable, so as adolescents they're way more conservative, and way more afraid. They're absolutely terrified to take risks.

Schools aren't helping matters when the system praises only the end result. Most teachers today are completely focused on assessments and numbers because their evaluation depends on their students' scores. They're trained to follow instructions, to obey. The whole educational model is based on not failing, not taking risks. If the students come to school with any grit at all, it is the grit to endure the system, not the grit of passion for something they love. I'm not saying all students lack determination and persistence, because it's clear to me and all teachers that many kids do have an admirable fighting spirit that serves them well, but I meet fewer and fewer kids who approach challenges the way Gady did. If they don't succeed, they look around for someone to blame. I swear, every semester my students walk into the beginning class looking like lambs. They're terrified. And they need help to find themselves and feel empowered. Learning comes when students are willing to take risks. Otherwise, it is called memorizing.

I'm not the only one who has noticed this change in student behavior. Recently, I visited Carol Dweck in her office at Stanford University. Dweck is one of the foremost experts when it comes to how we deal with setbacks. Her book, *Mindset*, first published in 2006, offered groundbreaking insights into the psychology of human success. Dweck describes two different belief systems, or mind-sets: *fixed* and *growth*. People with fixed mind-sets believe that our innate abilities are set. There are geniuses, and, well, not-geniuses, and there isn't anything they can do to change that. Why do they believe this? Because that's what parents and teachers taught them. As Dweck's research revealed, these subjects assumed "You were smart or you weren't, and failure meant you weren't. It was that simple."

On the other hand, people with growth mind-sets believe success is achieved through hard work and focus, and that failure is no reason to quit. People with this mind-set have been praised for their effort and dedication rather than their "brilliance." Subjects with growth mind-sets, Dweck explains, "knew that human qualities, such as intellectual skills, could be cultivated through effort . . . Not only weren't they discouraged by failure, they didn't even think they were failing. They thought they were learning." It sounds a lot like my mastery system: learning involves failure, and you should keep working until you get it right. Dweck's research has shown that teaching people how to have a growth mind-set completely changes their idea about the meaning of challenge and failure. The growth mind-set gives us grit — and it can be learned.

Dweck talked with me about a trend she's observed in her students. "I don't think helicopter parenting is making kids stupid," she told me. "It's making them ineffective. They've been chauffeured everywhere, given little to no freedom. So how are they supposed to do something in the world later? A lot of them aren't going for careers. They're doing little gigs here and there. And I don't blame them. Because all your life you've had to live up to this standard, you've been anxious, all you want to do is not be anxious anymore." Does avoiding anxiety sound like a good source of motivation, or the right mind-set for pursuing meaningful goals? Is it giving kids grit?

Dweck went on to tell me about a freshman writing seminar that she began teaching in 2005. She assigns her students a private essay each week — read only by her — and when she first started, she would have an occasional student who wrote about being nervous and afraid. "But around five years ago," Dweck told me, "all of them, male and female, were saying they were terrified of making a mistake, terrified of exposing inadequacies, terrified of being found out." The exact same thing has happened in my classes. Dweck's advice to those fearful freshmen: "You're terrified because you think Stanford admitted you because they thought you were a genius. Wrong. You're not a genius. Stanford thinks you have a *contribution* to make to the school, and then the world." When she says this to her classes, there's a huge, collective sigh of relief.

Business leaders tell me a similar story. Stacey Bendet Eisner, an accomplished fashion designer and the owner of Alice + Olivia, a high-end women's clothing store, believes it is harder than ever to hire the right people. "I always talk about wanting to bring up a generation underneath me that's better, that knows more than I do," she said. "I want to hire better workers. But there's been this generation of parenting that's about doing everything for your children whether you have the financial means or not. And then these kids get into the world and can't accept criticism, can't do things for themselves, they expect someone to hand them everything, and it's a workplace disaster."

Jamie Simon is the executive director of Camp Tawonga, an incredible wilderness camp near Yosemite National Park. The whole camp is built on grit: Kids are responsible to their groups and are given tasks ranging from making sure everyone is wearing sunscreen and has taken their medications to scheduling the group's activities and coming up with policies that encourage both fun and kindness. They even have seven-year-olds doing overnight camping where they pack and carry their own gear (including cans of bear spray), and prepare and cook their own food. I wish every kid could have an experience like this. Ironically, for such a grit-focused camp, Simon has noticed changes in her college-aged counselors. In the past, the resident psychologist would work exclusively with young campers, but now she has to see the counselors as well. Why? Because they're disempowered and depressed and, well, gritless. It's not their fault; it's how they've been raised.

There's another equally troubling problem, which is the extreme *inverse* of gritlessness. Picture your average tiger or helicopter parents who set countless, sky-high goals for their children. Sometimes it works. They do instill a brand of grit in a child who's expected to be number one in all activities. She will be the perfect student and get into the perfect college. She will be the next Mozart. There are many kids who rise to the challenge despite all the pressure. They meet these insane goals and even surpass them. They're incredibly tough and resilient and high-achieving. But for almost all kids in these circumstances, the source of their grit is fear. Fear of failure. Fear of not being loved by their parents if they bring home a B+. Fear of not actually being the next Mozart (which is virtually certain to be the case). Grit and determination work against them living with purpose and being happy. They are overprogrammed and overcontrolled, forced into a life where goals are supplied for them, where stepping off the track of predetermined achievement means they completely fall apart.

Contrast this with grit that arises from the child's own passion. These kids have parents who see their child as a human being with his own opinions and interests and purpose. That purpose might disagree with theirs, but it's his to choose. He's encouraged to pursue his fascinations and set his own goals. When he inevitably fails, he's taught that mistakes are a natural part of learning and that he should stay focused. Obstacles don't deter him. He becomes strong enough to tolerate anything in his path — failure, boredom, distraction, intimidation. He just keeps going, no matter what, because he's driven by passion instead of fear. His motivation comes from inner goals, not external forces. The kind of grit that results is what drives the most remarkable kids I meet today, like the seventeen-year-old software developer from Cairo who's making an app to assist deaf people. It's not an easy process, and I'm sure he's been discouraged more than once, but he's determined to succeed and determined to help the hearing-impaired. Basically, he's unstoppable.

This is what we want to bring out in our kids: grit that flows from unbreakable and keen drive and carries them through any obstacle. With resilience. Toughness. Never giving up.

This, to me, is the kind of grit our children need.

GRIT IS A TEACHABLE SKILL

On the east side of Stanford's campus sits Bing Nursery School, beloved for its classrooms filled with games and toys and a massive outdoor play area. In the spring of 1972, Susan had been a student at Bing for almost two years when she was asked to participate in an educational experiment that sounded like fun. Susan was four years old at the time.

"We had marshmallows today," Susan announced as we walked to the parking lot, "and I got *two*." She told me she had been in a special game room and had been given a marshmallow. "If I could wait and not eat it right away, I'd get a second one," she said. She was super proud of herself for her restraint being rewarded. She couldn't stop talking about those marshmallows.

I later found out that Susan had been a participant in the famous marshmallow experiment. If you Google it, you'll find over two million hits describing Walter Mischel's groundbreaking research. Mischel wanted to test children's ability to delay gratification and assert self-control, and he wondered how these qualities affected them in adult life. In a way, he decided to torture the nursery school students — but nicely. His team of researchers would lead children ages four to five into an empty room at the school. A treat — often a marshmallow, but M&M's, Oreos, and other goodies were sometimes used — was placed on the table. The child was told they could eat the marshmallow right then, or they could wait by themselves until the researcher returned (after fifteen minutes, practically a lifetime for a little kid) and get two marshmallows instead of one. Some kids succumbed right away. The marshmallow was just too tempting. The kids who waited the longest found all kinds of creative ways to distract themselves — singing songs, dancing, sitting on their hands, looking anywhere but at the marshmallow. But what was most striking were the follow-up studies. Mischel and his research team found over the course of forty years that children who could delay gratification at a young age were "more cognitively and socially competent adolescents," had lower BMIs (body mass index), and fewer interpersonal problems as adults.[9]

Just as I was about to pull away from the nursery school, one of the researchers ran up to the car and told me that of all the students at Bing, Susan had waited the longest for her marshmallow. He seemed very proud. Though I didn't understand the experiment at the time, it makes sense now. Susan is one of the most patient and logical people I know. She's also tremendously calm under pressure. Nothing fazes her. She has enormous self-control. She surrounds herself with employees that she trusts and respects. She had all these traits as a young girl, and not because she'd been born that way, but because she'd been practicing for years.

Grit is made up of many different skills. I think of them as pieces of a puzzle: each is important. One major key is knowing yourself well enough to control your emotions and your behavior so that you can stay the course and not be swayed. I didn't set out to do it, but I had inadvertently been teaching delayed gratification at home long before Susan was tested with a marshmallow. For instance, when it came to food, my daughters knew there was a particular order to follow. I'd give them a small piece of candy with their main course, but they could only eat it after they finished their dinner. No exceptions. Another tactic: Whenever they wanted something, I always suggested a way to get it — but it usually took time. If they wanted to go swimming, for example, I would say, "Should we wait until it's a little warmer outside before we go to the pool?" Or another common request would be, "Can we go outside and play now?" My response: "Did you feed Truffle (the dog)?" or "Did you finish the drawing you started last night?" I can't really say why I did this, but I had a hunch that they should learn to control themselves as early as possible, even when tempted with candy or other treats.

Patience is another piece of the puzzle. I taught that, too: waiting and saving were part of our lives. We didn't have much money when the girls were growing up, so we saved for what we wanted. They each had their own piggy bank, and they filled them penny by penny. Every Sunday we cut coupons from the newspaper. Anne even developed a special coupon organizing system so they were easy to find while we were shopping.

Here's the opposite of teaching patience: letting a kid be online twenty-four/seven, with her device, in the car, in restaurants, at the dinner table. If I recommended that you take away your kids' devices in the car and teach them patience instead, I would be going against what 90 percent of parents are doing on a daily basis. I understand.

In today's world it's just not practical or realistic. But my method might be worth a try every once in a while. Have your child share with you what she's doing on her phone, or make a movie about your trip. Try a "Go Back in Time" day where you pretend there are no phones or iPads and see what your kids come up with. You could announce: "Let's pretend we are Grandma or Grandpa when they were little. What do you think they did in the car?" Make sure you're ready to sing.

Even as you pursue goals you're passionate about, you're bound to encounter boredom. Learning to deal with it is another important step in building grit. In class, especially during lectures (yes, I do give lectures in my Beginning Journalism class, to teach basic skills) students would sometimes complain that I couldn't hold their attention. I have an open enough relationship with my kids that they feel comfortable coming right out and telling me, "You've talked for such a long time. I'm bored. Can't we do something else?" Okay, so that's not very encouraging when you're standing in front of the class, but I never get mad at them. I seize this as a learning opportunity. Here's what I say: "I want you to go home and ask your parents something important . . . Ask them if they are ever bored at their jobs. If you come back tomorrow with the answer that they are never bored, then you can skip my lecture." This usually gets their attention. "Being bored is preparation for life," I tell them. "You are practicing right now." They laugh, but they all get it. Life is sometimes, or often, *boring.*

But I also teach them that we can make the most of these kinds of moments. You can count dots on the ceiling, or you can dream. You can think about your goals. What are your next steps? What obstacles might get in your way? What are new things to reach for? Where do you feel the most excitement, the most hope? All of this thinking can happen during so-called boring moments. Boredom could in fact lead you to surprising places and your next, big passion.

LEARNING TO FIGHT BACK

Courage is one of the most powerful expressions of grit. It's a kind of selfless determination. It can involve self-restraint and patience, and it always requires a strong sense of self and a willingness to stand up for what's right.

After the horrific school shooting in Parkland, Florida, many students there and elsewhere started to stand up for the cause of safety. It takes courage for them to protest, courage to become public figures, and courage to enter into political debates with adults. Kids everywhere are now seeing what is possible; they too can stand up for what they believe in. They don't have to just accept what adults tell them. Another important lesson for all schools is the power of debate, journalism, and drama in the curriculum. These subjects taught the Parkland students skills that enabled them to speak out and exert some control. They wrote in blogs and online. They spoke at vigils. They took to the streets to demonstrate. A group of Parkland students are on a mission called March for Our Lives, traveling around the country demanding gun law reform, trying to bring the nation together. They are now powerful participants in the democratic process, and powerful examples for other students.

Six weeks after the Parkland shooting, on March 29, 2018, the office at Palo Alto High School got a dramatic call. Jenny in the main office answered the phone. On the other end there was a male voice that warned, "Someone on campus has a gun, and they are going to shoot up the school this afternoon."

The school went into lockdown. It was ninety minutes of hell for the students, waiting to see if their classroom, their school, would be the next in a string of shootings. The call turned out to be a hoax, but the students suffered during that ninety-minute period. *Verde* magazine, one of the ten publications put out by the Palo Alto High Media Arts Center, published its next issue with what looked like a bullet hole through the entire eighty-page magazine. No matter which page you turned to, you found that bullet hole. That is how we all felt — tragically affected. The magazine, edited by Julie Cornfield, Emma Cockerell, Saurin Holdheim (all seventeen years old), and their advisor, Paul Kandell, went national. It was featured on CNN, CNBC, and ABC. It illustrated the stress and fear that students nationwide feel on a daily basis. And it showed their courage to think critically, take control, and stand up with an unexpected and creative response to senseless violence.

We want to raise our kids to be the courageous ones, the ones who have what it takes to speak out, to stand up, to be heard. We can start by talking about brave people and having them share their stories of courage. All you have to do is watch TV any night to find examples of people standing up for what they believe. You as a parent can demonstrate courage by speaking out to protect the values you believe in, even if they are not popular. No need to be nasty about it; in fact, the impact is far greater if you are polite but persistent. That way your kids can see courage in action.

Encourage your child to stand up for what is right — from an early age. It's okay for kids to talk back, as long as they're being respectful.

Parents who silence their kids are teaching the wrong skills. They are teaching them not to speak up about things that matter to them. Respect is important, but so is having a voice. Teach your child to be friends with the kid no one else wants to be friends with; to be friends with the kid who may have different ideas than he does, to talk about them. Teach your child to help the teacher when it isn't seen as cool and to share with other students in class. When your child is courageous, be sure to acknowledge it. If he sticks up for the kid everyone is ridiculing, that shows courage and empathy.

Sometimes, though, despite all our tenacity and courage, grit means knowing when to quit. Grittiness is needed even when it's time to back down gracefully. It's the skill that gives us the strength to make a change. Susan learned this when she was working on Google Video, a free video hosting service from Google that launched on January 25, 2005. In 2006, she realized that there was a product out there called YouTube — and it was growing faster than Google Video. It was also a free video hosting service, but with some features Google Video didn't have. Susan had to make a very difficult decision: keep working on Google Video, on which Google had already spent a lot of time and millions of dollars, or acquire YouTube, the faster-growing product. Looking at the facts, she admitted that she had to change her plans. It was then up to her to convince Google management that they should buy YouTube. It was no small feat, because the price tag was $1.65 billion. It was the right decision, as we all know today, but at the time it took a lot of grit for Susan to give up her own project and risk buying the competition.

We need to let our children know that it's okay to give up and to fail if something isn't working out. There's wisdom in learning how to fail fast, figuring out and admitting quickly if a project won't work. Remember my mastery system in teaching writing? I assume that an essay will not be perfect the first time or even the second time. The same is true for coding; most of the time there are bugs at the start. Some parents have heard about the importance of failure and have actually asked me, "How can I help arrange a failure for my child?" I'm not kidding. This is coming from a good place, but this is not how learning works. It's not up to us to orchestrate a failure. What we have to do is allow kids to work on their own projects and make their own decisions about when to try something else.

Failure is a necessary part of learning, and learning involves doing it yourself. If you fail, you are not alone. The majority of people will fail at something at some point. It's the ones who get back up and continue who ultimately succeed.

GRIT AND ABUNDANCE

According to the National Center for Children in Poverty, 21 percent of American children live in households with incomes below the poverty threshold, and 43 percent of children come from low-income families that struggle to cover basic living expenses. Poverty is devastating; I know firsthand. But there is a silver lining in every cloud, and the silver lining of poverty is grit. If you have limited resources, or no resources at all, whatever you want is going to take a lot of imagination, and you have no choice but to use your creativity. When I was a teenager, I wanted a nightstand, and we had no money to buy one. So I took free orange crates from the grocery store, painted them in exciting colors, and made them into nightstands. They looked pretty nice. I only got one pair of shoes as a child because shoes were expensive. My father used to say: "Why do you need two pairs? You only have one pair of feet." I polished my one pair of shoes every single night. I was still poor, but my shoes always looked new. I am sure kids in poverty today can tell you better stories than mine about how they innovate.

The grit I developed as a child has stayed with me for life. It is a way of thinking about the world and how to make it better. If your family is in this situation, it's a constant struggle and a problem all of us should be working together to solve, but know that your children are developing important coping skills and grit skills as long as they stick with it. These are skills that will serve them their whole lives.

It's at the other end of the wealth spectrum where we have a grit deficit. Too many kids have too many toys. Electronic games, Lego sets, high-tech bikes, rooms so full of stuff that they can't use it all. Even some low-income kids have an abundance of toys. We all want to give our kids a better or abundant life, but overindulgence can rob them of the desire to work hard for something. If kids get whatever they want, they never struggle, they never understand the real value of pursuing something, and they don't develop their creativity and grit.

But it doesn't have to be this way. For one, stop buying all those toys! (A lesson I needed to relearn as a grandmother.) First make sure they enjoy the ones they already have. Since when did shopping become a principal activity with children? Just taking them to the store tempts them into wanting more than they already have. What about going to the park or on a hike? What about letting them do projects around the house or hanging out with their friends? What about simply spending time with them playing board games or cooking?

And if they like cooking, let them bake their own birthday cakes. It's tempting to plan an extravagant party, but some birthday events today border on weddings. I have seen full-fledged *Frozen* princess parties that included an actress posing as Elsa, and an elaborate circus party with ponies. Okay, the kids loved these parties, but you know what they would love just as much? Planning their own day, coming up with the concept, helping decorate, being in charge. Give them a budget, and let them decide how to put the day together. Let them go online and search for what they want. Make them compare prices and be smart shoppers. If they want a magic show, see if they can hire a neighborhood kid.

Children should be in charge of their education, too — no matter who's paying. When kids are in charge, they care. How well do you treat a rented apartment? How does your behavior change if you actually own that apartment? I'm not arguing that you shouldn't pay your child's college tuition. We were fortunate enough to be able to pay for our daughters to go to college, and we believed in the value of education. Yet we made them pay for their own graduate school. I remember Susan being upset when we told her we wouldn't finance her graduate education. We knew she could get scholarships or teaching assistantships. And if it wouldn't have been possible for her to find funding, I would have *loaned* her the money. Not *given* it to her. That's an important difference. She was our first child, and so what we did for her is what we would have to do for all three. We figured that they were old enough to manage, and they did. Both Susan and Janet paid for graduate education, or got scholarships. While it was tough for Susan, she learned a heck of a lot more balancing graduate studies and work than if we had paid for it. Not to mention that she also has an incredible sense of accomplishment, rightfully proud of herself. She did it.

If you've spent decades saving to pay for your child's college, do it. But here's my tip: Have the kid pay the tuition bill, even if it's from your account. They can write the check, and you can sign it. Just the act of writing that amount of money makes them realize what you're sacrificing. They'll see the real costs. It makes such a psychological impact. They will never forget that. I wish I would have thought of this back when my daughters were in college (even though they didn't really need it — they took their education seriously).

No matter the family income, I strongly suggest all teens get jobs. There is no better way to learn about how the real world works. All three of my girls worked during high school. Susan coordinated garbage trucks (as mentioned) and she worked as a hostess at the Fish Market in Palo Alto, a fun job because all of her friends came to eat there. Janet and Anne both babysat. Heidi Roizen, now a venture capitalist and entrepreneur, was doing puppet shows at birthday parties when she was in high school. She earned eight hundred dollars a month doing those shows, and only made a bit more — a thousand dollars a month — in her first job out of Stanford.

I love employing teenagers — they're some of the most enthusiastic, creative, forthright workers out there. They tell you what they think. My students designed my website, and I just hired a local teenager to water the garden. I love being a launching pad. They get their first job with me, and then they're off and running. Early on,

23andMe, Anne's genomic testing company, hired teams of my students to run conferences. My students even organized a swim meet at Stanford for competitors over age fifty. I'm proud that my grandson Jacob landed a job as a camp cook for ten weeks before heading off to college. He's on his feet eight hours a day, serving three hundred kids per session. I saw him in action — it's hard work. But he has a fantastic attitude, and he's learning a lot about grit.

Remember, too, that you get to decide what you model for your child. Money was tight in our household, and a lot of what I did was out of necessity. But these ideas will work with any child, from any background.

Grit was just part of my character. Living in Los Angeles in the late fifties meant you had to have a car. On my sixteenth birthday, I got my driver's license and I celebrated like all sixteen-year-olds in the L.A. area: my parents bought me a 1948 olive green Studebaker — heavily used — for three hundred dollars, and my dad, an amateur mechanic, taught me how to take care of it. His philosophy was that I had to do everything myself, since we could not afford to service the car. I learned how to change the oil, tires, and spark plugs, and do a pretty decent tune-up. Years later, when we were living on the Stanford campus, the neighbors were shocked to see me on the street under the car, changing the oil. I was known for climbing up onto the roof and cleaning the gutters. It was how I had been raised. My daughters were watching all of this. They saw their mother as someone who could do (almost) anything.

They also saw me as someone with a lot of persistence and self-control. I have enormous self-control when it comes to eating. I guess I learned how to value food growing up, when there was never enough for the whole family. I also realize that this is one thing I can control about my health: what I put into my mouth. No one else is in control but me. I can sit at a fancy dinner with amazing food and not eat it. My reasoning is that if I'm not hungry, I'm not going to eat. Period. I taught my daughters this same self-control. I didn't want them to use food as an emotional escape. Food was nutrition and sustenance in our house.

Another lesson in grit for my daughters: When I got an idea in my head, I would pursue it no matter what. My determination was unstoppable. Our kitchen and family room had linoleum floors when we moved in. It was my fault: I picked that linoleum, but I didn't know what high-quality flooring looked like. After a couple of years, I began to dislike those floors. I really, really hated those floors. I wanted them out — and I wanted hardwood. But there was no way we could afford expensive floors. We barely had any furniture; our budget was maxed out. Stan didn't see anything wrong with the linoleum, so it was hard to get him to support my idea. Then I took matters into my own hands. Slowly, over the course of a year, I saved a little money every week from our food budget. My daughters observed the whole process, all of my persistence and determination (in secret, of course). That summer, Stan went to Europe for two weeks, and it was time to execute my plan. I didn't want to give Stan a chance to argue, so I did it all myself. I had shopped around beforehand for the best price, I found a great company to do the work, and I scheduled the work to start the day he left. When he came back, he went into the kitchen/family room area and was absolutely shocked to see the beautiful hardwood floors. "Looks great, doesn't it?" I said. Stan was speechless. He was afraid to say he liked it at first, probably because he wasn't sure where I had gotten the money to do it, but he admitted I'd done a nice job and he was thrilled when he learned that I had paid for it. We have those same floors forty years later, and they still look great.

I also tried to show my daughters the value of being an intelligent shopper and how to speak up when they saw a problem in the store. I always had this attitude that you want to improve the experience for yourself but also for other people. Sometimes a store would advertise an item for a discounted price, but by the time we got to the register, the clerk would try to charge me more. "Sorry," they'd say. "The price has been updated," or "It must have been mismarked." That never worked for me. I fought, called in the manager, and insisted on the advertised price. I always brought in the ad with me. I figured that if no one complained, then the store would continue to do this to all the customers, not just me. I thought, *Why is it okay for them to misadvertise, to bring in a customer on false pretense?* My daughters would hide, they were so embarrassed. Now stores are very careful about the listed prices, and often if they ring up the wrong price, you get a discount. I think those policies came from people like me! And I like to think my daughters learned how to avoid being misled, and how to stand up for yourself and for the little guy, that a company has an obligation to advertise with integrity and treat customers fairly.

Perhaps the most powerful aspect of grit is that it becomes *you*. But while it's tempting to view grit as an individual quality, it's much more inspiring when we recognize how it can change not only us but the world — in both small and large ways. Gady did this by giving his all to everyone working on the paper, and the Parkland kids did it by using the enormous platform they had in an attempt to finally change the laws that affect us all. Success does not exist in isolation. Grit, then, is about fluidity and going beyond self-interest into the strength we can create in the world at large. When we have the flexibility to find strength in numbers, all boats lift on a rising tide.

COLLABORATION

6

Don't Dictate, Collaborate

IT WAS MY FIRST YEAR of teaching, and I was at a breaking point. Each day I taught 125 students in five classes of English and journalism, and I was supposed to police every one of them. They had to listen to me lecture — on anything from essay writing to grammar to journalism ethics — and I had to pretend I was interested in what I was saying. I love grammar as much as any English teacher, but I was forced to give the same lecture five times a day. That's what high school teachers do: You repeat yourself every period (if you're teaching the same subject). Some people are really good at that. I'm not. I get bored. I never did well with a script that tells me exactly what to do each day. It didn't matter if a certain class needed more of a challenge, or more time to understand a new concept. But even worse was having to present myself as the "authority" day in and day out. I wanted to work with my students, not against them.

When I wasn't lecturing, they were supposed to work independently. They all had their books, they (mostly) took notes, and they were to do the exercises at the end of each chapter. My hands were constantly stained purple from churning out extra exercises I made myself using a typewriter and running off copies on a mimeograph machine in the mornings. Why go through the trouble? Because if the kids finished the exercises in the book, I needed something to occupy them. You should have seen their faces when they finally finished the most boring exercises ever designed (the people who write grammar books should be required to take a class in creativity), only to see me approaching their desks with more drills on the same topics. "Learning" was memorizing, and we were all suffering through it together.

By November, I was so stressed out that I had stomach problems and a series of colds. One of the older teachers said to me, "You should take some time off. You look pretty sick." Well, I *was* sick, and I looked as bad as I felt. But most of all, I was confused. I'd been dutifully following the administration's instructions and what I'd learned in graduate school. I had the training that all teachers at the UC Berkeley School of Education had back in the 1960s. The main takeaway: The teacher is the boss. I took numerous classes on how to manage students. In fact, we had a book called *How to Maintain Control of Your Classes*. We were graded on classroom management — how well mannered the students were, how "on task," how often they raised their hands before speaking. The idea was for students to know without a doubt that the teacher is in charge. No question ever. One of the most memorable tips from my administration was "Don't smile until Christmas." I'm not making this up. Ask teachers trained before 2000, at UC Berkeley or any other school.

My students weren't just unengaged; they were afraid. Afraid of me punishing and maybe even failing them. I was supposed to be afraid too — of the mask slipping, of exposing my inner goofball, who was dying to make a joke, but I figured I'd get fired if I did.

When one student saw me coming and grabbed a pencil to look excited about another grammar exercise, I returned to my desk and took a deep breath. Right then and there I decided I had to make a change. I couldn't remain in control of everything and everyone while keeping my sanity. I considered my options: Quit to save my health, go to therapy to save my mind, or do what I wanted and wait to be fired.

Surprisingly, the decision was pretty easy. My first step: Stop lecturing full-time and let the students work in groups for some of the class. If they had to learn grammar from *Warriner's English Grammar and Composition,* which was about as exciting as it sounds, at least they could do it together. Mind you, this was not traditional or acceptable. It was sacrilege. Here I was the new teacher on the block, already trying to break some of the rules. Not a smart idea. But I couldn't teach these kids anything if I didn't make learning more interesting. So they picked partners and worked on grammar and spelling in groups.

I felt a little freer. My wild sense of humor started coming through. I made up crazy stories that belonged on some kind of sitcom and had them add the punctuation. I also had the students generate their own material. They'd walk into class on a Monday, and I'd say, "Tell me what you did this weekend. Write it out, and punctuate it with your partner." Kids had the option of telling the truth or wildly exaggerating. Either was fine with me. I got a lot of stories about beer pong (I now consider myself an expert, though I've never played the game), accounts of strange accomplishments (like a kid who ate twenty-five candy bars in a row), and — you guessed it — sex stories. That's where I drew the line, despite their protests. "Your parents think you don't even know what sex is," I said, "so don't get me in trouble!" There was a lot of laughter in that classroom, but I wasn't afraid of disciplining them. I had their attention — because I was always doing such wacky things — and I had their trust.

Then one day the principal entered my classroom unannounced, made his way to the back row, and took a seat. Scanning the room, he noted that my students were working in pairs, or in groups of three. I panicked. All I could think was: Lecture! So I ran to the front of the class and started expounding upon the beauty of semicolons. The kids looked at me like I was crazy. I mean, they always looked at me like I was crazy, but this time was different. They had no idea what was going on. I knew control was supposedly the most important thing, so I said, "Put down your pencils and listen to me," in my best Graduate School of Education style. Some kids listened, but two did not. The principal noted it on my "observation." "Class out of control and many students talking and not on task," he wrote. This was considered a serious problem.

The principal gave me three weeks to "get my classes under control." That meant silent students sitting in rows. No one talking when I was talking. Everyone taking notes. All period long. I was upset and again wondered if I should quit. Maybe I wasn't cut out to be a teacher. Many teachers today feel the same way. They're so pressured by the system to improve test scores that all they can do is teach the same material over and over. Today they use computers to help repeat the material, but the method remains the same. No flexibility, little creativity, and very few opportunities for the teacher to collaborate with the kids.

The rebel in me came up with an unusual idea. I decided to tell my students what was happening to me. The next time the principal came to evaluate me, they needed to be totally quiet or I was going to be fired. I actually told them that. I trusted them, and I had nothing to lose. "If you don't want the class to change, if you still want me as your teacher, you have to help me out," I said. It was a bold move to make them part of my scheme. But if we could work together, I thought, we just might pull it off.

The plan was to teach my way — collaboratively — until the first sign of the principal. At that moment, all students were to stop talking and face the front, where I would begin to lecture. We did a drill a few days later when I spotted the principal walking down the hallway. I bolted to the front of the class, and the kids stopped talking in an instant. Success! They loved the idea of being in on the plan. As my former student, now an assistant professor of sculpture at CSU Chico, Lauren Ruth, said: "One of the main things Woj did was deconstruct the hierarchy in the classroom. She was always breaking down systems. There was a special place that Woj could occupy that was different from a parent. She was a partner in crime. She trusted *us* enough to be that partner in crime. And there was something delightful about that experience."

Three weeks later the principal returned to observe me again, and the class was silent. I mean *silent*. It was like a morgue. And I passed with flying colors. "Glad to see you're in control," he said. He wanted to know how I had transformed my students in just a few weeks. I told him it was easy: "I made sure they knew I was in charge, and I stopped smiling, like they taught me in graduate school."

I got pretty gutsy after that.

In 1986, I walked past a store in the Los Altos Shopping Center that had a Macintosh computer in the window. "Hello" came up on its screen, like it was talking just to me. I had never seen anything like it, but I was pretty sure it was better than the Just-O-Writer typewriter that my students were using. It took hours to type up the stories in the school newspaper that they produced. I had to hire a student for a dollar per hour to type the stories for the kids who couldn't type. When there were mistakes, the stories had to be re-typed. That Macintosh looked like a godsend.

But I didn't have the funding. Then, purely by accident, I came across a State of California grant application for special funding. I filled out the request for seven Macintosh computers. My administration warned me that those grants were competitive. Not very encouraging, but guess who got the grant in the fall of 1987? Seven beautiful computers arrived at my portable classroom. I was thrilled, even though I couldn't figure out how to turn them on. For several weeks they sat in the back of my classroom until I announced to my students, "I'm so happy to tell you that I got a grant from the state, and now we have seven new computers!" They knew what computers were, but they'd never seen a Macintosh up close. No one at the school knew how to use them. The administration told me that these devices were "just a fad" and that they didn't have anyone to help me. Maybe I should have been discouraged, or even afraid — I had studied political science and English, not tech. Here's how ignorant I was: The first time I tried to use a Macintosh, I couldn't figure out where the words on my screen had gone. Turns out I scrolled too much. I didn't even know what scrolling was! But my students were way more skilled than I was, and they were excited to help.

"No problem," I told the administrators. "The kids and I will figure it out."

All of us spent extra hours after school and on weekends working on setting up the computers and learning to use them. I remember the Gill brothers — twins — and how they worked with the other students to figure out the mysterious science of Macs. Their father worked for Aldus Corporation and came in one Saturday to demonstrate how to use a program called PageMaker. It was perfect for the layout of the newspaper. We gladly took those Aldus disks — remember floppy disks? — and started using what would become a powerful digital platform for designing our newspaper, the *Campanile*. Then we had to figure out how to store our data. The kids did that, too.

It took us about six weeks to set up the seven computers, find a printer, network the machines, and organize our files. We were truly computer pioneers. Whenever something broke or we needed help (which was often), I would take a few kids and go to Fry's, the local electronics store. We got to know the store really well, and the kids became incredibly skilled in IT, way before that term became well known. If you haven't ever been to Fry's in Palo Alto, it is quite an experience. In the entrance there was a huge statue of a horse bucking on its hind legs. To me it represented the excitement about the coming tech revolution. Something big was happening, and we were part of it.

During that year I first got the idea to make T-shirts for the journalism program. Kids in sports got T-shirts, and we had a team, too. I'm proud to say there have been some amazing designs over the past thirty years, always done by the students: a graphic of me stomping on the school administration building, a shirt with a big coin on the front and TRUST IN WOJ on the back, and, recently, WOJ YOURSELF. The kids wear their shirts all over campus and Palo Alto.

What has happened in my classroom, from my first days teaching grammar to today's high-tech journalism, is all about collaboration.

Collaboration is only possible with a strong foundation of trust, respect, and independence. Kids also need a defined goal, one they feel passionate about. These elements have to be in place for students to work with one another, and mentor each other. My students practice these skills every day, and they've blown me away with their ability to support, educate, and inspire one another.

To produce a high-quality publication, my kids have to know journalism inside out. It isn't theoretical. They aren't memorizing material for a test and then forgetting it a few days later. They're writing and designing a complete newspaper, and they have to master the skills involved. I used to lecture on Adobe PageMaker and Photoshop, but the students would listen, take notes, and then go into the computer lab and have no idea how to use the programs. It never worked. You simply can't learn how to use a program by listening to somebody telling you how to do it. So I switched to a more interactive lecture where I would explain one aspect of the program and have them work on that function, and then we'd move on to the next step, alternating between lecture and practice. That worked better — but what worked best of all was having the students teach each other.

My idea was to pair each beginning student with an advanced student. We called the beginning students "cubbies." It was an affectionate term. Everyone had their cubbie. The advanced students got to pick whom they worked with, and they were responsible for making sure the beginning student knew how to do everything. I'd provide the structure, announcing, "Today we're working on improving our features," or, "Today we're improving our opinion pieces." Then we'd read examples together, and the cubbies would sketch a draft with an older student's help. Most of the time it worked perfectly, but not always. If a cubbie turned in work that needed further revision, I'd tell the older student, "Hey, your cubbie didn't write a very good news lead. Please go back and help him." Many times they would, but if they said, "I can't," or "I don't get it," then we'd talk about it some more — until they understood everything. Basically, I kept pawning off as much work as possible onto the students, and it turned out to be a tremendous success. Byron Zhang, one of my current students, who immigrated from China when he was in seventh grade, told me how important this mentorship was to his overall education. He was always a little shy about his written and spoken English, but his mentor helped him gain confidence in his abilities. He also valued the chance to be friends with students in other grade levels, which was rare outside of my class.

In all the years I've been doing this, I've never had a kid who didn't rise to the occasion. When you trust your students, and you help them structure their time and tasks, they can do it. But if you're fearful and don't believe in their abilities, well, they often can't.

Later I expanded this mentoring system to writing itself. It was impossible for me to give personal critiques to 150 students per day, but they could critique each other. And over the course of a year, students made significant improvements that both they and their partners could celebrate. Luckily, I got to provide feedback to Google on what was then called Writely, a new program that allowed my students to collaborate on their writing, and to edit each other's work. My students were some of the first users of what eventually became Google Docs, an application they, and millions of other students, still use today.

Again, I'm not saying it's always smooth sailing. There's an uncertainty factor anytime you're working with teenagers. Working with large, collaborative classes means you're going to have some chaos. But I happen to like the chaos. I guess I've developed a tolerance for it over time. There are times during production week when the kids play loud music and yell across the room and pay attention to three devices at once. I sit in the middle of it and do my own work.

It's hard to describe the impact this method of teaching has on kids. When students feel they can collaborate with their teachers, their self-image skyrockets and they feel absolutely empowered. They can do anything, because someone has their back. They can also weather disappointments, because they know they're a valuable member of the team no matter what. This year I have a very talented student who ran for editor in chief but lost. Sure, she was disappointed, but not for long. She has an important role as the school board representative, which means she attends all school board meetings and reports on the decisions that directly affect students. She also serves as a counselor in our journalism summer camp. She knows she's valuable to me and everyone else on the paper, and that's all the motivation she needs.

WORK WITH YOUR CHILDREN, NOT AGAINST THEM

It's unfortunate but true: A lot of people think the best way to educate kids both at home and at school is to be in total control. We think, *Children are young and know nothing. The parent has to show the way.* While kids like structure, too much structure doesn't bode well for their psychological health, according to some of the most important research done on parenting styles and their effects on children's behavior. In 1971, the developmental psychology researcher Diana Baumrind analyzed a group of 146 preschool children and their parents. She observed four distinct parenting styles: **authoritarian**, **authoritative**, **permissive**, and **uninvolved**. Let's break down the first two categories.

Authoritarian parents act like dictators. They focus primarily on obedience and following the rules. This is the parent who says it's my way or the highway, who is totally inflexible. By contrast, **authoritative** parents create a positive, warm, but firm relationship with the child. Most notably, these parents are willing to consider the child's opinions and engage in discussions and debates, which likely contributes to the development of social skills. As the Silicon Valley pediatrician Janesta Noland says, "An authoritative parent is one who sets some boundaries but does so through engagement — not your best friend, not a person who doesn't care about you, not a person who just wants to control you, but a person who is scaffolding you with expectations." Baumrind's original study found that authoritative parenting is associated with independent, purposeful behavior and social responsibility in both boys and girls.[10] Similarly, her follow-up study from 1991 found that authoritative parenting protected adolescents from problem drug use, proving that parenting styles have long-lasting influences on children.[11]

The last two categories are more self-explanatory: The **permissive** parent is prone to overindulgence and fails to enforce rules or expectations, taking a back seat in the child's life. Some people may misinterpret my philosophy as permissive or free-range parenting, but they're missing one important point: I never offer freedom without structure. I don't want my students to run wild in the Media Center; I want them to run wild with ideas for articles with a strong foundation in newswriting and a clear deadline. Big difference. I set high expectations. I just want the students to figure out how to meet them. The **uninvolved** parent backs away from his or her responsibilities, neglecting the child when it comes to attention, love, and guidance. Obviously a poor collaborator and a problematic caretaker.

There's a time and place for each kind of parenting, though the extremes are often excessive on a day-to-day basis. If you're in a dangerous situation, you might have to act like a dictator to command the attention and obedience you need from your child in the moment. You don't want to be consistently uninvolved, shoving your kids out the door and not knowing where they're going or when they'll be back, but there are moments when you do need to back off and keep your mouth shut. As far as authoritative parenting, I agree that you have to be firm with children when they're young and just starting to learn the elements of TRICK. It calms little kids knowing that someone is in charge. It gives them structure and direction.

But I think there might be another category. I'd like to call it the **collaborative** parent, someone who builds a relationship of mutual respect with their child once he or she is old enough to grasp the basics. For instance, if I were painting a child's bedroom, the authoritative style might be: "Here is the paint. Watch me paint first, and then you can do it the same way," while the collaborative style would give the child much more agency: "Let's go to the paint store and pick out a color. What color do you like? Now let's pick out brushes." This approach takes more time, but the child feels more like a collaborator than a worker. Giving them even a little choice can have a profound impact.

Kids seem to understand this naturally. We tend to think of toddlers as fixated on asserting their independence, but a study from 2017 found that kids as young as two experienced the same amount of joy when they achieved their own goals as when they helped another child achieve her goal.[12] Other research has shown that as children approach the age of three, they understand what it means to have obligations to a partner, and they can see their own perspective alongside others' perspectives.[13] It makes sense that collaboration is a natural impulse. Humans only survived because they figured out how to work together: there's strength in numbers. Collaboration is that powerful.

So why do we insist on dictating? Why are we so controlling? Aren't we trying to teach our children to function in a democratic society, to be able to live and work with others? The answer is we forget how important it is to let them practice having control, but that's what we have to do as parents, for the health of our children and the whole family.

THE PATH TO COLLABORATION

Like all the TRICK principles, collaboration starts with you, the parent. It's pretty hard to model collaboration if you don't know how to listen to others' opinions or if you're constantly attacking your partner because you think you know best. Remember, it's a team effort to conceive and raise a child. Your partner is your partner, not your adversary. And what you model is what you get. Kids are always watching.

But there will be disagreements. Kids misbehave and act completely crazy. They're not born with manners, and they are very self-centered. But as they grow they learn to think about others if that is what they observe. It's up to you to react in the moment, and that can be quite a challenge when your kid is throwing his food on the floor or having a meltdown in the toy store. Here's my suggestion: Try to avoid nasty fights with your partner (count to ten) and certainly don't have them in front of your child. But the annoyances and disagreements of daily life? Don't hide them. Seeing how you deal with them is exactly what your child needs. Kids learn from observing people airing their grievances and coming to some resolution. Don't hide the fact that you're upset, but model how to disagree in a way that helps resolve the issue.

Let's say your spouse comes home and wants to go out to dinner, but you have been cooking all day. Your spouse insists, "I'm tired of eating the same food all the time. I want to go out." A typical disagreement for couples. It's late in the day, you are both cranky. Your kids are watching! Your main objective? Find a compromise. That's what relationships are all about. Maybe you go out tomorrow night, or you save the leftovers for tomorrow and go out tonight. Don't blow the situation out of proportion. Keep your cool and find a solution. After all, this is really not an earth-shattering disagreement. Remember, kids watch us for a living. What kind of lessons are you teaching through your actions?

Collaboration in the home also depends on establishing the right pattern of communication. Talking to your child as a collaborator makes them feel like part of the team, and that's what families should be. This might seem subtle, especially when you're talking to little kids, but it makes a huge difference. Instead of commanding, "Put on your swimsuit. You're going swimming now," try a suggestion: "It's hot outside. Do you want to come swimming with us now?" Of course, sometimes you have to dictate. Some two- or three-year-olds would take over running the house if they could. But rather than dictating a child's afternoon activities, give him a say in the matter.

You are teaching them that they are heard and valued, even if they are little. "Do you want to go to the park or to the zoo? Would you like to play with your Legos or help Mommy prepare your snack?" I can just hear the likely answer: "I want to go get ice cream." And those kinds of answers have to be rejected. But the responses from kids can often be helpful. We need to avoid talking to them in ways we would never talk to our friends, especially when we're bossing them around. I see this all the time in public. I know how frustrated parents can get, but there are more collaborative ways to say "Get in the car," "Get off your phone," "Get over here." Also avoid saying things that can be hurtful long term, like "That was a stupid thing to do." We all make stupid choices, but saying this makes it worse. Keep the golden rule in mind: Would you want to be talked to the way you're talking to your child?

Collaboration doesn't have to be earth-shattering or huge in scope. Make it part of your daily living. For example, Susan and her family have dinner together every night. They go around the table and they all share one thing that happened to them that day. Even Ava, the four-year-old, reports on her day. It's a ritual that brings the family together and celebrates the importance of each child.

When it comes to chores and responsibilities, almost any task can be broken down into collaborative parts. At home, kids can play an important role in planning dinners: They can set the table, choose the recipes and help cook, and also clean up afterward. Keeping a home clean is a collaborative process, and the child should have a clear role in it. Who vacuums? Who does the laundry? Who takes the garbage out? Who's going to wash the car? Who's responsible for shoveling the snow? The overall idea should be that the house belongs to all of us, and we all need to work together to keep it nice. I'm not a servant, and you aren't either. Each of us has a responsibility to keep up our end of the bargain.

The same goes for school. I'm so impressed by the students in Japan who collaborate with each other to clean the classrooms, sweep the floors, and take out the trash. There are no custodians. They work together to keep their schools clean. We are a long way from the outstanding job that the Japanese kids do, but we at least try in most American schools by having the kids clean up after lunch. In the Palo Alto schools, students are responsible for separating their trash into the right bin (recycling or trash) and helping the custodians make sure the campus is in order. The kids in the journalism program take full responsibility for setting up the food for production nights when they stay late, and they clean up afterward. For the most part, they do a great job. And I make sure they know and value our custodians — we all share the responsibility, and we all care.

My favorite activity for teaching family collaboration is vacation planning — kids love it. You can offer a few options, and then the kids can research, pick a location, and choose activities. Here's the best part: Then you won't have to force them to do things. They will have planned it. In our family, Stan took the lead in planning our vacations. He had good ideas, and we trusted him to plan some pretty exceptional trips. We never took tours. Stan was the tour director, but always with input from the kids. Our daughters made suggestions every step of the way. We traveled to Spain when Susan was five years old, and I remember her picking out the restaurants. That kept her interested and excited. I'm not really sure how she made up her mind, but the meals we had were good. When we took hikes in the Swiss Alps, there were always choices, and we left it to the girls to make up their minds. "Should we take the longer route or the shorter one? Keep in mind, the shorter one is steeper. What's it going to be, kids?" They also chose which museums we would visit based on brochures. When they were part of the decision-making, they loved the museums. But I remember times when we didn't ask them. That was a mistake. Getting them into the museum was like taking them to the dentist! There were things Stan and I wanted to do too, so I would let the girls choose their time slot and activity. I'd say, "There's a whole day for us to plan, morning, noon, and night. You get to have input on one part — which part do you want?" They'd have an intense discussion and come to some consensus. We always honored it, though there was occasionally an exception when Stan argued, "I'm the oldest, and I might not ever get back here." The girls usually let him win that round.

I can't overemphasize the importance of friendships for children. Life is a series of collaborative relationships: first with parents, then with family and friends, then with teachers, and later on with mentors, colleagues, and the greater community. Every day my daughters had some kind of playdate or an art or science project with neighborhood kids. They were learning how to be a friend, how to share, how to get along. Most neighbors are a good and often unnoticed resource, easy to overlook in today's busy, overscheduled world.

And it doesn't always have to be kids. Children can be friends with people of all ages. We were great friends with an older couple next door who loved the girls, and so they would go over to visit whenever they felt like it. Turns out that our neighbor, George Dantzig, was a groundbreaking leader in the tech world, only we didn't know it for years, and he certainly never told us. He and his wife, Anne, were so friendly and down to earth. You never would have guessed.

But one day I noticed George had a study full of awards and honorary doctorates from countries around the world. *Hmm*, I wondered, *what did he do?* I learned that he'd developed the simplex algorithm, which solved the Internet's linear program problems, which then made the development of the Web possible. He was a humble man.

One evening when Anne was about two years old, she decided to take her doll for a walk and visit the Dantzigs. Our front door was unlocked, so she went out. The only problem was that she was stark naked, at a stage where she refused to put on clothing. Absolutely refused. It was summer, and it was hot. After hearing the door open from upstairs, I looked out the window and saw her wheeling her stroller up their driveway. At that moment I didn't have any more energy to explain the importance of clothes, so I just let her go. I figured they wouldn't mind. But later I found out they'd had dinner guests, some very distinguished people from France. Anne rang the doorbell, announced, "I am here to play," and then walked right in, naked, and sat down at the table. She created quite a sensation, and that story became a neighborhood classic.

As kids get older, sports become a perfect vehicle for teaching teamwork and being accountable to others. All kids should be involved in sports at some point. Individual sports teach grit, perseverance, and technical skills, but group sports are even better because kids learn that they're part of the team and that their performance matters to the group. My daughters joined the Stanford Campus Recreation Association swim team starting at about five years old. They would swim laps for an hour each evening. That really made them sleep well. On the weekends, they swam in relay races as part of the official team. Imagine a relay team of five-year-olds trying their best to swim the breaststroke, butterfly, backstroke, or crawl. It was pretty hilarious, but it was also great training for the real world.

Over the years, I watched how the attitudes they learned in swimming, tennis, and soccer carried over into other parts of their lives. They became more aware of each other, more understanding in the midst of disagreements, and more apt to help out. Though sometimes other parents worked against these lessons. Sports can become the parents' way of competing, if we allow our egos to get involved — insulting other teams, taunting other parents, or screaming at our own child because he missed a goal. Let's not forget to teach good sportsmanship, to always congratulate the other team on a good game, no matter the score. Easier said than done, but when in doubt, remind yourself: It's not about you.

Finally, don't miss giving advice as a chance to collaborate (*not* dictate). During high school, my daughters were not doing well in physics, of all things. You can imagine with their dad as a professor of physics, that was not cool. They didn't feel they were learning anything.

So I proposed three options and asked them to choose the best one: 1) Stay after school and get help from the physics teacher; 2) Have their dad help them, though he was very busy and didn't have a lot of time; or 3) Hire a tutor. They chose the tutor, so we posted an ad in the physics department and soon had a graduate student coming to the house three afternoons a week. Problem solved, together.

The same problem-solving happened when Janet decided to try out to be a cheerleader. She made the squad, and I was very proud of her. But there was a small problem: turns out she didn't like it. Again, I was the sounding board. "Well, what do you want to do?"

I asked. "I want to quit," she said. We talked about it. "How would it impact the team if you quit now?" I asked her. "And how would it feel to quit? They chose you for the year, so you might want to stick with it to hold up your end of the bargain." She understood my argument, and in the end she did finish the season.

There's no shortage of challenges that kids face on a daily basis. Every parent knows this: there's always some kind of problem to solve. The best thing we can do for our kids is to guide them and support them in their decision-making instead of telling them what to do. We have to be patient, and we need to stop being so judgmental.

COLLABORATIVE DISCIPLINE

All of this working together sounds good, but kids are still going to make mistakes, because they're learning. That's what kids do. They learn the most when they make mistakes. When problems arise, as they inevitably will, it pays to have an educational mind-set. Every issue, every misstep means a lesson has to be learned. And you guessed it: You're the teacher.

One of my grandkids was a biter. He actually bit one of his friends at school. This is more common than you might think. Biting, hair pulling, hitting — kids do all this because they don't know how to control themselves and are still learning how to interact. It's tempting to get mad. Really tempting. But you have to remain calm and reason with the child. And you have to be willing to talk with them.

That's what my daughter did with my grandson. She took him to a separate room, sat him down, and asked why he was doing it. She wanted to know what was making him so frustrated. Frustration is behind a lot of unwanted behaviors in little kids. In this case, he was upset because another kid was playing with his toys. For a toddler, that's tough. So she talked about how important it is to share with others so that they'll share with you. This is a critical skill for getting along in the world, and biting is not an acceptable way of voicing an opinion. While nothing works overnight, eventually this solved the problem.

When kids are a little older, I recommend they take some quiet time to write about what they're feeling and how they're behaving, in addition to having a discussion with parents. Reflective writing is a wonderful teaching tool; I used it all the time with my daughters. And if they can't yet write, have them draw a picture of what they're feeling. The point is to get them to reflect and express. Have them write a story from the perspective of the kid who is being bitten. That helps them have empathy and stop the unwanted behavior.

After that, move forward together. Don't carry grudges, especially against young children. They are learning. Instead, be your child's partner in learning. And if it happens again, repeat the process (without getting nasty). Identify the mistake, do your best to understand where the child is coming from, and have him write more about why he's acting out. He will learn, but it might take some time.

That is my way of solving many problems, but especially when dealing with plagiarism, which plagues teachers everywhere. When I used to teach English classes, I'd assign really unusual topics that made plagiarizing hard. But some kids still managed. I'm thankful I don't have a lot of problems with this in my journalism classes. I remind my students to think about all the eyeballs that will be on their story — and that does it. That's the beauty of a journalism program with real-world consequences. But when I had to deal with students who plagiarized, the main thing I did was talk to them. I gave them a zero on the paper and met with them after school, but I didn't give them a referral to the vice principal or they would have been dropped from the class or given an F. The school takes the issue pretty seriously. I figured it was between me and the student, not the administration and the student. Here's what I learned: Kids who plagiarize, like kids who cheat, are under a lot of pressure. I always treated it as a symptom of stress. Where is the stress coming from? Usually it's parental stress that the kid has to get an A or there's some kind of penalty. They're living in fear of punishment and fear of not knowing how to make the paper better.

I saw any kind of plagiarism as a teaching moment. First, I figured out why they did it, why they felt they couldn't complete the assignment themselves. Then I taught them what they needed to know to write the essay on their own. I explained why plagiarism is so bad, why it's unethical to take another person's words and thoughts and claim them as your own. "I want to know what *you* have to say," I'd tell them. "Not what CliffsNotes says." I also tried to help them see the bigger picture, the fact that the city was paying me to teach them. "Just think of all the money and time and effort you're wasting because you aren't taking advantage of this opportunity to learn," I'd tell them. This method was surprisingly effective.

The thing is, they were terrified. Terrified is an understatement. They were beside themselves. The penalty for plagiarizing at Palo Alto High School was harsh. But I never wanted them to learn that one mistake could ruin their school careers. I wanted to show them they were smart and didn't need to copy. That is why I don't give grades until they have revised sufficiently to get an A. Some kids revise twice and others revise ten times, but it doesn't matter. Each time they revise, they are learning. When I started this system, about twenty-five years ago, plagiarism disappeared from my classes and the motivation — and trust — went up.

But sometimes even if you trust kids, they do crazy things that damage the relationship, at least for a while. One such situation took place in the spring of Susan's sophomore year. It must have been 1994. My husband and I went away for the weekend and left our daughters home alone to take care of the house. They promised they would follow the routines, feed our dog, Truffle, and take good care of each other. Susan was sixteen, Janet, fifteen, and Anne, thirteen. Stan and I had a great time on our weekend trip and were so happy that we could finally leave our kids alone.

We were shocked to see how clean the house was when we came back on Sunday night. It looked spotless. Someone had vacuumed every room in the house. Wonderful, I thought. What great daughters. I was right to trust them. They even cleaned! The next morning was Monday, and I went to school as usual. In my first-period class there was a lot of giggling. I noticed a student wearing the exact same outfit that I owned — a matching blue shirt and skirt from Macy's, one of my favorite outfits. It looked great on her. I asked her where she got it. There was even more laughing.

"Janet gave it to me," she said.

"Really?" I asked. "Where did Janet get it?"

"In your closet. Didn't you hear about the rager?"

"What rager?"

"The one at your house this past weekend. I spilled a drink on my shirt, so Janet let me wear your clothes."

I almost fainted right there. I had a reputation of being a nice teacher, so I guess this student felt comfortable enough to tell me the truth. I think she enjoyed telling everyone that she had been invited to the party and was now wearing my clothes. How cool was that?

Well, it was pretty tense at our house that evening. Some of Stan's clothes were missing too. I wasn't sure how to tell my daughters I knew what had happened. I was fuming but trying to be calm, and I was not doing such a great job.

They all came into the kitchen for dinner, and I said, "Is there anything you guys want to tell me about this past weekend?"

They looked at each other, paused, and shook their heads no.

"Really? Well, in my first-period class today, I heard something about a rager."

"We didn't have a party," Janet said.

"Yeah," Susan chimed in. "We just wanted to clean the house."

"You had a party while we were gone," I said. "And I have evidence."

I told them about the girl in my class who was wearing my matching skirt and shirt. After that, well, I got mad. Finally, they admitted that more than a hundred kids had been partying at our house with no adult supervision.

"We're not leaving you home alone again," I told them. "You're having a sitter." They didn't fight back. Because they knew they had violated our trust, they were grounded for a month. We felt we had to make that point. But what was more important was having a serious conversation. Grounding wasn't the end of the process. "Let me tell you why it's dangerous to have a huge party," I said. "You have no control of these people, and you're really lucky that something didn't happen, because if someone gets hurt at your home, you're liable." They hadn't thought of that. Of course they hadn't. Teenagers don't think like lawyers.

In time I saw how clever they had been, and I had to laugh about how I figured it out. At least there hadn't been any damage to the house, beyond our missing clothes. And I had no idea their cleaning skills were so well honed. I also realized that leaving them alone for the weekend was a bad idea. Their friends knew we were out of town, so the pressure was on. By the way, we weren't the only parents who had this experience. If you have teenage kids, expect that they'll throw a party when you leave. Try to set them up for success by having a sitter. And make sure your favorite outfits are out of sight! (I did get my outfit back, by the way, but Stan's clothes were never returned.)

But let's say your child does something worse than throw a party, something like shoplifting, a common enough offense for teenagers. In these cases, discipline is in the hands of the police. All you can do is cooperate with law enforcement and let your child face the consequences. But afterward, it's again an occasion to talk and get to the bottom of what happened. Was your child acting out because of anger, stress, or lack of control? Or maybe they shoplifted because they wanted something and didn't have the resources. Those are problems that need to be addressed collaboratively, as a family. Sometimes teenagers are just after thrills, especially teenage boys, and they end up taking stupid risks. I've worked with dozens of parents over the years in this situation. Here, too, it's up to you to find the lesson you need to teach, and to work with your child to make sure he learns it.

It was 2005, during the week before school started, that a popular gym teacher at our local middle school was arrested for inappropriate sexual activity with a student. Everyone in our community was shocked and upset, especially his former students, many of whom were now at Palo Alto High. It was the kind of story that we absolutely had to cover in the paper. But the gym teacher's son had just joined the *Campanile* staff. He was a great student and a popular kid, and it was hard for the students and for him. As my former student Chris Lewis, then an editor in chief, says: "'Elephant in the room' doesn't begin to describe it." None of us wanted to make this student feel bad about himself. He was already devastated. What were we supposed to do? My students didn't know. I didn't either, but I told them they had a paper to run and they had to figure it out.

That led to many afterschool discussions. Lewis recalls: "I was surprised when Woj told us, 'You guys are the editors, this is your paper. It's your choice.' Never had I been given this much input or power — we could take the newspaper seriously and all, but this was a real-life, real-relationships, real-people situation with huge implications. We struggled with finding a decision, talked about it, and reached out for counsel. But eventually, the choice was ours." The editors had a talk with the gym teacher's son and asked how he felt. They let him be as involved or uninvolved as he wanted. In the end, they published a cover story about the gym teacher, but the son also wrote an editorial about the importance of presumption of innocence. It was a perfect solution to an almost impossible problem, but they figured it out on their own, and they did it as a group. If we give kids the opportunity to figure things out on a regular basis in high school, they will be ready for the adult world.

REAL-WORLD COLLABORATION

There's a misconception that life starts at eighteen years old when you can vote, that everything before then is just practice. Funny how you can vote at eighteen but not drink until twenty-one. Does anyone really believe that kids don't drink until twenty-one? Children are part of the real world from the day they are born. We just don't tend to think of them that way. Your child's life is already under way — they are running on a parallel track to yours, only on a different level, so why not have them join activities that reinforce this idea of parallels, that help them think in terms of the larger working world, that show them they are already a valuable participant?

In the summer of 2015, I got an email from my former student James Franco. He said he was interested in making a film with me and a group of teenagers from our community. I loved the idea . . . having kids make a full-length feature film with James and me as the teachers/coaches. Before I knew it, I was standing in the Media Center with James; his mother, Betsy, a children's book author; his brother Tom, an actor and artist; and Tom's girlfriend, Iris Torres, an accomplished film producer. The film was based on Betsy's young adult novel, *Metamorphosis: Junior Year*. It's a coming-of-age tale about the struggles of a sixteen-year-old boy, filtered through art and the myths of Ovid, the famous Roman poet. A perfect project for high school students.

On the first day, James and I started the workshop by handing out a script that Betsy had created from the book. The kids weren't afraid to share their opinions: "It doesn't sound real." "Teenagers would never talk that way." "The plot needs to be changed."

"Okay, guys, you rewrite the script," Betsy said. She's been teaching at the Children's Theatre in Palo Alto for years, so she knew a thing or two about working with teens.

The next time we met, the kids had revised the script. We went over it scene by scene, with James and Betsy leading the way. Then they read it out loud and continued to make changes, but only if they were approved by the whole group. It took time, a lot of time, but the script was amazing. They were all excited about it, and Betsy agreed that the revision was a major improvement on the original.

Then we had a movie to make. James, Tom, Iris, and I created forty roles — one for each kid. They all had a title of some kind, just like what would happen in professional films. We wanted them to have their own responsibilities and to contribute something important to the team. I'll tell you right now that this movie was probably the most complex project I've ever taken on, and it lasted a year. We had five directors, multiple actors and screenwriters, and kids running all kinds of departments, including casting, music, cinematography, editing, costume design, production design, cameras, animation, sound, and stunts. They were all working three days a week after school and on the weekends during the filming. I quickly learned that not only did we all need to work together, but we needed the equipment and the weather to cooperate too. Every day something went wrong: a kid showed up in the wrong place, brought the wrong camera, couldn't figure out how to work the lighting equipment. But they were all learning some of life's hardest lessons: how to make something work even when it doesn't work, how to work together with so many moving pieces, so many conflicting opinions. It was a real film, not a little attempt at a film, and in the end it turned out beautifully. It was even entered in multiple film festivals, including the Mill Valley Film Festival in the Bay Area.

This kind of experience is the real-world training ground we need for the professional world, where collaboration works in unexpected (and complicated) ways. As the CEO of 23andMe, Anne did a tremendous job of hiring top talent, but she never thought she'd be collaborating with her adversary. Yet in November of 2013, Anne learned that the FDA had deemed 23andMe's saliva-testing kit a "medical device" that needed to pass a daunting marketing approval process. Overnight, and after six years of business, she was banned from selling her product.

If Anne didn't have more grit than anyone I know, she never would have survived this. But she refused to fall apart. She was extremely strategic. And more than her toughness, it was her ability to collaborate that ultimately saved her company. In essence, she had to convince the FDA of the importance and validity of the idea behind her product, the fact that consumers could and should have their own genetic information and be able to make decisions about their health. There was no precedent for this type of product, so it was up to her to collaborate with the FDA about what she was doing and why.

Tracy Keim, 23andMe's vice president of brand and consumer marketing, recalls that Anne had "a constant drive to seek out the opinions of those within the FDA system and to understand them, to respect them. The realization that she never quite knew them at a human level made her want to get to know, understand, and respect those individuals." She set out to show the FDA that it was possible to educate consumers about the probability involved in calculating genetic risk. It was a major, company-wide effort. "The amount of collaboration and kindness that came out of that one moment in the company's history was unbelievable," Keim says. "While Anne balanced leadership with listening, this heightened sense of collaboration among the employees came into effect. Everyone wanted to win. Everyone wanted to win together."

23andMe successfully made their case, and in the spring of 2017, they received authorization from the FDA to sell tests that assess genetic risk for a number of diseases, and since have added other genetic markers, including the BRCA 1 and 2 genes associated with breast, ovarian, and prostate cancer. This was not only a victory for 23andMe but a victory for those who now had direct consumer access to their genetic information.

Anne realized through all of this that the FDA wasn't her adversary at all. It was a group of people with a different opinion about medical care, but like her, their objective was to protect the consumer. She wasn't a bulldozer, and she wasn't a dictator. She was a true collaborator.

In the current political climate, it wouldn't hurt any of us to take these lessons to heart: Respect your adversaries, understand where they're coming from, find common ground, and pursue collaborative solutions. We all want our country to be great, whether we live in the United States, Mexico, or China, and working collaboratively is really the only way to get there.

Finding common ground is more crucial than many of us realize. Perhaps today more than ever. It involves patience, flexibility, giving, and listening. It means noticing one another and taking each other into account. It also means tolerating chaos and uncertainty, especially when kids are involved. If we can do this, if we can learn to work together, we can solve complicated problems, navigate morally fraught decisions, and harness the power of many (often competing) opinions and ideas. We'll also become more aware of how we treat our children. Are they truly our collaborators? Do we value their ideas and passions? And what are we teaching them, through our own actions, about how to live in the adult world? This is one of the most important collaborations of all, because who we are as parents determines the people our children become.

And, of course, the people our children become determine the future of everything.

7

Children Hear What You Do, Not What You Say

CLAUDIA STOOD AT THE DOOR to my office, holding back tears. The prior weekend I'd had to break the news that she hadn't won the editor in chief election. I dread making those calls or having my editors make them. During my first few years of teaching, selecting the editors was easy because the class was so small, and usually one clear candidate emerged. Today is another story. In a recent election there were twenty-eight students competing for just five editor in chief roles. The campaigning is fierce. And consoling the losers? It's getting harder every year.

"I can't believe I didn't win," Claudia managed through sobs. She was a bright, accomplished student who'd written many important articles for the paper. I hated to see her so upset.

I let her cry and tried to reassure her that in the long run it didn't matter. "You'll get into college and do well even without having been editor," I said. I could tell she wasn't convinced.

The next day it was obvious that she was jealous of the kids who won. It was bad for class morale, and for her, so I decided to talk to her parents. When I got her mom on the phone, I was shocked to hear that she, too, was crying. "What did I do wrong?" she said. She interpreted this one election as a referendum on her own parenting and a reflection of her daughter's worth. I've seen this so many times, but it's always upsetting. She was obsessed with preventing this kind of failure from happening again. "How can I make sure my other children win?" she asked. I decided to break out my secret weapon: the Gady Epstein speech. I told her about how Gady lost the election, committed himself to making the paper great no matter his title, and ended up getting into Harvard. "It's all about learning to fail with grace," I kept saying. "That's so much more important than being editor."

But I wasn't sure that sank in, and I worried about whether Claudia would commit to the program for the whole school year. I've had students who couldn't recover and ended up quitting. I didn't want that to happen.

Claudia finally came through. She showed up smiling and ready to work and, as predicted, got into a good college. This was one of many instances in which I had to solve "the mother problem." Then, magically, the child was fine.

A few years later, I had a hardworking student who vomited every time she had to take a standardized test. She had a very challenging schedule with four Advanced Placement classes and afterschool tutoring. Her parents were immigrants from China, and she spoke highly of them, but she also overheard their discussions about her academic performance. She was under a lot of pressure. It didn't seem like a very positive situation.

The parents got so worried that they pursued the so-called 504 plan for their daughter, which provides testing accommodations for students with disabilities. They wanted her to be able to take the

SAT without the usual time limit. Alternative testing arrangements are necessary for students with learning disabilities — I'm not arguing with that. But there is an epidemic of worried parents who will do anything to make sure their children succeed. This student didn't have a learning disability; she had an emotional disability.

I met with the parents and suggested they might be projecting their own anxiety onto their daughter. They were immediately defensive. "It isn't us," they told me. "It's the school environment." This is a common defense — I hear it all the time. Parents don't want to think they're causing any problems for their children. I understand. But the truth is, they're wrong.

These parents eventually succeeded in establishing 504 status for their daughter. What was interesting is that as soon as she realized she could take tests untimed, her vomiting and anxiety disappeared. I didn't think it was about the timing at all. I saw that her parents relaxed, and in response, the daughter relaxed.

The parents in both of these stories made a common mistake: They forgot that when it comes to children, what you feel and what you model is what you get. This is so obvious, so automatic, that we just don't think about it. Both parents and teachers fall into this trap, despite the decades of research — and common sense — that prove this point. Kids pick up on subconscious cues as well as overt behaviors. Back in the 1960s, the famous Bobo doll study at Stanford found that kids who observed aggressive behaviors by adult models, like pounding a doll with a hammer, were more likely to exhibit aggression themselves. A 2010 study published in *Behavior Research and Therapy* found that children whose parents modeled anxious behavior and thinking showed greater anxiety and avoidance behaviors on academic tests — exactly what I've observed over the years.[14]

Other studies show that children learn to regulate their emotions through observing their parents, and that if parents are able to express a wide range of emotions, children are better equipped to manage their own emotions. Your child really is your mirror, for better or worse.

Modeling is often subconscious. We can see this in our own behavior as parents. For instance, my father had a rule: *Never bathe when you're sick*. It was a steadfast rule later in my own home, because I'd grown up with it. I never thought twice about it until my kids said, "What a silly rule, Mommy." Then I stopped and wondered why I was doing it, and where my father might have gotten that idea. Maybe it was wisdom from the Ukraine, where my father lived over a century ago. It probably was a bad idea to go outside in the frigid winter and take a bath if you were sick. But we were in California. We had heat and plenty of hot water. So the rule disappeared, but only because my daughters made me aware of its lack of sense.

Even if we're aware of what we're doing, we're pretty inconsistent. Some of us are downright hypocritical (myself included at times). We speed, but expect our teenage drivers not to go a mile over the speed limit. We check our phones during dinner, but yell at our children when they do the same. We lose our temper with them, and then wonder why they talk back. Any of this sound familiar?

And then there's anxiety and insecurity, some of the most debilitating behaviors we can model for our children, and unfortunately some of the most common. It starts when you first become a parent. I can't tell you how many times a new mother or father has come up to me at a conference and said, "I need to talk to you. I don't know how to be a parent. I need guidance." And they launch into question after question about sleeping, eating, discipline — you name it. I can see why. There's a real lack of understanding of what parenting is about. That's the reason I wanted to write this book. Because without the right support and information, we become insecure. We worry our child won't succeed because of our own deficiencies; we hover because we're afraid we've made a mistake. Test-taking anxiety among the children of parents who are obsessed with academic success is a perfect example of this — when parents project their own fears onto a child, the child can be so crippled by those fears that she can't perform. The same thing happens when young children are learning to sleep on their own. They pick up so many of the parents' insecurities that they can't do a simple, natural activity by themselves. It becomes a kind of codependency, a dysfunctional relationship where the boundaries between the two partners are blurred and each partner enables unhealthy behavior in the other. People usually think of codependency in the context of romantic partners, but the same thing can happen between parents and children. We can impair our children with our own anxiety. We can discourage and disempower them.

At the heart of all this anxiety and insecurity, all the inconsistency and confusion, is one simple wish: For our children to thrive. That's it. We want them to be better than we are, not to have the same hang-ups and habits, not to fail because of something we could have prevented. This is a noble goal, no question. But parents are only human. We all make mistakes. We all experience anxiety that our kids pick up on. We all have said or done something in front of our child that we later regretted. It's okay. It's bound to happen, and your children will turn out just fine. The last thing I want to do is make you more anxious. What I want to talk about is how we can be better models, and how we can make parenting a little easier for kids and adults. Because it's possible, as long as we're willing to examine our own behavior.

A CLOSER LOOK

One of the great gifts of parenting is that it makes you a better person. It's challenging and frustrating at times, of course. You have to grapple with long-held beliefs and patterns. You have to confront things about yourself that you might not like. But in the end, the experience of being a parent transforms you. It's the greatest opportunity available to us for positive change. With that in mind, I'd like you to consider the following behaviors. When it comes to this list, so many of us are modeling the opposite of what we'd like to see in our children. (I've done this plenty of times myself.) The point is to start to recognize what we're showing our kids and what we might want to change:

1) Are you generally punctual or often late to events and appointments? Punctuality shows respect for people's time. Being habitually late shows the opposite. Living in Silicon Valley, I'm pretty familiar with this. Wealth makes it worse. Somehow wealthy people think that just because they have money or fame, they can dictate the time they show up for appointments. It's as though they're saying, "I'm so busy and so important that I can set my own schedule, and the world will revolve around *me*." I've seen people show up two hours late or more and expect everything to go as planned. Unfortunately, they get away with it. And plenty of noncelebrities are habitually late and

disorganized. I try to teach all my students (and children, and grandchildren) that something as simple as being on time is important. If you can't make the appointment, at least call or text to let the other person know. It's common courtesy, and it's about being willing to see the situation from the other person's perspective.

2) Another simple thing: How do you present yourself in terms of clothing and grooming? The way you present yourself to the world says a lot about your confidence, capability, and respect for other people. If you wear basketball shorts to a cocktail party, that is showing lack of respect for the hosts. This has nothing to do with income or socioeconomic class — it has to do with self-esteem and respect for others, and understanding what's appropriate in a given situation.

The best way children learn this is by observing you. I'm not saying you need to teach them that looks are everything. I am saying you should teach them to look respectable and professional. I kept wondering why my daughters don't wear much makeup, and then I realized that I don't either, most of the time. This was never something I taught them or focused on when they were growing up. They didn't need to put on full makeup before leaving the house, but they did need to bathe, take care of themselves, and dress well. I always looked put together and professional, but never felt pressure to wear the latest high fashion outfit. That, too, influenced my daughters — except for that time Anne wore flip-flops to her interview. I guess she was still learning. Fortunately, they considered her accomplishments, not her clothes.

3) How do you interact with other people? Are you generally friendly? Do you invite guests into your home? How do you treat your children's friends and teachers? What about waiters and cashiers? How is your phone etiquette? Are you professional and courteous when someone calls?

Phone etiquette is a pretty reliable measure of what kids are learning. I tried my best to model this and have my girls practice so they knew exactly what to say. Maybe it's because I come from a humble background, but I always made a point of recognizing and thanking all kinds of people doing their jobs around me. I can guarantee you that I wasn't always perfect. Sometimes I lost my patience or simply overlooked someone in the rush of another busy day. But I always tried my best.

4) Do you clean up after yourself or leave a mess? I realize that there are a lot of families where both parents work and need to hire outside help. That's okay, but you can still clean some of the house yourself and keep it tidy on your own. I also suggest that you take on a monthly cleaning or organizing project with your children. This will help you model these important skills and reinforce your children's respect for the home they live in.

There will come a day when you leave the teens at home alone, responsible for taking care of the house and the pets. What if they don't know how to do it? One teenager I know who was left to take care of the house didn't know the difference between dishwasher soap and dish soap, and put the dish soap into the dishwasher. If you've never tried that, don't. It made such a sudsy mess that the floor had to be refinished.

When you treat your children as royalty, when you don't give them serious responsibilities, then you end up with a young adult who has no experience being responsible or keeping a house clean, and you're the one who has the pleasure of visiting them in their first apartment.

5) Do you have a healthy relationship with technology? This is a big one. Research shows that the average American checks their phone eighty times per day. Can you believe that? Actually, as a high school teacher, I can. This compulsive phone checking leads to what the technology expert Linda Stone calls "continuous partial attention." We're constantly in a state of doing many things at once, but we're not completely focused on any of them. We all know exactly what this feels like: eating lunch while typing an email while listening to a podcast. This behavior is bad for kids who need to concentrate on their homework, but it's even worse when it comes to parenting. A study published in *Developmental Science* found that young children whose mothers reported higher phone usage had more trouble recovering from emotional stress.[15] There's a clear connection between the amount of attention and care we receive and our ability to process our emotions. Additionally, a survey of over six thousand participants found that 54 percent of *kids* thought that their *parents* used their devices too frequently.[16] Thirty-two percent of kids felt "unimportant" when their parents were on their phones. *Unimportant.* That makes me really sad. And worried — and not just about children. How many of us adults have felt unimportant when someone

checked their phone during our conversation? I know phones are addictive, but for our children's sake and ours, we have to set some boundaries.

6) Do you have a healthy relationship with food? What about regular exercise and time in nature? Do you stay up late watching television and then wonder why your kid develops the same habit? Do you experience a lot of stress? If so, how do you manage it? Are you kind to yourself? Taking care of our own health is the best way to teach our kids how to do the same. Exercise, adequate sleep, and relaxation are so important. I've found that humor helps a lot in times of stress. And contrary to popular belief, we can actually say no when we're too overwhelmed to fit one more activity into our schedules. We also need to spend time with friends, do something fun once in a while, and have perspective when life gets difficult.

   When it comes to food, a lot of us parents can make better choices. In my family, we teach the grandchildren that not all food is good for you. They learn to read labels early, and they know to avoid processed junk food. In my classes, students know that I confiscate soda. No exceptions! The whole class gets the "anti-soda lecture" at the beginning of the year and then at intervals throughout the year, whenever I think it's necessary. Their health is important to me because I care about them as human beings.

7) How do you treat your relatives? To what extent do you prioritize family? How do you treat your former spouse? What

is your child learning about the importance of familial relationships? Even in divorced households, parents should model collaboration and cooperation for the benefit of the kids.

We're lucky because all nine grandkids live close by and are friends. They eat together, play together, vacation together, and sleep over at each other's houses. But my daughters did not grow up with family close by. They had cousins in Ohio but saw them only a few times growing up. So our family consisted of friends and neighbors we adopted. We spent holidays with them, went camping together, and shared meals every week. Many of them did not have family nearby either. Today they are still like my family, and I'm glad I was able to show my daughters the importance of creating and maintaining a community.

Prioritizing family also means sharing experiences, good and bad. Family members are instrumental in modeling how to cope intelligently, and they form a strong support system for the child. It means having someone to talk to, someone who can help you work out any issue, someone who will be there for you.

I've always thought that positive family interactions are critical to a child's happiness. The best way to teach the importance of family is to have fun together. The more positive experiences, the more support the child feels. It can be just playing a board game, or going to the park, or jumping on a trampoline. We are lucky to have my granddaughter Amelia (now seventeen), who is a very social person and one of the best organizers of kid fun. She has led the kids in imagining they were all on Mars, and dressed everyone up in funny costumes that she found in some adult's closet. We all sit down in the family room and watch them play, which usually turns out to be hysterical. Sometimes we just see Amelia out on the lawn with the kids all following her as if she's the Pied Piper.

8) Are you willing to discuss controversial topics? Do you model for your child how to talk about important issues, how to respectfully disagree with someone? Do you demonstrate the ability to listen and negotiate?

We always talk about what is going on in the world with the grandkids. We listen to and respect their opinions. Conversations around the table are lively. The current political climate means there is never a dull day — no one sits passively. A lot of the time we're debating with Ethan and Leon, both thirteen, who read the *Economist* every week. It isn't something we told them to read. They want to know what is happening in the world and they think the *Economist* is the best source. Inevitably, someone gets out-argued or proven wrong. Emma and Mia always add to the conversation by providing the devil's advocate view. These are the most instructive moments. As adults, we try our best to demonstrate our ability to change our minds and consider new information. We never shy away from a passionate argument, but we want to show that insights and ideas evolve, just as people do.

9) What about lying to your children? I think all parents lie to their children at times. We say things like "Don't think the ice cream store is open now," or "Daddy's really tired and wants to go home" when he really wants to do something else. After a

while, kids catch on — they're not stupid — but these types of lies aren't really harmful. It's the lies about significant issues that create lack of trust. Telling your child that no one else is going to the show is a big problem when they find out that everyone else went to the show. They will tend not to trust you, and we know that trust is the foundation of all our relationships.

10) Do you yell? Okay, we all yell at some point, but are you inadvertently teaching your children that yelling is an acceptable way of communicating? Do you curse but get mad when your kids use foul language?

No one is perfect, no one has total control, but some people yell more than others just because they are irritated. Yelling means raising your voice. Speaking in an agitated negative way might not be yelling, but it can still create an unpleasant situation for kids. We all need to be real with our kids — it does no good to fake or withhold your emotions — but it would help to realize that anger doesn't make things better. It's a choice and a way of life that we'd like our children to avoid.

11) How do you react to adversity? If you encounter an obstacle, do you stay committed to your goal and find another way to achieve it? Or are you easily defeated?

There are times in life when things go wrong. You turn right instead of left and end up in an accident. You break off a relationship when you should strive to keep it. We all make these kinds of "mistakes." But they aren't really mistakes; they're fate. Luck plays an important role in our lives. It is luck that puts you in the right place at the right time. I can certainly say that about Susan, who ended up buying a house in Menlo Park and then having to rent part of it to make the mortgage payments. If she hadn't needed to rent the garage, she never would have met Larry and Sergey, the co-founders of Google. There is a silver lining to almost everything, a lesson to be learned, even when that's hard to find.

12) Are you willing to learn and admit you're wrong? Are you willing to forgive? Many people aren't. But pride stands in the way of reconciliation. We all talk about kindness and forgiveness, but that doesn't mean we know how to practice them. In all my decades of teaching, I've learned to forgive my students no matter what. That doesn't mean no punishments, but it does mean that I always give them a chance to make something right. Though it's painful to admit I'm wrong, I've found it's less painful than trying to cover up a mistake I've made. No one can be right all the time, or even most of the time. This is where humility and open-mindedness come in. We can't be perfect models, but we can be aware of these qualities and how we illustrate them for our children.

WHAT TO DO IF YOU'RE NOT THE IDEAL MODEL (HINT: NO ONE IS)

So you have some flaws. You've identified some behaviors you want to change. Maybe you get irritated easily and often. Instead of feeling guilty or defeated, think about this: You are the best model possible for your child. Why? Because the process of change is an incredibly powerful lesson. A child can't learn this from a parent who's perfect all the time (and of course no parent is), and they won't learn it from a parent who repeats the same bad behavior over and over again. Consider yourself lucky: You have a golden opportunity. You can teach your child how to become a better person by being a living example. I'm not saying it's easy. Sorry to break it to you. It probably won't happen overnight. It might take a few months. But with time and patience, I believe anything is possible. If your child sees you working on your anger, she will learn to work on her own issues. Having the mind-set that behavior can be changed and then showing your children that you are working on it with their help proves to them it can be done.

There are all kinds of theories and methods out there, but change for parents comes down to these three principles:

BE AWARE AND WILLING. The first step to making any kind of change is awareness. You have to recognize the problem before you set out to solve it. Pause for a moment and study the problematic behavior. Why are you doing it? Is it largely unconscious? Did you pick it up from your own parents? Is it coming out of some anxiety or insecurity you feel about yourself when it comes to parenting? No matter the reason, try to learn from it. Identify a pattern that you might be stuck in. But then let it go. Forgive yourself. You'll save a lot of time and pain. I remember how difficult it was to admit to myself that I'd made mistakes with my daughters (and I made so many of them). I wasn't always who I wanted to be as a mother. There were times when I got mad, or punished my daughters the wrong way. I completely lost my patience. But this happens to all of us.

And, for my part, I realized I'd inherited this behavior over generations. Once I was aware of what I wanted to change, though, I was
committed. I believed in myself. I started by asking their forgiveness
and admitting that I was wrong (just like the time I looked at Janet's
diary). We keep learning as parents — in fact, we never stop learning
until we die. We can change if we set our minds to it. We can always
be better. Think about your children and how important they are to
you. They are worth the effort.

IDENTIFY AND SHARE YOUR GOAL. **Pick** just one thing to change
at a time, not everything. I suggest you start with the behavior that
most impacts your child. Maybe you need to be more patient when
your son is getting ready for school. Maybe you need to start exer-
cising and showing your daughter the power of healthy habits. Or
you want to repair your relationship with your mother, and in doing so, teach your children a profound lesson in forgiveness. Whatever it is, share this goal with your child. You can say something
like, "My goal is to be more patient with you in the morning. Can
you help me figure out what I should focus on first? What bothers
you the most? Why are mornings so difficult for us?" This definitely
makes you vulnerable and caring, and will get your child's attention. This is an opportunity for them to see that Mom and Dad are
real people with hopes and dreams and failures and imperfections.
And most kids want to help their parents. Sophie, Anne's daughter, always has great suggestions even though she's only seven. She'll
say, "Mommy, you can let me do more things with my friends by
myself," or "Kids know what they want to do. You just need to let
them do it." Explain that everyone is trying to improve, and so are

you as a parent. Also say *why* you want to make a change. What do you want to show your child, what lessons do you want to impart? And why is this so important to you? Why start with this goal? Why start now?

BE FLEXIBLE AS YOU PURSUE A SOLUTION. So you had the best of intentions, but you lost your cool with your son again. You worked overtime and didn't jog with your daughter like you'd promised. Things with your mother are even harder than you'd thought. It's okay. Like so many things, behavior change might not work on the first try. But that's not a reason to abandon your goal. Changing our behavior as adults is a lot like writing. You have to sketch out a first draft to get a feel for what you want to say. Then you have to go over it again and again, finding those run-on sentences and errors in logic. You'll feel a lot saner if you don't expect perfection out of the gate. Stick to your goal, but be flexible. Maybe the strategy you designed isn't working. Why not? What's getting in your way? How can you fix the problem and move forward? Is there a creative solution you haven't thought of? Can your children help you troubleshoot? Can they play an important role in the process? Maybe the night before school, your son can set out the clothes he wants to wear, or you can have him remind you to take a deep breath when he's running a few minutes late. Don't be afraid to enlist your child's help and support. In doing so, you'll show him how much determination it takes to change. And don't forget to keep a journal of your progress so you can look back and see how much change you've made. A written record will keep you motivated and committed, and writing can spark even more ideas about smart revisions to your plan.

THE SINGLE MOST IMPORTANT BEHAVIOR
YOU MODEL FOR YOUR CHILDREN

If you ask me, the single most important life skill we model for our children is our ability to have functional relationships with other people. The happiness we experience in life is determined by the quality of our relationships. This, perhaps more than anything else, sets our children up for success or failure as adults. For many of us, our most significant relationship is with a spouse or partner. But not everyone today has a long-term partner or fits into traditional definitions of family. If you're widowed, or a single parent by choice or circumstance, the same idea applies to you. The quality of your interpersonal relationships — with friends, family members, colleagues, and other caregivers — will deeply influence the relationships your child forges in his own life. Through observing you, your child learns how the world works, how people get along, and how conflicts are resolved. If you have acrimonious relationships in your life, your children will suffer the consequences. But if you relate positively to your spouse, partner, colleagues, and friends, you'll give your children the best chance to live happy, fulfilling lives.

I'm the first to admit that long-term partnerships aren't easy. No one who's been married for fifty-five years hasn't struggled. My marriage to Stan is still a work in progress, and by that I mean we work on the relationship every single day. When we were raising our daughters, we fought — over religion (Stan is Catholic; I'm Jewish), parenting styles (Stan is naturally more strict; I was more collaborative), and all the time we had to spend apart because of Stan's work. But we were committed to each other, and our goal was always the same: to provide a loving home for our children. We didn't have a perfect home, but it was a good home, and we built a good life for our daughters. As for our marriage, it isn't perfect either. But we love each other and are committed. There is no perfect marriage. Hollywood love stories only exist on film. That's one thing that young people have to understand. We fool ourselves by thinking there is "just one person for us" or that "love solves everything." Real life doesn't work like that.

Marriage is a compromise. This might sound basic, but it's worth repeating. In a marriage, both partners have to sacrifice. It's a partnership, not a competition. You shouldn't be keeping score: *I won that argument about the dishwasher, but he spent more of our money last month.* Sometimes one of you will give more than the other, but maybe the next year the situation is reversed. If you're constantly keeping score, you'll lose perspective of your goal, which is to get along and raise your children in a loving environment.

But marriage is also an incredible way to live a satisfying life. Stan and I share more than fifty years of memories: people we knew, trips we took, mistakes we made, ridiculous ideas we had. We can sit together and page through more than a hundred photo albums documenting our lives. It wouldn't be the same with a partner of five or ten years — we've accumulated so much life and experience, and we've done it together. We have memories of the early days, riding around Berkeley on Stan's Vespa scooter or the first car we bought (a VW Bug, so small that when I hurt my knee skiing, I couldn't even fit my leg in it). We drove around Europe, with Stan the driver while I was the navigator, though I couldn't for the life of me figure out where we were (sometimes it was Stan's fault, because he drove off the map!). And then there's the family we built with our girls, watching them grow up, our family then expanding with nine beautiful grandchildren. Who else can I talk to about all this? Who else can fill in the gaps in my own memory? No one. I hate to think what it would feel like to cut Stan out of my life. We would both lose so much. The whole arc of our lives would dissolve.

But so many relationships do end. I've seen it with my friends and family, and I'm sure you have too. Based on all my years, and all the relationships I've observed — marriages, friendships, parent-child relationships — I can tell you that no relationship functions without the principles of TRICK. You can see the deterioration of these fundamental values in all kinds of relationships, but especially between spouses. When couples separate, it's not always the big bomb everyone thinks about: infidelity. Sometimes it is, but infidelity usually happens because TRICK is missing. There are many other reasons that relationships fail — disagreement on common goals, different sexual needs, growing apart — but they're all a result of the absence of these basic human values.

LACK OF TRUST. The minute you stop trusting your partner is the minute the relationship starts to fall apart. But have they given you reason to be jealous and suspicious? If not, trust that you both have the other's best interests at heart. Trust in the commitment you made to each other. If there is an issue, resolve it. Remember, broken trust can be repaired.

LACK OF RESPECT AND LOVE. The number one cause of divorce is loss of respect, and once you lose respect, it is hard to get it back. Respect means that you value and admire someone. You are their number one supporter in all situations. You don't suddenly turn on that person because they made a mistake. When there's a problem, you first try to understand the issue and always give them the benefit of the doubt before accusing them. You don't jump to conclusions; you give them an opportunity to explain.

LACK OF INDEPENDENCE AND PRIVACY. Adults need some privacy, even if they are married. One of the fallacies of marriage is that everything has to be done in tandem all the time. In fact, people need some breathing room and independence. Too much togetherness is constricting. I've been married for more than half a century, and I realized long ago that my husband and I don't have to do everything together. We can go to dinner with friends without our spouse, and even travel with friends without our spouse. Many people wonder if that's a good idea. I think it is. Of course, my husband and I are together a lot of the time, but we have the freedom to act independently if we want. We also give each other privacy, but that doesn't mean we keep important secrets. It means we value a sense of autonomy and freedom.

LACK OF COLLABORATION AND COMMUNICATION. Relationships that involve parenting require so much collaboration, especially regarding how to take care of the child. Living together is nothing if not a collaboration, but sometimes people get so mad that they stop collaborating. They try the silent treatment, which avoids discussion, resolution, and continuing to communicate. One of the worst things a couple can do is to go to bed mad. Then in addition to not resolving their differences, they can't even sleep well. So many people know this rule, and yet they violate it. Too many of these negative memories, without forgiveness, mean the beginning of the end. The lines of communication have broken down, and no one wants to apologize or accept an apology. These are also the reasons that friendships and parent-child relationships break down. No matter the age, the causes are the same.

LACK OF KINDNESS. FAILURE TO FORGIVE. Kindness should be a daily habit in relationships. Smiling, helping carry heavy groceries, holding the door, cooking your partner's favorite meal — common courtesy. It's so important, so why do we tend to neglect the people closest to us when it comes to the basics? I guess because life gets busy, but really, how much time does it take to be kind? And how about forgiveness? If you can't forgive, you can forget being in any kind of relationship. Forgiving means being humble. It means letting go of grudges. It means prizing the relationship and the family over some petty disagreement, or even a bigger argument. In the end, what's more important?

Even if you and your spouse are working hard to keep the elements of TRICK alive in your relationship, children will cause strain. An eight-year longitudinal study found that parents showed a "sudden deterioration" in their marriage that was more drastic than married couples who didn't have kids, and this strain persisted throughout the length of the study.[17] Even the best relationships are put to the test. But additional research has shown that intervention programs and couples' workshops can help parents deal with the pressures of raising a family. In other words, you can work it out, as long as you're willing.

But it doesn't seem like a lot of us are: So many children have divorced parents these days. It's an epidemic. When I was growing up, divorce was rare, very rare. But today the national average is roughly one in two. It makes me wonder: Do we really value our marriage vows? People make a promise, but they don't prepare themselves for the major disruption kids cause. Then they're blindsided and come to the painful conclusion that separating is the only answer. But is that what's best for the partnership? And more important, is that what's best for kids?

I have witnessed how continuously painful divorce can be. It seems rampant in Silicon Valley, where sudden wealth contributes to the problem. That is why many children in divorced families are psychologically distressed. Experts say that younger children are negatively affected because they're still so attached to their parents, and adolescents, who are already in a rebellious stage, tend to feel betrayed, which only makes them pull away more. In a 2014 analysis of three decades of research on family structure and the well-being of children, Dr. Jane Anderson concludes that with the exception of abusive relationships, "children fare better when parents work at maintaining the marriage."[18] Dozens of studies point to the adverse effects of divorce, including reduced time with each parent, loss of economic and emotional security, decreased social and psychological development, impaired cognitive and academic development, and a decrease in physical health. Interestingly, additional research has found many of these same effects in the parents. This should certainly cause us concern, though there are other researchers who argue that children experience short-term negative effects of divorce that are usually not long-lasting. They argue that it's not the act of divorce itself that is so damaging to children but exposure to high levels of parental conflict during and after a divorce. I'm not a social scientist, but I'm not sure I agree with these researchers.

I have rarely seen a divorce where kids were happy about it; in fact, I have seen divorce destroy a child's motivation in life. I have seen divorce cause long-term depression. I have seen high school students fall apart when they hear that their parents are getting divorced. They're suddenly plunged into a situation of missing one parent or the other. Many couples today have joint custody, which means the children travel between houses and the burden is on them to move every few days or weeks. Some kids stop caring about school and start having dysfunctional relationships. They are looking for support and a group that cares about them. They are looking for stability. I have also seen incredible anger and conflict among divorcing couples. Divorce seems to bring out the worst, most vindictive nature in people. It's like we're trying to be so nasty that the other person — whom we once loved — completely falls apart.

And this is what we're modeling for our children: How to live an angry life. There are many things in life that make us mad. It happens all the time. The key is how you recover from these breakdowns and whether you hold grudges. Sometimes the breakdowns are small, but other times they are big. Either way, what lesson do you want your child to learn? Divorce shows kids that no relationship in life is forever; no relationship can be trusted. It's a sad and scary message for many children, especially younger ones. Divorce also teaches kids that if you don't like something, then you can run away from it instead of staying and solving the problem. We live in a society where everything happens quickly, where information travels at the speed of light, where the primary source of news is served in messages of 140 characters or fewer, and this all affects our willingness to put up with hard times. We're losing grit, and that's affecting our ability to deal with the challenges of long-term relationships.

So what am I recommending? Avoid divorce if at all possible (except in the case of abuse, untreatable addiction, or violence). I know that may be controversial to some people, but I mean it. At some point you loved your partner enough to marry them. Maybe you can still be civil to each other and fix things. Being civil doesn't mean you agree with everything your partner says or does, but it's important to show your kids that you can get along despite disagreements, that when a relationship is broken, it can be repaired. Everything, and I mean everything, can be forgiven — even infidelity. As the psychologist and best-selling author Esther Perel says, divorce is no place for haste: "The rush to divorce makes no allowance for error, for human fragility. It also makes no allowance for repair, resilience, and recovery." There is so much infidelity these days, and so much stigma. A woman is a slut for straying from her husband. A man is weak for staying. In the end, it's up to the couple and the couple alone. They should listen to what they think, listen to their hearts, and not be influenced by their friends.

And consider the fallout. If kids are involved, think twice. And it isn't just the kids who'll be upended. It's the whole family, the social network, the grandchildren. A divorce lingers for generations. It has an impact on years and years of your life. Reassess and ask whether this breach of trust, this breakdown of communication, is worth trading for a lifetime of alienation and discord, a lifetime that affects the happiness of you and your children. The pain does not go away after divorce. In many cases it intensifies. It's better to repair and forgive. So much unhappiness can be avoided for so many people. Of course, I realize that it's not always possible to fix things. My daughter Anne went through a very public divorce. When she told me there were problems in her marriage, I encouraged her to work it out. Both she and her partner tried, but the relationship couldn't be saved. It was time to move on, and to focus on making sure the children are affected as little as possible.

If you have already divorced, or if you have an acrimonious relationship with your former partner, it isn't too late to start to collaborate, to start to cooperate. Make it clear that you want to improve the lives of the kids and consequently your own lives. It is so much easier to drop the anger and look toward a positive future. That doesn't mean re-establishing the relationship; it means getting along. Your former partner wants the same thing you do — happy, healthy, productive kids. That is something you can agree on without concern about conflicts. Usually the conflicts arise from *how* to achieve this. Model those collaboration and negotiation skills that you want your kids to have. Everyone will be happier and you will be teaching them skills for their adult life. And if you have already reached a point where collaboration is no longer possible, then be kind to yourself, forgive yourself, and move on. That is also important to model for your children: moving on in life and being optimistic in the face of really difficult times.

It is important for kids to know that people change and that change is just part of life, sometimes in ways you do not expect. Some people change so much, they are unrecognizable. They want another life. There are illnesses, accidents, financial problems — so many changes that could happen. Most of the time these changes can be worked out with your partner, but if they can't, then there are always sensible ways to cope. That is the first thing you need to model and teach your child. *No matter what, you will find a good way to work it out and solve the problem.* We all have a choice: to be depressed or to be an optimist — and I choose to be an optimist and an activist. Take the necessary steps to feel better and to plan for the future. The alternative leads nowhere. I believe that things will get better, people will be nicer, and overall, human beings are fundamentally good — just believing it seems to make it happen.

On a positive note, divorce rates in the United States dropped between 2008 and 2015, and recently reached a forty-year low, according to the National Center for Family and Marriage Research. More people are aware of the importance of working it out for the benefit of the kids and for their own long-term happiness. The decline in divorce rates can be attributed to a number of factors, including the trend of marrying later in life, couples living together before getting married, and — thanks to feminism — the ability to marry for love rather than for financial support. People who find partners on dating websites also tend to have lower divorce rates. Perhaps it is because they look for people who have similar interests and backgrounds.

There are so many lessons in parenting and in relationships. Some are difficult, no doubt, but each one is an opportunity. An opportunity to make our own lives better, and to be better models for our children. All of us are capable of making positive changes. We just have to be willing.

KINDNESS

8

Kindness: Model It. It's Contagious

CARING IS KINDNESS; that is my mantra. In the fall of 2002, I got a call from my mother's doctor telling me she'd been admitted to the hospital. She was ninety-one, and she'd been sick and unable to walk for years. Recently, she'd been suffering from urinary tract infections and needed antibiotics almost all the time. I was really worried, so I flew down to see her at Eisenhower Hospital in Palm Desert. I remember how small she looked in that big hospital bed, but she was so happy to see me. My mother always had such a wonderful smile.

It didn't seem like much could be done for her. The doctor suggested that she be moved to a nursing home with a hospice wing. I didn't know at the time that "hospice" means palliative care for those considered terminally ill. I should have asked more questions. "They take care of the patient," he explained, "but they don't do any dramatic medical interventions." It seemed like the right decision for someone in her nineties. He promised they would take good care of her.

Once she was settled at the hospice, I flew home. A few weeks later, my daughter Anne decided to visit her. Anne always had a special relationship with my mother. After college, she went to Krasnoyarsk, Siberia, and visited my mother's hometown to see it for herself. My other daughters were close to their grandmother too. How could they not be? She was the kindest, most caring person I've ever met.

I always included my mother in as much as I could, but it wasn't easy. She couldn't travel because of her multiple sclerosis. It mainly affected her legs. First she used a cane, then a walker, until she couldn't walk at all. Anne, Susan, and Janet went to visit my mom in Palm Desert at least once a year, where she was living with my brother Lee. They'd all drive around together in a golf cart. They knew their grandmother wasn't well. They spent as much time with her as possible, wrote her letters, and called when they weren't with her. I tried to teach my daughters to be loving and kind to all people, especially the elderly. I made it clear that every single person is important, no matter what, and I modeled that behavior. I didn't just talk about it.

When Anne entered the hospice she saw the opposite of kindness. She heard a number of patients crying out and moaning. People in hospitals didn't normally cry out. Something was the matter. She scrambled to locate her grandmother. Then she realized that one of the patients in distress was her grandmother. Anne couldn't find any nurses. But when she did, they went the other way. None of the personnel seemed concerned. (Most hospice care is not like this, thankfully — it turns out we just had a really bad experience.)

This was not okay with Anne: her grandmother was not going to be treated like this. She took action. She called an ambulance, and it arrived within six minutes. She told them that her grandmother was on the verge of dying and needed to be transferred back to Eisenhower Hospital, that she was completely dehydrated and needed emergency care. The shocked nursing staff watched the entire process, dumbfounded. They said nothing as my mother was wheeled out. "Hard to believe you call this care," Anne said. "You're not taking proper care of your patients." And she was off with the ambulance.

At the hospital, my mother got an IV for fluid and was given some food. Apparently she hadn't eaten or had any water for hours. No wonder she was so incoherent. She started to regain some strength, and that was encouraging, but Anne knew from her work in the ER at San Francisco General Hospital that there was still more that could be done. She decided she needed new doctors on the case, so she found two and removed the previous one who had sent her to the hospice in the first place. The new doctors changed her medications, and within two days there was dramatic improvement. She was alert and talking.

Now the big question was how to care for her once she was released. How could we make sure this did not happen again? We lived in the Bay Area, and it was hard to monitor the situation from hundreds of miles away. My mother needed a family member who could oversee her care. She couldn't advocate for herself.

Always creative, Anne came up with a plan. We had to move my mother, but the cost of an ambulance was prohibitive. So she decided that we would drive her ourselves, with her IV drip and other medications. The hospital was shocked. "You are transferring a patient five hundred miles, and not in an ambulance?" they said. "That's dangerous."

"Well, not as dangerous as leaving her with people who don't care about her," Anne said. She figured out a way to do it, took responsibility for the medications, and rented a van and a stretcher. A few days later, at five in the morning, we got on Interstate 5 and drove my mother from Palm Desert all the way to the Bay Area, to a nursing home in Los Altos. It took eight hours, but my mother was fine the whole way. I had called them earlier to see if they would accept my mother, and they'd said yes, even though they had a waiting list. They were struck by the drama of the story.

Her new nursing home in Los Altos turned out to be great. They had daily activities, physical therapy, and a social hour, and they took good care of the patients. Our whole family celebrated Thanksgiving with her at the nursing home, a wonderful memory we never would have had if Anne hadn't stepped in. My mother lived another two years before passing away at ninety-three.

Anne's kindness, compassion, and persistence saved my mother's life. She came up with this innovative way to save her grandmother, and she took two weeks out of her work schedule to do it. Kindness is part of Anne's character. She doesn't just talk about it or think about it; she shows it. She was a very loving child, always socially aware, always concerned about the smallest kitten in the litter, or the dog that had a broken leg, or kids who didn't seem to have friends. In kindergarten, when she was asked what she was thankful for, she wrote, "I am thankful for Kenji," her friend. She is also a very caring mother.

Empathy and kindness had always been part of my way of looking at the world. I realized many years later that I was inadvertently teaching my daughters empathy, gratitude, and forgiveness by the way I behaved, the books I picked to read to them, the shows I suggested they see. Perhaps it also had to do with my childhood and hearing all those stories from my parents about their difficult lives surviving the pogroms in Russia, or perhaps it was because of losing my brother David. Whatever the reason, it was part of my life: warmth, concern, and empathy were a way of being.

Anne took those lessons to heart, but she wasn't the only one. Susan and Janet did too. They all worked in some way after college trying to make the world a better place. Susan was in India; Janet in South Africa. They did this on their own — no suggestions from me. During college, Anne volunteered in the emergency room of a local hospital and was shocked by the problems patients encountered. It made her want to volunteer even more. Patients couldn't advocate for themselves because they were too sick, and that often meant they didn't get the right treatment. Later she worked at San Francisco General Hospital and Stanford Hospital, thinking she would be a doctor. In the end, she decided that she would have more of an impact if she did something other than be a doctor confined to an examination room. She first wanted to establish a patient advocacy service to advocate for each patient since they were usually too sick to do so. She saw a real lack of kindness and concern. It wasn't that the doctors and nurses didn't care. It was more that they were overworked and just didn't have time. They were in medicine to be kind, but their grueling schedules didn't permit it. It is a major problem today.

Instead of establishing a patient advocacy service, she went way beyond that. She did something that would have a greater impact for all patients worldwide by starting a company that put people in charge of their DNA, the building blocks of their body. Understanding your DNA is the key to understanding your health and how to prevent disease. As the co-founder and CEO of 23andMe, she gives millions of people access to their own health information based on the belief that no one cares more about you than you, yourself. And she continues to fight for the best care for everyone. Someone she was particularly concerned about was her former mother-in-law, Genia Brin, who has Parkinson's disease. One of Anne's earliest actions was to join forces with the Michael J. Fox Foundation to study Parkinson's and find treatments. The company recently published the largest meta-analysis of Parkinson's disease to date.

One question I have is, *Are kids today learning how to be kind?* What is our national model when they read daily stories about an ICE raid, about infants and children being separated from their parents, about immigrants stalled at the border for days? I hope all parents, regardless of political affiliation, have empathy for immigrants and talk about it with their kids. But several studies suggest they aren't. When researchers at the Harvard Graduate School of Education surveyed ten thousand kids for the Making Caring Common Project, an initiative to help make kids more caring and community-minded, they found that 80 percent of children identified achievement or happiness as their top priority. Only 20 percent said "caring for others" was their top priority. This survey also revealed, "Youth are three times more likely to agree than disagree with this statement: 'My parents are prouder if I get good grades than if I'm a caring community member.'" Not very encouraging. Another study at the University of Michigan found a sharp drop in empathy in American college students after the year 2000.[19] One of my teaching colleagues had a similar finding when he did an informal poll with his students at a public school in the United States. He asked kids to raise their hands if they experienced TRICK in their classes. Starting with trust, most of the kids raised their hands — a great sign. Respect and independence: about half. Two-thirds of the kids said they had experienced collaboration. But no one raised their hands when asked about kindness.

We've fallen victim to the dominant style of parenting — helicopter parenting — that places no importance on kindness. Too many parents are focused on winning. Our main goal is to make our kids successful, and our main fear is that they can't succeed without our help. We're convinced that if they're not perfect, they'll fail in life, which is bad for them but even worse for our own anxieties and insecurities. When they fail, we fail — and we can't let that happen. Kindness has disappeared from our parenting goals. Amy Chua, Tiger Mom, even said in her talk with me in Puebla, Mexico, that she never worried about kindness or happiness. She just wanted her daughters to be number one.

But we're paying a price by focusing on individual success and perfection. We are inadvertently raising narcissistic children who lack kindness and empathy. We don't mean to do that, but that is what is happening. They don't have time to think about other people: they're too focused on performing. If they don't excel, they might not receive the love and acceptance they need from you, the parent. How kind is that? So they funnel all their energy into succeeding, which might produce perfect grades but does nothing for their independence and sense of empowerment, let alone their kindness toward others. And when it's all over, our kids end up entitled and self-obsessed in a society that values individual achievement above almost anything else.

Kindness doesn't factor anywhere into this kind of parenting, or this kind of society. I think it's because kindness gets a bad rap. It's often seen as weakness. When you're kind, the thinking goes, people will walk all over you. I have heard that throughout my decades as a teacher who tries to work with students instead of police them. When I was running the English department at Palo Alto High, at least half the faculty questioned my treatment of students. They didn't like my "punishments," in which I tried to understand where students were coming from and give them a second chance. My colleagues always told me, "They're walking all over you. They'll just break the rules again. You know what you are? A pushover." They didn't realize that kindness gets results. It makes your life better while improving the lives of everyone around you. I'm not saying you shouldn't be discerning when someone asks for help. Sure, some people are out to manipulate you, but you can usually sense when a person has ulterior motives (they're overly solicitous, they're asking for a lot of money, something they promise seems too good to be true). There is bad in the world, but that shouldn't stop us from trying to make the world better. We just have to be cautious.

Some of my students' parents have the same attitude as the teachers. How is kindness going to help their child get into college? I recently met with Marc Tessier-Lavigne, the president of Stanford University, and he told me the number one quality they're looking for in applicants is kindness and caring about others. These are the skills that determine a student's success both at Stanford and as a citizen of the world. Colleges say they don't want kids who are cutthroat and nasty. We may have fallen into a cruel and overly competitive system that rewards affluent students with top scores and top grades, but the tide is turning. Many colleges are dropping standardized tests and looking at the student as a whole, considering how their unique talents might benefit the community.

Kindness is now critical in the business world, too. When Google conducted an internal survey (called Project Oxygen), they found it was these so-called soft skills — not STEM skills — that separated their high-ranking managers from other Google employees. In fact, four of the seven top managerial skills were directly related to kindness: empathy, consideration for employees as individuals with different values and points of view, coaching and providing helpful feedback, and meaningful discussion of career development. Many companies today focus on kindness for employees and customers. Zappos is one, and another is Whole Foods. Jeff Bezos, CEO of Amazon, wants customers to be happy (though he freely admits that his employees face a demanding workplace — you don't hear much about kindness toward employees at Amazon). They are doing everything to be kind to customers. My daughters have taught me the importance of kindness at work firsthand. Janet has a similar story to Anne's in terms of fighting for people's health and well-being. She saw underserved communities decimated by chronic disease and wanted to do something about it. Her caring gave her access to real people in these communities, whom she has helped with advice about breastfeeding, managing HIV and AIDS, and tackling childhood obesity and other difficult health problems.

In Susan's professional life, kindness means taking better care of her employees. One important thing she did at Google was to help set up a daycare program. She wanted a top-notch program not just for her own kids but for as many employees as possible. She knew parents would be happier and perform better if their children were in good hands. She also fought for longer maternity leave for employees. It was major news when she succeeded in getting a fully paid eight-week maternity leave for parents at Google. She kept working to improve the policy over the years, and Google now awards eighteen weeks of paid leave for mothers and twelve weeks for fathers.

Google is a great example of how the best businesses are focusing on kindness for their employees. All people want to work in places where they feel the management genuinely cares about their health and happiness, and where they have a passion project. Google takes this idea to heart and provides free food, places to nap, and a collaborative work environment, and that's why it's consistently ranked one of the top companies to work for in the United States. Their generous policies have motivated other companies to change, and they've ushered in a whole new way of thinking about what it means to be an employee.

Kindness brings so much more than a college acceptance letter and a good job. Being kind makes the people around us happy, and ourselves as well. All kind acts have a bit of self-interest in them: they give us a sense of peace and meaning that can't be bought. We all have to go through life — why not make everyone's journey more pleasant, especially when we're so interconnected?

Today's drug addiction epidemic affords many opportunities for kindness. More people than ever are becoming addicted to prescription opioids, and more people are dying from drug overdoses than died from AIDS at the peak of that epidemic. It is a national tragedy. Finding a solution should be a national priority. So what does this have to do with kindness? Research shows that what addicts need most is kindness and love to help them cope and overcome their dependence. They need support from people they care about, not just support from therapists. Johann Hari's bestseller *Lost Connections* discusses the real causes of depression and anxiety, both of which can lead to addiction. Some of the risk factors he cites include disconnection from other people, from meaningful work and values, from status and respect, and from hope.

While everyone appreciates therapists and the care provided by treatment programs, another solution that works is a support network of friends and family. Sadly, many people struggle to find it because we all assume that the treatment program will take care of the problem. It just doesn't, as we can see from the statistics: Some studies have found that more than 85 percent of people who receive drug addiction treatment relapse within the first year. Twelve-step programs have helped many — and continue to do so — because they teach you to believe in yourself, but these programs need much more support from the outside world. One of the reasons people take drugs even though they know it is terrible for them is to alleviate emotional or physical pain; if family and friends can help mitigate the emotional pain, that, along with professional treatment, would make a difference. The true miracle cure for addiction is kindness.

I have seen tragic situations with teenagers addicted to drugs, which is why I always give my anti-drug talk in class. I don't call it that. It is a talk about how the most important organ in your body is not your heart; it is your brain. That is why you wear a helmet when you ride a bike. That is why you never want to do anything that impacts your brain, such as taking drugs. There are many other ways to get thrills that don't damage you for a lifetime. I also make sure they know that while they feel really empowered (which is good), they need to remember that their brain development continues through the midtwenties. Try bungee jumping or skydiving or car racing (on a track), but dump the idea of using drugs for excitement.

As parents, we can't brush off kindness as some nice-sounding but unnecessary skill. It's at the heart of what parenting really is: bringing children into the world and hoping they'll make it a better place.

INSTILLING KINDNESS

Kindness is a way of living. It's not something you do a few times a year, on Christmas, Thanksgiving, and Valentine's Day. It's an attitude, and it starts with common courtesy. Courtesy is an acknowledgment of someone else's presence. It's the perfect antidote to our self-obsessed culture.

"Good morning. How are you doing today?" So simple, but so effective. This should be a typical greeting when we walk into school or the office or someone's house. Say hello when your spouse, parents, relatives, or friends come in. Make sure your kids do that too. Sounds so easy, but it is missing in many families. Look people in the eye. Eye contact is important. And don't forget to smile. Here's a strange fact about families: Many people who practice these common courtesies outside the home don't carry them over to their own families. They walk in the door without a greeting. They watch a family member carrying groceries without offering to help.

Other easy acts on a daily basis include helping someone unload their car, holding the door for a mother and baby, making sure an elderly person gets off the bus safely, letting someone get in front of you in traffic, being a good listener. Even sending an email saying thank you is an important act of kindness. It seems so small — and it is — but it makes a difference.

As parents, we can teach our children by modeling common courtesy ourselves and guiding our children in making it part of their everyday lives. "Thank you" should be a common phrase in the home. I taught my daughters to thank me, thank each other, and thank everyone who did something for them, whether that was in person, on the phone, or in a letter. Every child should realize that even when they are little, they, too, can say nice things — to their friends, their parents, the adults in their lives. It starts with saying "Hello," progressing to "How are you?" and then to active listening.

Gratitude is part of kindness. It requires that you notice others, consider the ways in which they make your life better, and do something to show your appreciation. Based on what I've seen, a lot of kids today don't know what gratitude is. Perhaps it is because we are so focused on making sure our kids are happy. We do things for them all the time, and they take us for granted. One of the main issues that parents of teenagers have is that they regret having spoiled their kids by giving them too much. It is a common problem. The kids are not grateful for anything because they just expect all. They want more. It happens even in low-income families.

Gratitude makes everyone happy: the giver and the receiver. Many studies have found a connection between expressing gratitude and a general sense of well-being. A new study from 2018 found that being in a grateful state of mind increases levels of hope and happiness.[20] Another study published in the *Journal of School Psychology* found that adolescents who reported greater levels of gratitude were more optimistic, experienced higher life satisfaction, and had a decreased risk of developing depression.[21] Gratitude also improves our relationships with friends, parents, colleagues, business partners. When you are grateful for the people in your life, people want to be with you. It really is a powerful tool for not only creating kindness in the world, but becoming a better person.

To teach gratitude, model it yourself, the same way you do with courtesy and politeness. Those kids are watching you. You are the most powerful teacher. If you are grateful for what you have, your kids will be too. If you are always complaining, well, expect them to do the same. Here's a lesson that many parents need to take to heart: Make sure your kids appreciate the presents they receive for birthdays or holidays. I'm not saying giving gifts is bad. For some families, tons of presents under the Christmas tree could be a stroke of good luck because there wasn't enough money for presents the year before. In other families, kids open gift after gift without ever once saying thank you or understanding the time and effort that went into buying those gifts. We need to teach our kids that when someone gives you a present, you should always be grateful (even if you don't like it or you already have something similar).

Have children talk about their gratitude with you. What are they grateful for? Most kids are grateful for their parents. My daughters were grateful for their grandparents and wrote letters and thank-you notes to their grandfather in Poland on a regular basis (unfortunately, we couldn't thank him in person, and we couldn't call him, either, because he didn't have a phone). Some of the letters were pretty trivial, but they were sharing their lives with him. "I went to the park today and played with my friend Jessica. I missed you." They wrote to my parents and Stan's mother, too. They were always writing little notes, gift or not. It was a way to acknowledge someone else's effort, and to appreciate all the people who loved them. The art of writing thank-you notes needs to be revived.

The act of writing itself helps us to reflect on our life and actions. My daughters kept diaries, especially while we were traveling, and they learned to reflect on and be grateful for all their experiences. I recommend that kids write about their day and what they're grateful for every night before bed. It is a good way to practice writing, a good way to think about what you are grateful for, and a good way to keep a diary. It will be fun to read years later. Some of the entries can be pretty hilarious.

"I am grateful that I found a ladybug today."

"I am happy that my brother shared his ice cream."

"I am so excited that I went to a birthday party with a bouncy house."

It's a powerful ritual, and it's even been shown to increase gratitude-related activity in the brain. I also made sure to acknowledge my kids' actions when they did something around the house. "You did a good job of cleaning up with Mommy" was something I always said. "Your room looks very neat today. Good work." Even though it was far from perfect. It would be wonderful if we could all be grateful for what we have in life each and every day. I am like most people — I don't always have the time. Life is too busy. But my family celebrates Shabbat every Friday night, and that's when we think about our gratitude for the whole week.

At school, I tell the students that when they interview people for the paper, they should double-check all quotes for accuracy, and they should thank everyone who took the time to talk with them. We make a point of thanking our advertisers. So many wonderful businesses, including small ones, have supported the journalism program for years both with advertising and donations of food or services. I also remind the students to thank their parents for helping out with group dinners. Every three weeks, the students have dinner together for three nights in a row during production — sixty super-hungry students. The parents are so great to provide these meals. You can imagine the mess. Even though they clean up after themselves, there's still a lot of trash, so we make sure to thank our custodians, who are an important part of our program.

THE DEEPEST FORM OF KINDNESS

When my daughters were growing up, we had a Christmas tradition of buying the saddest tree we could find at the "Lucky National Forest," the lot at our Lucky grocery store. We'd buy the tree no one else wanted, the one left behind, and we'd take that tree home and do our best to make it beautiful. My daughters loved decorating our trees. The original ornaments were just cut-up egg cartons that they painted and put sparkles on, but as the years went by, the ornaments got more sophisticated. What we were building, without really realizing it, was a sense of empathy. Stan and I were teaching them to look beyond themselves and try to understand what another person (or, in this case, living being) was feeling. They comforted and cared for animals just as they did our Christmas trees. And those patterns naturally extended to all people, whether family, friends, a random patient in the ER who needed help, or a young mother in an impoverished neighborhood struggling to take care of her child.

There are many simple and enjoyable activities that teach kids about empathy. At home, parents can encourage pretend play. All you have to do is give a child the start of a story, a piece of clothing, or a toy, and she will invent her own characters, worlds, universes. It's free and kids love it. When kids pretend to be someone else, they learn what it feels like to be in another person's shoes. It gets them outside of themselves, a necessary state for having empathy. As the child development researchers Dorothy Singer and Jerome Singer point out, "Taking on different roles allows children the unique opportunity to learn social skills such as communication, problem solving, and empathy." So all those dress-up clothes, and that running around the house doing what looks like "crazy things," actually help your kids learn a very important skill.

Reading to your kids on a regular basis, especially books about kindness and empathy, is another helpful activity. We all need to remember the power of stories. Research has shown that reading fiction and considering other characters' feelings helps kids develop empathy. Some of my favorite books for children are *The Rainbow Fish*, about a beautiful fish who finds happiness when he learns to share, *Tikki Tikki Tembo*, in which a young boy rescues his brother, and Shel Silverstein's *The Giving Tree*, a classic story of love and selflessness. Kids love these books because the emotions feel familiar, and the characters are relatable. Just like with pretend play, they're able to imagine themselves in someone else's life. Be sure to talk about the characters and their decisions and feelings. Stan and I did this every night (well, almost every night). We'd read to the kids and reflect on the story. Talking about what you had read was what we did before the Internet. I didn't do it to build empathy specifically. I did it because I wanted to teach my kids about the world, other cultures, travel, history. But it had an added benefit.

Another tip for families: Get a pet. Pets are a wonderful way to teach compassion (and responsibility). We had multiple pets: a golden retriever named Truffle, two cats, and three rats. The girls had to take Truffle out every day. They took her for walks and fed her. They played with her, brushed her, and hugged her. They also took care of the cats and rats. Our pets were part of the family, included in everything. They even got Christmas gifts and birthday gifts. Because of this, my daughters were constantly thinking beyond themselves and making sure that everyone was well cared for.

One summer we decided to let Truffle become a mother. We bred her with a beautiful golden retriever in Oakland, and she gave birth to eight adorable puppies. It was so exciting. The girls couldn't believe their good luck, and they took this new responsibility very seriously. Every day they were taking care of the puppies and watching them grow up, and we moved our cars to let them spread out in luxury over the entire garage. The girls made sure that Truffle had plenty of food and water, that the puppies were nursing properly, and that they all had toys. We became the most popular house on the block. Two months later, my daughters helped find a home for each puppy and set up a way to keep in touch with the new owners. They wanted to make sure that all the dogs had good lives.

Empathy in children is natural. If we model it, our kids will follow.

HOW TO BE KIND WHEN KINDNESS IS HARD

Years ago I had a student, Dominic, who came from a poor family in East Palo Alto and accidentally entered my upper-lane English class as a freshman. He didn't really belong in that class, and he didn't sign up for it. The computer system had made an error. He performed below grade level, so he should have been in a remedial class.

Dominic was an angry kid, the kind of kid that the school considered hopeless. He was aggressive and unkind, seemingly for no reason. I could see that he was just reflecting the way he'd been treated all his life. I was worried about him from the start.

When I figured out the error two weeks into the semester, he had already bonded with me. I asked him if he wanted to move to the lower lane. "Absolutely not," he said.

"Well, you're going to have to do some catch-up work," I said. Dominic accepted the challenge. He was already beginning to see himself as another type of student, perhaps one who could make it in this world, just from receiving trust and respect in my class. I treated him like he was equal to everyone else, because he was. He'd just never been seen that way. The energy he was putting into being mean-spirited now went into catching up academically. It's amazing what a little kindness can do.

Dominic had more than a little catch-up work. He had to stay after school with me every day to work on his reading and writing for the whole year. Then he wanted to be in my journalism program. Here was a kid considered a below-average performer by the school district, now focused on not only getting to grade level but surpassing it. It was an amazing transformation.

Dominic did join the program. I gave him an old computer from home so he could keep up with the work, and he made a lot of new friends. The journalism program is a community of kids who all know each other and care about each other. He seemed pretty happy, but it wasn't all roses for him. Reaching the level of writing required by the paper was tough, and being evaluated by his peers was even tougher. But since everyone was in the same boat, Dominic did not take it personally and continued to work hard on his articles.

At a certain point, though, the pressure got to him. He wanted to perform, but he didn't think he could do it. One day, another kid in class reported that there was a plagiarized article. How did he know? He had read it online . . . the exact same article. I learned that it had been "written" by Dominic.

Dominic was embarrassed and apologized profusely. "I didn't have time and couldn't write it myself," he told me. "I never thought anyone would know."

We talked about the importance of doing your own work, and I decided to suspend him from the paper for one cycle. I had to make a point about the severity of plagiarism, but I didn't want to embarrass him or reignite the anger that he felt when he first arrived in my classroom. I knew why he'd done it. I could see things from his perspective. And what he needed most was some kindness and understanding if he was going to stick to this new path. He didn't need someone to lash out at him. He'd obviously gotten way too much of that in his life already. These are the most important moments in parenting and teaching: Instead of getting mad at the child, can you have a discussion and understand their point of view? Can you muster some compassion? Can you show them kindness even in the most extreme circumstances? I'm happy to say that my method worked: Dominic never plagiarized again.

As a senior, Dominic decided to go to college. He was the first person in his family to do so. I helped him get a scholarship to a college on the East Coast, and off he went. Today he works in retail in New York. He has not only changed his life, but the life and self-image of his family.

A few years after Dominic, I had another student on the verge of being expelled for drinking on campus. He and his girlfriend had been caught with alcohol in the darkroom. They were good kids, embarrassed by the situation. The campus supervisor was preparing to take them to the principal's office when I intervened and said, "Let me handle this one." If they went to the main office, they would be suspended for more than a week. Suspensions don't allow you to make up the work; this means you are permanently behind in your classes and all of your grades are affected. Imagine how devastating that is for kids.

Their punishment was my typical protocol: a conversation, writing, and staying after school and helping me. They also helped other students who needed additional support with their articles. I never took their behavior personally. Of course, I wasn't a pushover; I did have standards. It's just that my consequences were different from being suspended. I forgave their little adventure in the darkroom and allowed them a chance to make it right.

A big part of practicing kindness is remembering that kids are adults in training. They're learning — they're going to make mistakes. That's where forgiveness comes in. Teachers and parents need to know that violations and mistakes aren't necessarily attacks against us. Sometimes it's a case of typical teenager misjudgment. Yes, these mistakes can be hurtful and frustrating, but carrying a grudge, overreacting, and doling out harsh punishment only perpetuate the pain and anger. Try instead to show kindness and forgiveness. Remember what *you* did when you were that age. It doesn't mean you're weak; it doesn't mean you don't have standards. It means you stand firm but are also a big enough person to forgive.

But what if one child attacks another? It can happen in so many ways. I had a female student who was being bullied because she was overweight. She often wore unfashionable clothes to school — a T-shirt and ratty-looking jeans. Teenagers can be ruthless about appearance. They ridiculed her on Facebook. The student was crying and very upset. I tried to get the post removed, but that was pretty tough. (This was six years ago.) I submitted a request to Facebook to take down the comments, but they didn't respond. So I called up people I knew at Facebook, former students, and told them about the problem. The content was finally removed — and then we dealt with the bully. Not everyone has contacts at Facebook. I was lucky. Today Facebook and other social media platforms are working hard to decrease online bullying. Our children's mental health is at stake.

No one wants their child to be a bully. Most parents are horrified when their child is a perpetrator. Yet it happens all the time. According to the National Center for Education Statistics and the Bureau of Justice Statistics, 28 percent of sixth- through twelfth-graders in the United States have experienced bullying. It's likely much more common, since a lot of bullying goes unreported. And of course bullying now also extends into the digital sphere. A 2016 study by the Cyberbullying Research Center found that 34 percent of twelve- to seventeen-year-olds have experienced online bullying during their lifetime. Doctors point to bullying as arising from a number of causes: strained relationships with parents, low self-esteem, inconsistent discipline, and unsupportive peers. Sometimes bullies are victims of bullying themselves. Sometimes kids are modeling the behavior they see in their parents. And cyberbullying has gotten worse. It's because our comments are often anonymous. We can inflict cruelty without any consequences. We lose common courtesy because it's so easy to disregard other people. In a lot of cases, compassion and empathy completely disappear. And there are violent video games. What kind of influence does that have? Do our children really need to be counting the number of people they've killed? There are studies that claim video games don't have a negative impact on kids, but I question those studies. Violence in any form hardens kids. It teaches the exact opposite of kindness, and it can certainly promote bullying.

Something else I've learned in my decades of teaching: A sense of humor develops at a late age. Teenagers often don't understand what's funny and what's cruel. We used to do an April Fools' edition of the school newspaper, but I realized over the years that I couldn't trust my high school students to get the tone right. They thought making fun of someone's speech impediment was okay. I taught them that it wasn't. It was too hard to monitor, and so we stopped this tradition. They learn with time, but issues with humor can lead to cruelty in the adolescent years.

At its core, bullying is a breakdown in kindness that exposes uncomfortable truths about human nature. We seem to target those who stick out. Some of the kids who are bullied lack skills — academically or socially. Kids who are awkward in any way are especially vulnerable. They look funny, say the wrong things, and struggle to interact with their peers, and the other kids pick up on it. The term *schadenfreude* comes to mind, the act of taking delight in someone else's misery or suffering. It's sad, but it's part of human behavior.

Standing out in a good way can be a problem too. I had a student who won a statewide physics award and refused to tell the other students because she was worried that they would make fun of her or be jealous. It's envy, and as researchers have proven, envy is often the starting point of schadenfreude. You become jealous of someone else's success, and then you wait to pounce when they fail. Parents and schools should teach kids about these innate human tendencies. We might not be able to change our fundamental nature, but having conscious awareness could revolutionize how we treat each other.

Of course, even if all kids are aware, bullying will still happen. When it does, I do everything I can to stop it. If I see any type of negative behavior in my classroom, I start by giving a speech — forever the English teacher telling a story. Basically, I'll talk about a kid who was bullied and how it affected him for the rest of his life. I innovate every time, tailoring these speeches to what this particular class needs to hear. Kids don't think about the far-reaching implications of their behavior toward others in high school, but once I start talking about it, they stop and listen. Most important, the kids see me modeling acceptance on a daily basis. I don't care where you're from: China, Africa, or East Palo Alto. You belong in my class and your opinion matters. The only time the kids see forceful behavior from me is when I'm defending everyone's right to be there and be included.

I'm very careful not to single out the victim during these speeches. That kid doesn't need any more stress. Often I'll talk to him after class. I'll say, "Let's talk about what happened today in class. Is there something I can do to help you?" He'll usually respond, "I am not sure." And then I say, "Let's talk about it. I have seen this before, and I can help you." That usually works.

I'll also talk to the bully, again, after class. Bullies need kindness too. Their behavior is usually because they have been bullied or because they enjoy seeing someone suffer. They learned this behavior from someone else. What these kids need is someone who can understand where they're coming from, and why they act the way they do. They also need to know how hurtful bullying can be, how it can cause long-lasting psychological damage. Do they really want to be responsible for destroying another kid's life?

If your child is being bullied, this is the time to step in. Kids are too young and too vulnerable to handle vicious bullying on their own. Pursue every avenue you can. This is really tough, and there's no simple solution, but here are a few ideas. Talk to the school administrators and the teacher. All schools are actively working against bullying, but in spite of these programs, it still happens. Sometimes you won't get a positive response from the school, so you should try again. This is your opportunity to learn how to be a pest, to make enough noise so that the situation will be addressed. Be sure to talk to your child about why bullying happens, how it can affect people, that sometimes kids are mean and don't understand what they're doing. He needs to know that he's not alone, that many people experience bullying, and that he has the strength to stand up to it. Sometimes communicating with the parents of the bully can be helpful, as long as they're open to stepping in. You can also talk to your child's friends and their parents as a way of bolstering his circle of support. Above all, make sure your child knows he can come to you for guidance.

What's even worse than being bullied? Being excluded. One survey of more than ten thousand Australian students found that "social exclusion had a strong association with adolescents' psychological distress and low emotional well-being."[22] My students struggle with this all the time. Oliver Weisberg, one of my students back in the 1990s, was a great kid, but he found it hard to be accepted as a freshman. He'd transferred from another high school, and during his first year he wrote a reflection on being a freshman and how it felt to be excluded. He titled it "The Pain of Being Nobody." He wrote about how difficult it was to be the new kid in the class, how other kids would purposely invite someone to their house while Oliver was listening and not invite him. Or they would describe their fun weekend with friends and make sure Oliver overheard. I remember it so many years later because his essay was written from the heart, and it was true not just for Oliver but for all kids. Being excluded is one of the worst feelings there is. That's why excommunication is the harshest punishment in most religions, and why isolation is the worst form of punishment in prisons. Abandonment is one of the greatest fears kids face. Exclusion triggers it.

Watching isolated kids reminds me of how profoundly we need kindness and community. One of my main defenses against exclusion is to make sure that I do community-building exercises at the beginning of the school year. I want all kids to be included; it is one big family. Another exercise I started doing years ago in my freshman classes was to have them write on three-by-five cards the names of three other students they wanted to be in their group. I read all the cards and search for the kids whose names don't show up on any cards, and I purposely make sure these kids are put in a group and that the kids all get along. I also talk in class on a regular basis about inclusion no matter the ethnic background, their intellectual capabilities, or their looks. I talk about how diverse friendships are what makes life exciting, and I make sure they know that they don't want to be responsible for making anyone's life miserable or, even worse yet, ending it.

This spring I got a thank-you note from a student that said, "You're not just a teacher, you care about us as people." It's true. I care a lot. I care about what they eat, their emotional health, their plans for the future. I'm seen as a friend by my students. I know that many teachers don't think it is appropriate to be seen as a friend. Schools of education still recommend that teachers keep their distance, especially in today's world, where teachers are afraid to be too friendly.

I'm thankful that some schools are rethinking that philosophy. Kindness is about the world, not just our own personal happiness. It is about everyone's happiness. It is hard to be happy when others are suffering. What I do is simple: I show my students as much kindness as possible and hope they reflect it back to the world. A nice perk is that it always comes back to me. Dominic, the student who was placed in my class accidentally but more than earned his spot, is a great reminder of this. His mother has given me flowers every year since he graduated. She's never forgotten how my class turned her son around. Many teachers have stories like this. These are the memories that keep us teaching. There is nothing as gratifying as helping a kid succeed through kindness. You can change a life forever.

9

Teach Your Child to Give a Damn

JUST AFTER JANET WAS BORN in 1970 and we had moved into our new house on the Stanford campus, I went to the Palo Alto Library to check out a book. I was told that the libraries were for Palo Alto residents only. Stanford is not part of Palo Alto; it is an unincorporated area of Santa Clara County. They advised me to use the Santa Clara County Library instead, which was a few miles away. I was shocked, because kids from the Stanford faculty area went to the Palo Alto public schools. I thought, *This is really unfair to Stanford children. They have unequal access to important facilities.* I was angry and my mind went into action. What could I do to change this policy? With two kids in tow, I went to Palo Alto city council meetings as well as Stanford campus meetings and argued my point. I think having my kids with me helped. It was an easy battle to resolve, because fortunately everyone agreed. I got the impression they had all been worried about it even before I showed up, and I realized that some changes are easier to make than we think. In this case, all I had to do was notice the problem and communicate it to the people in charge. Today, all students in the Palo Alto schools, regardless of where they live, have access to the Palo Alto libraries, a wonderful resource.

When the girls were a little older, I took it upon myself to convince Stanford to build a neighborhood park. There were 160 families in our community, called Frenchman's Hill. We needed a place for the kids to congregate and for families to get to know each other. That's what parks are for, so why didn't we have one? I think they just forgot about it. I started agitating, wrote letters, made appointments, met with people, and got a petition signed by many parents. The Faculty Staff Housing Committee and the Land and Building Development Committee finally agreed to the park — if *I* designed it. Wow, I was thrilled. That was the fun part. I remember looking through mail-order catalogues of playground equipment and designing the best park possible. The Esther Wojcicki Playground was a huge success. The climbing equipment looked like a beautiful castle: Kids would crawl into a hole at the bottom and climb up inside of it, peeking out from little windows along the way. We installed high-quality swings and rocking horses, and a slide that was built into the side of the hill, a major attraction.

In 1975, because of a dire need for babysitters in the new faculty area of the Stanford campus, I started a babysitting co-op to solve the sitter scarcity. We had a rotating secretary every month, and all you needed to do was make a call, schedule another parent to come over and take care of your kids, and then return the favor when you were available. The babysitting co-op built a wonderful sense of community, and it also allowed so many parents to take a little time for themselves. I'm proud to say it lasted for over a decade. A few years later, in 1980, I oversaw a massive upgrade of the SCRA (Stanford Campus Recreation Association) swimming pool. I organized the re-piping and re-plastering of the pool, relocation of some of the play structures, and upgrading of the clubhouse.

I was always looking for what could be improved, where a help-ing hand was needed. I thought it was my duty to contribute and make our community better. I still feel that way. If everyone just sits around and talks, nothing gets done. I was always a doer. All of this influenced my daughters, not because I lectured to them about the importance of serving the community or even because I wanted to serve as a model—but just because I cared. I tried to show them through my actions what they could achieve. This atti-tude is important to leading a good life, but I didn't realize at the time the profound impact it has on children's well-being, which has been confirmed by a number of interesting studies. Teenagers who volunteer with younger children experience both decreased nega-tive moods and decreased cardiovascular risk, according to a study published in the *Journal of the American Medical Association*.[23] A 2016 study from India found that teenagers who performed volun-teer work were significantly less likely to engage in illegal behav-iors and also had fewer convictions and arrests between the ages of twenty-four and thirty-four.[24] Classrooms that emphasize social and emotional skills and help kids function as a community result in dis-advantaged students outperforming state averages on standardized tests.[25] We also know the opposite is true. Failing to build relation-ships and serve a greater community can impact both physical and mental health. Researchers have argued that loneliness is a bigger public health risk than obesity. One study found that participants with stronger connections to other people had a 50 percent greater chance of living longer.[26] Feeling like we belong can be a matter of life or death.

But how many of us think about this when it comes to parenting? How many of us take up causes and show our kids, through our own behavior, how to fight for our communities? How many children feel empowered to take on the biggest challenges of our time and find a way to contribute? Are we really showing our kids how to serve others, or are we teaching them how to escape into their own lives?

It's sad to say, but I've noticed more and more kids completely focused on *themselves*. Where *they* want to go to college, vacations *they* want to take, things *they* want to buy. Sometimes it feels like we're training a nation and a world of narcissists, and I don't think it's a stretch to say that helicopter parenting has played a big role in this. Kids are growing up feeling like they're the center of the universe. They're chauffeured by their parents, put into competitive activities that teach them being number one is the most important thing, and they're made to believe that if they're not perfect, if they don't achieve at all times, they'll be failures in life. No wonder kids are more self-centered (and anxious) than ever before.

As young adults, they're not only lacking grit and independence; they're wholly unprepared to take on causes that could make the world a better place. Instead they focus on money, because that, they think, will make them happy and fulfilled. It's the American idea: Get rich, then do nothing. Sit on a beach. Go out for an expensive dinner. Go to Las Vegas. But these kinds of pursuits turn people into narcissists and thrill addicts. There seems to be a number of them here in Silicon Valley, people who worry about themselves before anyone else. They don't prioritize the good of the community, they don't fight for social causes, and they aren't pursuing a life of meaning and purpose. As a result, they often end up isolated and depressed. I've met lots of unhappy millionaires and even some unhappy billionaires.

A lot of them probably started out as directionless kids. When talking with my friend Ken Taylor, former chair of philosophy at Stanford, he reflected on how confused students seem to be when it comes to living a good life. Taylor told me he can see kids' priorities just in the majors they choose. According to Taylor, 37 percent of all declared majors at Stanford, some 1,000 students, are computer science majors. Why? "Because if you get a degree from Stanford in computer science," he says, "you can step into the valley as a twenty-two-year-old starting at a hundred K per year, while believing that one hundred K a year is just a start, it's nothing." For some students this is the right choice because computer science really is their passion, but Taylor told me that other students in the program need to take the introductory course, CS 107, three times before they pass. Because computer science isn't their passion, or because their talents and skills are better suited to another field. Taylor says one of his main roles as a professor, especially when teaching freshmen, is to be subversive, to free students from the influence of their parents, who have in many cases modeled the idea that a well-lived life is "all about acquisition and status."

No wonder kids are confused. It's because their parents and teachers are confused too. The whole adult world needs to be aware of this. Why do you think that here in the States we have an epidemic of opioid addiction and depression and suicide? We don't seem to have the right information about how to live well, how to take care of ourselves and others. We don't seem to understand the point. We're chasing money and possessions. Not service, not purpose. If we have a purpose at all, it's to make *ourselves* happy. But if there's one thing I know, it's this: You're happiest — as well as most beneficial to society — when you are doing things to help others.

Bill Damon, the director of the Stanford Center on Adolescence and author of *The Path to Purpose*, thinks about this problem a lot. Damon is an expert in teaching kids the most important life skills. Here's what he has to say about self-centeredness and purpose: "Especially in these days of intense focus on individual performance and status, a real risk in the development of today's young is self-absorption. For the sake of both their mental health and their character development, all young people need to hear the message 'It's not about you' every now and then. Finding a purpose that contributes to the world beyond the self is a premier way of tuning in to that message." Thinking beyond the self—that's the key. How many of our kids are doing that?

When I visited Damon at Stanford, he told me about a formal dialogue he'd had with the Dalai Lama in Vancouver, in which he'd asked what parents can do to help their children find meaning in their lives. The Dalai Lama gave two recommendations: 1) Give your child a vivid sense of how empty and non-gratifying a life without purpose is. If you have nothing to believe in, you don't attach yourself to anything, you don't develop a purpose and follow it. You aren't serving others. Even though hedonism is fun for a little while, it gets old fast, and you get bitter. 2) You also must vividly portray the joy of living a meaningful life. Whether it's through stories, theater, religion, or modeling purposeful behavior yourself, we have to teach our kids what meaning looks like. And it doesn't look like a new Mercedes and a vacation home on Cape Cod. Meaning is connection, relationships, contribution, and service. That's what our children should understand about a life well lived.

But here's the thing: It goes way beyond your personal achievements. It's so much deeper than the meaning *you* derive from helping and serving other people, and how happy *you* become. When we talk about serving the community, creating social activism, and fighting for change, what we're really talking about is improving our culture and society at large. After all, isn't that the point of having children? To move the culture forward? To make us all more humane, more compassionate, more connected? And to bring us together to tackle the daunting problems we face as a species, such as combatting global warming, sharing access to clean water, aiding refugees, and confronting disease and nuclear war? If we're not working together, we'll falter. We may not even survive. That's how important this is. That's how vital these lessons are for children. You may be wondering whether all this is in the domain of parenting. It absolutely is. *It starts with the family.* Then your family connects to another family, to the larger community, and in the end to the whole world. Kids are instrumental when it comes to solving the challenges that await us, many of which we can't even predict. So I say, for the sake of us all, let's prepare our children in the best way possible.

BUILDING A SENSE OF SERVICE

For me, a commitment to social activism was inevitable given what I experienced as a child. After the death of my brother, and then seeing my other brother, Lee, struggle with dyslexia in an era when dyslexic children were classified as mentally challenged, I felt called to protect the underdog. My whole family was the underdog, uninformed and disempowered. We didn't know how to protect ourselves, and I never wanted that to happen to any other family. I also grew up in the shadow of my family's long history of persecution. My parents fled Russia and the Ukraine, narrowly escaping the pogroms. We lost so many people on both my mother's and father's side. When I visited Auschwitz, I learned that dozens of other women named Esther Hochman (my maiden name) had died in the Holocaust. For some reason, I had been spared. But I always knew that I could have been one of those other girls who didn't make it out alive.

And then there was my family's own activism. My father was an early member of the Sierra Club. My uncle was the head of the United Jewish Appeal in the eastern U.S., and both of my grandfathers were rabbis and community leaders. My cousin Rabbi Benzion Laskin was the first Lubavitch rabbi recently honored for his work in New York City with the Chamah organization, an international Jewish nonprofit that provides educational programs and humanitarian aid. One cousin on my mother's side owns a group of after-hours clinics in Portland, Oregon; another cousin on my mother's side, Tad Taube, is a philanthropist who donated millions to Stanford and UC Berkeley as well as the Polin Museum in Warsaw. I also have a relative who was the UN ambassador from Argentina. We all embrace the Jewish concept of *tikkun olam*, which means "repairing the world." We're here to make things better, in any way we can. For me, that meant taking up journalism and political science during the height of Berkeley's free speech movement. Studying political structures and writing about injustice became my way of making a difference. On Stan's side, his father, Franciszek Wojcicki, was one of the founders of the modern state of Poland after the war; his mother, Janina, was head of the Slavic division of the Library of Congress, and Stan himself spent his life trying to understand how the universe came to be and finding ways to explain it to all of us.

Your family may have similar stories and a natural impulse to serve. You might know exactly how I felt as a college student convinced I could change the world. But what if you don't? What if you were told to focus on personal success and don't really know where to start? Well, I have good news: It's not that hard. The main thing you need is the right attitude — toward yourself and your children. You can start small. Volunteer for one hour in your community. Go to a city council meeting. Research an issue that affects your neighborhood. At the very least, you can vote. While you're at it, you can teach your child about the importance of participating in a democracy. Once you have service in mind, you'll see opportunities everywhere. Everywhere there's a problem to be solved, someone or some group to support and champion. It really is a way of being in the world, and when it comes to our kids, it pays to shape this perspective as early as possible.

And I do mean early. Recently I observed my granddaughter Ava's preschool "graduation." At her preschool, all ages are given bird names. Ava was leaving the "Sparrows" to join the "Robins." The ceremony began with the Sparrows congratulating each other on a fantastic year together. There were twenty-five kids taking turns speaking in support of each other, with no interruption by the teachers. One little girl walked up to my granddaughter and said, "I love you, Ava, and I'm so proud of you." I couldn't believe it! Then the Robins officially welcomed each new student. It was so positive and supportive. At the end, Ava walked through a symbolic tunnel of Robins, who high-fived her and cheered her on. The caring, dedicated teachers, two men and two women, clearly had a great relationship with the kids. And they had built a powerful sense of community where every kid felt like she belonged. Imagine the foundation this was building, even in the youngest children. All preschoolers should have a feel-good experience like this where they can understand that they are part of a group. They will be supported by their peers, and together they are part of a larger goal: learning and growing up. Wouldn't you love to be a Sparrow or a Robin? I sure would. Perhaps your child can be. I am working with an amazing group of caring entrepreneurs who will be starting preschool centers called WeCare. Their goal is to help parents find preschool care by creating licensed homecare centers. This will open up more quality preschools, make it easier for parents to seek out help, and provide jobs for those who need them.

As kids grow up, parents should support them in finding outlets in their communities. All you have to do is look around. What problems need solutions? How could your children participate? They could care for the elderly, join environmental cleanups, or help at a soup kitchen, as some of my grandkids do. Here's a big one: Encourage your child to mentor another kid. Most students graduate from high school without having a single person as their champion. People might think this isn't true, but ask a group of teenagers in your neighborhood if they feel they have a champion at school, someone who believes in them and is looking out for them. If they do, they're lucky, because the majority of kids don't. Everyone — including a child — has something of value to offer to another person. I think this alone could change the world.

To be clear, I'm not talking about "community service" as some kind of punishment. I don't like that term and don't like it to be seen as a punishment, because it has such a negative connotation. Forced community service has marginal benefits. It might open kids' eyes to seeing how other people live, but they might also resist because they know they're being punished. I'm talking about kids enjoying helping others, and making it a rewarding activity to do with friends. I recommend scheduling one activity per week for kids that helps other people. Let them pick their cause, and let them join forces with friends and classmates. We want them to understand that contributing is fun and meaningful.

Another caveat: Please don't manipulate community outreach so you can pad your child's college résumé. Sure, it looks good on an application, but colleges are completely aware when kids only volunteer for the credit. That's one reason colleges have started doing interviews, because it's easy to sense whether kids have passion or not. You can tell if they really care or they only care about getting accepted. When we propose volunteering as a résumé builder, it sends kids the wrong message. It shows them that everything is for personal gain, which is exactly the idea we must fight against.

If you look around, you might be able to find a sense of social activism in unexpected places. Take summer camp. Sure, your kids could go to a tennis camp to perfect their game, but what if camps could instill important values of caring and service? One of the most effective groups for teaching social activism that I've seen in recent years is Camp Tawonga, located near Yosemite National Park in California. It has been in existence since 1923 . . . a long time, and for good reason. This camp is incredibly successful because their goal is to start kids out with, first, a positive self-image. Tawonga builds this through activities like arts and crafts, swimming, hiking, and soccer, as well as through responsibilities to the group, like serving dinner and cleaning up afterward. And they proceed to deeper lessons. They also show kids how to develop a "partnership with nature." Campers explore the beautiful area through overnight camping trips that teach how important it is to protect the environment. They're taught how to become advocates and return to their communities with a newfound respect and motivation to take care of their own surroundings. That's the point of the camp. Not perfecting some skill for personal benefit, but broadening horizons and learning what it means to be an engaged citizen of the world.

Here's another idea for families: Plan holiday rituals around helping others. Anything that helps all of you to think outside yourselves. Invite neighbors over for meals, provide gifts for kids who have none, donate time or money to homeless shelters, or support a foundation that works with the poor. If you go camping, invite the people in the next tent for a drink or to share your BBQ. My personal goal is to do more of this with my family in the coming years. We all donate to organizations through our foundations, and we give away clothing, furniture, and toys to local charities on a regular basis, but there's a lot more we can do. We still have too many possessions, and there are people who need them more than we do. Not all families are in this position of having plenty, but if you are, why not make giving an important part of holiday celebrations? Caring for the well-being of others rather than dwelling on the number of presents you give or get can be a powerful lesson.

All teachers want to support and empower others to make the world better, but most educators are forced into following an outdated curriculum. Instead of making kids memorize facts, we should as a community support a curriculum that will help them understand the "why" of what they're learning and how they might apply this to make the world a better place. I realized early on that it was important to talk to students directly about this, to put all of their high school classes in context. Palo Alto High School does this, and I am very proud to be part of that school; I also know hundreds of other schools are doing the same thing. We need to support all schools, all teachers in their efforts to provide a curriculum that explains "why" and gives students an opportunity to do a real-world project. The point is to serve others. I say that as often as possible. And I'm a living example. I have enough money to retire, but I'm still teaching and lecturing. Why? Because relationships and helping others are what matters to me, and they're what should matter to all of us. Not being number one, not getting rich, but making a difference. I'm not saying kids shouldn't have a goal of being comfortable in life. Of course that's important, but beyond a certain level, the real rewards come from service, from relationships, from knowing that you did something to improve another person's life.

Years ago I started giving what I called the "Power of One" speech, because so many of my students seemed defeated before they even started. They assumed that one person couldn't make a difference, so why even try? I'd tell them the exact opposite, that anyone can make a difference. One of the most powerful examples I could offer was the story of Varian Fry.

In the 1990s, the Holocaust survivor Walter Meyerhof, a professor of physics at Stanford, asked me to help him promote a book and create a movie to share Fry's incredible story. As World War II began, Fry, a young Harvard philosophy graduate, heard that hundreds of Jews were hiding in southern France and the French government would not issue them exit visas. It seemed like an impossible fight, but Fry traveled to Marseilles in 1940 with a plan to circumvent the Vichy government and forge visas for about a hundred Jews. When that plan succeeded, he kept going. He ended up staying for two years and rescuing between two and four thousand people, among them Walter Meyerhof and his famous father, Otto Meyerhof, who had won the Nobel Prize in Physiology and Medicine in 1922. Others rescued by Fry include Hannah Arendt, Marc Chagall, André Breton, and Marcel Duchamp. Here was a man completely committed to his cause. One day he was a student; the next, he was a one-man savior. What he achieved was nothing less than miraculous, and more students needed to know his story.

I helped create a study guide and traveled with Walter around the country, speaking at conferences about Fry and *Assignment: Rescue*, the book he published in 1968. We helped produce a film of the same title, which was narrated by Meryl Streep. I was the head of education for the Varian Fry Foundation for ten years and oversaw the distribution of the film to more than fifty thousand students. I can't tell you how much this incredible story influenced kids at Palo Alto High and across the country. Every year my students took this message very seriously. They came away with the conviction that they don't have to wait around for someone to give them permission. They can take action now.

Every child needs a passion for service, just as Varian Fry had. Families and schools can do a much better job of supporting kids in finding something they believe in, something to fight for. My colleague Marc Prensky wrote the book *Education to Better Their World*, in which he argues for allowing students to identify "problems that the kids themselves perceive in their own world, both locally and globally. School then becomes about finding and implementing solutions to those real-world problems in ways that fully apply the strengths and passions of each kid." It's so important to bring the world's problems into the classroom and into the home. Prensky continues, "The short-term positive result of this is a better world immediately. But the long-term result is far more powerful:

We produce a population of adult citizens who have been empowered, by their education, to actually create solutions to real-world problems." This is where education should be headed. Kids are so capable. Why not let them tackle the biggest, most complex problems?

Kiran Sethi, founder and director of the Riverside School in Ahmedabad, India, is now developing the largest gathering of children in the world at the Vatican in November 2019. Hundreds of middle school kids from more than one hundred countries will be hosted by the pope to work toward solutions for the UN's 17 Sustainable Development Goals for the World:

- No Poverty
- Zero Hunger
- Good Health and Well-Being
- Quality Education
- Gender Equality
- Clean Water and Sanitation
- Affordable and Clean Energy
- Decent Work and Economic Growth
- Industry, Innovation, and Infrastructure
- Reduced Inequality
- Sustainable Cities and Communities
- Responsible Consumption and Production
- Climate Action
- Life Below Water
- Life on Land
- Peace and Justice Strong Institutions
- Partnerships to Achieve the Goals

The objective is to realize these goals by 2030, and Sethi thinks kids are an important part of the solution. I agree. These issues should be part of every curriculum, every dinner table discussion. How are middle-schoolers going to solve worldwide poverty and hunger? I have no idea, but I can't wait to find out.

As your kids enter the professional world, help them see their work as connected to the greater good in some way, not just to profit margins, not just to their own pocketbook. Remind them that some of the best business ideas come from the wish to solve the world's problems. As Peter Diamandis of the X Prize and Singularity University says, "The world's biggest problems are the world's biggest business opportunities . . . You want to be a billionaire? Find a billion-person problem that you can make a dent in." Fantastic advice.

Having the right professional models makes a huge difference. Marc Benioff, the founder, chairperson, and CEO of Salesforce, is another progressive leader when it comes to how businesses can be a force for the greater good. He's famous for his "1-1-1" model of philanthropy, which requires that companies donate 1 percent of equity, 1 percent of product, and 1 percent of employee hours to the surrounding community. Benioff has talked about a broader shift in business toward a sense of service: "When I went to USC, it was all about maximizing value for shareholders. But we're moving into a world of stakeholders. It's not just about shareholders. Your employees are stakeholders — so are your customers, your partners, the communities that you're in, the homeless that are nearby, your public schools. A company like ours can't be successful in an unsuccessful economy or in an unsuccessful environment or where the school system doesn't work. We have to take responsibility for all of those things." He firmly believes that his company has a responsibility to the community and is capable of contributing in important ways. "Salesforce is the biggest tech company in San Francisco," he says. "We can unleash a power onto this city. All of these people can go into the public schools and volunteer, and they can work and make the city better. They can improve the state of the city, improve the state of the world. All I have to do is give them permission to do that." We want our kids to be leaders like Benioff, leaders who have a vision for how their companies move the culture forward and make all our lives better. You might think this idea is out of step with the corporate mind-set, but I see more and more CEOs moving in this direction, and hope that all kids will someday be part of this effort.

SERVICE IN ACTION

When kids have an awareness of the world around them and an interest in being of service, anything is possible. They find and champion their own causes. I've seen it thousands of times, and it's always incredible. The great advantage of teaching journalism for teens is that it gives them a voice and an audience, and they feel empowered to participate in a democracy and in the world. I tell them that news is a sophisticated warning, a way of informing people so they can have better lives. My students aren't just consumers: in my classroom they become participants with a duty to serve. They carry the burden of finding the truth and protecting the underdog, and I've found over the decades that they take the responsibility seriously.

Take Claire Liu, a recent student of mine who says she was "given the space and the agency to question the structures and norms so deeply ingrained in [her] surrounding environment, to look closer at things like class divides and racial tensions on [her] high school campus, to challenge ideas like dress code, to explore income inequality and the Bay Area housing crisis." After volunteering at a homeless center across from Palo Alto High School, Liu became interested in underserved communities. She had discovered an "interesting paradox between the local community and Silicon Valley. It was a wake-up call to the problems that existed in a community that always seemed comfortable and perfect."

In a SpotLight feature article for our newspaper, Liu wrote about the Buena Vista Mobile Home Park and how long-term residents, many of them minorities and working-class poor, were being relocated so the land could be used to develop upscale apartments for young tech workers. She interviewed many residents of Buena Vista to capture their stories, bringing along a friend who spoke Spanish and could serve as her interpreter. These people told her how they'd have to move far away from their current jobs because they couldn't afford to live anywhere in the vicinity. Children would have to leave their schools and friends. One resident contemplated going back to living in his truck. Liu also interviewed a local activist who spoke of the many problems with affordable housing in Silicon Valley. Liu cared deeply about this cause and kept searching for answers, for anything she could do to help. Her article ends with a question about the paradox of Silicon Valley. There's so much innovation and tolerance in our community, but none of it's being used to find solutions for people who struggle the most. Liu is now majoring in persuasive technology and political influence (a major that she designed herself) at Cornell University, where she continues to investigate, question, and search for justice. I can't wait to see what she contributes to the world.

Ben Hewlett, another of my former students, made headlines in

1996 for a groundbreaking discovery about our school board. It all started when Ben needed a story idea for the paper. I had picked up my mail from the office and was walking down the hall when Ben asked, "Woj, what should I do for a story for this edition?" I handed him the minutes from a recent board meeting and suggested they might contain something.

The next day Ben reported that they'd had a closed meeting for several hours before opening it at ten thirty p.m. and taking all of three minutes to pass several resolutions giving raises to the administrative staff. "Isn't that strange?" he said to me. "How could they pass three important resolutions in a few minutes if they hadn't been discussing them in private earlier?"

I agreed that it was strange. The associate superintendent had been promoted to deputy superintendent and given a nine-thousand-dollar raise during a year when the budget was so tight that the principals were teaching classes. "Deputy superintendent" was a new position that no one in the public had heard about. All very suspicious.

Ben was shy, and he wasn't sure he should "pry into the spending habits of the most powerful adults in the district." But I thought he should, that he must tell that story. As Ben remembers, "Without any hesitation, Woj said yes, it was a good idea — they were public servants, and if they had done something wrong, they needed to be held accountable."

This was exactly the kind of injustice I've dedicated my life to exposing, and I knew this would be a transformative experience for everyone on the school paper. I guess you could say I was pretty excited. James Franco was my student that same year, and he remembers my excitement vividly: "You should have seen the joyful/ mischievous flash in Woj's eyes as she pushed Ben and the student staff to get the story out . . . Ben Hewlett's story was not something that would be read by a teacher and then locked in a drawer; it was a story that engaged with the outside world."

It was wonderful to see Ben come out of his shell. "I had the luxury of soaking in every drop of excitement, apprehension, and righteous indignation that flowed from exposing what I came to see as violations of the public trust," he says. "I conducted interviews, and I reviewed and photocopied documents and slogged through late-night editing sessions with other students. And through it all, Woj was there, never so far away that I couldn't ask her for help, but never so close that I felt compelled to do so." It wasn't all easy. Ben and his colleagues were attending the board meetings, and at one point a board member said, "Why are you going to a boring meeting? Shouldn't you be doing your homework or hanging out with friends?" The insult only emboldened Ben.

Along with his fellow students, Ben discovered that all the administrators had credit cards that were not properly managed. In fact, some administrators had charges to Macy's and Lord & Taylor — for educational expenses? Not likely. The students investigated further and composed a dynamite article about overspending and administrative incompetence at the district level. The article came out in late May 1996, and there was an uproar. Everyone — students, parents, teachers — was watching the school board very closely. In June, the superintendent resigned. In August, the business manager resigned. The nine-thousand-dollar raise was reversed, and the administrative credit cards were canceled and never reestablished.

"It's a good feeling to have an impact on the community that you're in," says Hewlett. "I'm a very private person, so I did not welcome the personal attention, but it was nice to have the work recognized, and to have [the *Campanile*] recognized, too." As the teacher, I was very proud of Ben Hewlett, and proud of all the students who worked with him and did the research. They made an important contribution and showed us all that teenagers are much more capable than we think, that they can expose injustice and fight for causes that impact everyone. From then on, the community read the *Campanile* with renewed respect.

Students like Claire and Ben go out into the world and make their mark. But they never stop being someone's child. Don't forget that you're a model until the end of your life. How you live and what you do matters, even during retirement. Here's my problem with retirement: Most of us are retiring from a meaningful life, moving away from purpose, away from our communities. For Americans, retirement is usually a time to do whatever you want. You can get up late, eat whenever you like (and more than you should), and sit on the front porch for hours. Many people do exactly that. They travel a bit, watch a lot of TV. In time, this becomes boring and unfulfilling, and retired people often become isolated and depressed. No surprise there.

My suggestion is not to retire, ever. Instead, how about a mini-retirement rewiring of yourself as a volunteer or mentor? Focus on giving back and being involved. You always need some kind of purpose and some way to make a contribution, and this is such an important lesson for your adult children. For senior citizens in the United Kingdom, one such purpose came in the form of chickens.

That's right, chickens. A project called HenPower found that caring for chickens — a simple act — resulted in the elderly feeling less depressed and lonely and experiencing an increased sense of overall well-being. It makes sense to me, because that's what we all need: personal control, a sense of purpose, something to care for. Isn't this what we want to teach our grown children, who in many cases have children of their own?

Parenting is never just about children: it's about the adults they become. The citizens they become. The changes they fight for and the ideas they contribute. That's why we have to start instilling the TRICK values early on, and relearn them ourselves throughout our lives, as often as necessary. These simple values pave the way to success, producing radical results. Young children need someone to believe in them, and they need respect for who they are. Without that, they can't develop the independence that will be vital to their success as adults in a changing, unpredictable world. Throughout their education, all students need the same values. As it is, most of the schools that treat children with respect are private schools. Now the child is no longer in a prison — she's in a learning environment. But the other kids? They're out of luck. We shouldn't have to pay for respect. We can do better. Students need to master TRICK at home, and their teachers need to employ it at school. We *all* need to employ it in the workplace. I'm not saying that all schools must adopt TRICK — I'm saying all schools should have TRICK-like principles. We still need to have a typical curriculum to teach the basics, but within it, kids need some opportunity to feel respected and empowered, to work on projects that matter to them, to learn about the problems in their communities and the world. When they're given just a taste of this, they stop battling and fighting. They grow confident, and they commit themselves to important projects.

I can see business changing and embracing these values, and I know more will follow suit. Google was one of the first companies to treat employees like real people who needed to be cared for. Customers expect to be treated better by businesses now. Think about Amazon's return policy — so easy, lots of respect for the customer. Zappos gained market share in the same way: building trust with their customers and delivering on their promises. I hope all companies will take note. This is the future.

We face so many problems today — problems that require radical solutions — and more await us. We must stop thinking that what affects another country won't affect us. That's a huge mistake. We can't dismiss an inhumane policy or far-off war as a weather pattern that won't drift our way. We are all interconnected, and the biggest challenges we face will deeply affect us all. Climate change is the most urgent. Look at all the droughts and fires. More every year. One of the many pressures on Syria over a decade ago was a major drought that forced millions of people to leave their homes in search of food and water. And though Syria may seem far away, what happens in that country also happens to us. What about refugees, disease, and air and water pollution? We can't have millions of stateless people wandering the globe; it makes all our lives miserable.

We can't escape these problems, and we can't solve them on our own. We need to plan intelligently together, to think about ways that we as a planet can work toward collaborative solutions. We have to be unified. This is a plea for us to use TRICK in all our interactions — *all our interactions.* If our politicians won't embrace these values, our communities have to organize and make our voices heard; we have to model the use of these values ourselves. We want to move forward, not backward. We have to resist and fight for what is right, not resort to violence.

Because in the end, this is the meaning of our full lives: improving ourselves, each other, our communities, the planet. Parenting may start small, but it has profound implications. We all share the future, and the way we treat our children is the way they'll treat the world.

Conclusion

IT WAS A WINTER afternoon in New York when I met Stacey Bendet Eisner, a prominent fashion designer and the founder of Alice + Olivia clothing stores. We planned to talk about her life and work, and what it's like to train millennial employees. I'm always curious about how younger workers are faring, how their parenting and education prepares them — or doesn't — for managing adult life.

Stacey walked into the restaurant looking glamorous in her teal overcoat. With her was her seven-year-old daughter, Scarlet, who was wearing some very fashionable kids' clothes. *Well,* I thought to myself, *this is going to be a different kind of meeting.* I figured we would have to pay lots of attention to Scarlet.

We all sat down, and Scarlet whipped out her drawing pad and pen and proceeded to draw with a smile on her face. I was immediately impressed. Stacey started talking about the new generation of employees, and how many of them lack grit and empowerment. "It's tough to find employees with creative ideas," she said. "Their biggest fear is making a mistake. And it's hard to be creative if you're afraid." We both agreed that it almost always comes down to parenting — my favorite topic. We talked about trusting kids and giving them more independence and responsibility, and at least some control over their lives — how important those skills are to succeeding in school and in life. I told her about the time I let my grandkids do their own shopping at Target and how upset my daughter had been. Stacey loved the idea, but admitted that it seemed harder and harder to give kids even small freedoms. Our afternoon meeting lasted about an hour and a half, and during that time, little Scarlet said not a word. By the end she had a portfolio of beautiful drawings. There were colorful maze designs as well as pictures of what looked like ice cream cones. I was amazed at her ability to concentrate and told her so.

Recently, I heard from Stacey again. She told me how much she appreciated my advice, but more important, how much Scarlet loved my advice. I didn't think Scarlet was paying attention, but apparently she was. Turns out she heard every word I said. *Every word.* Now whenever she and her two sisters want to do something on their own, they say, "Esther would say it's okay." Even in the middle of New York City, they've been crossing the street on their own to buy Italian ices at a nearby restaurant. They've gained a lot of independence just over the course of a few months, and Stacey has watched them become more empowered, more confident, more capable.

This family is a great example of how minor changes can produce major results. I'm happy our conversation had such an impact, and honestly, I'm not surprised. I've never met a kid who disliked what I've said, who didn't want more respect and freedom, who didn't immediately take to my method. That's because it's natural: it works *with* kids, not *against* them. All children want to be recognized and respected. They want to help other people and have an impact. They're innately optimistic and idealistic — the most wonderful qualities in children. So why not nurture the best in them? Why not encourage them to become empowered and compassionate? It will improve their lives as children and as adults, as well as the lives of everyone around them. Any step toward the TRICK values is a step in the right direction. And you can start at any time. It's never too late to say to your child, "I believe in you." It's never too late to step back and let the world teach its own lessons.

I know this because I've lived it, and I've seen it work every time. As I write this conclusion, another school year is starting. This is the thirty-sixth year that I've watched a new group of sophomores and juniors enter my journalism classes. Like so many high-schoolers, they're worried about whether they can handle the class, what grades they're going to get, and if they'll make friends. They've heard about the media arts program and all its offerings, and they've been told that the teachers in the program are different — there are now six of us — but the students still don't know what to expect. Until the first day, when they see that the Advanced Journalism class is being taught by their peers. That catches them by surprise.

My fellow teachers and I give a lot of speeches throughout the year, but the first time we address the students, we tell them that this class is unique, that the purpose of our time together is to empower them and give them the opportunity to learn the most important skills for life: TRICK. These are just words in the beginning, and kids have heard a lot of words by the time they are in high school. The difference is that they actually see this happening and realize they are going to be in charge. Just like seven-year-old Scarlet, they are thrilled to be empowered, thrilled to have control and the ability to choose their own projects.

Over the next two years, my fellow teachers and I watch as they transform from timid sophomores to young adults with voices and agency. After Beginning Journalism, they get to pick which publication they want to write for. There are now ten publications and even more coming. My colleague Paul Kandell started a new Entrepreneurial Journalism class in the fall of 2018, in which kids can come up with their own ideas for publications, and just as with a startup incubator, they can apply for funding. No matter the publication they choose, they will write articles that influence our community. The paper, the *Campanile,* has a tradition of being an important voice in Palo Alto, and one of the greatest lessons for students is how to make their voices heard. That is also true for the other student publications at Paly: *Verde, C Magazine, Voice, InFocus, Agora,* and *Proof.* They will become writers and thinkers who impact their world.

Throughout this process, they form a community that lasts after they graduate from high school, a community they can rely on for support. As one of my former editors said, "It's like a big family." We always have a party during the school year's final production week. It's a send-off for the seniors and a celebration of the great work everyone has done together. We wish them the best and tell them to keep in touch. Most of them do.

My program works at Palo Alto High School, and it can work in all schools and all homes worldwide. Consider a school called Centro de Capacitación Integral (CCAI) in Monterrey, Mexico, which is supported by the Vicente Ferrara Foundation and directed by Marco Ferrara (Vicente's great-grandson). I first met Marco five years ago when I was giving a talk in Puebla, Mexico, at the Cuidad de las Ideas Festival. He loved what I said about empowering students and asked me to be a mentor and advisor to the school. I happily agreed.

The school is built on a former dump site called San Bernabe, and the students are adults who somehow missed out on their education and have no job skills. The focus is on real-world learning based on TRICK and the moonshot philosophy described in my first book. More than half a million people are living in extreme poverty just in the Monterrey area, and the goal is to help these people out of poverty and subsequently improve the country. In the eleven years since the program first started, they have educated fourteen thousand people and will educate over ten thousand more in 2019. Each one of the students is promised a job after the program, which can take from six months to three years. It isn't just a job, though; it's a lifestyle. They focus on the whole person: self-esteem, nutrition, ethics, finance, sports, and more. They understand that self-respect, belief in oneself, and kindness are the most important life skills. Their motto is *Give a man a fish and you feed him for a day. Teach a man to fish and you feed him for a lifetime*. CCAI is raising successful people of all ages and striving to make a difference despite the odds. The world needs more goals like this.

And then there's my former student Kristin Ostby de Barillas, president and CEO of Boys Hope Girls Hope in Guatemala. Kristin works with kids who have some of the worst experiences imaginable. But they, too, can succeed if given a supportive environment that emphasizes TRICK. As Kristin says, "Young people growing up in poverty gain grit and resilience by force. If they can find a community of people who care about them, who help them to become lifelong learners and develop key life skills, they become the motivated, persistent, creative, team-oriented leaders our society needs today. They have the character that young people growing up with privilege need to develop." The organization has educational and residential programs in Guatemala City, and is making a difference one child at a time.

Today in the United States there are more than 4,300 Boys & Girls Clubs serving kids in poverty. Even here in Palo Alto, we have families living in RVs on El Camino Real, unable to afford housing anywhere in the area. In every city in America, rich or poor, there are opportunities to serve others. Legendary baseball player Alex Rodriguez was helped by the Boys & Girls Clubs, and now he is giving back to the Boys & Girls Club of Miami. We all can find a way to be of service. We all need to support the kids in our communities, in schools, in organizations like the Boys & Girls Clubs, in programs like CCAI in Monterrey, Mexico, and in our lives. TRICK works for all ages, all stages of life. Everyone needs to be trusted and given respect for who they are. Everyone needs to be given freedom and taught how to work with others. Everyone needs to be shown kindness so they can reflect it back to the world.

Because that is the real meaning of raising successful people: shaping the next generation, teaching the skills we all need to make life better for everyone. And that is what Steve Jobs wanted for his oldest daughter, Lisa, when he put her in my program in the early 1990s (he even showed up to interview me in advance — glad I passed!). As he famously said, "The people who are crazy enough to think that they can change the world are the ones who do." Perhaps he saw me as "crazy enough," and by the way, so do my own kids. Well, I feel "crazy enough," but I need many more crazies to join me in using TRICK regularly to give our children the power to change the world. TRICK only seems "crazy" to a system that is truly flawed and destroys the creativity, ambition, and dreams of students. Parents always want what is best for their children but so often what is seen as "loving" or "supportive" parenting is actually stifling the child's innate capacity to learn and grow. We are the crazy ones who will change the world by truly trusting and respecting our children enough for them to develop independence, to collaborate, and to be kind. This is what the future needs from them. This is what the future needs from us.

This book is part of a movement to change the culture of education and to help support the first educators: parents. Parents and teachers are always asking how they can help young people succeed. Well, here is the answer: rediscovering and teaching the core values in all of us and, by the way, in all religions — TRICK *with love*. That has been the core of every religion — including Judaism, Christianity, Islam — throughout history. Let's remember that. I hope you will share this book with other parents, educators, grandparents, therapists, coaches, caregivers — anyone who is responsible for the minds and hearts of young people.

Success begins with our kids and us. Let's all believe we are "crazy enough" to change our world together, and we will.

Acknowledgments

This book came about by accident. I wasn't thinking about writing a book until I had so many people asking me how I raised my daughters. They wanted to know the techniques and tricks I used. I considered it, but that was all I did — until one day when I met my amazing literary agent, Doug Abrams, founder of Idea Architects, at a book reading. It was through his vision and guidance that the book became a reality. I have numerous people to thank and acknowledge, people who helped me in many ways along this path. The first is Doug Abrams for helping me bring this book to you today. I couldn't have done it without his wisdom and guidance. Alongside Doug is my editorial assistant, Amy Schleunes, who was there for me day and night to challenge my ideas, help me clarify my thoughts, and make sure my writing actually made sense! Also, I would like to thank writer Katherine Vaz, who was a third pair of learned eyes, giving me invaluable suggestions and guidance that made a huge difference. Bruce Nichols, my editor, understood the book's vision from day one and has been a great collaborator all along.

On a more personal level, I would like to thank my husband, Stan, who tolerated and supported me when I was holed up for days, even weeks and months, on a bright red beanbag chair with a computer on my lap, writing this book. While he did wonder aloud, "What happened to my wife?" he did the shopping, made me dinner, and accepted my new reclusive lifestyle with grace. The same thank-you and appreciation go to my daughters, Susan, Janet, and Anne, my son-in-law, Dennis, and my nine grandchildren, who complained about my absence from family events ("Where is Nana?") but supported me when I explained what I was doing. "It is taking you such a long time, Nana," they lamented. Time moves more slowly when you are a kid. My children, being somewhat less tolerant, consistently reminded me of how many family activities I was missing, but nevertheless, they encouraged and supported me when they realized it was really going to happen.

This book would not have been possible without the support of hundreds of former *Campanile* students who sent in stories and memories of being in my class dating back to 1984, when I first started. I couldn't include most of them because of word constraints by my publisher, but I so appreciate getting all of those stories. I would particularly like to thank the editors in chief of the *Campanile*, who over the years have helped me shape the program and given me so many ideas about what could be better. It was their ideas that helped make the program what it is today. Some of the students are included here in alphabetical order, and I am sorry if I left out your name. Every student is important to me and you all know who you are: Karina Alexanyan, Lisa Brennan-Jobs, Aaron Cohen, Ben Crosson, Gady Epstein, James Franco, Ben Hewlett, Maya Kandell, Forest Key, Chris Lewis, Jennifer Linden, Claire Liu, Aidan Maese-Czeropski, Bilal Mahmood, Andrew Miller, Kristin Ostby, Lauren Ruth, Tomer Schwartz, Jonah Steinhart, Sammy Vasquez, Michael Wang, Oliver Weisberg, Andrew Wong, Brian Wong, and Kaija Xiao.

A large part of this book is devoted to the journalism program that I founded and the pedagogy that I developed at Palo Alto High and expanded through the years starting in 1998. Much of my success with the expansion of the journalism program is the result of a concerted devotion by my colleague, Paul Kandell, without whom I never could have built the program we have today. He took over *Verde*, a newsmagazine, in 2000, and *Voice*, an online publication, in 2002 and supported my efforts as I continued to add publications to the program to accommodate the interests of hundreds of students. He has provided me with interesting ideas and great conversations about using journalism as a way to empower students in the twenty-first century. The program now encompasses eight magazines as well as television, radio, and video production, and I am indebted to everyone who has contributed to the *Campanile* (www. thecampanile.org), *Verde* (https://verdemagazine.com), *C* Magazine (https://issuu.com/c_magazine), *Viking* (https://vikingsportsmag. com), *In Focus* (https://www.infocusnews.tv), *Voice* (https://paly voice.com), *Proof* (https://issuu.com/proofpaly), *Madrono* (https:// palymadrono.com), KPLY Radio (https://www.palyradio.com), *Agora* (https://issuu.com/palyagora), *Veritas Science*, and *Veritas Travel* (no websites for the last two — yet!). There are five other media teachers, all of whom have been incredibly supportive: Rod Satterthwaite, Brian Wilson, Paul Hoeprich, Brett Griffith, and Margo Wixsom. I am blessed to have such an exceptional group of colleagues.

I would also like to thank all those who took the time to be interviewed, some of whom talked with me informally on a regular basis. There are so many people who have helped me shape the ideas in this book. I tried to include all of them but I may have missed some. Forgive me if I inadvertently left you out:

Karina Alexanyan, MediaX Stanford

Stacey Bendet Eisner, CEO of Alice + Olivia

Marc Benioff, CEO of Salesforce

Gary Bolles, eParachute.com

Danah Boyd, President of Data & Society

Andrea Ceccherini,
    President of L'Osservatorio Permanente Giovani

Freedom Cheteni, President of InventXR LLC.

Ulrik Christensen, CEO of Area9

Shelby Coffey, Vice Chair of Newseum

Jessica Colvin, Director at TUHSD Wellness

Bill Damon, Professor of Education, Stanford University

Linda Darling-Hammond, Professor Emeritus of Education,
    Stanford University

Carol Dweck, Professor of Psychology, Stanford University

Charles Fadel, Professor of Education, Harvard University

Marco Ferrara, President of Vicente Ferrara Foundation

Cristin Frodella, Head of Marketing, Google Education

Ellen Galinsky, Bezos Family Foundation

Khurram Jamil, President of Strategic Initiatives, Area9

Heidi Kleinmaus, Partner, Charrette, LLC

Julie Lythcott-Haims, Author, Former Dean of Admissions,
    Stanford University

Ed Madison, Professor of Communications,
    University of Oregon

Barbara McCormack, Vice President of Education at Newseum

Dr. Max McGee, former superintendent of Palo Alto Unified Schools

Milbrey McLaughlin, Professor Emeritus of Education, Stanford University

Maye Musk, Mother of Elon Musk, Supermodel, Nutritionist

Dr. Janesta Noland, Pediatrician

David Nordfors, Co-Founder of i4j Summit

Esther Perel, Author, Psychotherapist

Marc Prensky, President of Global Future Education Foundation

Todd Rose, Professor of Education, Harvard University

Dan Russell, Google Search Quality & User Happiness

Sheryl Sandberg, COO of Facebook

Bror Saxberg, Vice President of Learning Science, Chan Zuckerberg Initiative

Michael Shearn, Compound Money, LP

Jamie Simon, Executive Director of Camp Tawonga

Peter Stein, CEO of Reunion

Jim Stigler, Professor of Psychology, UCLA

Linda Stone, Writer, Speaker, Consultant

Ken Taylor, Professor of Philosophy, Stanford University

Jay Thorwaldson, Former Editor of *Palo Alto Weekly*

Tony Wagner, Professor of Education, Harvard University

Ann Webb, Compound Money, LP

Veronica Webb, Supermodel, Speaker, Actress

Lina Williamson, Director of Entrepreneurship & Innovation, Brigham and Women's Hospital

Eddy Zhong, Co-Founder and CEO at Leangap

I want to give special acknowledgment to former principal of Palo Alto High Kim Diorio and my former student Dr. Karina Alexanyan, with whom I talked at length about my ideas for innovation in education and about student engagement and success. They are involved my new nonprofit GlobalMoonshots.org, the foundation I have set up to promote TRICK worldwide.

It has been an intense experience writing this book over the past year and a half. I am grateful to all those who supported me in my passion to spread TRICK to everyone around the world, especially to parents, families, and teachers.

Notes

1 "Mental Health Information: Statistics: Any Anxiety Disorder," National Institute of Mental Health website, last updated November 2017 (https://www.nimh.nih.gov/health/statistics/prevalence/any-anxiety-disorder-among-children.shtml, accessed October 22, 2018); "Major Depression," National Institute of Mental Health website, last updated November 2017 (https://www.nimh.nih.gov/health/statistics/major-depression.shtml, accessed October 22, 2018); Claudia S. Lopes et al., "ERICA: Prevalence of Common Mental Disorders in Brazilian Adolescents," *Revista de Saúde Pública* 50, no. 1 (2016): 14s (https://www.ncbi.nlm.nih.gov/pmc/articles/PMC4767030, accessed October 22, 2018); Sibnath Deb et al., "Academic Stress, Parental Pressure, Anxiety and Mental Health Among Indian High School Students," *International Journal of Psychology and Behavioral Science* 5, no. 1 (2015): 26–34 (http://article.sapub.org/10.5923.j.ijpbs.20150501.04.html, accessed October 22, 2018); "Mental Disorders Among Children and Adolescents in Norway," Norwegian Institute of Public Health website, last updated October 14, 2016 (https://www.fhi.no/en/op/hin/groups/mental-health-children-adolescents, accessed October 22, 2018).

2 L. Alan Sroufe et al., "Conceptualizing the Role of Early Experience: Lessons from the Minnesota Longitudinal Study," *Developmental Review* 30, no. 1 (2010): 36–51 (https://www.ncbi.nlm.nih.gov/pmc/articles/PMC2857405, accessed October 22, 2018).

3 J. A. Simpson et al., "Attachment and the Experience and Expression of Emotions in Romantic Relationships: A Developmental Perspective," *Journal of Personality and Social Psychology* 92, no. 2 (2007): 355–67

(https://www.ncbi.nlm.nih.gov/pubmed/17279854, accessed October 22, 2018).

4   Isaac Chotiner, "Is the World Actually Getting . . . Better?" *Slate,* February 20, 2018 (https://slate.com/news-and-politics/2018/02/steven-pinker-argues-the-world-is-a-safer-healthier-place-in-his-new-book-enlightenment-now.html, accessed October 22, 2018).

5   Ian M. Paul et al., "Mother-Infant Room-Sharing and Sleep Outcomes in the INSIGHT Study," *Pediatrics* 140, no. 1 (2017): e20170122 (http://pediatrics.aappublications.org/content/early/2017/06/01/peds.2017-0122, accessed October 22, 2018).

6   Jean M. Twenge et al., "Increases in Depressive Symptoms, Suicide-Related Outcomes, and Suicide Rates Among U.S. Adolescents After 2010 and Links to Increased New Media Screen Time," *Clinical Psychological Science* 6, no. 1 (2017): 3–17 (http://journals.sagepub.com/doi/abs/10.1177/2167702617723376?journalCode=cpxa, accessed October 22, 2018).

7   Ryan J. Dwyer et al., "Smartphone Use Undermines Enjoyment of Face-to-Face Social Interactions," *Journal of Experimental Social Psychology* 78 (2018): 233–39 (https://www.sciencedirect.com/science/article/pii/S0022103117301737#!, accessed October 22, 2018).

8   Lingxin Hao and Han Soo Woo, "Distinct Trajectories in the Transition to Adulthood: Are Children of Immigrants Advantaged?" *Child Development* 83, no. 5 (2012): 1623–39 (https://www.ncbi.nlm.nih.gov/pmc/articles/PMC4479264, accessed October 22, 2018).

9   Walter Mischel et al., "Delay of Gratification in Children," *Science* 244, no. 4907 (1989): 933–38 (https://www.ncbi.nlm.nih.gov/pubmed/2658056, accessed October 22, 2018); Dr. Tanya R. Schlam et al., "Preschoolers' Delay of Gratification Predicts Their Body Mass 30 Years Later," *Journal of Pediatrics* 162, no. 1 (2013): 90–93 (https://www.ncbi.nlm.nih.gov/pmc/articles/PMC3504645, accessed October 22, 2018); Ozlem Ayduk et al., "Regulating the Interpersonal Self: Strategic Self-Regulation for Coping with Rejection Sensitivity," *Journal of Personality and Social Psychology* 79, no. 5 (2000): 776–92 (http://psycnet.apa.org/doiLanding?doi=10.1037%2F0022-3514.79.5.776, accessed October 22, 2018).

10 Diana Baumrind, "Current Patterns of Parental Authority," *Developmental Psychology* 4, no. 1 (1971): 1–103 (http://psycnet.apa.org/doiLanding?-doi=10.1037%2Fh0030372, accessed October 22, 2018).

11 Diana Baumrind, "The Influence of Parenting Style on Adolescent Competence and Substance Use," *Journal of Early Adolescence* 11, no. 1 (1991): 56–95 (http://journals.sagepub.com/doi/abs/10.1177/0272431691111004, accessed October 22, 2018).

12 Robert Hepach et al., "The Fulfillment of Others' Needs Elevates Children's Body Posture," *Developmental Psychology* 53, no. 1 (2017): 100–113 (http://psycnet.apa.org/record/2016-61509-005, accessed October 22, 2018).

13 Michael Tomasello and Katharina Hamann, "Collaboration in Young Children," *Quarterly Journal of Experimental Psychology* 65, no. 1 (2011): 1–12 (https://www.ncbi.nlm.nih.gov/pubmed/22171893, accessed October 22, 2018).

14 Marcy Burstein and Golda S. Ginsburg, "The Effect of Parental Modeling of Anxious Behaviors and Cognitions in School-Aged Children: An Experimental Pilot Study," *Behavior Research and Therapy* 48, no. 6 (2010): 506–15 (https://www.ncbi.nlm.nih.gov/pmc/articles/PMC2871979, accessed October 22, 2018).

15 Sarah Myruski et al., "Digital Disruption? Maternal Mobile Device Use Is Related to Infant Social-Emotional Functioning," *Developmental Science* 21, no. 4 (2018): e12610 (https://www.ncbi.nlm.nih.gov/pubmed/28944600, accessed October 22, 2018).

16 "Kids Competing with Mobile Phones for Parents' Attention," AVG Technologies website, last updated June 24, 2015 (https://now.avg.com/digital-diaries-kids-competing-with-mobile-phones-for-parents-attention, accessed October 22, 2018).

17 Brian D. Doss, "The Effect of the Transition to Parenthood on Relationship Quality: An Eight-Year Prospective Study," *Journal of Personality and Social Psychology* 96, no. 3 (2009): 601–19 (https://www.ncbi.nlm.nih.gov/pmc/articles/PMC2702669, accessed October 22, 2018).

18 Jane Anderson, "The Impact of Family Structure on the Health of Children: Effects of Divorce," *Linacre Quarterly* 81, no. 4 (2014): 378–87 (https://www.ncbi.nlm.nih.gov/pmc/articles/PMC4240051, accessed October 22, 2018).

19 Sara H. Konrath et al., "Changes in Dispositional Empathy in American College Students Over Time: A Meta-Analysis," *Personality and Social Psychology Review* 15, no. 2 (2010): 180–98 (http://journals.sagepub.com/doi/abs/10.1177/1088868310377395, accessed October 22, 2018).

20   Charlotte vanOyen Witvliet et al., "Gratitude Predicts Hope and Happiness: A Two-Study Assessment of Traits and States," *Journal of Positive Psychology,* January 15, 2018 (https://www.tandfonline.com/doi/abs/10.1080/17439760.2018.1424924?journalCode=rpos20, accessed October 22, 2018).

21   Jeffrey J. Froh et al., "Counting Blessings in Early Adolescents: An Experimental Study of Gratitude and Subjective Well-Being," *Journal of School Psychology* 46, no. 2 (2008): 213–33 (https://www.ncbi.nlm.nih.gov/pubmed/19083358, accessed October 22, 2018).

22   Hannah J. Thomas et al., "Association of Different Forms of Bullying Victimisation with Adolescents' Psychological Distress and Reduced Emotional Wellbeing," *Australian & New Zealand Journal of Psychiatry* 50, no. 4 (2015): 371–79 (http://journals.sagepub.com/doi/10.1177/0004867415600076, accessed October 22, 2018).

23   Hannah M. C. Schreier et al., "Effect of Volunteering on Risk Factors for Cardiovascular Disease in Adolescents," *JAMA Pediatrics* 167, no. 4 (2013): 327–32 (https://jamanetwork.com/journals/jamapediatrics/fullarticle/1655500, accessed October 22, 2018).

24   Shabbar I. Ranapurwala et al., "Volunteering in Adolescence and Youth Adulthood Crime Involvement: A Longitudinal Analysis From the Add Health Study," *Injury Epidemiology* 3, no. 26 (2016). (https://www.ncbi.nlm.nih.gov/pmc/articles/PMC5116440, accessed October 22, 2018).

25   "Setting School Culture with Social and Emotional Learning Routines," KQED News website, last updated January 16, 2018 (http://ww2.kqed.org/mindshift/2018/01/16/setting-school-culture-with-social-and-emotional-learning-routines, accessed October 22, 2018).

26   Julianne Holt-Lunstad et al., "Social Relationships and Mortality Risk: A Meta-Analytic Review," *PLoS Medicine* 7, no. 7 (2010): e1000316 (http://journals.plos.org/plosmedicine/article?id=10.1371/journal.pmed.1000316, accessed October 22, 2018).

Index

ZUBIN MEHTA

The Score of My Life

Zubin Mehta
with Renate Gräfin Matuschka

Translated from the German by
Anu Pande

With a foreword by
Pandit Ravi Shankar

AMADEUS
PRESS

An Imprint of Hal Leonard Corporation
New York

Amadeus Press
An Imprint of Hal Leonard Corporation
7777 West Bluemound Road
Milwaukee, WI 53213

Trade Book Division Editorial Offices
19 West 21st Street, New York, NY 10010

Originally published in Germany in 2006 by Droemer Verlag; published in India in 2008 by Roli Books

Published in 2009 by Amadeus Press

Photograph credits: Page 8 of photo section (top): Rothschild Photo. Page 12 (top): Isaac Berez. Page 12 (bottom): David Weiss Photography. Page 13 (top): Wilfried Hösl. Page 13 (bottom): David Weiss Photography. Page 14 (bottom): Wilfried Hösl. Page 15: Nancy Mehta. Page 16 (top): G. Luca Moggi / New Press Photo / Archivio Teatro del Maggio Muiscale Fiorentino. Thanks to Teatro del Maggio Musicale Fiorentino, Florence. Page 16 (bottom): Farrokh Chotia. All other photographs are from the collection of Zubin Mehta.

Printed in the United States of America

Book design by Snow Creative Services

Library of Congress Cataloging-in-Publication Data

Mehta, Zubin.
  Zubin Mehta : the score of my life / Zubin Mehta with Renate Gräfin Matuschka ; translated from the German by Anu Pande ; with a foreword by Pandit Ravi Shankar.
    p. cm.
  Includes index.
  ISBN 978-1-57467-174-2 (alk. paper)
  1. Mehta, Zubin. 2. Conductors (Music)--Biography. I. Matuschka, Renate v., 1943- II. Title.

ML422.M24A3 2009
784.2092--dc22
[B]
                                    2008055132

www.amadeuspress.com

CONTENTS

FOREWORD

Chiseled features, dashing smile, handsome, dear Zubin Mehta—one of the greatest conductors of our times. As a fellow Indian, musician, and friend, I have more reason to admire and love him. I first met Zubin in the early sixties when I went to Montreal to perform, where he was the music director of the Montreal Symphony Orchestra, but I came to know him better a year or two later in Los Angeles when he became the director of the Los Angeles Philharmonic. This was after the Monterey Pop Festival period, and I was also living in Los Angeles at that time. Both Zubin and I met often at parties and on different occasions. Along with the classical fans of ours, we also had such wonderful times with the vibrant young and loving hippy crowd!

Later we got together again, when he was the director and conductor of the New York Philharmonic. We decided I should write my Concerto No. 2 for sitar and orchestra to be performed by the Philharmonic and conducted by Zubin. I cherish the memory of those few months in New York.

I was living in New York near Gramercy Park with Sue Jones, and our daughter Geetali (Norah) was only a few months old. On Zubin's suggestion, I used to go in the mornings to Lincoln Center, where Zubin would rehearse the pieces to be performed in the evenings. This, he said, would help me know the musicians and their proficiency with the instruments, which it really did, and it helped me bring different sounds into the musical structure. This was a wonderful brief period in my life, and Zubin and I really had a great time.

Zubin loves spicy food and hot chillies. In fact, he always carries a little metal box with him in his pocket, and this box contains some hot chillies. He asked me to write some "hot chilli parts" in the concerto, which I did— like the first movement in the Indian mode known as Raga Lalit, which has a minor second and seventh, both the fourths, and no fifth note. It also has parts in rhythmic cycles of five-and-a-half and thirteen-and-a-half beats!

Zubin is also a very caring and sensitive person. Recently he heard my daughter Anoushka perform in Switzerland. After the concert, he phoned me immediately to say how well she did. It was a wonderful gesture from him, and I was deeply touched.

Being eighty-eight and still performing (though much less than I used to), I keep track of Zubin's glorious conducting tours all over the world. My love and admiration grows stronger for him, and I feel so much closer to him. May God bless and protect him always.

—*Pandit Ravi Shankar*

AUTHOR'S NOTE

Writing about my own life—taking my own measure, so to speak—is a venture that at first I had to be persuaded to undertake. I hesitated for a long time, because this is a task that requires intensive retrospection, which is certainly not one of my favorite pursuits.

For the last fifty years, I have been practicing what seems to me the most beautiful profession in the world. I am a conductor. I am constantly surrounded by a world of masterpieces and beauty. And yet I always have to look ahead into the future before each musical project and concentrate on the current objective: the next opera production, an upcoming concert, a planned tour, a new soloist, or a composer's new work. In music, even what is supposedly "old" is new, in the sense that music is fleeting even in the moment of its creation. The note just heard leads to the next one, and the development of the whole work can never be captured in an instant. Nevertheless, the hearer should be able to have an impression of the whole work at the end. This is why there is a constant need to rehearse and practice, to discuss, and perhaps also to improve before each performance. For me as a conductor, this implies a very detailed and thorough study of the score so that I can achieve a satisfactory result with the musicians, even if I have several decades of practice behind me and a very thorough knowledge of the work. This is precisely why I find it so difficult to deal with the past and to look back in time, instead of looking forward into the future. And yet my musical career has given me so many remarkable experiences and lucky encounters that I would like to share them with others. Perhaps I might even be able to convey some of my musical knowledge and encourage young musicians to persevere in what they feel called upon to do—namely, to make music and to spend their lives with it.

Much of my maturing as a musician and conductor in my first thirty years I owe to the superb musicians that I encountered as a young conductor in Montreal and Los Angeles and later to my colleagues at the New York Philharmonic, with whom I spent the most wonderful thirteen years. Since I conducted most of the important works in the repertoire with my first two orchestras in Montreal and Los Angeles, I cannot express enough how much I profited from the advice given me by the outstanding artists of these two fine ensembles.

In California my wife Nancy has created an atmosphere of utter serenity for us, spanning more than four decades. It is from this haven that we have traveled the world over, both professionally and on adventurous holidays that Nancy has conjured up, many of them at first with our children. Even though the children have grown up on the other side of the continent, I have taken as keen an interest as I possibly could in their development, and I am very proud today to see what fine human beings they have turned out to be, with adorable grandchildren that I, as a grandfather, enjoy with each encounter.

Although Nancy and I still live in Los Angeles, my work in Israel and Europe takes a lot of my time, but whenever we land in L.A. we are glad to be home—the supreme contradiction being that I still feel equally at home when I land in my Mumbai.

ZUBIN MEHTA

1

MY EARLY YEARS
IN INDIA

I was born in India on April 29, 1936, during politically turbulent times. My parents provided us with so much warmth and security, though, that as a child I hardly noticed the tremendous political upheavals that India was undergoing in the 1930s, nor the work that it faced, work that was to continue for decades. At the time of my birth, British rule in India was already long in dispute, and it continued to be until much later. Mahatma Gandhi led the Indian independence movement as the president of the Indian National Congress in 1924. His philosophy of nonviolent resistance was eventually successful, but in 1936 the country was still in turmoil. In fact, it was to remain so for a long time, even after it achieved independence in August 1947.

My early life was untroubled by all these events, and I grew up protected and happy. My earliest memories center on a tenderly loving and caring mother and a wonderful father. I can't recall exactly when I was first exposed to music. I was a perfectly normal young boy, mischievous and not at all averse to taking part in the usual boyish pranks and fights, as well as the usual childhood pleasures. I got my first scar in the course of a wild scuffle at the age of nine. Later I developed an active interest in cricket, which I played all through my school years.

My father, Mehli Mehta, was born in 1908, the heir to a cotton mill and groomed from quite a young age eventually to take his place in the family business. But he soon developed a tremendous passion for music. Needless

1

to say, music was not nearly so readily available in the 1920s and 1930s as it is today. The only way to hear music of a high level was to attend concerts by great artists on their way to China and Japan. One such artist was Jascha Heifetz, the most important violinist of the twentieth century. Another was the Czech violinist Jan Kubelik, father of the conductor Rafael Kubelik, who often went on extensive concert tours, stopping over in Bombay on his way to Shanghai. These concerts must have made a deep impression on my father. He saw an entire musical cosmos opening up before him, one to which he felt himself more and more strongly drawn. He had an innate sense of belonging in this world, a world that was to come increasingly to determine the direction of his life. So inspired was he by what he heard that he desperately wanted to learn how to play the violin himself. For a young Indian trained as an accountant, this was not easy. My father came from an old-fashioned Parsi family. In those days musical ambitions were certainly much better tolerated among the Parsis than in other Indian communities, but his immense passion for music was definitely unusual even in his circle.

However, my father was determined to fulfill his dream. He got himself a violin and learned to play it—without any instruction, and without a teacher, not counting the occasional suggestion from an immigrant Italian music teacher; he simply taught himself. He was extraordinarily musical, and as determined as he was talented, so that he soon mastered the instrument to the point where he was able to play the Beethoven Violin Concerto.

This was the environment in which I grew up—my father practicing music in the living room and scores lying all around the house. I liked looking at them, even though I could hardly read. My father had something else that was marvelous: a record player on which we could listen to some lovely music.

Of course, this gramophone was a real monstrosity. The records back then had an absurdly short playing time, barely five minutes, so that if one was listening to a symphony or a quartet one had to put on one new disc after another. (Vinyl records, with their hair-thin grooves on which one could record long works, did not exist back then, not to mention the compact disc.) It took four or five of these things to record some symphonies. As a result, to hear a symphony in its entirety one had to constantly run to the record player and very carefully put on one after another of these breakable and easily scratched black discs. This was in the 1940s.

My father's record collection was quite impressive by the standards of his time, which enabled me to listen to the most magnificent music all the time. Since in the beginning I couldn't read at all, I could only tell one piece from another by the records' different-colored labels. From early on I heard symphonies and became familiar with Beethoven and Brahms. I also heard a bit of Mahler. Later I would often miss my favorite sport, cricket, to attend one of my father's string quartet rehearsals.

My father founded the Bombay Symphony Orchestra in 1935 and also the Bombay String Quartet, which rehearsed at our home. In fact, I was enveloped in and surrounded by music. Music was my daily pleasure. The records, the quartet rehearsals, my father playing music—all this meant for me no more and no less than a premature access to paradise. I entered this musical pleasure garden as a very young person, and so far nothing and no one has ever managed to drive me out of it.

I come from a traditional Parsi family. Outside India this requires some explanation. Parsis come from a religious community whose founder, Zarathustra, lived in Persia, in the area north of modern-day Iran, around 1200 B.C. in a region corresponding to present-day eastern Iran. This ancient religion, Zoroastrianism, was the state religion under numerous dynasties until the seventh century A.D. After the Muslim conquest of Persia in the seventh century, faithful followers of Zarathustra's teachings migrated to India around the ninth century and settled in the area north of Bombay (or Mumbai, as it is now known). There they came to be known as Parsis because of their Persian origins. In its basics this monotheistic religion, characterized by the opposition between light and darkness, between truth and lies, resembles aspects of the Jewish Apocalypse. However, whether the Jewish faith was really influenced by the Parsi religion is still highly contested among scholars.

The name Zarathustra comes from two words, *ustra* (camels) and *zarath* (those who are in good health), which refers to the fact that he came from a family of cattle breeders. This historical person has almost no relation to all the myths and legends that much later came into circulation through Kant and Nietzsche.

Zarathustra's guiding principle has been accepted by the Parsis for 2,500 years as the highest maxim. It can be summed up briefly as "Good thoughts, good speech, good actions." Today there are no more than approximately eighty thousand Parsis worldwide, and I am one of them. When I am in India I am a Parsi first and an Indian second, though it is exactly the opposite abroad. One cannot become a Parsi by converting; unfortunately, in fact, one can only inherit the religion through the father. This is one reason the Parsi population is steadily dwindling. There are two utterly contrary trends in the community, liberalism and conservatism, which leads to some conflict. I count myself among the liberals: I believe that a child can be a Parsi even if one of the parents is not, provided both parents basically agree. Conservatives, on the other hand, believe that the faith can be passed on only to children both of whose parents are Parsis. Under these conditions, I am afraid that in a hundred years no more Parsis will exist anywhere in the world.

Many languages and countless dialects are spoken in India. Mine is a dialect of Gujarati, named for the federal state of Gujarat, north of Bombay. Incidentally, Gujarati was also Mahatma Gandhi's mother tongue.

My father, who was very self-critical, knew that he had to improve his violin playing. He also knew that he needed a teacher to educate him further, to mold him anew after the great Russian school of violin playing. So in 1945, in the last phase of World War II, he decided to board the first available ship to the United States in order to seek out such a teacher in New York. My mother, Tehmina, remained in Bombay with me and my brother, Zarin, who is two years younger than I. She raised the two of us all by herself for four years while my father studied in New York. He had a scholarship from a Parsi charity foundation, the J. N. Tata Endowment, but since he was already too old for the renowned Juilliard School he had to take private lessons. But he had the good fortune to come under the tutelage of Ivan Galamian, one of the most important violin teachers of his time. Galamian, an Armenian and a great exponent of the famous Russian Leopold Auer school, was a legendary figure. He had taught the likes of Michael Rabin, Itzhak Perlman, and Pinchas Zukerman, who later reached great heights of fame.

These four years were certainly a difficult time for all of us, but most of all for my mother. It was not easy for her to have her husband in New York and to bring up two young sons all alone. I was nine years old when my father left for America. My mother was not burdened with any serious financial problems, since she came from a rather well-off family. At the same time, however, she could not count upon any financial support from her husband, since he had to manage rather frugally himself. We sublet a room in the house to a tenant, and my mother managed to cope wonderfully with the situation.

In New York my father had the opportunity to further develop his innate musical talent under the strict training of this great teacher. He sent us programs of all the concerts that he attended in New York, along with his comments on the works performed.

In Bombay I attended a school run by Spanish Jesuits. This might seem an odd choice, but the reason behind it was simple: schools run by Jesuits were considered the best in India. Moreover, we were taught in English, something to which my parents attached great importance. Above all, the experiences I had there were formative for my life. St. Mary's High School accepted boys from a tremendous range of backgrounds, particularly in respect of religion. This was both exceptional and at the same time representative of the matter-of-fact way in which religion is dealt with in

India—though this unfortunately does not apply to the ancient conflict between Hindus and Muslims. The approximately forty students in my class belonged to six or seven different religions. Hindus and Muslims, Parsis and Sikhs, Jews and Christians—we all got along perfectly well. Nobody tried to convert us to Catholicism. We studied the gospels as literature, and that was all. I believe that this inculcated in me a keen appreciation of the great diversity among people and taught me early on to respect the differences between us. I learned from the example and experience of my surroundings that people from completely different circumstances could coexist in peace as long as they bore in mind that difference did not automatically imply strangeness, which leads so easily to mistrust.

It seems to me that a facet of my later life, which saw me traveling all over the world and coming into contact with a wide variety of people, had its roots here. At the same time, though, I still consider myself to be Indian. This is why I never gave up my Indian passport. Now as ever I feel a sense of belonging to my homeland—India.

After his return from New York my father paid even more attention to Bombay's musical scene. He gave many concerts, organized performances, and engaged prominent artists. Once again there was music at home. He opened new horizons to me, including score reading. I was thirteen years old and a quick learner, and I soon I knew all the important symphonies really well, many of them simply from piano scores. This proved to be of some advantage later, though I realize now that I missed something crucial: opera.

In any case, I loved orchestral music and even as a very young boy imagined becoming a conductor. In truth, I became a conductor because deep down I wanted to conduct Brahms's four symphonies and Richard Strauss's tone poems. I knew these pieces backward and forward from records and also from orchestral scores. Naturally, the recordings available in those days did not have today's sound quality, but my father's steadily growing record collection at least gave me the opportunity to listen to all the prominent conductors: Arturo Toscanini (of whom there are only a very few recordings), Leopold Stokowski, and Wilhelm Furtwängler. I heard recordings of Jascha Heifetz, along with a large part of his violin repertoire. All of these were for me a musical revelation. For my father, they served as models whereby he improved his understanding of music.

My father was often quite strict with me about musical matters. When I was about fifteen years old, Yehudi Menuhin came to Bombay. Menuhin was a friend of the Indian prime minister, Jawaharlal Nehru, and very pro-India, and he expressed his willingness to play with the Bombay Symphony Orchestra. This orchestra, founded by my father, consisted of a very colorful assortment of musicians, most of whom were definitely not professionals. There were several immigrants among them, some of them quite talented, but by and large the orchestra was not equal to many demands in those days. The Parsis were all dilettantes. A few Christian professional musicians, mostly string players, came from Goa. Woodwind and brass players were provided by members of the Indian navy band, who showed up for concerts in their uniforms. My father tried to prepare the orchestra as well as he could. They were supposed to accompany Menuhin in Brahms's Violin Concerto, and they practiced tirelessly, with my father playing the solo part in the rehearsals while I was instructed to hold the orchestra together—in other words, to conduct. This was my very first experience as a conductor. But no matter how carefully I tried to listen and how well I knew the score, the whole experience was pretty miserable. I was severely reprimanded for forgetting to give the third horn or the oboist his cue. This, then, was the first time that I stood before an orchestra, and the result was not at all encouraging.

Once again my father, the autodidact, got to work. Just as he had taught himself how to play the violin, he now also taught himself how to conduct. This capacity for fully independent learning was a special talent of his. In his four years in New York he probably went to a concert every evening; he saw and heard a lot and also observed the great conductors.

The first time I really conducted in public was when I accompanied my father at a radio recording session in Bombay. He played Bach's Concerto in A Minor and I conducted the orchestra—from memory. I had studied the piece endlessly with my father and had a very specific idea of how it should sound. Whether I actually conducted it correctly is hard to say today, but for me it was a beautiful experience. Besides, playing music with my father was a special experience no matter what.

Some time later Yehudi Menuhin came again to Bombay and played Bach's Double Concerto with my father. Once again the already legendary Menuhin was humble enough to play with Mehli Mehta!

All this might seem to point toward my later musical career, but at the time that was unthinkable. It's true that I was supposed to improve my piano playing—I had already given up the violin when my father left for America—but I have to admit that I never saw myself as an instrumentalist. Besides, I always had to be more or less forced to practice. In short, I was lazy, and to be honest, I sometimes preferred cricket, a game I loved with a passion, to the piano. Cricket is still a passion with me.

Following in my father's footsteps and becoming a musician was out of the question, for my family had decided that I would study medicine. In India it was simply a given that one would accept decisions made by the family. Tradition and family cohesion are deeply important, even decisive for Indians. Hence, my brother was sent to London at the age of sixteen to study accounting, while the medical profession was chosen for me. Traditionally there are only a few professions considered acceptable for the upper middle class in India, but these two were among them. So I began unprotestingly to study medicine, a decision made for me that I accepted completely as a matter of course.

It was already clear after two terms, though, that medicine was not the right choice for me. I was fortunately able to tell my parents this and to express my wish to devote my life to music. In the end my parents agreed. They have always stood by me whenever I have asked them for advice or faced major decisions, either encouraging me or discussing what would be in my best interest. In the end they consented to my becoming a musician, and from then on my whole life took a completely different and very unusual course.

I had begun to study music theory, as my father wished me to do. He had sent me to the same elderly Italian teacher, Oddone Savini, from whom my father had taken classes earlier. Savini lived in Pune, which meant that once a week I had to travel three hours by train in order to pursue my studies.

However, my parents had other plans for my real training, plans that took me far from home to a foreign country on another continent. I was to go to Vienna, where my cousin Dady Mehta was studying piano with Bruno Seidlhofer, a leading authority.

So I set out at the age of eighteen for Austria, which eventually became a second home for me in many respects, one that to this day gives me energy and inspiration, the true musical foundation of my profession.

2

MY STUDENT YEARS
IN VIENNA

I n 1954 the journey from Bombay to Vienna was still a big adventure. It was time consuming and had to be made in several stages. Up till the day I boarded the ship in Bombay that took me to Genoa, I had been a more or less well-protected young man living a sheltered life in his family circle in Bombay. I didn't have to see to the various details of daily life, and I didn't have to worry about my livelihood. All that changed with one stroke.

My parents had chosen Vienna for my musical schooling in part because my cousin was there. He had been living abroad for a long time, first as a piano student in Paris and then in Vienna. My parents probably hoped that Dady, who was somewhat older than I, would take care of me and help me settle into this completely new and unfamiliar environment. In retrospect, it's hard to say who took care of whom. Dady recently retired after decades as a highly reputed professor of piano at the University of Michigan. He has two sons, Bejun and Navi. Bejun is a countertenor who is in great demand worldwide and sings in all the major opera houses. Navi is a successful violinist and conductor in San Diego.

And so I was sent off on this long journey. Everything was new and exciting for me. On the ship I met other young men who were also headed to Europe. We were all very young and utterly inexperienced, but of course we felt very grown-up. Upon arriving in Genoa we fooled around a little. After all, we were on our own for the first time, free from parental supervision. We were off the leash, and there was no one telling us what to do. We experienced unbounded freedom, I suppose like all young people left entirely on their own for the very first time. Naturally we had girls on our minds, and not necessarily the kind of girls we would have met in school or under our parents' watchful eye back in Bombay. But this was definitely a part of our emotional education—or whatever you want to call it.

From Genoa I took the train to Vienna. I didn't know any German, and my English didn't get me very far in the Vienna of the 1950s. I didn't really think too much about the future, about dealing with what was to come. I knew that my cousin was expecting me and trusted that I would somehow manage. But I did know what I wanted to do: I wanted to go to the Musikakademie in Vienna and dive right into my studies. I wanted to finally and properly learn all those things I had learned to love in India over the past several years and with which my father had so inspired me that I was going to turn them into my profession. From now on music would determine the rhythm of my life.

I arrived in Vienna at the Westbahnhof on a gray day in November 1954. Everything was a little strange. Bombay's overflowing liveliness was a far cry from the well-ordered traffic and the remarkable peacefulness that marked Vienna. At least, that was my impression. I hadn't been able to form any idea beforehand of what the city would be like. Most of all I had not realized that there were still so many bombed-out ruins in the city even nine years after the end of World War II. Vienna was a European city wounded by the war but kept alive and thriving by its people, who seemed to me to be looking toward the future with a sunny optimism in spite of their cheerless circumstances.

I simply accepted this picture of Vienna that presented itself to me. What else could I do? I made good use of youth's prerogative to accept the given as obvious, and otherwise to concentrate on myself, my life, and my musical future, as well as on the many new experiences that awaited me here: the surroundings, the people, and the language.

Naturally, the most beautiful thing was that I could listen to music here, music that was actually being played at the exact same time I was listening to it. That sent me into a kind of culture shock: a lot of this music sounded entirely different from what I knew. I went to concerts thinking that I knew the works on the program. But my sources were my father's records, and the sound quality of those recordings was exceedingly poor, nothing like the real thing. I heard symphony concerts and solo recitals and opera. I knew nothing about opera. I had never heard any, partly because my father had little interest in them. I didn't know any arias at all, neither by Mozart nor Verdi nor Wagner, nor even by Richard Strauss. Furthermore, in the early 1950s recordings of complete operas were rare. Hence, when it came to this genre I had no previous training. The very first opera I ever heard was Beethoven's *Fidelio*, under the baton of the great Karl Böhm.

I had one advantage over my fellow students, though: I knew a whole lot more chamber music than they, since I had had the chance to listen to it practically every day when my father met with the rest of the Bombay String Quartet at our home to rehearse. I knew many quartets by Haydn, Mozart, Beethoven, and Schubert. This had been my daily bread, so to speak, and was certainly also excellent training for my musical sense.

I can never forget the first symphony concert I heard live. It was given in the famous Vienna Musikverein Auditorium by the Vienna Philharmonic under Karl Böhm, and one of the works on the program was Brahms's First Symphony in C Minor. This was a piece I knew inside out—or so I thought. I had heard it often at home in Bombay and was familiar with the score, and I thought I was well prepared. But what I got to hear that day in one of the most beautiful auditoriums in the world—and I feel this way about the Musikverein Auditorium even today—was so different from what I had learned off of those scratchy records that I could hardly believe it. What an experience it was to listen to one of the best orchestras in the world live, with nothing between me and the music and with a great conductor at the helm! I had never heard such a sound before. Gradually it became clear to me what an adventure I would be embarking upon if I decided to become a conductor. Because this had always been the real

13

source of my desire to learn music: to be able someday to conduct Brahms's four symphonies.

Times were difficult politically in postwar Austria. The country was still occupied, and Vienna was divided into four occupation zones. The Russians in particular were no laughing matter. I remember encountering Russian soldiers as I walked around in the city. They seemed to me incredibly alien, the sight of them brought home to me what occupation really meant for Austria. One of the worst disasters from the war years was the bombing of the Vienna State Opera House. The structure was destroyed in March 1945, when the war was almost over. The stage was completely burned out. The reconstruction of the State Opera House began in 1948, and it was scheduled to reopen in 1955. I attended my first operas in their temporary home at the Theater an der Wien.

As for lodging, I subleased a room near the city in a region called the Wienerwald. It was modest but affordable with what my mother could send me each month—half of a small legacy from her father. My brother, Zarin, had to survive in London on the other half. We managed, even if it was always a little tight at the end of the month.

My one and only wish came true whereby I could justify my presence in Vienna: I was accepted at the Musikakademie. Conducting was obviously out of the question during the first year of my studies. I needed to decide upon one instrument to start learning and a second one to master, and I chose the double bass. In addition, I needed to study to get a thorough grounding in music theory. I had a lot to catch up on and some obstacles to overcome. I had heard a lot of music with my father, but as a violinist, he was not in a position to give me any analytical training.

One of the teachers I most admired was Karl Schiske, a remarkable musician. I have known few people as supremely musical as he. He was a fantastic pianist and could take any theme you gave him and play it as a

Bach fugue or in the style of Brahms, as a Chopin nocturne or a Schubert waltz. His modulation and the ideas he developed in his playing were unbelievable. I have never come across anything like it since. As a teacher he was strict and severe, but he also had a superb way of giving his students all the musical fundamentals.

I chose the double bass out of simple pragmatism: for me it was the quickest path to playing in an orchestra. This was my most ardent wish: to play in an ensemble and to study and observe the conductor's art from an orchestral player's point of view.

I had an excellent bass teacher, Otto Rühm, who was also a great human being. He was the solo bass player in the Vienna Philharmonic. This meant that I found myself in the extremely enviable position of being able to attend all the orchestra's rehearsals. Rühm opened up a completely new, wonderful, and breathtaking musical world to me. He was my bridge to the renowned Vienna Philharmonic, whose members soon became my friends.

Many years later, very shortly after I started conducting, Rühm played the bass solo in Mahler's First Symphony in one of my first concerts with the Vienna Philharmonic. He later told me that he'd been particularly nervous.

A musical experience from my early years in Vienna is still vivid in my memory. Barely a month after I arrived in Vienna, I was passing by the Musikverein Auditorium when, on a sudden whim and driven by curiosity, I darted into the rear entrance. I heard music—Tchaikovsky's Fourth Symphony. It was the same old story: I knew this piece from a record my father had of the Boston Symphony under Serge Koussevitzky, but what I heard through the doors of that auditorium sounded completely different. Once again I felt a sense of wonder at this pure and direct form of music. I ran along the corridor a little farther and came to a door with a small round window through which I could look into the auditorium. There stood Herbert von Karajan. I had never seen him in person and recognized him only from pictures, but it was undoubtedly he. I crept in through the door as quietly as I could, slipped into a seat, and listened in amazement.

Nobody discovered me there; nobody threw me out. There I was, and there I stayed. This is how I experienced Karajan for the first time. Once again I had the overwhelming feeling that my ears were straining to open up so that I could listen to this real music in the right way.

This is how I came to know music I thought I already knew. I cannot express it in any other way. Everything I thought I knew now became truly clear to me now for the first time. This new listening was often a very far cry from what I had been used to. Time and again I made new discoveries. I felt like Columbus on a musical expedition. I was setting foot on territory that was completely new for me, though I already knew its outlines. It was during this rich and marvelous time that the foundation for everything I later achieved was laid.

I had listened to a lot of music in Bombay, but because of my father's personal preferences, a certain bias in the selection of music was inevitable. Hence I discovered Mozart, for example, only in Vienna, and then thankfully in the right way.

It is remarkable that I heard so little Bach during my studies. This profoundly Protestant composer wasn't really played very often in those days, unlike the Catholic Haydn and Mozart, whose sacred and church music could be heard everywhere. Baroque ensembles such as the Concentus Musicus Wien were a long way off, and there weren't even any baroque specialists. I have to acknowledge that initially there was a gap in my musical education regarding Bach. I later studied intensively and conducted the *St. Matthew Passion*, the Magnificat, and several cantatas with the greatest of reverence. I did recognize this as a deficiency at first, and even though I conduct Bach from time to time, I prefer to leave this job to my colleagues.

Apart from my studies at the academy, the instrumental lessons, and the theoretical training, I was also a member of the Vienna Singverein choir. I got in pretty easily soon after I began studying and had a chance to witness some wonderful performances. Imagine having a chance to sing Mozart's Requiem under the great maestro Bruno Walter! Many years later, long after I became the head of an orchestra myself, I met him in

America and told him about it. Naturally he did not remember me, but I have a photograph of that performance in which I am recognizable right at the edge of the picture.

My first concert with the Singverein was Beethoven's Ninth Symphony, conducted by Karajan. In the meantime I had learned a bit of German. I could make myself understood quite respectably, but Friedrich Schiller's *An die Freude* (Ode to Joy) was still a real tongue twister for me. I also didn't really understand what it meant. So I had a huge scare when, after the first rehearsal, Karajan declared that starting the very next day we would all have to sing from memory. I was terrified that I would not be able to learn the text and spent half the night reading the ode again and again and memorizing "Freude, schöner Götterfunken." Somehow I was able to pull it off; at least, I don't remember embarrassing my fellow choristers.

Some crucial political developments took place in Austria during my first year there. On May 15, 1955, an international treaty was signed in Vienna, the Austrian State Treaty, granting Austria once more full sovereignty and independence. And in compliance with the terms of the treaty, the occupying forces pulled out of Austria. I remember a convoy of cars driving past me on that memorable day up to the famous Schloss Belvedere, where the treaty was signed by the foreign ministers V. M. Molotov, John Foster Dulles, Harold Macmillan, and Antoine Pinay, after which Austria declared its permanent neutrality. It was a great moment, even for a non-Austrian like me, when Leopold Figl, Austria's foreign minister, stepped out onto the balcony of the Belvedere, the peace treaty in his hands, and proclaimed, "Austria is free!"

Never in my wildest dreams could I have imagined that fifty years later I would be giving a "Concert for Europe," expressing the Austrians' gratitude to the signatory countries, in this very city with the Vienna Philharmonic. The idea would have seemed utterly absurd. But this is precisely what happened in an open-air concert on an unseasonably chilly day in June 2005 before an audience of 90,000 in one of the gardens of Schönbrunn, the palace of the Habsburg monarchs.

In any case I wasn't much more than a young man from India in 1955, learning music in Vienna and preparing like mad for the test for the conductor's course the following fall.

After the first couple of semesters in Vienna many of my fellow students went home or on holiday somewhere. Not me. My limited means did not allow for any traveling, so I stayed in Vienna. Besides, I had a lot to do. I was planning to apply for a place in the master class of Hans Swarowsky, the best conducting teacher at that time.

Even today I am very grateful to Swarowsky, and I owe it to him to describe him here in greater detail. He has become famous as a conductor, and even more as an extraordinary and inspiring teacher. Entire generations of conductors have been taught by him, including my colleagues Claudio Abbado, Mariss Jansons, Giuseppe Sinopoli, and many, many more. Swarowsky's understanding of music was marked by a deep respect for musical authenticity. He believed in absolute fidelity to the work and brooked no experiments. Born in Hungary, he had studied composition alongside Arnold Schoenberg and Anton Webern in Vienna. He was a student, and later also a friend, of Richard Strauss. He also counted Clemens Krauss and Felix Weingartner among his friends. In his lessons he was able to give his students firsthand experience, so that for each of us the learning process was unique. There are two kinds of lessons. Either one learns the theory and then somehow learns how to deal with the subject, or one meets a real master and becomes his disciple, his apprentice, developing close ties with him, which makes the teacher-student relationship an unusually close one. This is an extremely personal and intimate way of learning. Knowledge thereby becomes a kind of experience, or even a piece of reality, communicated by the teacher to the learner, something that simply cannot be achieved by theoretical means. Swarowsky had mastered this way of teaching, this direct passing on of knowledge, to an exceptional degree. Especially where music is concerned, one can learn best by absorbing unmediated and very personal experiences. Who else could have told me how Richard Strauss had conducted Mozart, not to mention his own works? Who could have imparted to me Schoenberg's ideas and reflections on *Moses und Aron*?

Swarowsky was severe and inexorable. He criticized us aspiring conductors, but he also encouraged us whenever he considered it appropriate. Despite his old-school strictness, he was a man of our times. His friendship with the members of the Second Viennese School alone made him quite modern. He kept the flag of this altogether new music flying very high indeed—and this was in the mid-1950s! But as far as the classics were concerned, his unvarying credo was that Mozart's andante could never be an adagio. He was all for quick tempi and in this respect was completely different from many other conductors of his time.

Swarowsky had been adopted by a Viennese banker, and he always made a secret of his real origins. There was a rumor, one he enthusiastically promoted, that he was an illegitimate son of some branch of the Habsburg dynasty. I don't know whether this was true, and in the end it doesn't matter.

Swarowsky saw to it that his students not only learned to conduct in class, but got the opportunity to perform at concerts. We organized concerts with other students from the academy under the motto "Students giving concerts with student conductors." These were a good opportunity to get some experience. My first attempts at conducting were decidedly terrible. I had always been attentive to Swarowsky's lessons. I had studied the technique of indicating the beat thoroughly and had mastered whatever one needed to know. However, when you suddenly find yourself on the stage with the orchestra in front of you, the novelty of the situation overwhelms you, and in the excitement you tend to forget everything you've learned. In these early concerts I looked like a combination of Böhm and Karajan, the two conductors whom I had seen and heard the most in Vienna. I threw my arms around wildly—I still remember that—and my movements were violent and over the top. At the end of a concert I would be totally exhausted. So Swarowsky once asked me to consider what I would do if I had to conduct Wagner—that is, for five hours or longer. In his opinion I would never be able physically to sustain the entire performance!

So one time, after a rehearsal with the student orchestra, he came up to me, grabbed the sleeve of my jacket, and held on to it, forcing me to use only my wrists. He wanted me to finally learn to give up my wild gesticulations. That experience taught me how to conduct only from the wrist. Of course, it is particularly motivating for the musicians, but it can be done. One doesn't always need both hands to conduct. Now I often keep my left hand down by my side in a relaxed posture. That relaxes the orchestra too.

I enjoyed my studies with Swarowsky. My parents visited me in Vienna for the first time in the fall of 1955. My brother also came from London, and we were all finally able to see each other. My father played a violin concerto in the Brahmssaal, to very good reviews. He wanted to remain in Europe, since the musical opportunities in Bombay were now inadequate for him. Our circumstances were not particularly good at the time, but still, it was simply wonderful to have the whole family together again.

Around this time a major event took place that the four of us enjoyed together. The reconstructed Vienna State Opera House was finally opened on November 5, 1955, starting with *Fidelio* under Karl Böhm. We were there in the standing-room section, of course; we couldn't afford anything else. What a performance it was! There were Anton Dermota and Martha Mödl as Florestan and Leonore, Irmgard Seefried as Marzelline, and, to top it all off, the orchestra of the Vienna State Opera. I had managed to get hold of tickets for almost all the performances, and the day after *Fidelio* I heard *Don Giovanni*, also under Böhm, with Dermota and Seefried as Don Ottavio and Zerlina, Lisa della Casa as Donna Anna, and Walter Berry as Masetto. Berry also sang *Wozzeck* a few days later, again under Böhm. Those were really festive days. I simply couldn't get enough of the music. One morning Bruno Walter conducted Anton Bruckner's Te Deum and his Ninth Symphony. I will never forget that concert in Vienna.

Fifty years later, on November 5, 2005, I participated as a conductor in the fiftieth-anniversary celebration of the reopening of the Vienna State Opera House. The three-part program included extracts from the six inaugural premieres of November 1955. I conducted extracts from *Don Giovanni*. Somebody who knew that I had been there fifty years ago in the standing-room section as a student said, "Mehta is still *standing* at the State Opera"—albeit under somewhat different circumstances.

That fall of 1955 my father went to England and found a job as a violinist in Glasgow. Soon thereafter my mother joined him. For my parents this was the beginning of a completely new life, one that would bring them many surprises in the years to come.

I went often and regularly to the reopened State Opera. I remember wonderful shows and also some very strange ones—for example, a *Boris Godunov* with George London, who sang the title role in Russian while everyone else sang in German. At that time a good many operas were sung in German, even the Italian ones, which was complete nonsense from the standpoint of the rhythm of the language. As far as I know it was Karajan who finally put a stop to it when he performed *Tosca* in Italian. Strangely enough, I hardly worked on any operas with my teacher Swarowsky, apart from *The Marriage of Figaro*. This influenced my later conducting career. It was only long after my studies that I dealt with the opera thoroughly. In fact, even when I was leading an orchestra in Montreal and at the same time one in Los Angeles, I hadn't progressed terribly far in my study of opera.

I received my entire orchestral education exclusively and definitively in Vienna, and everything musical that I carry within me is a legacy from that world. I learned a tremendous amount there, not only because of the excellent training I received, but also because I constantly listened to everything there was to hear. At the risk of repeating myself, I have to say this: one can learn either through theory or, like me, by listening—and today, more than ever before, through recordings. But the best and the only real way to understand music is still through live performances. I urge this particularly for all those who want to make a career in music, especially aspiring conductors.

The main reason I managed to learn so much was that I went to all the rehearsals within my reach. That's the only way one can learn by oneself. It amazes me these days when I see young students coming to my rehearsals without the score. If one wants just to listen to the music, that can be done at home. One has to read along in the score in order to understand everything down to the last detail—including the kinds of mistakes that are made.

At any rate, I missed some of my classes in the academy because I was constantly running off to rehearsals. If there was a class on the history of music or the theory of musical form, then I was likely to be listening to Brahms's Piano Concerto in D Minor elsewhere. I was always very close to Swarowsky. I admired him unreservedly, and I still consider him the greatest intellect I have ever encountered. He was my idol in so many ways.

Apart from Swarowsky, another conductor with enormous charisma was Karajan. In those days he used to conduct the Vienna Symphony. At that time the old rivalry between Furtwängler and Karajan was still quite marked. It didn't end even with Furtwängler's death. Since then rumors have circulated suggesting that Furtwängler had a real persecution complex as far as Karajan was concerned. After Furtwängler died, my bass teacher, Rühm, said that the Viennese would remain loyal to him—unlike the Berliners, who didn't even wait for the last nail to be hammered into Furtwängler's coffin before calling in Karajan. A short while later, in 1956, however, Karajan did come to the Vienna State Opera. From that time on he worked well with the opera orchestra. There was a sort of reconciliatory concert, for which Bruckner's Eighth Symphony was programmed, and after that everything was basically fine. I have lived through the entire Karajan era in opera. It began with *Tosca*, then continued with *Die Walküre*. I greatly admired the way he conducted. His beat was extremely clear. In addition, he could really motivate the players. Swarowsky also respected Karajan a lot, although he was often bitter. Because of the war and other things, he never managed to attain his professional peak, unlike Karajan and some other conductors who had become famous. They were all there in Vienna at that time—Rafael Kubelik, Dimitri Mitropoulos, Karl Böhm, Hans Knappertsbusch, Josef Krips—and I heard them all. Just watching these musicians always gave me new ideas and showed me both what and how I had yet to learn.

⁓

The many rehearsals that I went to were not only impressive, but also extremely important for my progress. I was even able to see how Mitropoulos rehearsed Richard Strauss's *Alpensinphonie*. That was something new for me, and it naturally influenced me. It certainly also taught me a lot that contributed later to my own work in music.

Swarowsky's strictness was sometimes difficult to bear. The utter fidelity to the musical work and the discipline that he expected created some problems for us. However, although I sometimes listened to pieces differently from the way that he had taught us, I am thankful for the clarity his rigorous approach brought to our still unripe musical ideas. There was never a careless moment with this teacher. He was exact to the last detail with himself as well as with us, his students.

One of my first performances as a student conductor was one in which students performed for and with students. I had come up with a pretty ambitious program. It was scheduled for the Brahmssaal, a small auditorium in the Musikverein in Vienna—the one where my father had played a violin recital in 1955. Naturally, there was no money for renting the hall or paying the musicians. I thought for a long time about how to get financing. The program was a real Arnold Schoenberg evening. Among other things we were playing the First Chamber Symphony, with fifteen solo instruments, and *Pierrot lunaire*, for voice and five soloists. These were rather difficult pieces, and on top of that the program was a fairly daring one for the time. *Pierrot lunaire* is one of Schoenberg's most important atonal works, unbelievably difficult to perform for the vocal and instrumental soloists alike.

23

While I was casting about for a source of financing for rental of the hall, I had what I thought was a good idea. There was a teacher of the theory of musical form in the academy named Erwin Ratz who was also the general secretary of the Mahler Society. I asked him if the Mahler Society could take care of the hall rental. Ratz enthusiastically agreed and even said that I would be paid something too. I really didn't think that was necessary. My honorarium was basically the opportunity to conduct and to take on the colossal challenge of Schoenberg's pieces. But when Ratz insisted, I asked for a copy of the facsimile of Mahler's *Kindertotenlieder*. At that time Ratz was the custodian of Mahler's scores and had them all stashed under his bed. I actually got this "fee," my first ever and probably the most exciting one I have ever received.

The concert was an unqualified success. Someone even remarked that it was the first-ever performance in Vienna of *Pierrot lunaire* since Schoenberg conducted the work there himself. A local newspaper reported that it hadn't been heard there in fifty years. After the concert I went to meet Ruth Vasicek. She worked in the office of the Konzerthausgesellschaft and always tried to help young artists along. I asked her if she could do anything for me, and that was the beginning of a long and happy association. She not only promoted me as a musician, but for many years also negotiated all my contracts. Her last job for me was in 1995, when she settled a contract for me to accept the position of general music director at the Bavarian State Opera in Munich.

Every year there was a kind of summer festival in Bad Aussee where innumerable students from the various state academies played together and celebrated music. The atmosphere was wonderfully cheerful. We played music, cooked, drank, laughed, and went sailing and swimming. All of us had big plans for our future—but that would, after all, come later. In 1956 I had just turned twenty and had fallen in love with Carmen Lasky, a Canadian voice student in Vienna who was a few years older than I.

My father, who hadn't been particularly happy with his work as a violinist in Glasgow, found a new challenge in the form of a job as violinist in Manchester's reputed Hallé Orchestra under Sir John Barbirolli. When he joined the orchestra he was seated at the back of the first violin section. Within three years he had moved up to the position of assistant concertmaster.

I didn't spend the summer of 1956 studying by myself in Vienna. I was able to attend a summer course conducted by Carlo Zecchi at the Accademia Chigiana in Siena. I hadn't left Austria since I began my studies in Vienna, two years earlier, so of course I was eagerly anticipating my stay in Tuscany. Everything would be new there—the people, the teachers, the surroundings—and I couldn't wait to see what might lie in store for me there.

Not only did I learn a great deal in Siena, but I also met musicians from all over the world. The guitarist John Williams took me along to meet the legendary guitarist Andrés Segovia. Many other musicians became my friends, and at least two of them still are. One was Claudio Abbado, with whom I soon felt connected by a very close bond. The other was Daniel Barenboim, who has become one of my closest friends. I call him up as often as I can wherever the two of us might be. We exchange views and discuss our ideas, and we also talk about political issues.

How I met Barenboim is a story that deserves to be told. On a hot day in August, when the entrance test for the course was held, I walked into a dimly lit auditorium and saw a little person on the stage—at least, that was how it seemed to me—and he was conducting Robert Schumann's Fourth Symphony. Upon coming closer I realized that the person standing on the podium was still almost a child. I was dumbstruck. This young boy conducted with such control and such a beautifully balanced tempo that I could hardly believe my eyes. A little later we found ourselves together in a class. This was the beginning of Daniel's and my friendship—a friendship that has continued to this day.

Daniel was just thirteen years old, so his parents had come along to Vienna with him. They soon accepted me into their family circle and in fact more or less adopted me. Till the end of their lives they remained affectionate and caring people who always looked after me whenever we met. They were a tremendous help to me especially in later years, when I began going to Israel, and they remained in every way warmhearted and supportive friends.

Despite the difference in our ages, a genuine friendship developed between Daniel and me. He too wanted to become a conductor, and I was greatly impressed that he had already been in a master class with Igor Markevitch in Salzburg a year ago. Daniel had studied piano only with his father, but he had already given a concert in New York with Mitropoulos and the New York Philharmonic.

We didn't meet often over the next several years, but the connection between us was never severed. Our friendship has survived for many decades, complemented in later years by the phenomenal cellist Jacqueline du Pré, Daniel's first wife, who died so tragically in 1987. They were joined by Pinchas Zukerman and Itzhak Perlman, with whom I formed an intense and musically intimate friendship. We played a lot of music together, and we also got through some politically and personally difficult times together.

After our first summer course in Siena, Claudio Abbado also came to Vienna. He attended a master class with my teacher Swarowsky and went with me to the choir of the Gesellschaft der Musikfreunde. Not only did the two of us get to sing under the greatest conductors of that time, but we were so stuck-up that we only went if Bruno Walter, Josef Krips, or Karajan was conducting. One of Krips's favorite pieces was *The Book with Seven Seals*, by Franz Schmidt. Schmidt, a Viennese composer, is largely forgotten today, but I remember that I enjoyed singing it.

Our arrogance in deigning to sing only under the great and important conductors had a disastrous and embarrassing consequence. Right in front of Karajan and the orchestra, the choirmaster, Reinhold Schmidt, told Abbado and me to leave the stage. He said that we were interested only in cherry-picking, that we came to rehearsal only when there were "big names" conducting, never to any of his, and told us to stop it right away. What he said was true, but it was still really embarrassing to be given such a public dressing-down.

With this my role as a choral singer—a bass, incidentally—was over. There still remained my role as a bass player, which I was equally uninterested in playing forever, even though for now it brought me small sums of money from time to time and my parents thought it could at least provide me with a steady income and some small degree of security. That was more than I could expect in the extremely risky (or so it seemed to them) profession of conducting. However, I still wanted to wait and see. I wasn't too worried about my income in the near, or even in the far, future. Music was everything to me, and I definitely wanted to continue with conducting in whatever capacity I could. About that I had no doubt whatsoever.

In the fall of 1956 I had another chance to fulfill my desire to conduct, but it was occasioned by a political tragedy. The Hungarian Revolution of 1956 brought innumerable refugees to Austria. Someone came up with the idea of consoling these desperate people, thousands of them living in camps, through music. Under such miserable circumstances this could only have been cold comfort, but it was worth a try. I was chosen along with other students at the Musikakademie to play a concert near the Hungarian border. I remember it as a very moving occasion. A Hungarian priest, also a refugee in the camp, blessed all of us at the end of the concert. Many decades later, in California, I happened to meet a Hungarian couple who had been present at this concert in the camp.

3

THE VITAL YEARS

There is an institution in Vienna called Jeunesses Musicales—Jugend Österreichs. It was part of the Jeunesses Musicales International, one of the largest youth music organizations in the world, which was founded in Brussels in 1949. Jeunesses Musicales is aimed at giving young people access to music and creating opportunities for aspiring musicians to perform onstage, opportunities that would otherwise largely be closed to young soloists and conductors. Swarowsky had recommended me to Jeunesses, and so I got another chance to conduct professionally. At that time I was of course happy about every opportunity that came my way. I was still a student and had hardly any experience.

The most important thing was being asked. Once the invitation came, naturally one tried to put one's best foot forward in the hope of being asked again. In 1958 I was sent in an exchange with a Yugoslavian conductor to do a concert in Belgrade as the Jeunesses representative from Vienna. However, none of these early invitations meant that I would actually have a career as a conductor. (Later I was invited back to Belgrade, and much later, after I had achieved some measure of success, I did one or two concerts each season for Jeunesses.)

Swarowsky's master course officially ended at the conclusion of the summer term in 1957. The final concert was held in the world-famous Musikverein

Auditorium with Vienna's Tonkünstlerorchester Niederösterreich. The concert attracted very little attention and generated no reviews—a pretty big disappointment to all of us young conductors, including Claudio Abbado. The opportunity to perform onstage with a renowned orchestra meant a lot to us, not to mention the musical effort involved. Given the big names in music who performed in Vienna in those days, though, we were simply too insignificant to merit any notice at all. This is probably par for the course.

In 1957 I again spent the summer in Siena with Abbado. This time Alceo Galliera conducted the course. He was completely different from Zecchi and occasionally drove me almost to despair, he was so impossible to please.

I had good news, though, from my parents in England, the biggest piece of which was that my ninety-one-year-old grandfather Nawroji, whom I absolutely adored, was going to move to Manchester to live with my parents. It was unimaginable. My parents wanted to bring him over because he was completely alone at home, and they worried about him constantly. Yet my grandfather had spent his entire life in India, and I was worried that at his advanced age he might not be able to bear such an enormous readjustment in his life. He arrived in the cold, wet climate of northern England at the beginning of winter. As it happened, he died soon after coming, in early 1958—a day after my wedding to Carmen Lasky.

When I came back to Vienna that fall of 1957, I had to think seriously about my future. I occasionally played bass in the orchestra, but my engagements were few and far between, and my income was unimpressive.

Then I heard of a competition for conductors in Liverpool. The winner would be given a chance to work for a year as assistant to Sir John Pritchard, director of the Royal Liverpool Philharmonic. I decided to take a chance and enter. If I won, I would get to spend a year in Liverpool—close to my parents, who were still in Manchester, and to my brother, who was in London.

The competition was held in March 1958. To my great joy, I won and became Sir John's assistant for the 1958–59 season.

My studies in Vienna were over, and my wife and I were expecting our first child. I now had to earn my living, and so we set out for Liverpool, England.

⁓

Life with Pritchard and the Liverpool Orchestra turned out to be very difficult for all concerned. The head of the competition jury was William Steinberg, at the time the director of the Pittsburgh Symphony Orchestra. I later learned that he had liked my resolution of the fermata in the first movement of Beethoven's Fifth Symphony, which made me particularly happy because I had played it the way Swarowsky had taught me. It was Steinberg, not Pritchard, who was actually responsible for my winning.

Pritchard left the conducting of many concerts that season to me, despite my youth and inexperience. I was expected to prepare for most concerts with just one rehearsal. Even today that would be far too little for me, but back then it was impossible for me to pull the concerts off to everybody's satisfaction—either the musicians', the director's, or the audience's. I had not yet discovered what could be achieved with a three-hour rehearsal, nor how best to get the result I wanted.

While in Liverpool I was again invited to conduct in Belgrade, giving me the extraordinary and wonderful opportunity to play with yet another orchestra. For that I had four rehearsals, and it was only then that I realized what was missing in my work with the Royal Liverpool Philharmonic. The experience in Belgrade gave me confidence, though, that I could do absolutely anything if I was just given enough time.

I still remember clearly my first program in Liverpool: the Overture to Verdi's *La forza del destino*, Glazunov's Violin Concerto in A Minor, the Adagio from Mahler's Fifth Symphony, and Tchaikovsky's Sixth Symphony. It was a colossal program, and if you bear in mind that the orchestra did not know either Glazunov or Mahler at all, then you can imagine how much work it meant for me. By pure chance, I at least was familiar with Glazunov. And here my father came to the rescue, for he had often practiced the concerto in Bombay.

On the whole, the orchestra was as dissatisfied with me as I was with the work I was doing. The only really welcome event in my life during this time was the birth of Carmen's and my daughter, Zarina. I had brought my wife to stay with my parents in Manchester, where she was in much better hands than she would have been alone with me in Liverpool. My mother in particular took loving care of her. After the news of our daughter's birth reached me in the middle of a rehearsal, I took the next train to Manchester to see my wife and child. The terrible conditions I found in the hospital's maternity ward were shocking—poor hygiene and an impersonal atmosphere.

Sometimes Pritchard would simply call me up in the morning and ask me to take over one of his rehearsals. In such a situation even a more experienced conductor than I would not have been able to please the musicians. In some areas of life it's probably a good thing to just dive in, but music is not one of them. I still remember how one of these rehearsals was assigned to me. The program, chosen by Pritchard, included Edward Elgar's First Symphony, Richard Strauss's *Ein Heldenleben*, and Schoenberg's Variations for Orchestra. I knew these pieces but was not prepared to take over the rehearsal and could not direct the orchestra well.

My experiences with Pritchard and Liverpool taught me a valuable lesson: never expect an assistant to achieve what he or she has not been able to prepare for well in advance. More than anything else, I think, one needs time to mature. One certainly cannot accomplish much simply by trying things out and improvising in rehearsal—the results are bound to be at best insipid.

This was an important realization for me, but it wasn't much help at the time. Liverpool proved to be something of a disappointment, for me as well as for the musicians.

After that year I returned to Vienna with my young family. It was the beginning of some hard times for us. I now had a wife and child to take care of. Every now and then I got a small assignment through Jeunesses Musicales International, but on the whole I had little to do. My parents pitched in and supported us as much as they could. We were subleasing our apartment, and our future was uncertain.

At least through Jeunesses I gained recognition in some circles. This got me an invitation to conduct on a small tour organized by one of my former fellow students from the Musikakademie. I went to Sarajevo, Ljubljana, Skopje, and then Norway, where I gave a guest performance in Trondheim.

Jeunesses also had its own concert series, during which I conducted one of my first concerts with the highly regarded Tonkünstlerorchester Niederösterreich. All through the summer of 1959 I worked on the scores of Brahms's First Symphony and First Piano Concerto, often while sitting in a city park in Vienna, my little daughter beside me in her baby carriage. My soloist for the concerto was Alfred Brendel. We were acquainted in the way young students are, running into each other every now and then. During one of these chance encounters in a bookstore, I asked him almost in passing if he wanted to play with me. He agreed immediately. It was by no means his first concert, but for me the program was completely new.

I conducted one or two concerts each season for Jeunesses Musicales until 1960, thanks to its director, Joachim Lieben, who in the meantime had become a close friend. In fact, this is what I was doing in Brussels on February 10, 1960, when I was informed of the birth of my son Mervon in Vienna.

In the summer of 1958, before my year in Liverpool, I attended summer school with Claudio Abbado in Tanglewood, in Massachusetts's Berkshire Hills, where the Boston Symphony has its summer home. We had both been accepted as students there. It was sheer paradise for us. The region was delightful, and the music we got to hear was wonderful. Charles Münch was the conductor of the orchestra as well as the director of the Berkshire Music Center, now known as Tanglewood. It was a wonderful time. That summer Abbado and I won first and second prize, respectively, in the Koussevitzky Competition, named for Serge Koussevitzky, the conductor of the Boston Symphony from 1924 to 1949.

In Tanglewood I met the Berlin-born American composer Lukas Foss. He seemed to really like me. In fact, it was probably he who spoke about me to the famous music agent Siegfried Hearst, also originally from Germany. I didn't know Hearst, but I knew that he represented many prominent and famous musicians, such as George Szell and Leopold Stokowski. This was a world that was galaxies away from my life.

Hearst, whose cultural sensibilities were unparalleled, got me my first professional concerts in America in August 1960. I don't know what Foss said about me or even what happened to bring me to Hearst's attention, but on his recommendation I was invited to conduct the CBC Orchestra in Toronto. It was my one and only concert with them, but I believe my work was appreciated. I always got along extremely well with Hearst, and it is to him that I owe some important advances in the early stages of my career.

Back in Vienna with my wife and children, I didn't have much to do. Then one day Hearst called up and offered me the chance to conduct the Philadelphia Orchestra in one summer concert and the New York Philharmonic in three others. This was an unexpected opportunity for me, and a very important one. American orchestras always have a summer season during which they play away from their regular venues. These concerts, aimed an audience that does not frequent large concert halls, have a wonderful reputation and often feature excellent musicians as soloists and conductors. I was overjoyed to get a chance to conduct such first-rate orchestras. The audience must have been a little surprised at first to see an unknown Indian conductor, but the concerts were a huge success. For the first time in my life I got genuine reviews: Philadelphia—excellent; New York—so-so. Since this was the real beginning of my career, I would like, just this once, to quote what the Philadelphia newspaper wrote about me: "The sky is the limit for this man."

All this traveling cost a fortune, and it took some fancy footwork and a lot of salesmanship to get the necessary financing. I had to lobby everyone

I could think of. I approached the Indian High Commissioner in London, Mrs. Vijayalakshmi Pandit (the sister of the Indian prime minister, Jawaharlal Nehru), and asked for help. She immediately put in a request to the Indian government, which very kindly paid for my trip to the United States and back. Mrs. Pandit and I remained friends for a long time, and I was very moved when she asked Nancy and me to sit next to her at Indira Gandhi's funeral in New Delhi in 1984.

It all made me exceedingly happy. I had the feeling that the whole world was open to me, along with the skies above. Stokowski, who was supposed to conduct in Philadelphia as well as at the summer concerts in New York, was not really in good health. So Hearst asked me if I could also take over three concerts in Lewisohn Stadium, the summer home of the New York Philharmonic.

Hearst, I believe, played his cards right, and that was how I got the chance to play with two such renowned and world-famous orchestras as Philadelphia and New York. I suppose that he first suggested one of the biggest names in music—Stokowski—but since he could no longer work much, I, a young, unknown Indian conductor from Austria, entered the picture as a substitute.

In 1960 I met Frederic R. Mann, a prominent patron of the summer concerts, in Philadelphia. He was a wonderful person, very affluent and very interested in music. In later years we became close, and we saw a lot of each other when I took up my musical commitments in Israel. Without him, an untiring friend and patron, many of the developments with the Israel Philharmonic Orchestra would not have been possible, and the orchestra would never have got an auditorium in Tel Aviv, the Frederic R. Mann Auditorium.

The summer of 1960 was a formative time for me. There had been so many unexpected developments, and I'd had such marvelous experiences and met such wonderful people, in music as well as in my personal life. Suddenly the whole world seemed to be opening itself up to me.

My wife and children had come with me to the United States, but now they went to Canada—to my wife's hometown of Saskatoon, Saskatchewan, to be precise. We wanted to return to Vienna that fall, though. After all, Vienna was our hub, and besides, my next conducting appointment, in Linz, had already been set.

While I was still in Vienna, before the summer, I had asked Leonard Bernstein if by any chance he could use me as an assistant. The job seemed tempting, and with it I might be able to secure my future. I had been introduced to Dimitri Mitropoulos at one of his concerts in Vienna, and I asked him what he thought. He was not too wild about the idea. To my surprise, though, I received an answer from Bernstein, and we met while I was in New York for the summer concerts. He offered me the post of assistant. Bernstein had always had three assistants, but he was inviting me to be his only one. I asked for some time to think it over. Mitropoulos had advised me not to become an assistant, no matter how fantastic it might be to work with Bernstein. So now I was unsure.

Then, before I could make up my mind, something happened that turned my entire life upside down. The orchestra in Montreal had a wonderful and enterprising manager, Pierre Beique, to whom I had been introduced by my good friend Eugene Husaruk, a violinist who had been a colleague of mine while we were students in Vienna. Beique knew how to bring good conductors to Montreal regularly, even though at that time it was not the best locale for musical events. A confirmed Wagnerian, he was obsessed with music, knew his field thoroughly, and took great care to make sure that the Montreal orchestra was always in good musical hands. He regularly went to the various summer festivals in Europe, where he heard all the important concerts and operas with interest, listening to everything with great acumen and very sound understanding.

A concert was supposed to be held in Montreal in October 1960 with Igor Markevitch as conductor. But Markevitch canceled this concert on short notice, supposedly because he was unwell—although it was said at the same time that he was well enough to conduct in Paris. Beique was a friend of Hearst's, and the response to the concert in Philadelphia had been excellent. Maybe Charles Münch had recommended me; he was conducting in Tanglewood when Abbado and I had been there, and he was also a friend of Beique's. In any case, some reports about me had reached Montreal, where they were desperately looking for a substitute conductor for the concert in October. The really big names were obviously not available on such short notice, and so they asked me to take Markevitch's place. At the time I was vacationing with Carmen and our two children at my parents' home in Philadelphia.

I agreed enthusiastically, quite overwhelmed by the multiple opportunities I was being offered all at once. The contrast with the dreariness of waiting in Vienna in the vague hope of getting an offer or engagement was pronounced. In addition, my father's efforts to find a new job had finally borne fruit, and he was now teaching young people at the New School of Music in Philadelphia and playing in the Curtis String Quartet, for which position he had been recommended by his former teacher, Ivan Galamian.

And now I had this offer from Montreal. It was a bit too much all at once. But then, what young conductor could possibly have refused? I went to Montreal, where I conducted Hector Berlioz's *Symphonie fantastique*, among other works, and the musicians and audience gave me a very friendly reception.

To my immense surprise, the morning after the concert Beique offered me the post of permanent conductor of the orchestra starting in the fall of 1961. Never in my wildest dreams could I have imagined that my trip to America would produce such results. I didn't need much time to make up my mind. I was overwhelmed by the offer, and my wife and my parents were also exceedingly happy. It seemed that sometimes it paid off to be stubborn and wait, to be willing to take risks such as accepting musical challenges at the last minute, stepping in for someone else, and deciding matters on short notice. Finally I was going to present everything that I had learned, practiced, rehearsed, and studied. Now I had a chance to prove myself and my capability.

Astonishing as these events were, each one following as it did hot on the heels of the last, things weren't over yet. During the substitution concert in Montreal, Hearst, a good judge of character and an experienced agent who knew all the tricks of the trade, heard from Georg Solti. Solti, another of Hearst's clients, was going to be the musical director of the Los Angeles Philharmonic starting in the fall of 1961. This famous and very busy conductor had committed himself to several weeks per season in Los Angeles, apart from his engagement at Covent Garden in London, and was looking for an assistant. Hearst suggested my name.

The problem was, I had just rejected exactly the same kind of offer from Leonard Bernstein. Now, after the Montreal offer, taking such a position seemed even more difficult. I had to turn down the offer. What would I do in Los Angeles? I had unexpectedly got a wonderful job in Montreal, and now I wanted to go back to Vienna to arrange everything. Basically it was impossible for me to accept a job like the one with Solti, and I saw no reason to pursue something that was out of the question from the very beginning. But Hearst—who was, incidentally, the only real agent I had during my entire musical career—suggested a way to handle the situation. He told me that under no circumstances should I turn down the Los Angeles offer right away. One never knew what it might lead to. A rehearsal in front of Solti was far from the worst thing a young, inexperienced man of twenty-four could do at the beginning of his conducting career. An opportunity like this didn't come along every day, and at my age it wouldn't hurt to get a bit more exposure. And so it was that I flew to Los Angeles. So many new things had happened in the preceding months that I simply followed Hearst's advice and dove headlong into this adventure too.

When I conducted in front of Solti, I was once again confronted with an unfamiliar orchestra. My audition program included Brahms's First Symphony and Mozart's "Prague" Symphony. Solti liked the Brahms but thought the Mozart much too fast. However, he immediately offered me the post of assistant. Every American orchestra employs an assistant conductor who conducts youth concerts and performances outside the city—all those supposed trifles that the boss has no time for.

Solti's offer landed me in a dilemma. After all, I'd never intended to accept the job even if he offered it. With a guilty conscience, I explained that it was not possible for me to be his assistant and apologized, saying that I had been offered a job as conductor of the orchestra in Montreal just the evening before and that it would be impossible for me to manage both Montreal and Los Angeles. Solti understood, and I was happy that we had at least been able to meet one another. This, it turned out, had been the whole point of Hearst's not altogether aboveboard game.

⁓

Finally it was time for me to fly back to Vienna. There was hardly any work waiting for me there, but thinking about next fall spurred me on and allowed me to take the upcoming financially hard times in stride. I was going to have a permanent post. I was going to have my own orchestra, which I would be free to organize my way. This seemed to be quite enough for the moment.

Shortly before Christmas I got a telegram from George Kyper, the manager of the Los Angeles Philharmonic. Fritz Reiner, who was scheduled for a concert in January 1961, had fallen ill, and Kyper asked if I could substitute for him. This was really incredible. Two unemployed months ago I had thought I would be staying in Vienna, and now, all of a sudden and with no prior notice, I was going to substitute for a great and famous conductor in three weeks of concerts! Obviously, I said yes.

Reiner was a renowned conductor in the United States who had elevated the Chicago Symphony Orchestra to international standards. Like George Szell, Ferenc Fricsay, and Solti, he was Hungarian by birth. I knew none of the pieces Reiner had selected for the program, and I had very little time left to study the scores. I had to get them out of the music library as soon as possible, because in a short time I would be expected to present all of this music knowledgeably and convincingly to a great orchestra.

I suggested a couple of changes in the program, since it seemed altogether too reckless to dive into the deep end yet again and only then find out whether I could float. I added some pieces to the program that I was familiar with—Anton Webern's Six Pieces for Orchestra and Stravinsky's *Petrushka*. Richard Strauss's *Don Quixote* had also been on Reiner's list, but I did not know it at all. This program meant that I had to immediately begin studying really hard if I was going to meet the expectations everyone would have of me. All in all I had to substitute in four concerts. Beyond that I really didn't know what to expect.

During my stay in Los Angeles I had a moving encounter with Bruno Walter, who lived in Beverly Hills at that time. I had heard that a recording had been scheduled with him and the Los Angeles Philharmonic and requested permission to attend. I had seen Walter in July of that year in Vienna during the centenary celebrations for Gustav Mahler, whose music was hardly ever played in Vienna in those days. Walter had conducted the Fourth Symphony. I remembered it clearly. Now, meeting him in California, I told him how impressed I had been with the concert in Vienna. To my surprise, he had already heard of the "Indian" Mehta, who had conducted Brahms's Third Symphony there. I asked him how he knew about it, since there had never been any international interest in me, and he said that he subscribed to a Viennese paper in which I had been mentioned in a review. He then agreed to go through the score of Mahler's First Symphony with me and answer all my questions. He was extremely kind and helpful and impressed me tremendously, both as a musician and as a human being. He was sometimes homesick for Vienna, he said, but he fought it by putting on a Boskovsky recording of waltzes; that made him feel completely at home. Sadly, Walter died in February 1962—a great personal loss to me, for I had felt a very warm camaraderie with him.

It was impossible to predict how the public in Los Angeles would react to me. Webern had never been performed there before, so in a sense he was new for the musicians too. I probably had faith in God and courage, coupled with a certain youthful cocksurenesss about my ability to do anything. That included convincing the musicians, many of whom were head and shoulders above me in experience and knowledge. I think that was when I first learned how much a conductor, and not only a young conductor, can learn if he is ready not to overplay his own position and instead to listen very carefully to what the musicians of an orchestra have to say. This is another piece of advice I'd like to give aspiring conductors: listen, pay attention, and fall back on the experience of musicians who love their job and can guide you, as it were, by means of their skills and talent. A conductor should always be prepared to accept this kind of advice from orchestra members.

I have always had the good fortune of working with musicians who allowed me to share their vast musical experience. One can learn a lot this way, and I believe I have done it often and well whenever I could.

I arrived in Los Angeles more or less well prepared. When I was there before, in the previous fall, I never thought I would return so soon. I started rehearsing with the orchestra and realized I could work very well with them. It made me happy to see how the musicians received my suggestions. They were all quite dedicated, and during the three weeks I spent there, never once did any disagreement or misunderstanding arise between us. Even the audience accepted to some extent without complaining that instead of Fritz Reiner up there on the podium they were seeing some unknown.

I do not know what fate or the gods—it is not for me to decide—had in mind for me. In any case, once more some very strange things happened. After the Fritz Reiner concerts, there were to be some concerts scheduled with Markevitch. He too had to cancel, also because of illness. Markevitch's cancellations were something I was familiar with, and since I was already in Los Angeles, the musicians, the management, and the president of the administrative board, Dorothy Chandler, thought that to simplify matters I should take over his concerts as well. It was a lucky break for me in every way imaginable. The young conductor who had been unemployed in Austria was suddenly not just sought after, but also in great demand. In another piece of luck, in his program for Los Angeles Markevitch had included Béla Bartók's Concerto for Orchestra, which I had already worked on thoroughly the last time I had substituted for him in New York. It could not possibly have been more convenient. All in all I was in Los Angeles for three fruitful and musically very eventful weeks.

Toward the end of this time Dorothy Chandler asked me if I would be interested in becoming associate conductor under Georg Solti. It would mean that my presence would be required—in fact, compulsory—for six weeks every season, far more responsibility than the assistant's post Solti had offered earlier. This arrangement was intended to reduce the workload for Solti, who wanted to spend twelve weeks per season in Los Angeles as music director. At least, this was how it was explained to me. I was also told that the orchestra was really happy with me and that this solution would be in everybody's best interest. As an associate conductor—that is, a kind of subordinate conductor—I would have to conduct six subscription concerts during the season. And since Solti could not be convinced to spend any more than the stipulated twelve weeks in Los Angeles, something that his commitments in London did not permit, it was suggested that I come for eight weeks to compensate for the times when Solti could not be present. This seemed absolutely practicable to me. I had a contractual agreement to spend sixteen weeks in Montreal; I could easily fit in eight weeks in Los Angeles. It was an appealing idea. I of course inquired whether Solti agreed with this arrangement and was assured that everything would be in order. Still, I had turned down the offer to be his assistant, and now I was suddenly getting in through another door and in a completely different capacity.

In the end I didn't worry about it too much and left the negotiations with Solti up to the responsible parties in Los Angeles. I returned to Vienna overjoyed with the professional opportunities I had been offered.

All this happened at a time when intercontinental communications were much more difficult than they are now. Even long-distance calls were enormously complicated. We had no telephone in our rented apartment, and calling the United States from Austria was nothing short of a small adventure, not to mention that the average citizen could hardly afford to pay for such calls. I bring this up because nowadays, when agreements like this have to be worked out, one simply phones or e-mails to make sure all parties concerned approve of the deal.

But this was 1961, and I flew back to Vienna in high spirits. I had a full-time job in Montreal and a part-time one in Los Angeles. It was a splendid feeling. It never even occurred to me that Solti might possibly be surprised at my new position in Los Angeles, or that he might not have been consulted at all about this arrangement involving me.

Today, as I look back, it is incomprehensible to me that I didn't bother to check further into the whole matter. I was back in Vienna, but I knew that my time there was finally coming to an end. I had spent seven years in this city, and it had been instrumental in my development. However strongly I might now perceive myself as an Indian, I still have to admit that it was in Austria that I matured and developed into a musician. Accordingly, I felt that that was where I belonged. In the meantime I had developed a good command of the language, and I had met people in Vienna who played a focal role in my life. Most of all, however, everything I had ever learned musically was deeply influenced by Vienna. This is something that has never changed.

Vienna has a specific notion of sound that relates to what's known as *Wiener Klassik* (Viennese classical music) and the First and Second Viennese Schools. This notion of sound refers in equal measure to various small details such as Viennese brass and bass instruments, which have a very particular timbre and are played and heard only in Vienna.

After I returned from America in such a good mood, there wasn't much for me to do besides preparing myself emotionally to leave Vienna and begin my work in Canada and Los Angeles. So I was a little surprised to read in *Time* magazine one day that Georg Solti had resigned from his post in Los Angeles even before taking up his duties—and that he was deeply annoyed with me and the way I had been brought in as his associate conductor. It might sound naïve, even incredible, but this is exactly how I came to learn of Solti's resignation from Los Angeles.

What had happened was that nobody in Los Angeles had asked Solti if he had any objections to my working there only four fewer weeks than he, putting me almost on a par with him. He had obviously been presented with a fait accompli, and he didn't like it. He must also have found it peculiar that after turning down his offer of an assistant's job just a short while earlier, suddenly I was by his side again, and under completely different circumstances. He objected to my spending so much time in Los Angeles, and he was extremely irritated that nobody had consulted him before making me this offer. His reaction was more than understandable, really. I had been too trusting and inconsiderate of a senior colleague. Solti had also been too passive; he could have initiated a dialogue just as easily as I. The whole thing was caused by a string of misunderstandings and clumsy moves, and Solti did not forgive me for many years. I deeply regretted the whole thing. In later years I made some attempts to make up for it so that we could deal with each other in a friendly way and let bygones be bygones, but I was only partly successful. We were connected to each other for many years in a kind of technical relationship. Not only did we both work with American orchestras—Solti having in the meantime accepted the music directorship of the Chicago Symphony Orchestra—but we were also under contract to the same record label, Decca. The president of the company always gave Solti precedence whenever a repertoire was being recorded. For me this was a given, and I did not mind at all. Our relationship was quite strained for twenty years. But during Solti's last year with the Chicago Symphony Orchestra, it had normalized to the extent that I could take over the conducting of the orchestra for both the Brahms piano concertos, with Daniel Barenboim as soloist.

There was a big scandal and a lot of excitement in Los Angeles. People obviously wanted to placate the extremely angry Solti. It was suggested that my time with the orchestra be shortened, in the hope that this would solve the problem neatly. However, Solti stuck to his decision to quit. He would not accept any compromise, and the whole affair ended in a rather shabby and distasteful way.

The upshot of it all was that I was offered a full-time position, beginning in 1962, as Solti's replacement. This was a bit much for everyone. Not only did those responsible in Los Angeles have to bite the bullet and end up with a young, unknown conductor and a lot of trouble, but also Montreal, where I had a contract starting in the fall of 1961, had to be approached about letting me work in Los Angeles at the same time. On the one hand, Montreal was not happy with this solution. On the other, they couldn't offer me as many weeks of work as Los Angeles. Obviously they could not prohibit me from commuting. It was a very dicey situation. Even Hearst, who had been involved in the whole business, was quite surprised by the way things developed. Originally he probably just wanted to help this young, unknown, Austrian-trained Indian. He eventually finalized the contract with Los Angeles for me. Unfortunately, he died two years later. I am deeply grateful to him for everything he did for me.

And what about me, the main person involved in this muddle of changing offers and ideas? For most of 1960 and 1961 I had not been regularly employed and had been trying to acquire as much experience as I could by substituting for others and conducting here and there, struggling to earn a living for myself and my young family. And now, success was coming to me all at once in almost unstoppable waves. Suddenly I found myself, all of twenty-five years old, with two permanent jobs in the bag. I was in the happy situation of having to adapt to the extremely demanding life of a conductor with two different orchestras. It also meant that I had to study incessantly and painstakingly to prepare for my upcoming concerts.

During one such guest conducting engagement in Brussels, when I learned of Mervon's birth in Vienna, one can only imagine with what zest and celebration I conducted Bartók's Concerto for Orchestra. Of course, the orchestra had also been told the happy news and responded to my enthusiasm with equal delight.

A lot of things fell into my lap, particularly in 1961. Sometimes, thinking of Schiller's claim that "Freude, schöner Götterfunken" (joy, the beautiful spark of the gods) is not granted to any mortal, I ask myself if it has been granted to me in excess.

I was still caught up in this whirlwind of events when something else completely unexpected happened. This time it was a telegram from a sender who called himself, mysteriously, "PALPHILORC." The telegram said that Eugene Ormandy had had to cancel his conducting of the Israel Philharmonic Orchestra and asked if I could perhaps take over the scheduled concerts. First of all, of course, I had to find out who the strange

45

sender was. I learned that ever since the state of Israel was founded in 1948, the orchestra there had been officially known as the Israel Philharmonic Orchestra, but the cable address had never changed. Something like this could hardly happen nowadays: the acronym PALPHILORC stood for Palestine Philharmonic Orchestra.

Naturally I accepted. (My entire musical progress seemed to be connected to the illnesses and cancellations of my renowned colleagues. It was becoming more and more uncanny.) I went to Israel with my wife, Carmen. It was completely new to me, and back then I was really ignorant politically. However, I felt at home as soon as I arrived in Israel, particularly because I was welcomed so affectionately by all the Barenboims. They looked after me during my stay there. Israel—it was again love at first sight, on both sides. In those days the orchestra consisted mainly of immigrants who had fled Austria or Eastern Europe before and after the Holocaust. This meant that I was immediately greeted with "my" sound, that very European sound that was so familiar to me and that I knew so well. From the outset Tel Aviv, with its organized confusion, reminded me of Mumbai. Everyone talks at the same time, constantly offers advice, and has a decided opinion. Open a window in Mumbai and you see thousands of people all doing something or other. This is what I had been missing in Vienna, and so experiencing a mini-Mumbai in Tel Aviv made me feel very much at home.

Musically, I felt as though I had never left Vienna. I had chosen a program for Israel—Kodály's *Galánta Dances*, Stravinsky's Symphony in Three Movements, and Dvořák's Seventh Symphony—that I would be conducting there for the first time. I quickly became acquainted with the orchestra. The program was new for them too, and none of the musicians knew these pieces. We had only had four rehearsals together—scarcely enough time to prepare such an ambitious program. The Stravinsky piece went surprisingly well. The Dvořák, on the other hand, was really difficult. I can no longer remember the reactions to the concerts; I just know that we played the same program thirteen times. Yet even though we did not necessarily improve with each performance, we had a good time together and got along well despite the difficulties. Once again I met musicians who taught me something I could not have learned in the academic system: that music comes as much from the heart as from the head, as well as from a mastery of the basic technical prerequisites.

I was impressed by the strength and will one sometimes needed in order to survive under the most difficult of circumstances. Making music in Tel Aviv and in a number of other places in Israel meant sustaining the hope for a more peaceful life, or at least for a better understanding among people.

That year, 1961, was really pretty rough. Not only did Ormandy cancel in Israel, but he also had to cancel his concerts with the Vienna Philharmonic. I was connected to the Vienna Philharmonic in a number of ways—as a frequent member of the audience, as a student of my double bass professor Otto Rühm, and as a singer in the choir, even though my exit from this last had been somewhat inglorious. So it was really special for me when the artistic director of the Vienna Festival, Egon Hilbert, invited me to conduct, instead of Ormandy, at a festival concert with the Vienna Philharmonic. I was truly overwhelmed by this offer.

On June 11, 1961, the ninety-seventh anniversary of Richard Strauss's birth, I conducted the Vienna Philharmonic in the Golden Hall. We had a program that even now seems to me extremely demanding: Stravinsky's Symphony in Three Movements, Beethoven's Third Piano Concerto (with Friedrich Gulda as soloist), and Strauss's *Don Quixote*. At that time it was a little unusual for the Viennese to play Stravinsky, but it went quite well. I had already conducted the Strauss in the United States, so I was well prepared for this difficult piece. I think this is when the love affair between the Vienna Philharmonic and me began. It continues to this day and has informed my work with every other orchestra I have ever been associated with.

It is interesting to look at this concert from today's perspective. At that time the orchestra was still very deeply entrenched in the Viennese tradition, influenced by conductors such as Furtwängler, Knappertsbusch, and

Krauss. When Karajan conducted Debussy's *Pelléas et Mélisande* in Vienna for the first time, he revealed an entirely new world to the musicians. Today the Viennese are completely different. Practically no other orchestra in the world has such an impressive repertoire. They know everything and can play just about any style, including the entire operatic repertoire.

The concert seemed to be a success, though I found myself in the somewhat strange position of having some of my former teachers among the members of the orchestra. In any case, I was invited the following year to take over two more Vienna Philharmonic engagements while I was busy with my commitments in North America. This time it was a festival concert with Nathan Milstein and a concert at the Salzburg Festival featuring Bartók's Second Piano Concerto (with Géza Anda as soloist), a Mozart symphony, and Dvořák's Seventh Symphony. But I'm taking a giant leap in time in my narration. These things were yet to come.

For me 1961 was a seemingly endless chain of coincidences and unforeseeable events. An angel seemed to be watching over me and repeatedly bringing me into contact with people who seemed to be interested in my well-being.

I have already mentioned my German-born agent Hearst—a true professional and a real connoisseur of the musical scene in America and Europe. Through him I suddenly, at the age of twenty-five, had two contracts as an orchestra conductor. I was penniless and completely unknown outside Austria when I started substituting for colleagues who had fallen ill. This took me from Vienna to the United States and Israel, and then back to Vienna. Moreover, I also had the chance to conduct the Berlin Philharmonic in that miraculous year entirely on my own merits—in other words, without having been called to substitute for anybody. The director of the Berlin Philharmonic at that time, Wolfgang Stresemann, was the son of Gustav Stresemann, the national economist and later chancellor and foreign minister of the Weimar Republic, and a friend of Hearst. I still do not really know what Hearst discussed with Stresemann, but that engagement made me the youngest conductor ever of the Berlin Philharmonic. This, by the way, was my very first trip to Germany.

It is hard to say now whether the concert in Berlin was good or bad. However, I still remember that I conducted Gustav Mahler's First Symphony for the first time in my life. In retrospect, I feel that I had a lot of guts at that age to attempt this enormous work with an orchestra like the Berlin Philharmonic. To place myself, with no more experience than I had, in front of such an excellent, sensitive orchestra—and with Mahler, whom I had not really mastered—could only have come about through a combination of courage and megalomania. Also on the program that evening was Schumann's Cello Concerto, with Enrico Mainardi. The concert took place on September 18, 1961, shortly before I finally went to the United States with my family. Incidentally, this concert is the source of a somewhat embarrassing anecdote. Mainardi was trying desperately to tell me something urgent before the cello concerto began, but I didn't understand him and simply ignored his attempts to get my attention. It was only after the end of the concerto that I understood what Mainardi had been whispering to me: "Pantaloni son aperti"—your fly is open.

I had seven years of life in Vienna behind me. I had felt at home in this magnificent city. But now a new life was beginning, a life that was going to bring me new challenges and new experiences. I could hardly wait to tackle whatever it had in store for me.

4

NORTH AMERICA

Montreal, Los Angeles, and More

In the fall of 1961 my wife and children and I boarded an ocean liner at Cherbourg and crossed the Atlantic to Canada to start our new life there. In the dramaturgy of events this voyage turned out to be an apt beginning. Upon finally arriving in Montreal, we met with a very warm reception.

I was rather poor but still had to support a family of four. Here Pierre Beique came to the rescue. He was a wonderful person and soon became a good friend. He arranged for the Montreal Symphony Orchestra to buy us a house. For the moment our worst financial worries were over.

My wife was overjoyed to be back in her native country. As for me, my first major job was awaiting me, and I was impatient to begin.

When I take stock of that year, I have to acknowledge that in 1961 everything that would determine the rest of my life fell right into my lap. That's something for which I'm really grateful. Between August 1960 and September 1961 I conducted all the orchestras that have since become my musical homes. I have remained faithful to them all my life, and they have become landmarks for me. I became acquainted with the Montreal and Los Angeles orchestras, had already conducted the orchestras in Vienna and Berlin, and had been invited to Israel and Florence for the first time.

I am a very loyal person. If I make a friend, I keep that friendship for life. It's the same way with orchestras. I remain loyal to them too, because I don't believe in playing here and there with ensembles I don't know, only to reach a partly satisfactory result after a few rehearsals. I feel that I simply cannot meet with an orchestra three or four times for two and a half hours each and thereafter conduct the best "Jupiter" Symphony of my life; it just doesn't work, even if the orchestra is world-famous. That's why I have never conducted some orchestras even though I've been invited by them several times, and even though by turning them down I've upset some of my colleagues. For example, I have never conducted the Boston Symphony, the Cleveland Orchestra, or the San Francisco Symphony. I have to feel comfortable with the musicians; I need to know them and to have worked with them. I have to know that I can rely upon them, and they also have to know they can rely upon me.

It is always different when a conductor plays with his own orchestra. He knows the orchestra through and through, and the orchestra in turn knows all the conductor's nuances and his musical tastes. Even if they have not played together for a few seasons, the orchestra musicians know what the conductor wants. Obviously it is all there in the score, but each and every member of the orchestra must also know what the conductor wants and exactly how he wants it. One cannot reach this level of understanding with just a few rehearsals—not even with a first-rate orchestra. At least, I can't do it, and I don't even want to.

My loyalty to orchestras is also related to the artistic standards toward which I strive and requires a great deal of perseverance on my part. I always like to remain with musicians I know and with whom I have played often, and I feel that I may have played a part in their careers. With some orchestras I have had quite a long association. I was in Los Angeles for sixteen years, I have been acquainted with the Israel Philharmonic Orchestra since 1961 and have been their musical director since 1969, and I was in New York from 1978 to 1991 and in Munich from 1998 until the end of the 2005–6 season. I have personally recruited many of the musicians in these orchestras—at least eighty-six in the Los Angeles Philharmonic alone. Naturally, this allows me to follow the musicians' progress. Having been together for such a long time makes it much easier for me to achieve what I want with them.

I was unfaithful to my principle of loyalty just once—in 2005, when I conducted the Concertgebouw Orchestra in Amsterdam for the first time. The program included Anton Bruckner's Eighth Symphony. Memory and sentiment played some part in my decision. I had heard this orchestra as a student in Vienna in 1956, and I was simply thrilled to experience it now as a conductor. This event made a deep impression on me. The Dutch love Bruckner and made me aware of that feeling in no uncertain terms.

Going back to Montreal, to the beginning of my life as a conductor: I found a good second-tier orchestra there, with, however, some wonderful soloists. The first horn player, Joe Masella; the concertmaster, Calvin Sieb; and the brothers Otto and Walter Joachim, on violin and cello respectively, were excellent. Pierre Beique had long tried to get a first-class conductor, but as I mentioned, there were problems with that. Not even a superb conductor can bring an orchestra to the heights of technique and expression with just a couple of rehearsals followed by a concert. Montreal also had some serious financial issues, which didn't make the orchestra's day-to-day operations any easier.

When I first came to Montreal, all the concerts took place in Plateau Hall, a hideous 1,200-seat space that looked like a high school auditorium. It most certainly was not the concert hall of my or any other conductor's dreams.

At my first concert Alfred Brendel played Brahms's First Piano Concerto, the same one we had performed so successfully in Vienna. Unfortunately, we didn't perform with each other as often as I would have liked to. Daniel Barenboim, who had a lot of experience with American orchestras, also came to Montreal as a soloist. He had already performed as a soloist in New York in his early youth.

I had to be diligent and concentrate entirely on Montreal, because I was expected eventually to build up a repertoire. There was so much that I did in Montreal for the first time and so little time available. On top of that, beginning in the fall of 1962 a new job awaited me in Los Angeles.

The season in Montreal was relatively short. I tried to bring some sparkle to the city's musical life by inviting guest conductors. Claudio Abbado came, and my old teacher from Vienna, Hans Swarowsky, also did me the honor of accepting. Even Charles Münch accepted my invitation. He loved Montreal because of its French ambience.

A new auditorium was inaugurated at the Place des Arts in September 1963, a multifunctional concert hall with much better acoustics than Plateau Hall, and much more pleasant aesthetically as well. This too was Pierre Beique's doing. He just pressed ahead with his mission, planning and organizing tirelessly.

Carmen and I separated in 1964. We had met as students in Vienna and lived there, and our two children, who were a source of infinite joy for us, had been born there. But a lot had happened since those days. In short, a separation was unfortunately unavoidable. I moved out of the house, which I eventually gave to Carmen and the children. I still deeply regret that I could not contribute much to the upbringing of my children.

About two years later my brother, Zarin, who had by then settled in Montreal, developed a serious relationship with Carmen, and they married in 1966. They went on to have two children, Rohanna and Rustom, and Carmen now has six grandchildren.

Professionally, I was now doing double duty and serving two masters—I had two orchestras to conduct and build up, and moreover, they were an entire continent apart. Montreal and Los Angeles were the two fixed points of my young professional life. Working with these two orchestras made enormous demands on me and on my musical ethos. I studied constantly because I had to conscientiously prepare new repertoire each week, and I had to learn how to deal with the vast complex of responsibilities I had got myself into. Beyond that, I had to constantly expand my repertoire and prove myself as an orchestra conductor at every rehearsal with each orchestra. Maybe this was all to be expected, but in my case there was also the considerable distance between my two places of work, musically as well as geographically, which meant that I always had to be on the move.

This, then, was the beginning of my professional life as a conductor. I learned not only how much internal and external flexibility an international career demanded, but also how continually to transform that flexibility into a springboard for some new initiative. I considered it an unmitigated privilege to be able to do that which is for me of the greatest beauty: to make music with my two ensembles, and to build a rapport with the public of both cities and eventually win their confidence.

In Los Angeles I found the same lack of perfection that marked the orchestra in Montreal. However, working out a variety of musical problems with this orchestra also gave me infinite joy. Besides, I myself was still very far from a perfect conductor.

For historical reasons, there were a lot of long-serving musicians in both orchestras who had come to the United States and Canada as immigrants, bringing with them their European musical traditions. They knew how music was played in Berlin or Vienna and could therefore hold some sway through their very European style of playing, which was very different from the North American way. But my sheer delight in this circumstance was marred by its depressing historical background, in which a lot of suffering and misery was hidden and which had brought about dramatic changes in the course of some lives. These people had been forced to emigrate because they were persecuted and their lives threatened under the Third Reich. They found protection here in their new home, but they were never completely free of their inner misery and the trauma of having been uprooted.

I remember that I came across a first bassoonist who had played under Arthur Nikisch in Berlin at the age of eighteen. I met old and wise musicians in Los Angeles who had played Beethoven's Seventh Symphony under countless conductors. And there I was, a young man, who was supposed to tell them how things should be done! This was yet another challenge for me.

Orchestras have a definite musical memory, and a conductor must see it as something being offered him by the orchestra. This kind of memory should never be underestimated; instead, it should be utilized as much as possible. Nor should one ever be intimidated by the prospect of conducting an orchestra that has already worked under major figures of the musical world (in the case of my orchestra members this meant Furtwängler, Bruno Walter, Otto Klemperer, and Josef Krips). I took the musicians' vast experience as a challenge, and yet it was also a wonderful chance for me to pick up the thread of this musical history. If a conductor realizes this while he is still young, it helps him get past his uncertainties and doubts, not to mention the mistakes he will inevitably make.

What is needed is a willingness on the conductor's part to take the musicians' experiences and memories seriously and even to incorporate them, no matter how many years it may take. Only then can a conductor attain the necessary maturity, insight, understanding, and feel for the music he wants to perform. These qualities are just as important as all the analytical skills.

In Montreal in 1964 I conducted an opera for the first time, Giacomo Puccini's *Tosca*. Before this I had been purely a concert conductor. Never really having studied any operas with Swarowsky in Vienna except *Figaro*, I was now all on my own, so I really had to work hard. Of course, I had heard and seen *Tosca* umpteen times in Vienna, but it's a long, hard trek from simply listening to actually playing and conducting.

My early experiences in Bombay did not extend to opera, since my father had not been interested in the genre. Once again, opera to me meant Vienna. During my studies there I had heard and seen everything there was to hear and see, and I also had some ideas of my own. At the time I was in the grip of a kind of Karajan complex: I told the director and the stage designer exactly how I pictured each and every detail of the production.

I don't know whether they always found my input helpful, but I can say with certainty that I exerted as much control over the design and execution of my first opera as I could.

I also had wonderful singers: George London sang the part of Scarpia; an American soprano, Ella Lee, was Tosca; and the Canadian tenor Richard Verreau was Cavaradossi. It must not have been too bad, because Rudolf Bing, the legendary director of the Metropolitan Opera in New York, saw this *Tosca* in Montreal and congratulated me very warmly on the production. Afterward Bing invited me to conduct *Aida* at the Met.

So it was that I had my debut at the Met in 1965 with *Aida*. After that I went back there as guest conductor once each year until 1971, either with a new production or with a piece from the repertoire. The new Met was inaugurated under Thomas Schippers at Lincoln Center on September 16, 1966, with Samuel Barber's *Anthony and Cleopatra*. Leontyne Price, who was really made for this opera, was in the cast.

My *Aida* was scheduled for the first evening after the official opening. It was to be the first performance of the season: a remounting of Puccini's *Turandot* in Cecil Beaton's fantastic production. The magnificent cast included Birgit Nilsson, Franco Corelli (who was famous as Calaf), and Teresa Stratas as Liù. I had studied this opera while on a completely unplanned tour of Australia and New Zealand with the Israel Philharmonic Orchestra—but I'll come back to that later.

That same season I conducted the premiere of Marvin David Levy's *Mourning Becomes Electra*. Unfortunately, it was not a success, despite a splendid cast that included Sherrill Milnes, among others, and despite the wonderful director, Michael Cacoyannis, whose film *Zorba the Greek* had been an international hit.

The following year I conducted Giuseppe Verdi's *Il trovatore* for the first time. I have had some very interesting experiences in the course of my work at the Met. This *Trovatore* was staged with a first-rate cast: Leontyne Price, Grace Bumbry, Plácido Domingo, and Sherrill Milnes.

At the Met I always had the chance to work with famous singers—for me an entirely new situation. I didn't quite realize at that time what a wonderful blessing this was for a young and relatively inexperienced conductor like me. Here I had world-class singers and orchestras available to me, and I simply accepted them as if they were just a fact of life. Later in life, while conducting normal repertoire performances in Munich, I often thought about all the superb casts I was exposed to as a young man and all the international stars I had had a chance to work with.

Obviously things were not always this good. For example, I simply did not succeed with *Otello* at the Met. I had enough rehearsals but somehow could not really master the opera. George Szell, a giant of a conductor for whom I had a lot of respect, sat in Bing's box at the premiere and pointed out to him all the details that were wrong. Bing had a huge store of experience at his disposal but was not a musician himself. Having been informed by Szell's criticism, he came to me after the unsuccessful premiere and told me down to the last detail what had been missing from my performance as if he had thought of all this himself.

Incidentally, Rudolf Bing was one of two Austrians—though he always introduced himself as an Englishman, he was in fact Viennese to the core and loved it when I spoke to him in Viennese dialect—who were very influential on the American musical scene. The other was Kurt Herbert Adler in San Francisco, a musician through and through.

After the first successful attempt in Montreal, I suggested staging an opera each year. Beique immediately accepted my suggestion, and I was able gradually to build up my repertoire of operas—*La traviata*, *Aida*, *Otello*, *Carmen*, and *Tristan*.

In 1964 I was invited to conduct Verdi's *La traviata* in Florence for the first time. The artistic director of the Maggio Musicale Fiorentino had invited me as a concert conductor several times over the past few years, but now I was going to have my opera debut in Europe. It was a bold combination: an Indian conductor, trained in Austria and the head of two North American orchestras, conducting an Italian opera in Italy! People were more or less satisfied with me. These collaborations with the orchestra of the Maggio Musicale Fiorentino, undertaken early in my career, were resumed some years later and led to a close musical and personal bond between the orchestra and me.

Even though I was increasingly satisfied with my operatic progress, I was still very far from having an impressive repertoire. To this day I have always conducted almost all Italian operas from memory. Wagner, however, is another matter. Wagner's language is too difficult for me; I simply cannot completely memorize the alliterative texts. This is to some extent connected, no doubt, to the fact that I was not exposed to Wagner's range of expression when I was young. One could argue that I didn't grow up with Italian either, but this language is closer to me in its vocabulary, and it is certainly not as difficult as Wagner's language. In fact, the text of a Puccini opera is as understandable as the Italian normally spoken on the streets.

I have conducted concert performances of operas at one time or another in Los Angeles—*Fidelio*, for example, with Jon Vickers, a renowned Florestan. Some years later I conducted the first act of *Die Walküre* for the first time in my life with him. I have learned a lot from this very experienced singer. On that occasion he gave me some great advice, saying I should not "milk" Wagner's music too much.

Back then there were no operas in Los Angeles; there was no budget for staging them. The only operas staged were guest performances from San Francisco or from the New York City Opera. There was one time when my wish was granted to put on a staged *Salome*, but the staging was just improvised. Musically I was lucky to have an experienced Salome, the excellent soprano Phyllis Curtin.

I consider this work with operas to be more or less my first steps toward the genre. I had absolutely no experience and therefore did not produce anything really remarkable. My real domain was still concerts.

I conducted many works for the first time in Los Angeles. During the first four seasons I never once repeated a piece. At that time I had to learn everything from scratch. On the one hand, it was a huge task, but on the other, it was also a great blessing for my curiosity, since I was free to do whatever I liked.

I have already mentioned that my entire basic musical training and understanding were influenced by Vienna. I carried within me a very specific, Viennese sound ideal. Wherever I went, I had a vision of the so-called Viennese sound. Whether I always succeeded during these first few years in living up to my own standards, though, is an open question.

In order to bring the orchestra as close to this ideal as possible, I tried to import some instrumental elements from Vienna to America. Sometimes I would play records of the Vienna Philharmonic for certain individual musicians in Los Angeles to try and make them understand what I expected of them. Initially some of the musicians were deeply insulted by this approach, but in time they all understood me.

I also brought along trumpets from Vienna—German, or rather Austrian, trumpets, which are completely different from American instruments. In fact, I was the first conductor to introduce these trumpets into North American orchestras. The Austrian trumpet has a much warmer sound than does its American counterpart, which is rather piercing. The legendary Helmut Wobisch, trumpeter of the Vienna Philharmonic, gave me his mouthpiece, and I had it reproduced in Los Angeles so that I could get exactly the sound that I wanted. I am grateful that my colleagues in Los Angeles were willing to try this new experiment. They became so adept that they played these new instruments on our recording of Bruckner's Eighth symphony.

Whether a warmer tone is preferable naturally depends to a great extent on the piece, but it is always preferable for Central European classical music. Viennese trumpets can be played loud without any loss of that warmth. The mouthpiece and breathing technique are equally important for the sound. Since the technique is so fundamentally different, the musicians get a doubling fee when they play Viennese trumpets. Musicians in my other orchestras, such as the Israel Philharmonic Orchestra, are also required to use these instruments.

There should be no coarseness at the end of a Bruckner symphony or in Brahms. The brass should blend smoothly with the orchestral sound, to which trumpets are very important. When a Viennese symphony, whether by Haydn or Mahler, nears its climax, it is the trumpets that provide the last jubilant flourish.

In the case of the double bass, a distinction is still made between German and French bows. The French bow is an oversized cello bow and is used in Italy and France as well as in the United States. The resulting sound differs fundamentally from that produced with a German bow. The French bow is heavier, so the player uses less pressure, which in turn makes the sound correspondingly lighter. It is very good for many French pieces, but in my opinion it is not suited to Brahms, Bruckner, or Mahler. The German bow is played with greater force, and the player needs much more strength to manage it. The two bows are also shaped differently and thus have to be held in different ways. The German bow is gripped underhand, whereas the French bow is held between the fingers and played overhand. The Scherzo of Beethoven's Fifth Symphony or the beginning of *Die Walküre*, with its eight basses, can only be played authentically with the German bow, in my opinion. It was and still is common for German orchestras to use it exclusively.

I recommended the German bow to the musicians in Los Angeles. Understandably, it was difficult for some of them to make the change, and I had to settle for a compromise.

I also introduced the Viennese clarinet in Los Angeles. My American clarinetist, Michelle Zukowsky, had to entirely change her style of playing, since here too the Austrian system is completely different. She still plays on this instrument, with stellar results.

I even tried to teach the string musicians to mellow their playing and produce a more chamber music–like sound. This is possible only if the musicians listen to each others' playing very carefully and rehearse a lot. In Los Angeles I tried to prepare the musicians for each performance by getting them to play the selected program as often as possible. A Schubert symphony had to be played like a quartet. For this reason I have always recommended that orchestral musicians play as much chamber music as possible.

My engagement with the Israel Philharmonic Orchestra came, in addition to my existing workload, in the mid-1960s. I had first worked with them in 1961, when I substituted for Eugene Ormandy, and was subsequently invited as a guest conductor in 1963. In 1966 I went on a tour of Australia and New Zealand with the orchestra—once again because of a cancellation, this time by Carlo Maria Giulini.

Here I should again mention all my early career successes that I owed to cancellations. For a no-name conductor, substituting for a famous colleague does not necessarily lead directly to anything except, of course, a wonderful chance to work with a good orchestra. It is always a tremendous challenge, though, and sometimes it can go horribly wrong. If the performance flops, the opportunity is gone for good, and the conductor will never be asked to work with that particular orchestra again. Everything has to be just perfect when a young conductor steps into a well-known colleague's shoes. The musical communication has to flow smoothly, and the orchestra must be convinced of the conductor's artistic intent. In short, they have to have good chemistry if anything worthwhile is to come out of it. The orchestra must also want to work with the conductor again; otherwise all his efforts will have been in vain.

There was excellent chemistry between the Israel Philharmonic Orchestra and me just about from the very beginning. We liked each other almost immediately. Later political developments, particularly the Six-Day War in 1967, strengthened my bond to the country and its people, and I went to Israel several times as a guest conductor. In 1969 I became music director of the orchestra, and finally, in 1981, I was appointed music director for life. But I'll talk about all this in more detail in another chapter.

It has often been alleged that I went to Los Angeles because of the glamour associated with the city or because I was attracted by the international flair of the glossy world of cinema. This is utter nonsense. The strange circumstances of my appointment there and the fact that Georg Solti was originally supposed to direct the Los Angeles Philharmonic contradict this allegation, as should the list of all the famous guest conductors who were there before me.

I have always looked upon my time in Los Angeles as one of intensive learning. Of course I also had the pleasure of meeting actors, directors, filmmakers, singers, and jazz musicians—in short, the whole variety in the cosmos of geniuses and lunatics that Hollywood represents. I was a young single man, even though I felt a deep sense of commitment toward my children, who lived with their mother in Montreal. It was always with a sense of great joy that I tried to meet my parental responsibilities toward them.

I love my children deeply. We always used to spend the summers together. Sometimes we went to Israel on vacation. After I married Nancy we went on more adventurous trips—hiking in Kashmir or going on safari to Africa. Once we even spent two weeks in the Amazon basin.

When I became director of the orchestra in Los Angeles, the city was still a cultural desert. This also meant that the spaces available to the orchestra were extremely limited. Just as in Montreal, there were hardly any real music venues in Los Angeles where the acoustics came up to ordinary European standards and where serious music could be performed. The auditorium in Los Angeles where we first performed was part of a Baptist church, and it was simply terrible. Renowned conductors such as Otto Klemperer, Eduard van Beinum, and Bruno Walter had also conducted in this less than mediocre hall, where I spent two seasons with the orchestra.

However, it was much easier in Los Angeles than in Montreal to mobilize people and raise funds for such a huge project as a new concert hall. This too was Los Angeles: movie stars, popular singers, Hollywood moguls such as Walt Disney, and in fact a whole range of powerful and influential people were willing to be roped in for a worthy goal and to support a good cause.

Even today there is a sharp difference where such initiatives are concerned between the cooperative and privately funded orchestras in the United States (and also Israel) and the state-subsidized orchestras in Europe, particularly Germany. Undeniably, the situation there needs to be rethought. Greater involvement on the part of the people is necessary if the high standards to which audiences have become accustomed are to be maintained. Actually, I welcome this development. People value a major achievement much more highly if their own efforts go into it than if it is subsidized by a higher authority and served up to the public in bite-sized morsels.

Thanks to the monumental zeal of Dorothy Chandler and her indefatigable fund-raising, promoting, and planning, the Music Center in Los Angeles was completed and inaugurated in 1964, finally giving the orchestra a suitable setting for their performances. Chandler, who was married to the publisher of the *Los Angeles Times*, played a crucial role in Los Angeles's cultural life. She pulled a lot of strings and accomplished a great deal in the face of tremendous opposition. The great city of Los Angeles profits from her achievements to this very day. Shortly before the Music Center was inaugurated, work on a new concert hall was completed in New York. However, it was very soon acknowledged to be an acoustic catastrophe. That made Los Angelenos even more nervous about the reaction to their new auditorium. It was known that the dreaded New York critics would attend the premiere, and there was a strong possibility that envy might lead them to find fault with the new hall.

The inaugural concert, which was to feature a festive program, was the first time I performed with Jascha Heifetz. It was his recordings that had initially exposed me to the violin, so for me it was frankly thrilling to have him as a soloist. After the intermission he played the Beethoven Violin Concerto. Rehearsals with him had not gone altogether smoothly. He had his own ideas about tempi, ideas I didn't always share. As a result, in the first movement, Heifetz began playing during the four bars when the orchestra plays alone, before the soloist comes in again, because he found my tempo too slow. "My four bars are already over!" he explained. He also expressly requested that I not conduct from memory.

In addition to this very remarkable concerto, I had picked a work by an American composer, Richard Strauss's *Festfanfare*, and Ottorino Respighi's *Feste romane*—truly a festive program, with its rich tapestry of sound, intend to express everyone's jubilation over the orchestra's new home. Today this hall, now just a part of the Music Center complex, is called the Dorothy Chandler Pavilion. I must emphasize that in all those years, this obviously very influential woman never once tried to impose her musical ideas or personal tastes on me.

At the opening I just gave one short statement: "We like the acoustics." My intent with this sentence was to forestall any possible criticism. Incidentally, the acoustics were very good, far better than those of the new hall in New York.

I took a sabbatical in 1967, and with this my engagement in Montreal ended. The orchestra had found my successor in Rafael Frühbeck de Burgos. Montreal had been my first appointment as the head of an orchestra. It did me a lot of good, and I still look back upon my time there with gratitude.

At the opening of Expo 67 I brought together my two orchestras, the Los Angeles Philharmonic and the Montreal Symphony Orchestra, for the first time. This was also my first tour with the Los Angeles Philharmonic. The two orchestras first performed individually under my direction, and then, after the intermission, they played Hector Berlioz's *Symphonie fantastique* together. I have always believed that Berlioz would have approved of this, since he always imagined exaggeratedly large orchestras that aren't normally found in the music industry.

In later years I brought some more orchestras together, but they were always orchestras I knew well. I find such experiments interesting, but they should never be done purely for show. Only very rarely have I deviated from this principle.

The tour with the Los Angeles Philharmonic lasted nine weeks. We went all around the world and had a terrific time with each other, though I am convinced that some of the spouses are still upset with me because we were away for so long.

One of the stops in this tour was Vienna. My Vienna! It was the city in which I had my roots, at least in some respects, the city that had put its indelible stamp on me and given me everything. I performed Bruckner's Seventh Symphony in the Musikverein Auditorium with my American orchestra. I wanted to display what I had achieved with the Los Angeles Philharmonic, to show what a tremendous improvement in sound I had accomplished with them. I felt a bit like a student wanting to demonstrate to his teachers that he had taken to heart everything they had taught him.

Our tour took us to Europe and Asia, where we performed in large and small halls for audiences with different levels of interest. The U.S. State Department sponsored the whole tour, which was called, appropriately, the State Department Tour. We played a concert in Tehran on the occasion of Shah Mohammad Reza Pahlavi's imperial coronation and another in Cyprus for Archbishop Makarios. We also held concerts in Greece, at that time still a monarchy under King Constantine; in India; in Hong Kong; and in Sarajevo, where the small planes in which we were traveling had to fly over the runway a couple of times before the sheep cleared the landing strip. The young André Watts came along with us as a soloist. He played Liszt, Brahms, and the American composer Edward MacDowell, who had studied with Debussy and in Germany as well. It was not unusual for American orchestras to be sent all around the world on what one might call official missions to demonstrate what *else* Americans were capable of. This project was discontinued in 1976.

But the crowning moments for me were our concerts in India. This was the first of what turned out to be many trips to my native country, taken every few years with different orchestras. It was a dream come true when we landed at Santa Cruz airport in Bombay. I felt at home immediately. When I wasn't being hounded by the press or a legion of supposed relatives, I went for long walks by myself, drinking in the atmosphere I remembered so well from my youth. I visited my former home, which made me feel very nostalgic, especially since my mother had flown in from Los Angeles. Only my father was missing. I think he had felt so strongly about leaving India that he thought going back would just be too emotionally overwhelming for him. (It was also many years before my brother could bring himself to go back home.) The visit was all the more joyful because it coincided with the annual Hindu festival of Diwali. We could hear the traditional firecrackers all through Mahler's First Symphony. Everyone had a great time, and they especially enjoyed all the Indian food.

I had, and still have, an inclination to experiment that is occasionally misinterpreted. Sometimes it is even perceived as a joke, something not to be taken seriously. This I consider extremely unfair and in fact very shortsighted as well. One can very well prove the seriousness of music by pointing out its funny side, its entertaining aspect, the pure delight in beauty and the joy inherent in it.

In 1970 the now legendary Ernest Fleischmann took over as managing director of the Los Angeles Philharmonic. He was as passionate about experimentation as I, and during our endless discussions we came up with various quasi-revolutionary program concepts. One was a twelve-hour Beethoven marathon to celebrate the bicentennial of the composer's birth. Then there was the infamous "Star Wars" concert at the Hollywood Bowl, which was originally intended for a children's audience. One such experiment led to a crossover concert on NBC television, a mixture of rock and classical music, which was not at all common in those days. The show featured a motley assortment of groups and orchestras. Some of the bands, such as the Who and Santana, went on to become internationally famous, but at the time they were still at the beginning of their career.

We, the Los Angeles Philharmonic, had to hold our own against an impressive spectrum of artists representing totally different notions of music. The orchestra performed one of J. S. Bach's Brandenburg concertos, Stravinsky's *Rite of Spring*, Lalo's *Symphonie espagnole* (with Pinchas Zukerman), and Carl Orff's *Carmina Burana*. We played one piece after the other, always alternating between rock and classical music. All in all, it was an interesting mix. Our participation in this huge event met with a great deal of disapproval in some quarters. But I believe that even something like this can serve the cause of musical education and familiarize people with all kinds of music. And perhaps that will create a demand for more.

The Beethoven marathon was a minor sensation and a resounding success, and we had a lot of fun. Today similar marathons are organized everywhere.

I traveled again with the orchestra in 1976, this time through the whole of Eastern Europe, again at the instigation of the State Department. Again we were on a cultural diplomatic mission, trying to show the whole world that the United States represented more than the world of high tech, fast food, and cars. This was a special agenda, intended to coincide with the U.S. bicentennial celebration.

One of the stops on our tour was the Soviet Union. A Russian government official made a special trip to Los Angeles to discuss all the details with us. Even clearing all the logistics took a long time and a lot of effort. By then I had long been engaged in Israel, to which Soviet Jews had been allowed to immigrate more or less unrestricted since 1971. I could not stop myself from heartily congratulating the official, who constantly affected an air of importance, and thanking him for his country's generosity, because of which the orchestra in Israel had acquired so many excellent musicians. I could not have addressed myself to a more fitting man. He pretended not to understand what I meant, suddenly pleading communication problems and refusing to talk to me anymore. The next day, furious, he called up the director, Ernest Fleischmann, and declared that the orchestra could perform but certainly not with this conductor, this Mehta. Fleischmann answered coolly that in that case unfortunately nobody would be able to come. So the USSR part of the tour was canceled. Later I learned that this official had been a prominent KGB man.

~~~~~

Los Angeles and Israel—much farther apart than Montreal and Los Angeles—increasingly became the reference points of my life. Between them were engagements in Berlin and Vienna that had become a tradition. I conducted at the Metropolitan Opera in New York until 1971, was invited to Salzburg every year, and went on a tour with the Los Angeles Philharmonic. I could do what I loved most: make music, live with music, and perhaps also bring joy to people. I could bring people together and divert them from their cares and their hostilities for at least two hours.

It was important for me at that time to present not only classical and late-romantic music to the Los Angeles audience, but also twentieth-century repertoire. This is still one of my main musical concerns. I have always wanted to make the music of the Second Viennese School as accessible as that of contemporary American composers. My attitude has not always been understood, and it seems to me remarkable that some people have interpreted my attitude as some kind of joke or viewed it as a trivialization of the repertoire. I couldn't understand it back then, and it's a perspective that even now I just do not want to deal with.

In Los Angeles, for the benefit of the audience, I began to provide commentary on largely unknown pieces before concerts on which they were programmed. In my opinion this is often essential, particularly at first performances or for completely unknown works. It can also contribute to a better understanding of familiar works. I do not formulate my introductory remarks according to any specific analytical concept. Rather, I try to keep it as uncomplicated as possible so that the audience can have better access to the music they are about to hear.

One of my earliest attempts to explain a piece of music came when I presented Schoenberg's Variations for Orchestra, in my opinion one of the most difficult pieces ever composed. Schoenberg based this work on his highly developed twelve-tone technique. The concept for the variations is a strictly classical one; the only difference is that it uses the twelve-tone system. It was difficult even for the orchestra to grasp this piece, and I had to discuss everything with the musicians first. Schoenberg himself had written to Furtwängler before the premiere saying that he didn't consider the work "excessively difficult when played as an ensemble," but the "individual parts," on the other hand, were "mainly very difficult, so that the quality of the performance depended on how well the individual parts were performed."

I was not aware that Stravinsky was in the audience that day. He had started using with the twelve-tone technique quite late in his compositional career—in his last creative phase. But then he became a devoted follower of Schoenberg and Webern. I really regret that I couldn't greet him and had no opportunity to get in touch with him later either. Stravinsky's passion for Schoenberg and Webern developed under the influence of Robert Craft, who became Stravinsky's colleague and closest adviser in Los Angeles.

Unfortunately, Craft and I had little to no contact. He was even able to set Stravinsky against me, so that there was never any kind of personal or musical exchange between us. I have always been passionate about playing Stravinsky's works, and in 1980 I organized a Stravinsky evening on the occasion of his eightieth birthday. But I was not generous enough to overlook some misunderstandings that arose between us or to fulfill some of his personal requests. I still regret that today. I am convinced that had I had an advisor such as Ernest Fleischmann at my side, this painful situation with Stravinsky would never have developed.

All my life I had a deep, loving, and close relationship with my parents. They gave me so much and were always ready to economize so that Zarin and I could have a good education and fully develop our potential. Moreover, our shared love of music created a very special relationship between my father and me. For me he was and remains a model of willpower, energy, and stamina. Respect for parents, family cohesion, and a strong faith in the security that results are generally a matter of course for us Indians. We depend on each other and help each other wherever we might be on this planet. I am very thankful that my parents were granted a long life. My father died in 2002 at the age of ninety-four, and my mother died three years later, shortly before her ninety-seventh birthday.

My parents had moved to the United States at around the same time I began working in North America. They lived in Philadelphia, where my father taught highly gifted students at the New School of Music and also played in a quartet. Hardly anyone could have been as good as he at inculcating an interest and enthusiasm for music in young people, at training them carefully and guiding them, and at paving their way to a career in music. Because of his experience in chamber music as well as orchestras and conducting, he had a comprehensive understanding of music and a wide range as a musician.

Shortly after I began working in Los Angeles, I finally had a chance to do something for my father. I recommended him for the position of director of the American Youth Symphony, a renowned artistic institution run by Maestro Merenbloom, who had just announced his retirement. The mandatory auditions and tests went off perfectly, and my father was entrusted with this wonderful job. My father was engaged at the same time by UCLA as a violin teacher, and he also took over the helm of the university orchestra. Now, after being separated for so many years, I was able to have my parents living near me again. In fact, they both lived in Los Angeles until their deaths.

One of my main concerns has always been to bring music closer to children and young people, to interest those who are truly gifted in music at a young enough age, and above all to give them a chance to learn and get good training. In the course of my career as a conductor I have been able to realize these goals in different ways, some more successfully than others. But I never want to forget the importance of early exposure to music and how formative it can be. I have experienced it personally in the most exquisite way.

In Los Angeles I started a program that allowed gifted children from economically disadvantaged backgrounds to take lessons from orchestra musicians for the fee of one dollar. The funds for this program, called the Minority Training Program, were authorized by the administrative board, since it was required to make up the remainder of the musicians' lesson fees. Primarily intended to benefit African Americans and Hispanics who would not otherwise have been able to afford a good musical education, the program met with an enthusiastic response. In addition, the orchestra and I played once a year with the choir of a church in Watts, an economically underdeveloped Los Angeles neighborhood. For these occasions I enlisted the talented composer Joe Westmoreland to write music for choir and orchestra, which we performed enthusiastically. He was also appointed director of the Minority Training Program. My aim was to show solidarity with people who, for a variety of reasons, were not in a position to come to the concert halls. I know that such programs can only represent the proverbial drop in the bucket, but I still think they are a good idea. The program was discontinued soon after I left for New York in 1978.

The musical education of young people, whatever their social and economic backgrounds, is of great interest to me. I like to engage personally with children and youth. I encourage them where necessary, give them my advice when it is asked for, and warn them against overinflated expectations. One such youngster was Gil Shaham, a violinist who played with the Israel Philharmonic Orchestra before he had reached his teens—first at children's concerts and later on tours, where we used him sparingly on a few occasions so as not to exploit him in any way that might harm his future development.

During a 2005 tour of South America with the Israel Philharmonic Orchestra I attended a concert of young people who were performing in one of São Paulo's *favelas*. It was heartwarming to see the passion and dedication these young players brought with them. Often they have to overcome enormous opposition and terrible external circumstances. I met a young double bass player on this tour who impressed me so much with his musicality and his talent that I immediately arranged to have him placed in a training program in Israel so that he could attend the Buchmann-Mehta School.

These small, seemingly unspectacular achievements give me great joy, and I find them well worth the investment of my time.

5

NANCY

A Love Story

I n this book I am giving a synopsis of my private and my musical life. It is a story of the circumstances under which I grew up, of my family, of musical engagements and priorities, and of the sense of fulfillment I derive from my profession. Some aspects of it are not important enough to discuss in detail, while there are others for which this space is not enough.

But there is one event that I have to chronicle in greater detail, something that helped shape my life even though it was not directly connected to my musical career. This was my meeting Nancy Kovack in 1968. We have been married since 1969, and for four decades now she has been my irreplaceable companion, friend, and partner. Nancy and I share an unshakeable, immutable relationship in which she has often had to summon up great forbearance and understanding, as well as patience and stamina.

At this point in my story I would like to yield the floor to her and let her describe how and under what circumstances we met. Luckily for me, she did not persist in her initial resistance to meeting me. But I'll let her speak.

~

The sweetness of the life I led in the small Michigan town in which I was born gave my later years a pervasive calm and quietude. I was an only child, and flamboyant imagination filled my days. My desires were prayers of a sort that were answered later in life. My father, of Czechoslovakian ancestry, was the first generation of his family to be born in America, and my mother sailed as a babe in arms from the country of her birth, Poland. My family belongs to various ethnicities ruled by the Hapsburg Empire in the nineteenth century—Poland and Czechoslovakia, but also Ukraine and Hungary.

My mother dearly missed the artistic opportunities she had to leave behind when she settled in Michigan. New York afforded her the weekly opera and symphonic works she so loved, and she lamented repeatedly that her child had no access to these sources of inspiration. Therefore, she insisted that I avail myself of the Saturday broadcasts of the New York Metropolitan Opera. The problem was that I, with my dog, could always be found in an apple tree several acres away reading a book.

She couldn't see me, but I could hear her calling me. Thus was thrust upon me my first moral decision: whether to pretend I didn't hear or to respond and suffer through the opera.

I chose the latter. It interests me to consider the prayerful thought of a mother for her child. She never learned that I now listen to either operas or symphonic works every other evening, and that I love them. Is this something a seven-year-old could have foreseen?

Years later I entered the University of Michigan at fifteen, then graduated on a scholarship just after I turned nineteen.

The following day a classmate's wedding drew me to New York. The day after the wedding I heard the words "cattle call" for the first time and found out what they meant when I went to an audition with 1,475 other girls. I was one of ten chosen from this group and the only one who didn't already know Jackie Gleason. His television show initiated me into a business I had never considered and for which I was not professionally prepared. However, after live TV drama and multiple other shows, my agent insisted I do Broadway. This, like the opera, was something I was not at all interested in, but it led to my signing a contract with Columbia Pictures.

In the early 1960s I went to Italy to do a film in Capo di Palinuro. It was extremely remote (we arrived by donkey) and somewhat primitive. To entertain myself, I read old magazines that happened to have a number of articles on Iran. I became fascinated with that country. One couldn't read about it back home in the United States. Once a rare essay appeared, and I wrote the Iranian Embassy in Washington to ask about its accuracy. The reply totally negated every observation in the article.

Financially, I couldn't afford to leave my apartment and live in Iran, but believed that if one expected an idea to materialize, one should proceed as though it would. So I enrolled in a UCLA language course to learn Farsi, the language of the Iranians. Having made multiple unproductive attempts to visit the country that had so obsessed me, I finally released my striving to leave the matter in God's hands. One day soon after that, I received a call from someone I had never heard of in Iran inviting me to do a film in Tehran. Gleefully, I asked my agents, the William Morris Agency, to draw up a contract, which they reluctantly did.

The character I was asked to play was the daughter of an English mother and Iranian father. This fitted my American-accented Farsi perfectly, since the film was shot in that language. I was deliriously happy to venture to these wilder shores, ecstatic to be introduced to a new culture which was so rich and artistically beautiful, and to immerse myself gently into Islamic culture.

The people who took me in embraced me fully. Never had I arrived at a dinner party only to have every woman in the room come up and kiss me. All of them were highly educated and magnificently arrayed, and tremendous decorum always prevailed.

At one point I was invited by the American Embassy in Afghanistan to come to a Thanksgiving dinner. On the plane I read a *Time* magazine, on the cover of which was someone named Zubin Mehta. Hmmm, thought I—how did I miss him in California? By the time I reached Kabul, though, I was so repelled by the character portrayed in the article that I knew I could never have any interest in him.

During this time I returned to the United States once a year for tax reasons, always taking a different route. Once I traveled east, through Afghanistan, India, Cambodia, Thailand, and Japan. The next time I went west, through Iraq, Yemen, Israel, Turkey, and finally Uzbekistan, to enter into Russia through a port that was to be closed for entry thereafter. After that I purchased a ticket for the first passenger ship to sail for Antarctica.

In 1968 friends Denise and Vincent Minnelli invited me to the opening of the Philharmonic season in Los Angeles. I was thrilled to go until Denise said she would like to introduce me to Zubin Mehta at dinner.

Explaining how genuinely I would love to enjoy the opening, I added I could not come because I didn't want to meet Mr. Mehta. At this time in my life I was "cleaning up" my social life. I had been dining every night with someone different. Now I decided that if I didn't think he had the qualities I might want in a husband, I was being dishonest, wasting both his time and mine. I would graciously thank the caller for thinking of me but preferred really to be alone.

Denise called again in a few weeks inviting me to another party. It would be very informal—we would all just be sitting around on the floor and eating pasta. Happy to be asked to join in such simple pleasures, I thanked her, after which she said: "And you could meet Zubin here." Sadly, I told her I could not accept. "You're a fool," she said, and hung up the telephone.

A month later she phoned again: "Please, please come sit with Vincent, you're the only one he loves to talk with. I am giving a party upstairs at The Bistro." "Oh, I'd love to come," said I, since I in return adored talking with Vincent.

The room was very dim, illuminated only by candles. At Vincent's table I talked first to him and then to the man on my left, at which point I heard a voice announce decisively: "Tehran was magnificent at the coronation." Who is this latter-day visionary, I thought. I had said that a month ago in Los Angeles and everyone had ignored me, totally uninterested.

I turned. It was Zubin. Denise had won.

He referred to the Cufic writing around the mosques. We disagreed. He left for the airport in the middle of the meal.

Some weeks later he called from another country and I opened: "And furthermore, the Cufic writing. . . ." Zubin asked if we could meet in two weeks between 4:00 and 5:00 P.M. And this type of conversation has gone on between us now for forty years.

That is how it was, and that is how it is still. Perhaps because our lives are so complex, our schedules so completely filled, we've really only been married twenty years!

But it has been a grand journey, and we stand in awe of it continually. We laugh and laugh. We are continually amazed at our way in the world and how it touches us. We feel enwrapped in beauty, perhaps because we are constantly alert to it. It is a richness which is a gift from outside ourselves for which we express gratitude endlessly.

And some aura of love permeates our being, in that it underlies our every waking moment. A feeling that we are both loved, cared for, watched over, and that this embrace precedes us wherever we go and is the basis for whatever happens to us. It is omnipresent.

I felt some significance in his asking me not to use my ticket to Antarctica. Softly, he said we might do it together one day. And in fact we did.

On July 19, 1969, the first day Zubin had free in his schedule, we were married—once in a Christian church, and thereafter, at a precisely calculated moment at sunset, again in a Parsi ceremony. I do not recommend two weddings in one day!

I feel strongly, and always say when I am asked, that our marriage was divinely authorized.

I didn't seek it, didn't program it, surely never entertained the idea. But the question always presented itself: was I drawn to Iran and its culture because I needed to be prepared to better understand this Asian man, or was I drawn to Zubin because by then I understood so much of his culture?

I shall never know the answer.

People ask if I'm a musician, and I respond that I'm here to bring balance off the podium. I swim in the luxury of glorious music but don't involve myself in the business of it, and I really don't love hearing about it over dinner, if anyone's listening.

One of the richest revelations I've had, one that truly freed me, was that one can't work out the life of another. The no-free-lunch adage applies. We each pay for our own lives. This understanding left me free to fly forward with Zubin, shoulder to shoulder, smiling all the way.

It takes uninterrupted attention to protect our personal time. Basically, it's difficult to describe a life determined by other people. I think the lives of politicians come closest to this kind of scheduling.

I have not been reluctant to note that the things I fought hardest against, music and Zubin Mehta, have ultimately brought me the greatest joy.

All marriages embody change, but ours, I believe, has seen profound metamorphosis. These monumental changes have always brought great inspiration to my life, and experiencing them steadies one with ever-present hope. Maybe that's what life is—expectation. Remember that old commercial, "Getting there is half the fun"? Or perhaps the lesson to take away from our life together is "Faith is the evidence of things unseen."

Zubin has enriched my life enormously, as I hope I have his, and my profound love embraces him.

⌒⌐

At this point I want to say something fundamental about my personal life, something I consider worth sharing. Most of all I would like to talk about my two children from my first marriage, my daughter Zarina and my son Mervon, who have already given me grandchildren. Zarina lives in Canada. She is a nurse's aide, caring for the sick in a completely self-sacrificing way, and has two children, Daniel and Shenaya. Mervon started out as an actor—a good one, I thought. After years of appearing off-Broadway in New York; at the Canadian Shakespeare Festival at Stratford, Ontario; and in various successful freelance opportunities, he accepted a post in management at the Ravinia Festival in Chicago at the invitation of my brother before moving to Philadelphia with his wife, Carey, where he is now the vice president of programming at the Kimmel Center for the Performing Arts. Our youngest grandchild, Zed, was born to them in 2003. Both my children are workaholics in the true Mehta tradition.

I have a very good relationship with my children and feel very close to them despite the innumerable commitments that make my life so tumultuous. For this, again, I have to compliment my wife. Nancy accepted my children from my first marriage completely and was always there for them whenever they needed her.

I also want to talk about my two children born outside of marriage. There has been quite a lot of gossip on this topic. Much has been said on condition of anonymity, quoting supposedly reliable sources. My daughter Alexandra Payne, who lives in Los Angeles, was born in 1967 from a relationship that I had between my two marriages, and she already has three children. I see them all whenever I am in Los Angeles. Nancy has cared for Alexandra even from a distance with sympathy and understanding.

Zarina, Alexandra, and Nancy all share a good relationship—a situation that makes me very happy.

However, I deeply offended my wife and hurt her unendingly when another son, Ori, was born to me in Israel in 1990 after a brief affair. It must certainly have been dreadful for Nancy to find out about it, first from me and then from the newspapers, and I know that I inflicted a lot of pain on her. I can hardly thank her enough for bearing it and not leaving me, hurt and humiliated. The fact that she did not leave helped me a lot in dealing with my mistake and the difficulties that followed from it.

Ori grew up with a wonderful family, the Zislings, in a kibbutz in the north of Israel. As a young child he only spoke Hebrew, a language that I have not learned even after working in Israel for so many years. Now he speaks very good English, so we can talk to each other perfectly. He started his army service in 2008.

Another wonderful human being entered our lives quite by chance when a young lady helped Nancy to do inventory at one of our homes in California and brought along her little niece, Darla. Nancy and this wonderful child of eleven took to each other immediately, and with my full blessing Nancy started a concerted education program for her. This was almost twenty years ago. Darla is a working mother today, as close to Nancy and me as ever, with two wonderful children, Juaan and Makayla. They live very near to us in Los Angeles and are a constant source of joy to me and my dearest wife.

One more member or our family that we are all very fond of and close to is our sister Julie, who lives with her husband, Simon Thorensen, and daughter, Allegra, in New York. She is my father's child from his period in New York, and he was in touch with her until the very end.

6

ANOTHER LOVE STORY

The Israel Philharmonic Orchestra

I was invited back by the Israel Philharmonic Orchestra two years after my first stint with them in 1961. I chose an unusual program that was not in their repertoire: Anton Webern's Six Pieces for Orchestra and Bruckner's Ninth Symphony. Webern was not played very often anywhere back then, and not at all in Israel. This was also true of Bruckner, despite the country's many emigrants from Austria and Poland, for the most highly regarded conductors in Israel in those days—Koussevitzky, Paul Kletzki, Leonard Bernstein, even Charles Münch—only rarely performed any of his work. (On the other hand, there is a famous recording of Mahler's Ninth Symphony with Kletzki and the Israel Philharmonic Orchestra.) Apparently this program did not faze the musicians, for I continued to receive invitations from them. The next one came in 1965, and I accepted it with the greatest pleasure.

In those days I was deeply apolitical and didn't really know anything about Israel's extraordinary geopolitical situation. During my years in Vienna I had hardly met any Jews. The only one I knew had been in my school in Mumbai. They were from Iraq, and I couldn't really talk to them since they spoke Arabic. I only gradually understood, through reports and narratives, what the Holocaust must have meant to those who escaped to Palestine.

The Israel Philharmonic Orchestra, originally called the Palestine Philharmonic Orchestra, was founded in 1936 by the great Polish violinist Bronisław Huberman. Foreseeing more clearly than most the disaster the National Socialists were about to unleash upon the Jews, Huberman convinced approximately seventy-five musicians to emigrate. The conductor of the first concert of this orchestra, on December 26, 1936, in Tel Aviv, was none other than Arturo Toscanini.

My path crossed the great Toscanini's many times, though only spiritually. I was born on April 29, 1936, the day Toscanini conducted his last concert with the New York Philharmonic—the same orchestra whose head I became a good forty years later. And the year I was born Toscanini also conducted the other orchestra with which I have been connected for decades and which appointed me director for life—the Israel Philharmonic Orchestra.

The years following that first concert were difficult and full of privation for the musicians, as one can well imagine. It was a time of political conflict, turmoil, the Holocaust, and World War II.

When the state of Israel came into being in 1948, the orchestra was renamed. It was now called the Israel Philharmonic Orchestra, IPO for short, and formed an integral component of Israeli life from the very moment the state was founded. The orchestra played the national anthem, "Hatikvah," on May 14, 1948, in the museum of Tel Aviv. In November of the same year a very young Leonard Bernstein conducted a moving concert before five thousand soldiers sitting on the hills in the desert of Beersheba.

In the following years many famous conductors came to conduct the orchestra in Israel—Celibidache and Fricsay, Giulini and Markevitch, Mitropoulos and Kubelik, Krips and Koussevitzky, and of course the great Leonard Bernstein. Later on wonderful colleagues of my generation—Daniel Barenboim, Lorin Maazel, Claudio Abbado—have often come to Israel, although not as often as I would have liked. The newest member of our musical family is Gustavo Dudamel, whom we all adore. Acclaimed soloists—Rubinstein, Heifetz, Arrau, Piatigorsky—were also regular favorites. And then there was Isaac Stern, one of the orchestra's greatest friends, whose spirit was tremendously influential in the development not only of the orchestra, but of young Israeli talent. It is very important to note that almost none of these artists ever took any remuneration for their work in Israel. The list of artists to whom we are indebted for their services could go on and on. It is so wonderful when great souls give of themselves to the orchestra and benefit a country so in need of this cultural infusion, whose entire sixty years of existence have been mired in terror and crisis. To this day the orchestra has to struggle really hard to survive financially and therefore cannot afford to pay lucrative fees.

At the end of the 1950s the orchestra finally got its own auditorium in Tel Aviv thanks to the generous support of the Philadelphia arts patron Frederic R. Mann. The Mann Auditorium is still the home of these excellent musicians.

In the years after my debut at the Salzburg Festival in 1962 I was regularly invited to conduct concerts there. In 1965 I was asked to conduct an opera, Mozart's *The Abduction from the Seraglio*. Although back in 1962 Herbert von Karajan had objected to my being invited to the festival, he now telephoned me himself and asked me to take over the new production of Mozart's opera. Paradoxically, in 1962 he had asked me to come to conduct for him at the Vienna State Opera. At the time I had refused. I had to; I had not yet conducted any opera, and to do so there would certainly have been a disaster. Although Karajan had been very enthusiastic and even promised to take me under his wing, I explained to him at the time that I wanted to become thoroughly familiar with this genre before trusting myself to undertake such a responsibility.

Three years later I had made my first few forays into the field of opera, and it was growing on me. Of course, my repertoire was still very small, and only gradually was I able to expand it. So far I had never performed a Mozart opera, so I was very pleased to receive the invitation to conduct the *Abduction*.

That summer in Salzburg was notable for me in a couple of respects. I did a concert with the Vienna Philharmonic, with Daniel Barenboim as the soloist. He played Mozart's Piano Concerto in C Minor, K. 491, and I conducted Brahms's Second Symphony. And then came my very first Mozart opera, a fantastic production by Giorgio Strehler that stayed in the repertoire for years, with Reri Grist as Blonde, Anneliese Rothenberger as Konstanze, and Fritz Wunderlich as Belmonte. Michael Heltau, the famous actor at Vienna's Burgtheater, the former Imperial Court Theater, had the speaking role of Bassa. After the first performance Karajan complimented me on my composure and said that he agreed with my tempi. Naturally I felt pleased to receive praise from an older, more experienced colleague. But the day after the premiere, I met George Szell. He had always been very critical and in all matters musical was unyielding and unerring. Not only did he not compliment me, he completely shattered me, saying that he had not liked my performance at all. Yet I continued to conduct this opera for the next six or seven seasons.

After the 1969 performances I intended to prepare myself thoroughly for *Turandot*, which I was supposed to conduct the day after the official opening of the new Met in New York. Once again something completely unexpected happened. I received a frantic telegram from Israel saying that Carlo Maria Giulini, one of the two conductors for the Israel Philharmonic Orchestra's upcoming tour of Australia and New Zealand, unfortunately had to cancel due to illness and asking if I could perhaps take over. The other conductor was Antal Doráti.

Naturally I agreed, even though I had had quite different plans for my time before the premiere in New York. I boarded a plane in Munich that took me directly to Adelaide, where I met the Israeli musicians. We had several programs on this tour, and over the course of the many rehearsals that were therefore necessary we got to know each other very well. It was during this long trip that I really melded with the orchestra.

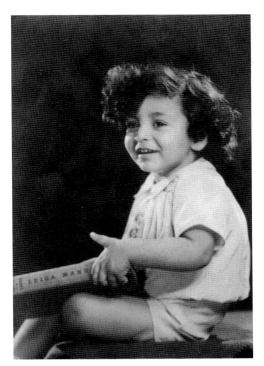

My earliest
childhood
memory.

The family prior to the departure of my father, Mehli Mehta, for America, 1945.
Left to right: me; my mother, Tehmina; my brother, Zarin; and my father, Mehli.

A visit to our Parsi fire temple with my mother in Bombay, 1967.

Nancy and me at our wedding, 1969.

With Nancy, my caring companion, friend, and wife of forty years.

Nancy loves
to wear saris.

With my brother, Zarin, and our parents at the beginning of the 1990s.

The family in the mid-1980s. *Left to right*: my grandson Daniel; my brother, Zarin; my daughter Zarina; my father, me, and my mother; Nancy; and my son Mervon.

My son Mervon with his wife, Carey, and son, Zed.

My daughter Zarina with her children, Daniel and Shenaya.

Arthur Rubinstein's conducting debut with the Israel Philharmonic Orchestra.

At a rehearsal with Arthur Rubinstein. Pierre Beique is in the background.

Jascha Heifetz at the inauguration of the Dorothy Chandler Pavilion in Los Angeles, 1964.

With my close friend Teddy Kollek, mayor of Jerusalem.

With Shah Mohammad Reza Pahlavi of Iran and Empress Farah Diba, after a Los Angeles Philharmonic concert in Tehran celebrating their coronation, 1967.

With Israeli Prime Minister Golda Meir.

With Indian Prime Minister Indira Gandhi, 1967.

A protest concert against the Vietnam War on the UCLA campus.

The Victory Concert in Jerusalem, after the Six-Day War, 1967, with Daniel Barenboim and Jacqueline du Pré.

A joyous moment after accompanying Daniel Barenboim in a concert.

At the Bavarian State Opera with its general director, Sir Peter Jonas.

Conducting Itzhak Perlman and Pinchas Zukerman with the Israel Philharmonic Orchestra.

With Isaac Stern.

Dressed as Albert Einstein after a performance of *Die Fledermaus* in Munich, 2005.

With about 200,000 penguins on the island of South Georgia during an Antarctic cruise: finally, an orchestra large enough to play Mahler's Eighth Symphony! The photo was taken by my wife, Nancy.

With the Orchestra del Maggio Musicale at a concert in Mumbai, 2005.

The first results of the Mehli Mehta Music Foundation's efforts in Mumbai—who knows, maybe with a Heifetz in the making?

My work in Israel strengthened my friendship with Daniel Barenboim still further. As long as they lived, Daniel's parents looked after me very lovingly whenever I was in Israel. Over and above our personal relationship, Daniel and I have a lot in common musically, and we enjoy playing together. Since our respective engagements always take us to different parts of the globe, we try at least to talk on the phone regularly.

We played some remarkable concerts together, including one with the Berlin Philharmonic in November 1964 at the commemoration of the tenth anniversary of Wilhelm Furtwängler's death. We performed his only piano concerto—an unbelievably difficult piece seventy minutes in length. Daniel played it from memory, and it was a tremendous challenge for him as a soloist. The concerto is very beautiful, and in it one can detect a lot of Brahms, Bruckner, and César Franck. Unfortunately, it has now largely sunk into oblivion.

I knew Barenboim primarily as a pianist. It was at first difficult for me to imagine how he could juggle being both a pianist and a conductor. Since 1967 his conducting has taken more and more of his time as he has gotten more and more offers from the great orchestras, and he has become one of the most important Wagner interpreters of our times. Music obviously always makes up a large part of our conversations, but we also talk about political problems and their consequences for all of us. We have discussed how we can readjust our musical lives to resolve the seemingly impossible situation in the Middle East. My parents also loved Daniel a lot, and it was a red-letter day for us when Daniel appeared at a fund-raising concert with my father for his American Youth Symphony. Daniel became a great fan of Parsi cuisine and loved my mother's cooking.

In May 1967 there was a sharp escalation in the Middle East crisis. Egypt, Jordan, and Syria concentrated a massive contingent of troops on their respective borders and blocked access to the important port of Eilat. Israel, practically encircled by Arab armies allied with each other through various military pacts, felt extremely threatened. The Six-Day War began on June 5 with a preemptive strike by the Israeli air force on the Egyptian airfields outside Cairo, and they were practically destroyed before a single plane had taken off. The prevailing international opinion was completely in favor of Israel, which then went on to destroy its neighbors' armies in a less than a week.

At that time I was in Puerto Rico for the Pablo Casals Festival. When I heard what was brewing in the Middle East, I knew I had to go back to Israel immediately. In these grim times I wanted to stand by the country and the people I knew there. In addition, I had heard that a well-known conductor who had come to Israel as a long-term guest conductor had fled the country, leaving the orchestra waiting for him at the 10:00 A.M. rehearsal. I simply wanted to be there. It was so important to me that I left Puerto Rico in a hurry and flew to New York, hoping to find a way of getting from there to Israel. I even had to cancel two performances in Paris and Budapest, something I had never done before.

As an Indian I still need visas for nearly all countries. Getting one for Israel at a time of such incredible tension was practically impossible, but I managed to get one in the shortest time possible with the help of Isaac Stern's wife, Vera, and her contacts. In fact, Vera Stern put me on the plane to Israel herself. I knew that Daniel was already there, along with Jacqueline du Pré, and I was impatient to join them.

We were flying over the Mediterranean Sea when the pilot announced that war had finally broken out in the Middle East and that he would therefore have to land in Rome, since passenger flights were no longer allowed to land in Israel. I really did not want to go to Rome, so I tried to contact the Israeli ambassador immediately after landing. I wanted to ask him to help me reach Israel somehow. The situation was a little delicate, since I did not have a visa for Italy, and the ambassador did not seem too interested in helping me get to Israel even though I had told him that it was urgent that I reach his country's orchestra. He probably had other, bigger concerns at the time than following up immediately on my request. But I apparently got on his nerves so much that he just wanted to get rid of me. He found a way of putting me on a flight to Israel fairly soon, so I had to reach the airport as fast as possible. This was exactly what I wanted. The airport was full of Israelis, all of whom wanted to go back home to help their country and their families or because they had been called up for military service. I boarded an El Al flight that was supposed to take us directly to Tel Aviv. On my flight there were only a journalist, a correspondent from *Newsweek*, and the director of the Bank of Israel.

It was not very comfortable on the plane; we had to squat on some boxes stacked one on top of another, which were supposed to compensate for the missing seats. But none of us was concerned about our comfort—we all just wanted to get to Tel Aviv as soon as we could. Shortly before we landed at a blacked-out airport, a member of the crew came by and asked us casually if we knew what we had been sitting on all that time. Of course, nobody had the slightest idea. It was then that we learned we had been flying in a plane filled from cockpit to tail with neatly packed boxes of ammunition. I don't dare think about what could have happened to us had the aircraft been hit by a stray bullet.

After we arrived safe and sound in Israel, where Daniel was waiting for me, we stayed in the cellar of a house where the guests of the orchestra had been accommodated. I began rehearsals the very next day; they had been brought to an abrupt halt by the previous conductor's departure. It was relatively calm in Tel Aviv—the fighting was far from the city—but everybody was on high alert. In spite of this we played music. Daniel's parents were also there, since he and Jacqueline wanted to get married in a few days' time. The tension in the atmosphere was almost unbearable. It was only by making silly jokes and feigning high spirits that we could avoid succumbing to worry and fear. Like all Israelis, we too presumed that the armed forces would pass this test of strength, but the truth was that our survival, our very existence, was depending on it.

While the fighting was still going on I went to Jerusalem and stayed in the famous King David Hotel. Hopefully this divided city was finally going to be reunited without any major casualties among either the soldiers or the many invaluable historical places. This was a very high priority for the Israelis. Daniel, Jacqueline, and I had already thought up a program for a Victory Concert: we wanted to perform Beethoven's Fifth

Symphony with the Israel Philharmonic Orchestra; after that Daniel would play Beethoven's Fifth Piano Concerto, and Jacqueline would play the Schumann Cello Concerto.

I spent a night in the King David Hotel, disturbed only once by a remarkably loud crack that made me sit up suddenly but did not interrupt my sleep otherwise. When I woke up the next morning I noticed that the picture above my bed seemed to be a little crooked. While trying to straighten it I suddenly saw that it had a bullet hole in it. I must have really had a guardian angel. I was apparently also blessed with the sleep of the just, for I had not even realized that a shot had been fired into my room.

The King David is right next to the old Arab part of the city. When I went into the city that morning, I met a soldier, who called out to me that Jerusalem had been reunited. The bullet in the wall of my room must have been a stray shot fired during the last phase of the fighting.

At that time Teddy Kollek was mayor of Jerusalem. Originally from Vienna, he was known all over the world for his ability to combine politics with an inherent humanity. I had met this legendary man several times, and we had gotten along well right from the start. Kollek loved music and art. He particularly appreciated his "children," as he always called us: Daniel Barenboim, Lenny Bernstein, Isaac Stern, and me. Kollek had a brilliant sense of humor, and his understanding of the most sensitive and complicated contexts, whether political or purely human in nature, was impressive.

I met him for the last time in the fall of 2004 in a nursing home in Jerusalem. Seeing him again moved me deeply. His mind was as sharp as ever, but physically he was very frail, and it was difficult for him to carry on a long conversation. He was terribly tired, and his age weighed heavily upon him. I talked to him about earlier times, about our many encounters with each other, about all the fun that we had had together. Among other things we were connected by our special shared knowledge of Vienna, of what makes that city so unique and sometimes so unbearable as well. We understood each other: he, a Jewish survivor who had risen to a position of great honor in Israel, and I, an Indian conductor who loved the country in which Kollek had found refuge and a home.

After this visit Kollek wrote me a heartwarming letter that I will keep with me always as proof of his affection. His sentences carry a tone of farewell, but there is nothing tearful about the letter. Rather, it is marked by a wise acknowledgment of the finiteness of life. He wrote that my visit had come as a breath of fresh air into his rather drab and monotonous days, and he had felt refreshed by it.

But back then, in 1967, I rushed to Kollek's office right after the happy end of the war and congratulated him on now being the mayor of the whole of Jerusalem. When I entered the office, the already very elderly David Ben-Gurion was sitting there. Ben-Gurion was wise enough to foresee that the addition of the new territories of Gaza and the Golan Heights would bring immense problems in their wake. As far as the reconquered Western Wall was concerned, he was of the opinion that Israel would never again relinquish it.

The day after the war ended, I was allowed to accompany Abba Eban, Israel's foreign minister, and his entourage to the Western Wall. In those days there were still some run-down Jordanian barracks in front of the wall. A journalist asked Eban what this war should be called. After a slight hesitation, Eban suggested calling it the Six-Day War. Incidentally, I was the first civilian to go through the Mandelbaum gate to East Jerusalem, which, having been closed to Jewish residents for decades, had been a symbol of divided Jerusalem. It was pure chance that I became not only a witness to this great moment, but also a participant in it.

Just four days into the war, the news we were receiving was so positive that, foolhardy as it may seem, we were already planning the Victory Concert. We discovered a terrific setting for it: a natural amphitheater near Mount Scopus. However, our suggestion was promptly shot down by some higher authority. Apparently the entire area was so heavily mined that it was impossible for a few thousand people to gather there. We couldn't argue with that, so we wound up staging the concert in Jerusalem's main concert hall, Binyanei HaUma.

I have to admit that I was a little offended when Leonard Bernstein gave a huge concert at that very spot nine months later, after all the rubble left by the war had been cleared away. Bernstein's concert then went into the annals as *the* Victory Concert.

Apart from the general jubilation over the political situation, there was also a private cause for celebration—the wedding of Daniel Barenboim and Jacqueline du Pré. Jacqueline converted to Judaism so that the wedding could be held according to Jewish rites. I was one of their witnesses, but since I was not Jewish I had to temporarily be renamed Moshe Cohen, which made me a "kosher" witness. We celebrated the wedding just at the time Israel had to demonstrate its resistance to attack from outside its borders, when it once again ensured its political survival. All of us thought it was a good sign. We had hardly any presentiment of the problems the conquered territories were going to bring to Israel, though some prescient politicians perhaps foresaw it more clearly than we did.

A few weeks after Daniel and Jacqueline's wedding, we decided to organize a tour of the United States with the Israel Philharmonic Orchestra. The whole world needed to be made aware that Israel needed some assistance, and we wanted to help the country and the musicians. We performed in many American cities, with the proceeds from the concerts going to Israeli relief funds. Many artists supported us on this tour and gave us their cooperation.

Since the Six-Day War my relationship with the musicians of the Israel Philharmonic Orchestra had strengthened considerably. Nothing could have separated us, and I tried to spend as much time with the orchestra as my other obligations allowed.

My engagement in Montreal ended in the fall of 1967. Once it was over, at least I no longer had to lead and be fully responsible for two orchestras. I was the head of the Los Angeles Philharmonic, I regularly conducted at the Met and in Vienna and Berlin, and I also went to Israel twice a year.

The Israel Philharmonic Orchestra is like family to me. With just a few exceptions, I have chosen and appointed the musicians myself from among candidates short-listed by a special committee. I know every minute characteristic of this orchestra, just as they know me down to my smallest gesture. Conducting is to a large extent communicating. And when there is such complete understanding between the conductor and the players that they understand each other without anything being said, before he even begins to conduct or they to play—as there is between the Israel Philharmonic and me—it is always possible to reach a true musical consensus. It is not a matter of finding the lowest common denominator, but rather of our combined efforts enabling us to reach our highest potential.

It is easier for me to reach this level of communication with the Israel Philharmonic Orchestra than other orchestras, even though it is not exiled Poles or musicians from Vienna and Hungary anymore who call the tune. Right now most of the orchestra members are from Russia, and unfortunately I cannot communicate verbally with them. But even so, we understand each other perfectly on a musical level.

During my first few years in Israel, I got to know many of the musicians personally. We met outside the concert halls as well as inside, and they even invited me to their homes. I think that for some of them I played a role that was part confessor, part psychologist, and part career counselor.

It is an extremely interesting phenomenon for me, and very stimulating for my work, to see that musicians from different parts of the world understand music in completely different ways. I have repeatedly emphasized the strong musical influence on me of Vienna. I matured there musically in a very particular tradition and internalized its entire cosmos, from Haydn to Webern. I may even have gone so far as to sacrifice precision in favor of a warmer sound. Similarly, in Israel I tried to convey my notion of sound to the musicians, particularly when it came to music of the nineteenth century. This is possible even with Viennese waltzes, which are more difficult to play than one might imagine. I will rehearse a Strauss waltz with the Israel Philharmonic Orchestra again and again. Of course, this is not these musicians' native tongue, musically speaking, but it is important for me to make them understand even music to which they don't take quite naturally. I try to explain the right tone and style—for example, the fact that the many accompanying figures in a waltz do not have to be played exactly as printed, that everything must be played in a slightly messy way, though this mess has to be very controlled and specific. This is very difficult to explain outside Austria—even German orchestras don't always know exactly how this organized sloppiness works—so I actually had it written into the parts for the Israel Philharmonic Orchestra. I like such exercises, for they bring some freshness into the orchestra. Besides, they're fun. And then, when the whole auditorium shakes with delight, all of us feel rewarded too. But I have to admit that waltzes are perhaps still somewhat unusual in Israel.

A similar exercise is connected to chamber music. It is a European tradition, far more than an American one, for orchestra players to play chamber music. I have tried to encourage musicians of all the orchestras I've worked with to play chamber music—in New York as well as in Tel Aviv. One necessarily plays differently when one is part of a small group. Chamber musicians have to listen to each other much more sensitively, which then helps them enormously when they go back to their large ensembles. The fact that chamber music is played without a conductor obliges the musician to interpret all aspects of a masterpiece, from the tempo to the most minute intricacies. This makes the musicians more receptive and enables them to play together much more intimately. The consequent influence on their orchestral playing is entirely positive.

In 1969 the Israel Philharmonic Orchestra appointed me their "music adviser." This rather peculiar designation can mean everything or nothing, but there was a simple legal reason behind it: I was already the music director of the Los Angeles Philharmonic and could not have a similar title anywhere else. So the governing board of the orchestra in Israel (orchestras in most non-European countries are run cooperatively through these kinds of governing bodies), which wanted me to be closely associated with them, came up with this rather remarkable-sounding title.

I was appointed music director of the Israel Philharmonic Orchestra in 1977. This was a brand-new title. Finally the close relationship between the orchestra and me was formally sealed. When my work in Montreal came to an end the officials in Los Angeles had hoped that I would not take up another leading post elsewhere, but I couldn't help it that I had so much stronger a wish to be connected to the Israel Philharmonic Orchestra. Eventually the people in Los Angeles consented to my appointment as music director of the orchestra in Israel.

At this juncture I want to come back to Teddy Kollek again and to an experience we shared. In 1968, one year after the Six-Day War, he and the mayor of Bethlehem had an unusual idea for an orchestra program. They wanted to organize an open-air concert in the large square (now a parking lot) in front of the Church of the Nativity in Bethlehem. It was really uplifting to see thousands of people—Jews, Christians, and Arabs—gathered together at this historically and religiously significant square to listen to Verdi's Requiem. This most dramatic choral masterpiece is a work of colossal dimensions. It ends with a "Libera me" that Verdi had at one time intended for a requiem dedicated to Gioachino Rossini but eventually became part of another requiem—for the great Italian writer Alessandro Manzoni. The text means something different to each and every person, and all who heard this concert must have been deeply moved.

I often think back to this concert and wonder if we should not have tried to talk to everyone there that day in order to better understand their worries, to give them new hope, and to show them new ways of seeing things. Maybe it is naive, but I feel that the Israelis simply threw away many chances to communicate and understand. It is true that the brutal reality of those times also stood in the way. Kollek had taken me aside before the beginning of the Requiem to warn me that there could be a terrorist strike by Al Fatah at this public performance. He asked me to keep my cool and not lose my nerve or run away from the podium in case some unforeseen incident in the middle of the concert started a panic. I was supposed to remain as calm as possible. The most important thing would be to reassure the public. I myself, however, was not at all reassured, and a couple of times during the concert I had the uneasy feeling that someone was going to head for me with a gun or something. I have to say that I feel relatively safe in such situations simply because I believe myself to be on the side of justice.

In earlier years the orchestra had often played an ancient Roman amphitheater in Caesarea. The city is historically very significant: it is said that each stone in Caesarea, once the largest seaport of the East, symbolizes two thousand years of history. At the same time, the city also hints at the beginning of the oppression and extermination of the Jews and their long struggle against Roman rule.

The beautiful amphitheater, built by Herod the Great, is a wonderful place for listening to music, and we played there on several occasions with great success. We performed unforgettable concerts and operas, including Schoenberg's *Gurrelieder*. This great work marks the true end of the great post-Wagnerian romantic era and seems almost to have been made for such a setting. In 1977 we appeared there with *Fidelio* under the direction of Otto Schenk, with Gundula Janowitz as Leonore and Jon Vickers as Florestan. The Roman theater suited the dungeon scene in particular like none other; it was really impressive. The Israel Philharmonic Orchestra's home, Mann Auditorium, was not particularly suitable for staged performances, and there was still no separate opera house in Tel Aviv in those days. So we had to play concert versions of operas, a practice we still maintain.

There has now been an opera house in Israel for several years, and in it are mounted seven or eight productions a year. The Israel Philharmonic Orchestra is not connected with it, though we are good neighbors. For a long time now I have been performing a concert opera each season with the orchestra, and each time I find it particularly challenging. Of course, one needs much less time to prepare for an opera that will be performed in concert. And for me it is a great advantage musically when the singers are nearby. I can then stage everything exactly the way I picture it to myself. I do not have to struggle with grotesque or unmanageable stage directions, nor do the singers have to sing coloratura flourishes while climbing a mountain or standing on their heads. Of course, I know that this attitude is inconsistent with the actual nature of opera, and many operas also do not take well to a concert version. But when the music of the opera targets the unconscious, as Puccini's does, for example, I believe one can venture to play it in concert.

It has to be admitted in all honesty that there are repertoire performances in opera houses that are actually no more than concert performances in costume with a bit of movement. There are some things that are difficult to perform, and not many singers have mastered the art of singing and convincingly enacting a role at the same time. Ultimately it is frustrating for both the director and the conductor if a performance is simply static.

There are very difficult operas, such as *Il trovatore*, that make unusually tough demands on singers. On the other hand, there are also exceptionally talented singers—Maria Callas and Jon Vickers were two of the foremost examples—who are able to master both the acting and the singing. Today more and more of the new generation of operatic performers are proving their mastery of this ideal combination, and it gives me much pleasure to observe the goings-on from my place in the orchestra pit. One must rehearse a lot so that the singers are truly of one mind about the general concept of a particular scene. But sometimes I'm happy if the singers just manage to stand there and sing correctly. I don't mean this to sound cynical. Everybody knows how much I enjoy conducting operas. It would be really ridiculous if, as the head of an opera house, I did not love the acting as well, with body and soul. But I often make a virtue of necessity, and so I also enjoy giving concert performances with the Israel Philharmonic Orchestra.

I am often asked how I deal with it if I cannot work with a particular singer. This obviously happens sometimes. I try not to show any personal animosity; the singer is after all under my protection, so to speak, as long as we are working together, and it is my duty to convince a singer of my intentions and bring out the best in him or her. There are some conductors, though, who bare their misunderstandings or disagreements with a soloist before the public. Bernstein did it once before a concert with Glenn Gould when their rehearsals for Brahms's First Piano Concerto had not gone well.

Bernstein announced to the audience that as a conductor he did not agree with Gould. I personally do not hold with demonstrations of this kind. However, I happened to accompany Gould in the same work a few months later, and I must say I agreed entirely with Lenny!

Another major event around this time was the Israel Philharmonic Orchestra's first visit to Berlin in 1971, during our major European tour. The members of the orchestra and the three-member governing board discussed whether a concert tour of Germany was possible at all. There were so many bad memories, so many objections, and such overwhelming feelings were expressed. Some of the musicians had a really hard time dealing with the idea. They could not forget their personal experiences, nor could they suppress their memories of the suffering of their family members and friends. Could they really go to the country that was responsible for the Holocaust? The discussion took a very emotional turn. There were strong arguments in favor and against, but eventually we decided to do it as a sign of understanding and reconciliation.

With the passage of time, relations between the Berlin Philharmonic and the Israel Philharmonic Orchestra normalized to the extent that the former was able to visit Israel with Daniel Barenboim. As long as Karajan was the chief conductor in Berlin, such a visit was unthinkable because of his past affiliation with the Nazi party. Back then both Daniel Barenboim and I were occasionally asked to give a guest performance in Israel with the orchestra, but we could never accept. After the Karajan era, though, there was no reason to oppose a musical exchange, and so the orchestra came to Israel. Daniel conducted all of Brahms's symphonies, and at the final concert I led a performance by the two orchestras together. Before the break the Berliners and the Israelis each accompanied, respectively, an Israeli clarinetist, Sharon Kam, and a German violinist, Vivianne Hagner. In the second half the two orchestras together performed Maurice Ravel's *La valse* and Beethoven's Fifth Symphony. This concert was naturally supposed to be symbolic, and the audience reacted with great enthusiasm, as they had the previous evenings to Daniel's performances. The concert was intended as a sign of reconciliation, and it also corresponded to my credo completely: we gave the audience a chance to forget their troubles and their disagreements for at least a couple of hours.

⁓

At the first performance of the Israel Philharmonic Orchestra in Germany in 1971, we played a concert with Dietrich Fischer-Dieskau and another one with Daniel Barenboim at the opening of the Berliner Festwochen. Fischer-Dieskau sang Mahler's *Kindertotenlieder* from the depths of his heart. It was a wonderful performance. He often came to Israel and therefore knew the orchestra very well. He was very moved after the concert, and once backstage he could hardly hold back his tears.

Even for the rest of us this concert was a very emotional experience. Perhaps it helped that I, who am neither German nor Israeli, led the orchestra. I could to some extent parry the enormous tension, which was constantly palpable and understandably weighed heavily on everyone. Out of the 115 members of the orchestra, only two refused to take part in this guest performance in Germany. It was left up to each member to voice his or her opinion, and personal reasons for backing out were naturally accepted.

After the *Kindertotenlieder* we also played Mahler's First Symphony. The audience in Berlin thanked us for it with a standing ovation. The musicians and I were impressed by their enthusiasm and very happy with the way the orchestra was received. After lengthy applause we decided to give an encore and played the Israeli national anthem, "Hatikvah," which most of the audience did not know. I had decided on this at short notice. It seemed to me to be a conciliatory end to an evening that had been marked by so much emotion. I felt that we had progressed a little bit further on the road to a new friendship. I was perhaps able to make a comparable contribution in 1994 when I performed with the Israel Philharmonic Orchestra in my homeland of India for the first time.

Our first tour of Germany also took the Israel Philharmonic Orchestra to Bonn. Johannes Wasmuth took care of us over there. Wasmuth had become a legend through his work in music. He was not only a highly circumspect impresario who kept an eye on everything, but he also displayed great empathy and a high level of musical competence. He turned the famous Rolandseck railway station to the south of Bad Godesberg into a mecca for chamber musicians. Members of the Israel Philharmonic Orchestra later performed there on several occasions. The respect with which Wasmuth treated people really deserves the highest appreciation.

That year the Israel Philharmonic Orchestra was invited for the first time to participate in the festival concerts in Salzburg. This was the beginning of a long series of guest performances with great soloists. Pinchas Zukerman played the Brahms Violin Concerto at the first concert. Later Itzhak Perlman, Maurizio Pollini, and Maxim Vengerov also performed with us.

As in Los Angeles and New York, I tried to include contemporary music in the Israel Philharmonic programming. One of my major concerns is to familiarize a larger audience with more recent music. Whether what I choose to play from the vast abundance available will have a lasting impact is not always easy to say. It will be the next generation, at the very earliest, that will be in a position to judge. During the 1970s I had tried to promote contemporary music with a concert series called Musica Viva. It was not easy, and unfortunately we had to discontinue the series after a few years owing to poor response and a lack of financial resources. Even in regular concerts I constantly try to stage a premiere of an indigenous composer, or at least to perform a contemporary work, since it is hardly possible to come across new music outside the concert halls. In my opinion it is also our responsibility as conductors to make sure that we do not always perform only the well-known classics that people already have at home on CD.

This is also one reason I support a good professional musical education that gives young people thorough training. In 2004, at the request of a generous donor, I willingly lent my name to a music school in Israel that aims to promote young talent by training them in the art of orchestral playing. Moreover, it wants to keep talented young artists in the country: Israeli musicians are often compelled to go abroad because they find more favorable conditions there. The Buchmann-Mehta School was founded at the University of Tel Aviv in cooperation with the Israel Philharmonic Orchestra. Thanks to the generosity of Josef Buchmann, a concentration camp survivor and for many years now also a close friend who is currently a prominent real-estate developer in Frankfurt, this institute has been provided for financially for some years. Just as at the Curtis Institute in Philadelphia, here too the best are chosen through an extremely competitive audition process and given scholarships to enable them to study under the principal players of the Israel Philharmonic Orchestra.

There are many promising projects worth supporting. If I cannot pursue them as fully as I want to, it is only because of the limited time at my disposal. The West-Eastern Divan Orchestra, founded by Edward Said, a Palestinian, and David Barenboim, an Israeli, is one such project that has become famous worldwide. It aims to enable and facilitate an Arab-Jewish dialogue, at least in the field of music. There are also other small projects that are quietly growing and, to some extent, thriving. I support a project called the Israeli Music Celebration / Tempus Fugit—Biennial for Contemporary Music, during which Jewish members of the Israel Philharmonic Orchestra and young Arab instrumentalists and singers perform together.

We need to do everything possible to overcome differences and promote mutual understanding. This is the only way to get beyond all our political and historical obstacles.

In October 2004 I went to the music school in Ramallah, which is funded by the Barenboim-Said Foundation, at the invitation of Mustafa Barguti, an internationally renowned Palestinian physician. I wanted to look at projects that could be further developed with his help, and I also hoped to get some idea of the living conditions there. As it turned out, I was able to see a lot of the oppression people there constantly live with.

During this visit I also organized a children's orchestra in connection with the foundation. I wish the musicians of the Israel Philharmonic

Orchestra could have come with me. Perhaps it would have helped both sides to understand each other better. Unfortunately, Israelis are not allowed to travel to the West Bank or the Gaza Strip. The enthusiasm, interest, and courage I found there, which never slacken despite the deplorable living conditions, are impressive. On the evening after this visit I had to conduct a gala for the American friends and patrons of the Israel Philharmonic Orchestra in Tel Aviv, and it was difficult for me to detach myself from the images and impressions of the day.

In probably no other country in the world are differences so sharply delineated and so rigidly adhered to as in Israel. And not just political, but also social differences. The orchestra and I must take this into account if we do not want to end up ignoring reality and making the enjoyment of art possible only for a small social elite. We gave a concert of Beethoven's Ninth Symphony in July 2005 in a kibbutz near Nazareth, in the north of Israel. We sold tickets to approximately two thousand Israelis from neighboring kibbutzim—and also to around four hundred Arabs. Obviously the acoustic conditions were miserable, but it pleased me to see Arabs and Jews sitting together again. Unfortunately, this does not happen very often in Israel. While performing the last movement, I could only pray that the Jews and Arabs who were there might take to heart Schiller's words—"Alle Menschen werden Brüder" (All men will be brothers). I believe that feelings of hatred can be overcome at least for a short while with such concerts, because music and hatred are mutually exclusive. And if this is true, then a lot will have been achieved by such events. Unfortunately, economic realities seldom allow us to give this kind of concert.

The orchestra and I have gone to border areas in Israel, however, in regions into which a big philharmonic orchestra normally does not stray. One of these was a concert held in January 1982 at the border between Lebanon and Israel, in the middle of a tobacco field. This is how the concert came about: There were mostly Christians living in southern

100

Lebanon, particularly in the years after a civil war erupted. Initially they were supported by Israel and protected from being encroached upon by the Palestine Liberation Organization. It was a more or less peaceful phase in the relations between Lebanon and Israel. The "good fence policy" was put into effect there in the border areas starting in 1977. The Maronites from southern Lebanon found work there, and they were taken care of in times of need. They could ship in goods from the port of Haifa, and free medical attention was available. All in all it was a project that was evidently functioning well.

The commander of the border police, Zvi Bar, was a close friend and a keen music lover. I arranged with him to give a concert for the people living on the border. Zvi Bar later became the mayor of Ramat Gan, near Tel Aviv. Even today he is held to be one of the most important authorities on the Arab-Jewish conflict.

The musicians and I went with all our equipment to the border, where the commander had prepared everything for a concert in the middle of a tobacco field. He had even erected a sort of stage and surrounded it with the army's sun-blocking shields, while the audience, most of them Lebanese, sat in the open. After the concert people came up to us and embraced us. They felt a brotherly bond with each other and were inspired by a new hope for a happier future. Naturally, we did not play a Beethoven symphony or any other kind of heavyweight fare. It is better to play some "lollipops" on such occasions, since they are meant for pure entertainment, and their only purpose is to bring joy to the public. It was a very peculiar and special experience to stand and play in the middle of a tobacco field. In June 1982, after the Israeli military incursion into Lebanon, I went all the way to Beirut with Zvi Bar, accompanied by Rafi Eitan (one of the Mossadniks who arrested Adolf Eichmann) and Vidal Sassoon. It was a thrilling and very moving experience. We were greeted as friends in most of the villages, and there were Israeli and Lebanese flags hanging all along the streets. It seemed as if people had simply been waiting for this moment to finally reach across to each other. Little did we know that things were going to take a 180-degree turn soon and that the Israelis, who had initially been greeted as saviors, after a few months would be looked upon as invaders. But this is something that cannot and need not be discussed here.

When I work with the orchestra in Israel, we naturally also perform concerts in other parts of the country. The auditoriums in outlying areas neither correspond to conventional notions of satisfactory acoustics, nor do they come up to our aesthetic standards. The entire orchestra travels by bus to the north of Israel or to the southern regions and plays under adverse conditions without the smallest complaint. This is how we bring music to people who sometimes spend an hour or more traveling to the venues.

The rather naive notion that a musically knowledgeable and experienced conductor flies to a concert venue, puts on his tailcoat, makes a bit of music, and then disappears again into a high-end luxury hotel is based on ignorance of our profession. In the case of Israel, it also stems from of a complete lack of knowledge about the conditions there.

We had a performance once in Kiryat Chaim, in the north of Israel. We played Beethoven's Fifth Symphony in an auditorium with all the charm of a 1950s movie theater. It is always a great pleasure for us to perform at such places, since we get to meet an enthusiastic audience that is longing to listen to an orchestra concert and clearly lives the music with us. This kind of feeling is contagious. It vibrates through the whole auditorium and communicates itself to the musicians. A group of about sixty Arabs and Jews who met regularly as a choir came to this concert, and for them it was a great experience to see and hear this famous orchestra.

In the case of the Israel Philharmonic Orchestra the fact that things like these are organized and that appointments, travel plans, dates, and logistical issues are carefully coordinated—in short, that everything associated with such an enterprise is meticulously synchronized so everything goes smoothly once we are there—is thanks to Avi Shoshani, the secretary general of the orchestra. There is nothing Shoshani cannot do. He can reconcile a Latin American tour with a performance in Jerusalem effortlessly. He works out the travel details, hotel reservations, and instrument transportation, and most important of all, he negotiates the highest fee possible for the orchestra all over the world. Over and above all these functions, he also acts as a social secretary for Nancy and me during our extensive tours. There is virtually no problem for which Shoshani cannot come up with a solution almost before the question even arises. The fact that he occasionally also manages a financial tightrope act on behalf of the orchestra makes him one of the most important people in the orchestra hierarchy (apart from the musicians, of course). He works in close contact with the three members of the elected council of the orchestra, whom the members vote on every two years. This council also works with Avi and me on all musical matters. And he manages all this not with some huge staff, but with only the help of two highly qualified women who work as tirelessly as he. I am also very attached to him personally, and he and his family are my friends. He is also my advisor, and I consider him and my brother to be the finest orchestra managers in the world. Zarin has also recently been named president and executive director of the New York Philharmonic.

After a concert such as the one in Kiryat Chaim, described above, it is usually long past midnight when I come back, utterly exhausted, to my hotel in Tel Aviv. I need to calm down before I can sleep. The tension does not wear off easily, and I really need to relax. Usually I eat something, phone friends and family, and watch a good game of soccer or cricket on television.

The anniversary of the founding of the state of Israel is always celebrated in a big way, and the Israel Philharmonic Orchestra has contributed at each important anniversary by playing a musical tribute suitable to the occasion.

Two remarkable celebrations in particular made a lasting impression on me. The first took place in 1978, on the thirtieth anniversary of the founding of Israel. Once again Teddy Kollek, the brilliant mayor and mediator, had his finger in the pie. He had chosen the famous square between Old and New Jerusalem called the Sultan's Pool for a concert with the orchestra.

The old city of Jerusalem is bounded on the east by walls that were renovated in the sixteenth century by Suleiman the Magnificent, who built the Sultan's Pool. The adjacent amphitheater lends itself wonderfully to concerts and open-air performances of all kinds.

At that time this historically significant place had just become usable again after all the armed conflicts and political disturbances of the 1960s and early 1970s. Kollek's idea of organizing a big anniversary concert at this venue was utterly brilliant. Thanks to him we managed to engage world-class soloists for this concert—Leontyne Price, Mstislav Rostropovich, Jean-Pierre Rampal, and Isaac Stern—all of whom gave memorable performances.

Ten years later another, even more significant place was chosen for the fortieth-anniversary concert: Masada, one of the first sites of the Jewish people's struggle for survival. At the end of the celebrations the Israel Philharmonic Orchestra played Mahler's Second Symphony, the "Resurrection," a monumental work that was uniquely perfect for the occasion and the venue. In the last movement Friedrich Gottlieb Klopstock's verse, which gives the symphony its name—"Auferstehn, ja auferstehn wirst du, mein Staub, nach kurzer Ruh" (Rise again, yes, you will rise again, my dust, after a brief rest)—captivated the huge crowd. There were famous Russian immigrants among the audience, the so-called refuseniks, such as Ida Nudel and Anatoly Sharansky, who later became a cabinet minister. After many years of struggle Nudel and Sharansky had made it out of the Soviet Union, and they were accorded heroes' welcomes upon their arrival. It was very moving when, after Mahler's great symphony, a six-year-old boy stood alone on the stage with his violin and played "Hatikvah."

It was a grand event, and Jews from all over the world had come to attend it. Now, far into the night, they listened to this music, filled with the hope of a more peaceful future. At my request Gregory Peck and Yves Montand gave an opening address that went out to the whole world. Both were my friends, and I am grateful to them that they agreed to take part in this unique performance.

There was something else that I managed in connection with this concert that gave me a lot of joy and also a bit of satisfaction. There was an immigrant from the Soviet Union named Anna Rosnovsky in the orchestra. She had left the Soviet Union legally, but her sister still lived there. This sister was an electrician, and I had met her earlier during a guest performance in Leningrad. She had given me a grief-stricken account of her situation: she was refused permission to travel to Israel since, with her profession, she was obviously in possession of state secrets! This, she told me, was absolutely preposterous; the only secret she possessed was an excellent recipe for borscht. In addition, her son was to be drafted into the military soon. That evening I arranged a phone call to Leningrad from the stage in Masada before an audience spread out over several continents. In the course of my conversation with the young woman I expressed the hope that she would soon be able to be reunited with her sister in Israel. We were counting on the Soviet authorities to listen in, of course. Our gamble paid off, and fifteen days later the woman and her son were in Israel. It was actually a trifling action, but it had huge consequences for those directly involved.

My acquaintance with actors such as Gregory Peck, Sophia Loren, Yves Montand, and Danny Kaye should not lead anyone to assume that I am interested in knowing the who's who of Hollywood. I have repeatedly been accused of having a superficial interest in stars from the world of movies and entertainment. But believe it or not, even famous film stars are often avowed music lovers—Gregory Peck, for example. And Sophia Loren has a very gifted son, Carlo Ponti, who is well on his way to becoming an established conductor. One of my particularly close friends, Louis Jourdan, is not only a music connoisseur par excellence but also one of the most cultured and well-read persons I know. Louis has almost perfect recall: at the drop of a hat he can sing parts of Schoenberg's *Gurrelieder*, recite Shakespeare's *Henry V*, or break into a medley of Frank Sinatra songs.

Under these circumstances it is only natural for people to come together to organize an event, particularly for a good cause. One big name can draw in more donations than many unknown ones with equally good intentions. This is also why I sometimes give concerts for a good cause at places that may strike people as a little odd. I will come back to this topic later, since it is very important to me.

In connection with my musical activities in Israel, I have to talk about the reception of Richard Wagner there and my stand on this issue. There is no official ban on playing Wagner in Israel. The earlier Palestine Philharmonic Orchestra had decided no longer to play Wagner in view of the horrors of the war and the Holocaust, and especially out of respect to those concentration camp survivors who were still living in Israel. Wagner, after all, was Hitler's favorite composer. However, CDs of Wagner's works can easily be bought in any record store in the country, and he is also played on the official Israeli radio station, Kol Yisrael. There is an enormous discrepancy between the official rejection of Richard Wagner and the actual reception of his music. But in my opinion there are other inconsistencies as well. After all, one could use the arguments against Wagner to reject many other artists. And conclusions about Wagner often are based on a goodly number of prejudices and clichés, many of them simply passed on from one generation to the next. On the other hand, it simply flies in the face of common sense, not to mention ordinary human decency, to expect someone with a number tattooed on his or her forearm to appreciate Wagner. Volumes have been written about the different arguments in favor of and against his music, and it will certainly be a while before a balanced attitude to his music can develop naturally. Wagner is played neither in the concert halls nor in the opera in Israel. At the same time, the history of music over the last 150 years would be unimaginable without him. This is simply not in serious dispute.

In the 1960s there was a public debate about Wagner in which Gideon Hausner, the lead prosecutor in the trial of Adolf Eichmann, and I represented two completely opposing points of view. In 1981 I thought of a way to break this impasse. After an ordinary subscription concert I stood before the audience and announced that we would play the Prelude and Isolde's "Liebestod" from *Tristan und Isolde*, and whoever did not wish to listen was welcome to leave the hall.

The orchestra started playing softly, very softly, as is called for in the beginning of Wagner's score of the Prelude. Suddenly somebody in the auditorium shouted, "You will not play Wagner!" and began calling us names. Some people became enraged and tried to come up onto the stage. The orchestra stood its ground and kept playing. The concertmaster, Chaim Taub, was visibly unnerved by someone who kept pulling at his sleeve while he was playing. But we kept playing in spite of the chaos. The powerful crescendo in the Prelude drowned out the worst shouts, as I knew it would, and the pianissimo of the "Liebestod" calmed everyone down. The performance ended in triumph. The next day I repeated the attempt. I simply wanted to try it again and not let myself be put off by these emotional objectors. But to my dismay they were much more organized, entering the auditorium after the concert and creating such a brouhaha that we had no choice but to stop the music.

It is impossible for me as a musician to separate the historical and the musical significance of Wagner's importance, and I was convinced that Israel, a democracy, would not tolerate this kind of musical hooliganism. In hindsight, I think I simply failed to understand how painful the very sound of his music is for Israel's Holocaust survivors. I still believe that Wagner's music will be played in Israel at some future time. For now, though, we must respect the feelings of the survivors, with whom any intellectual debate on the subject is quite impossible.

The concert was the subject of much public discussion for several months. To some people I was a hero. Many, however, accused me of callousness and said that I had no idea what the Holocaust had been like. One night around the time of this incident I was driving home from a dinner with my first bassoonist at 2:00 A.M. when a policeman stopped me at an intersection for running a red light. He went on to reproach me for not understanding anything that had gone to make up Israel. He said his father had been a victim of the Nazis and still had a number tattooed on his arm.

Feeling completely helpless against the officer's outburst, I found myself unable to reply. Yet he didn't give me a ticket.

Perhaps I was insensitive. I don't really know. Maybe I should not have tried to introduce this kind of educational measure. I had used a kind of force to get something done that I thought was right. In any case, intellectually I still cannot understand what happened that day.

Around this same time a politician in the Israeli Parliament stated on record that Israel had done enough for my career and it was time I left the country. I was shocked when this harsh attack came to my attention. I thought that if this was what people really wanted, I would have to submit to their wishes. What happened next was completely unexpected. To my great surprise and joy, the orchestra responded by offering me the post of music director for life. Daniel Benyami, the principal viola and a representative of the governing board, approached me at an organized gathering to put forth the proposal. Deeply moved by the offer, I accepted gladly.

I have held this post since 1981, but the length of my tenure never appeared in my contract. It does not really need to be. Every five or six years I ask the orchestra if they still want me. I would prefer to be told directly and straightaway if they change their minds, and for this we do not need a contract. Maybe the musicians would like to have another music director some day. And who knows, maybe someday it will all be too much for me too. Even though the Israel Philharmonic Orchestra is like a part of my family, we still sometimes have disagreements and quarrels; but then, these happen in all families. It would be hypocritical to behave as if we were always of the same opinion. Still, everything can be sorted out if we basically get along.

I do not generally like talking about honors, medals, and awards I have received, but I would like to mention just one. This is the Israel Prize, awarded by the government of Israel. So far I am the only non-Israeli to whom it has been awarded. Incidentally, the same politician who had wanted to get rid of me was present at the award ceremony in the Knesset. We did not look at each other, nor did we shake hands.

Israel is very important to me, and I perceive my work there as an integral part of my professional life. I am always ready to devote myself to this work, but at the same time I am also prepared to be critical when necessary.

I really believe that the authorities in Israel must learn to accept compromises and realize that the long-term solutions for their fundamental problems do not lie in walls and barriers. On the other hand, the shelling from Gaza of defenseless towns such as Sderot creates such antipathy that the response from the Israeli side, though understandable, is often exaggerated. Many of these arguments may seem contradictory. But right now the two sides are so intransigent that only some kind of future compassionate inspiration will be able to solve this immense human tragedy, one that touches both peoples.

After all these years I feel myself to be a part of Israel, though by the same token I also feel I have the right not to agree with everything the country does. However, Israel can count upon me whenever the situation calls for it. I am always willing to serve the country in any way I can. For the most part, though, I can do little more than be there with my music.

When the first Gulf War erupted in 1991 I put the patience of my wife and of my colleagues in New York to a very difficult test. I was on my way from Vienna to New York to work with the New York Philharmonic when I heard that a war in the Middle East was imminent. The deadline for the Iraqi army, which had invaded Kuwait, to retreat had expired. There was nothing else to do but cancel my ticket to New York. I called Nancy and told her that I was canceling my New York trip and taking the next flight to Israel. She was terribly angry. She thinks I should not try to play the hero, though that was not my intention at all. The powers that be in New York were placed in the awkward situation of finding a substitute to conduct the concerts for the next two weeks, but if they were terribly upset, I never knew about it.

The mayor of Tel Aviv at that time, Shlomo "Cheech" Lahat, went up and down busy Dizengoff Street with me to show people they did not need to be scared. Actually, they had good reason to be. Saddam Hussein's Scud missiles were aimed at Israel, and nobody was sure of their intended targets or how accurate they were. The atmosphere was again heavy with the pragmatic fatalism that always distinguishes the Israelis in troubled times. Still, it was a very uncomfortable feeling, and the small concrete shelters in high-rise buildings and hotels where people were supposed to go during a bomb attack were not exactly welcoming.

I arrived completely unannounced and with no intention of conducting. Once the Scuds started raining down on us, we couldn't play normal concerts, since there were mandatory blackouts every evening. We performed free concerts in the mornings in places that were never intended for music. This was my little contribution toward giving a little peace of mind to the Israelis at least for a few hours every day. I hope we succeeded, even if only in a small way. Isaac Stern, Daniel Barenboim, and Yefim Bronfman flew in immediately. We did what we could—we played music.

There is so much to tell about the many years I have spent with the Israel Philharmonic Orchestra in Israel and on tours. Since my debut in 1961 I have led the orchestra for more than forty years in 3,098 concerts. I have never been so intimately connected with any other orchestra. That this collaboration always leads to extraordinary situations is largely because of the unusual external circumstances. I was rather apolitical when I first came to Israel and began working with the orchestra. Now I try to take a stand politically whenever it seems crucial to me to do so.

But I will not compromise myself. If I were ever asked to conform to any politically motivated stipulations that I believed to be ethically wrong, I would categorically refuse. I stand by the opinions I have developed for myself and don't allow anybody to talk me out of them. The frequent political changes that go hand in hand with each change of government do not affect me. I have no choice but to accept either a right-wing or a left-wing coalition. But I am not indifferent when I'm confronted with something I cannot reconcile with my sense of justice and democracy.

I like speaking up for minorities. After all, being a Parsi in India, where we are but a fraction of the population—80,000 among 1.2 billion—

gives me some authority to speak on the subject. Even during my student years in Vienna and at the beginning of my career I was often referred to as "the Indian." It may have been meant as a kind of endearment, but in fact it was nothing but a form of exclusion.

I think people should try to talk to each other instead of shooting at each other. I have the ability to communicate through music. If I can stop people from being enemies for just two hours, or if I can at least help them to forget their hostility, then I feel I've achieved something. This is the driving force behind a lot of the activities I have undertaken in my life. I cannot say for certain whether I was successful or whether this success could be measured, but it is a part of my nature to try to do it again and again.

7

FRIENDS IN MUSIC AND MUSICAL ENCOUNTERS

I deeply regret the fact that some great artists are not willing to come and perform in Israel, but I am truly grateful to the ones who are. My encounters with such artists are often connected to special musical events. Some stand out in my memory because of their uniqueness, and some simply because there was something particularly funny associated with them.

One of the true friends of the Israel Philharmonic Orchestra was Arthur Rubinstein, who often accompanied the orchestra on tours and also came to Israel once a year. He used to enjoy playing with Daniel Barenboim and would often perform with him outside Israel. Rubinstein's playing was technically perfect, yet that technique was always put to the service of musical interpretation. He achieved a level of perfection in his playing that corresponded to my notions of music and musical expertise.

Rubinstein's fidelity to the musical work always impressed me. Unlike some other soloists, he never reinvented the music every eight or ten bars, never overinterpreted it. He always played each piece as it had been composed and allowed it to flow freely through his hands. This philosophy fit perfectly with my education under Swarowsky in Vienna. For me, listening to his playing was almost like hearing a musical miracle. Everything acquired an amazing naturalness in his hands, as if the way he heard the music were simply self-evident. His mastery over Chopin's rubato and the way he played Brahms or Saint-Saëns—they were all musical revelations.

The first time I worked with him was in Los Angeles. He had been scheduled to play under Fritz Reiner but did not seem at all upset when told that he would instead be playing with a replacement, a completely unknown conductor from India.

I clearly remember the rehearsals for our first performance together, which was Brahms's First Piano Concerto. Rubinstein was very strict and precise in rehearsal. Moreover, he was one of those soloists who understand something about orchestras. Many soloists are simply content to master their own parts and leave everything else up to the orchestra and the conductor. However, those soloists who work very carefully and thoroughly—such as Nathan Milstein, Pinchas Zukerman, Isaac Stern, and Daniel Barenboim, to name just a few along with Rubinstein—know all the orchestral details and are satisfied only when everything is perfectly balanced according to their own concepts. Rubinstein played Brahms like no one else of his generation. When it came to this music, his vast experience from his time in Berlin at the turn of the century made him, as an interpreter, incomparable.

Toward the end of his life, when Rubinstein was once again rehearsing this Brahms piano concerto with me and the Israel Philharmonic Orchestra, he expressed an unusual wish: he told us he would give anything to be able to conduct an orchestra once in his life. He wondered if it could be managed without too much waste of time and without giving the musicians too much trouble. Who could possibly want to deny this great pianist his wish, a man with whom the orchestra had been associated so closely and who had so often provided ample proof of his friendship? So the orchestra prepared itself to read through Brahms's Third Symphony, the piece Rubinstein had chosen. He was ecstatic, and the musicians, though ultimately somewhat exhausted, were pleased that they could make him happy, even if both sides rated the effort less than 100 percent successful.

Rubinstein's sense of humor was as legendary as the good cigars he smoked after a concert. His jokes and storytelling would extend far into the early hours of the morning. Once, when he had included both Beethoven and Saint-Saëns in the same program, he was asked in what order he wanted to play the works. His answer was typical: "First we go to church with Beethoven and then to a brothel with Saint-Saëns."

I really liked working with Rubinstein. We performed all five of Beethoven's piano concertos, the two concertos by Brahms and the two by Chopin, the Concerto in D Minor by Mozart, and the Concerto in G Minor by Saint-Saëns. Regrettably, we were able to record together only once; we were under contract to different record labels, and it would have been extremely complicated to reach an agreement on sharing the rights. Shortly before his death Rubinstein insisted upon making a recording with the Israel Philharmonic Orchestra and me. RCA released him from his contract for this one occasion, he waived his royalties, and we recorded Brahms's First Piano Concerto together for Decca, the label to which I was under contract. It was his last record.

During her heyday Jessye Norman came to Israel twice. She was supposed to sing some arias from Bizet's *Carmen* and Saint-Saëns's *Samson and Dalila*. I had already warned her at the rehearsal that the audience would certainly expect an encore and that she should be prepared to sing one. The evening arrived. She sang like a goddess and looked like an African queen in her stunning gown. Norman's rich, sensual voice, her musical skill, and her erotic charisma took everyone's breath away. As I had expected, the public raved about her and demanded an encore. It struck me that some years ago, after one of those unforgettable concerts with the New York Philharmonic in Harlem, she had performed as an encore an a capella spiritual. She immediately took my suggestion, went back onstage, and sang "Were You There When They Crucified My Lord?"—in front of an audience of a couple of thousand Jews. Nobody took offense, and she later said that at the moment it had been the only thing that came to mind.

Besides such almost comical events, there were also many seminal meetings with musicians from whom I have learned a lot. I am very fortunate to have had the chance to work with some of the major soloists of the twentieth century, people who embodied the music of their times and conveyed it to the world.

One of these was certainly Yehudi Menuhin, whom I had heard during my childhood in Bombay. Rehearsals with him were always an education. His good nature and the patience with which he tried to explain everything and respond to each musician, which I first witnessed when he played with my father in India, were wonderful. Rehearsing and performing Beethoven's Violin Concerto with him was a lesson for the entire orchestra. He was never unduly severe; instead, he allowed the musicians to share in a very natural way in his musical experience, his great knowledge, and his musical skill.

Those were great moments—when Menuhin explained Edward Elgar's Violin Concerto in B Minor or Bartók's Violin Concerto, both of which he had worked on with the composers. He could therefore offer an approach to these works unmatched by any other artist. There is no substitute for this kind of authenticity. Working with him was like being given a contemporary history of music, and I was fortunate to be able to experience it firsthand.

When speaking of encounters and influences, I obviously have to mention my teacher Hans Swarowsky. I owe my early musical career to him. Even today all his students remember him with love, respect, and appreciation. There is no dearth of occasions on which to pay small musical tributes to him. One of his students, Uroš Lajovic, the director of the Belgrade Philharmonic, regularly organizes commemorative concerts in that city. Swarowsky has been dead for more than thirty years now, but his impact and influence on generations of conductors remain undiminished.

It is to Swarowsky that I primarily owe my early acquaintance with Schoenberg, because Swarowsky had studied composition with both him and Webern. My ability to put my heart and soul into conducting works by Schoenberg, Berg, or Webern is attributable primarily to Swarowsky's influence.

This is also true of Schoenberg's *Gurrelieder*, which I have been conducting all over the world for decades. Again it was Swarowsky who taught me to appreciate this immense and beautiful work. The first time I was to perform *Gurrelieder* in Los Angeles, I was able to obtain the services

116

of the legendary baritone Hans Hotter for the spoken part. It took some time to convince him to undertake this venture. I had heard countless performances by Hotter at the Vienna State Opera during my youth and considered it an immense honor that he was willing to collaborate with me. The rhythm and pitch for this part have been precisely defined in a technique called *Sprechgesang*—speech-song—and it is very difficult for most actors to manage. Toward the end there is a single note that the speaker has to sing. Thus I can say that the great Han Hotter did perform one note under my direction.

~~~~~~~~~~

Despite all the sacrosanct seriousness associated with music, it occasionally has its comical, bizarre, and even amusing aspects. For instance, at my first subscription concert with the Vienna Philharmonic Orchestra, in 1963, we were supposed to perform Schoenberg's Five Pieces for Orchestra. I was working with youthful zest and fervor with the musicians at the first rehearsal, which was held in the Brahmssaal in Vienna. The excellent concertmaster was Willi Boskovsky, the legendary and unmistakably Austrian conductor of the Vienna Philharmonic's New Year's Eve concerts for almost two decades. When he played Johann Strauss, the entire world became Viennese. At the Schoenberg rehearsal, though, there was no talk of Viennese charm. On the contrary, Boskovsky looked at the music— which, incidentally, is very difficult just to read, let alone play—stood up, and said in the broadest Viennese dialect, "We don't like it, we're not going to play it," and walked out. The trumpeter Helmut Wobisch, who was president of the orchestra council at the time, tried to persuade him to come back but couldn't. We decided not to change the program and to look for a substitute concertmaster instead. No one ever mentioned another word about this incident, and in later years Boskovsky and I collaborated often and with great mutual respect.

Incidentally, I later made the acquaintance of Schoenberg's widow, Gertrud, in Los Angeles. She and her two sons lived nearby, and her door was always open to me. From time to time I also ran into Schoenberg's daughter Nuria, who was married to Luigi Nono and living in Venice. I still treasure my friendship with this family.

I firmly believe that conducting cannot be learned through recordings, although it is perfectly possible to be inspired by them. So I would be exaggerating if I claimed that my father's record collection in Mumbai taught me the basics of music. At the same time, the stimulation they provided me, which I have already discussed in detail, should not be underestimated. This is why I feel the influence of conductors, younger as well as older colleagues, whom I have never heard in concert and know only from recordings.

The recordings of Toscanini and Furtwängler, for example, gave me some unique musical insights. I have also heard recordings of Sir Thomas Beecham and many of Leopold Stokowski. Stokowski was one of those conductors who took an early interest in the technical possibilities of the world of recording. His recordings sounded wonderful even on our old-fashioned record player in Bombay. His conducting of Shostakovich and *Gurrelieder* influenced me tremendously as a young man. Stokowski was a revolutionary. He had performed *Wozzeck* in Philadelphia—a sensation in those days—and made the Philadelphia Orchestra the orchestra with the most beautiful sound in the whole United States. He led this orchestra for a very long time, from 1912 to 1936.

It never fails to amuse me when Europeans arrogantly claim that a particular orchestra sounds too American. I always reply that it was actually the great European conductors who built up orchestras in the United States. Mahler and Toscanini were both music directors of the New York Philharmonic. Later Toscanini led the wonderful NBC Symphony Orchestra, Koussevitzky the Boston Symphony, Stokowski the Philadelphia Orchestra, and Fritz Reiner the Chicago Symphony Orchestra. William Steinberg conducted the Pittsburgh Symphony and Otto Klemperer was beloved in Los Angeles. Strictly speaking, before Leonard Bernstein came along there was no one of world renown leading an American orchestra who was born in the United States.

The most meaningful stimuli for me, though, came from music that I heard live. My idols were therefore those great conductors, most of them of an older generation, whom I had a chance to hear in concert. I went to every concert by Krips and Erich Kleiber that I could. Karl Böhm was one of my idols, along with Herbert von Karajan. Seeing them evening after evening during my years in Vienna was for me not only an extremely vivid lesson in conducting, but also pure inspiration.

Performances by Karl Böhm are among the earliest memories I have from my student days. I heard him innumerable times. Many years later we got to know each other better and developed a great deal of affection for each other, even if it was sometimes put to the acid test. Meanwhile, I have the Arthur Nikisch ring in my possession. This is actually a woman's ring—a South Sea pearl set in diamonds—that Böhm was given by the descendants of this prominent German conductor. Böhm bequeathed it to me in his will, and I feel deeply honored to have received this mark of distinction from him. Böhm always kept it with him in the pocket of his waistcoat as a kind of good-luck charm. Unfortunately, I am so forgetful and careless that I would never dare to carry it around with me.

Böhm could become extremely annoyed if things did not go his way. I saw this once for myself. I was supposed to conduct Richard Strauss's *Salome* at the Vienna State Opera in a co-production with Böhm and Jürgen Rose. It had already been some time since the premiere when Rudolf Gamsjäger, the director of the Vienna State Opera, sent me an invitation to take over the opera. I accepted happily, never realizing that Böhm had not known about the offer and was consequently very upset about it. Gamsjäger called me up after Böhm protested and asked me to turn the offer down. He explained that he didn't want to unnecessarily upset the old man. Of course I agreed; I would have hated to get involved in that kind of tug-of-war. But Gamsjäger spread the word that I was sick and therefore unavailable—which then made me look bad because I was conducting a concert with the Vienna Philharmonic at the same time. On the other hand, I suppose he could not very well have said that Mehta had been asked to withdraw because Böhm was upset.

In the end we were able to reconcile the whole matter. Böhm called me up and invited me to lunch at the Hotel Sacher, in the course of which he explained everything to me. He said he had objected to my taking this job because he had put so much of himself into the production that he felt only he could carry the concept through and bring it to life in performance. I did not contradict him; I respected his achievement too much to do that. Then Böhm told me about a similar episode from the distant past. Franz Schalk, director of the Vienna State Opera from 1918 to 1929, also had once prohibited a young conductor from taking over a new production that he, Schalk, had rehearsed. The young conductor was Wilhelm Furtwängler. The story made me feel better, since of course I didn't mind being compared with Furtwängler.

The whole affair caused quite a stir at the time and generated a lot of gossip, but I took no further notice of the incident. Böhm and I were still friendly and cordial whenever we met, mostly in Salzburg, and often sat together after his performances. Whenever we went out to eat together each of us paid his own bill. Once I even "studied" with Böhm for a couple of hours. I had gone to him with the score of *Die Fledermaus*, and he was kind enough to go through the whole work with me. Encounters like these are invaluable for a young conductor because the advice of a seasoned conductor is like a musical manual. The advice is not necessarily binding, but it is very inspiring for a young conductor. To work through a masterpiece with a great and experienced conductor, to go over a score with him and get his personal remarks on it, is a priceless gift.

I had a similar experience with Herbert von Karajan when he worked through the entire score of *Tristan* with me during a visit in Vienna. Karajan was frankly of two minds in his assessment of my musical potential. He was not at all impressed with the concert that I conducted in 1962 with the Vienna Philharmonic in Salzburg. In fact, he wanted to stop me from conducting it. But later he invited me to conduct *The Abduction from the Seraglio* in Salzburg and even asked if I wanted to come to the Vienna State Opera as second conductor. That concert in 1962 with the Vienna Philharmonic was not a success. The program consisted of Mozart's "Prague" Symphony,

Bartók's Second Piano Concerto (with Géza Anda), and Dvořák's Seventh Symphony. I simply was not experienced enough to make good use of the rehearsal time available. Karajan heard the concert but never commented on it. Soon after, when he was working through the score of *Otello* with me, he didn't say a word about it. His silence spoke volumes.

Years later, in the 1970s, Karajan tried to persuade me to come to the Deutsche Oper Berlin. Even then it was too early for me. Apart from my experiences at the Met and in Montreal, I knew very little about opera and had hardly ever performed Wagner or Mozart, so I could not possibly have worked in Germany. It was only much, much later, in 1998, that I finally felt mature enough to take over the responsibility of a German opera house—the Bayerische Staatsoper München—as its music director.

One person who was difficult to deal with musically was Nathan Milstein. He was a wonderful violinist and a marvelous musician, but if he did not like something it was entirely possible that he would just leave the stage in the middle of a rehearsal. I had to pass a few endurance tests with him. The first time I worked with him as a soloist was in Montreal with the Tchaikovsky Violin Concerto. He seemed to be quite satisfied on that occasion. However, a rehearsal in Vienna for the Beethoven Violin Concerto was a real catastrophe. Milstein wasn't happy with anything and found fault with the orchestra over something or other every couple of bars. One has to bear in mind that the Vienna Philharmonic can play Wagner's *Götterdämmerung* with no rehearsal whatsoever, but in the early 1960s it was not really accustomed to playing with soloists. That might have been because of the peculiar way that orchestra was managed. The orchestra of the Vienna State Opera is supported by the state, whereas the Vienna Philharmonic is a private company made up of members of the State Opera orchestra. A musician must play for at least a couple of years in the State Opera orchestra before he—and now also she—can become a member of the Vienna Philharmonic, which gives concerts in Vienna and the rest of the world as a completely independent cooperative.

So Milstein carped at everybody and was downright insulting toward the musicians. He asked me aloud in French, "And this is supposed to be the Vienna Philharmonic?" Mercifully, the next rehearsal went much more smoothly, and he was more than happy with the concert.

It was very moving for me to perform with Jascha Heifetz once again at the opening of the Los Angeles Music Center. However, it wasn't entirely free of conflict, since Heifetz, an extraordinarily sensitive artist, had his own very particular demands. I have already spoken of our different notions of tempo in the Beethoven Violin Concerto. Heifetz would not express his wishes directly and openly, choosing instead to convey them in roundabout ways, which made things a little difficult and sometimes very complicated. It so happened that in the course of preparations for the concert one of his employees made a lunch appointment with my father under rather mysterious circumstances to submit a request that was actually addressed to me: Heifetz asked that I not conduct this concerto from memory. No reason was ever given. Naturally, though, I acceded to his wishes. It really did not make any difference to my ego, and I was happy to grant his request if it could put this giant of a violinist at ease.

Before the concert Heifetz invited me to his home in Los Angeles, where he taught at the University of Southern California. But he didn't really want to talk to me. Instead, he just played the entire violin concerto for me in a kind of private audience.

When Heifetz came for the first rehearsals, he was always unhappy with this or that. He forbade people to address him as "maestro" and responded to a violist's request to photograph him by taking away the man's camera. In addition, he wanted my podium to be a little lower. These were minor details that people took very seriously, and nobody got upset.

This meeting was of profound personal importance for me, since Heifetz had been a part of my earliest experiences of music: my father owned every single recording he had ever made. Heifetz liked my father, and my father in turn worshipped him. Heifetz had the reputation of being a technically perfect musician who, however, didn't play from his soul. On just seeing his playing, one could easily believe that he played without any emotion whatsoever, but anyone who listened to him carefully understood that he was a highly emotional musician. Performers are very personal when it comes to what they want to show of their innermost feelings. I, for example, cannot conceal my love for music and the emotions that move me while performing and am therefore often misunderstood as being too flamboyant.

Arthur Rubinstein, Jascha Heifetz, and the cellist Gregor Piatigorsky were also partners in a trio. Cynics called them the "million-dollar trio" because their fees reached dizzying heights even for those days. But these musicians were such exceptional figures that, in my opinion, their fees were completely justified. Unlike some of the figures now in the music industry, they were not soloists who had briefly been glorified as stars and had then forgotten that an artist cannot afford to stand still. Instead, Rubinstein, Heifetz, and Piatigorsky worked seriously on their craft all their lives.

I had a very special relationship with Isaac Stern, who often came to Israel. He was one of those soloists, like Henryk Szeryng, who knew every detail in the orchestra backward and forward. Rehearsals with such a musician are not restricted to a simple "The orchestra is too loud" or some other vague observation. Instead, they make it possible to work on the sound of the orchestra, taking into consideration all the parts. Stern was president of the America-Israel Cultural Foundation, which helped bring Israeli students to the United States and facilitated cultural mobility and exchange. Stern was also a highly gifted public-relations man. It is thanks to him and his untiring efforts that New York's Carnegie Hall was saved from the wrecking ball. He performed all over the world; only in Germany and Austria did he consistently refuse to perform, for political reasons. When I got to know him his behavior toward me was that of an uncle toward his nephew. Eventually we became more like brothers. Even today during concerts I sometimes remember how Isaac would spin a particular phrase and then, having executed it in his own inimitable manner, look at me adoringly with that special satisfied twinkle in his eye. I miss him tremendously and often tell young violinists how old Isaac would have interpreted this or that phrase.

Henryk Szeryng performed Alban Berg's Violin Concerto with me in New York. Working with him and the musicians of the New York

Philharmonic was enormously profitable because of the analytical manner in which he rehearsed. After the performance Szeryng made me a gift of his score, in which he had noted down his detailed remarks.

It is in such rehearsals that one finds out about other artists' concepts. Very often they are radically different from one's own. This can bring greater lucidity to one's own analysis and open up a whole world of new ideas.

I was also fortunate enough to encounter some of the greatest pianists of the postwar era. In the early 1960s I had the opportunity to lead the Vienna Philharmonic in Wilhelm Backhaus's performance of Beethoven's Third Piano Concerto. At first I was extremely nervous. This quiet old gentleman sat at the piano, carefully listening to the orchestral introduction. He then tore into the first C minor scales with such vehemence that it brought out the best in the orchestra and me, and the rehearsal turned into a great show of musical camaraderie. I felt as though we had been making music together for ages, the old sage transmitting his musical wisdom to a novice with hardly a word spoken. Once more I received an education.

Wilhelm Kempff was another such artist with whom every encounter was a musical revelation.

One great artist with whom I never performed was Sviatoslav Richter. My loss. However, I did play with Emil Gilels quite often. We often performed Rachmaninoff's Third Piano Concerto, and we even recorded the Tchaikovsky Piano Concerto in B-flat Minor together. I have learned a lot from Gilels. His tone emanated not from his wrists alone, but rather from his shoulders and upper body. His immense sound and his approach to music were always an unqualified inspiration.

Another great soul with whom I was closely associated was Rudolf Serkin. He was shy, quiet, and always very kind; it was difficult for him to criticize anything he didn't like. His life had been scarred by the horrors of the Third Reich, and he managed to survive only because he fled Austria just in time. I often met him outside musical circles too. Serkin celebrated his one-hundredth appearance with the New York Philharmonic in 1972, a rare milestone for any musician.

The musical giants I have mentioned above sound like a massive exercise in name-dropping. But as music director in Montreal, Los Angeles, New York, and Israel, I was in a position to invite them every season.

All these great soloists and many others had a profound influence on me, an influence that will continue for the rest of my life.

Meeting Daniel Barenboim in Siena in 1956, when he was barely a teenager, was one of the most important things that ever happened to me. Out of it came a lifelong friendship that began with music but grew to include a personal and, as far as Israel is concerned, a political perspective.

I have already talked about our experiences during the two wars in Israel in 1967 and 1973. Our friendship naturally expanded to include Daniel's first wife, the cellist Jacqueline du Pré. Jacqueline was like a sister to me. She fought her illness with admirable bravery before eventually succumbing to it in 1987. I can never forget that day in October 1973 when, as Daniel and I sat together in a hotel room in Tel Aviv hugging the phone to our ears, an English doctor explained what multiple sclerosis was. Just the previous May Jacqueline had played Elgar's Cello Concerto with me; it was to be her last concert in England.

For over two decades now Daniel has been married to the lovely and talented pianist Elena Bashkirowa. They have two adorable and equally talented sons, David and Michael. Elena is the artistic director of the important and highly successful Chamber Music Festival in Jerusalem. Pinchas Zukerman and Itzhak Perlman are also a part of our inner circle, and we have played together consistently for many years. Zukerman and Perlman are among the soloists who like coming to Israel yearly and performing with the Israel Philharmonic. Perlman regularly visited Tel Aviv for more than ten years as my soloist, when we made many records together.

I have a relationship with Daniel that is firmly anchored and that nothing can ever alter. In all these years there has never been a harsh word between us. His musicality inspired me on that very first day in Siena, when I immediately noticed what a deep understanding he had of conducting.

He is never sensational, not in so much as one single bar. When playing with him, one senses that he completely understands the essence and the structure of each piece and each phrase deep within himself. It is always interesting to rehearse with Daniel, even if it is a piece we have played together often. He never stops reflecting on music, which obviously influences him as a conductor. When playing, he compels the conductor to reflect with him and in this way exercises tremendous influence over the musicians in the orchestra as well.

This constant rethinking is of great importance in music. It is the only way to avoid routine, boredom, and, most of all, a sense of déjà vu, which is the absolute death of music. Music has to be constantly brought to life. Naturally, certain basic concepts need to be in place whenever a piece is played. However, at the moment of performing experienced artists are always able to strike a balance between the rehearsed and the innovative.

Most of all it is the details that are always new. By details I mean that there are various personalities within an orchestra—that is, the orchestral musicians—whose ideas and musical concepts have to be taken seriously. But these details should be part of a comprehensive concept. Ideally, they will accord with the conductor's basic concept of the work so that everything blends smoothly into his or her overall artistic vision.

My friendship with Daniel is comparable to this way of constantly approaching well-known music with new interest. Our friendship is always fresh, and it is further deepened and developed through our keen exchanges. That is the beauty of it. It is precisely because we have known each other for so long that we can stimulate each other and give each other new ideas. I admire him for his work with the West-Eastern Divan and appreciate his stand on Israel.

Toward the end of the 1960s Barenboim had the idea of organizing the South Bank Summer Music Festival, a festival in London devoted mainly to chamber music. The famous Promenade concerts in the Royal Albert Hall had been going on for a long time, but the Festival Hall and the Queen Elizabeth Hall were unused in the summers—symphony concerts were given there only during the season. Why shouldn't this gap be filled?

The negotiations reached a happy end: Daniel was entrusted the artistic responsibility for the festival, and the first concerts took place there under his direction from 1968 to 1970.

At that time Daniel, Jacqueline, Zukerman, Perlman, and I were close friends. Zukerman also played in a trio with Daniel and Jacqueline. We also liked each other and helped each other wherever we could. In retrospect, I view this as one of the most intense and happiest times of my life.

In 1969, immediately after my marriage to Nancy in Los Angeles, where Daniel was my best man, he played Brahms's Second Piano Concerto at the Hollywood Bowl, the summer home of the Los Angeles Philharmonic. Then Nancy and I went to Hawaii for our honeymoon, after which we proceeded immediately to London for the South Bank Festival. That summer Daniel thought of playing Franz Schubert's "Trout" Quintet with all of us. For me it meant performing as an instrumentalist again, taking the bass part. Everything was really unusual at this performance. The entire concert was filmed by Christopher Nupen using a new kind of camera that operated silently. What emerged was something of a rarity in documentaries. That August of 1969 it was not merely a concert that was filmed; the documentary did not begin with the appearance of the musicians on the stage and end with the last note. Rather, the five of us were filmed from the very first moment of rehearsals, which began days before the concert, through the performance, and even as we made our way backstage at the end of the concert. Together we had a lot of fun—and not in the usual, banal sense of the word. It was rather an exuberant joy at playing together that never left us young artists in all that time. This documentary, called *The Trout*, became the most frequently broadcast film on classical music of its time. It is still broadcast on television and is now available on DVD.

After the "Trout" Quintet I conducted Schoenberg's *Pierrot lunaire*, in which all my friends participated. The actress Vanessa Redgrave was kind enough to read the poems in English before the performance. It was a magnificent performance, one that in my opinion also deserved to be filmed.

Plácido Domingo sat in the audience with my new wife, Nancy. I am almost tempted to say that I discovered him, though strictly speaking that's not true. In 1968 I engaged the very young Domingo for a concert performance of *Carmen* in Israel. At the end of Don José's Flower Aria in the second act, I had real tears in my eyes. Josef Krips, who was present in the audience, was thrilled to hear this incredible tenor. I had also conducted Domingo in Verdi's Requiem at the Pablo Casals Festival in Puerto Rico. Casals had never met him, but he had heard of Domingo's mother, a very well-known zarzuela singer.

Domingo's Met debut was occasioned by Franco Corelli's cancellation. That was in 1969, when I conducted *Il trovatore* for the first time in my life. In any case, Plácido was already well established at the New York City Opera and had just been engaged to be part of the Met ensemble. Since then we have become close friends.

It is no secret that I have a great affinity for Mahler. Thus, when the opportunity to meet Alma Mahler-Werfel came up, I was naturally eager to talk to someone so closely associated Gustav Mahler's life and works. I had read a lot of what she had written about her life with Mahler, as well as what others had thought and written about her, so I had good reason to meet with her in New York.

Her home was in itself impressive. I remember that when I entered I felt for a moment as if I'd been transported to Vienna. The rooms were crammed with dark furniture, and the place was decorated with memorabilia of her husbands and lovers: a framed Kokoschka fan, architectural designs by Gropius, and a score by Mahler. There was an air of theatrical pathos hanging over everything. Alma Mahler-Werfel had lived in the reflected glory as well as in the shadow of the many men whom she had gathered around herself, and whom she had been able to keep attached to herself with charms that were undiminished even in her later years. At more than eighty years of age, she really had enormous charisma to which I couldn't help succumbing. Her personality made quite an impression, and she radiated a strong individualism. In the course of our conversation I remarked quite in passing that I found her granddaughter in Los Angeles very beautiful. This *grande dame* replied succinctly that in her opinion the young lady had a very big bottom.

I listened to her stories with a great deal of interest. She could tell me about events from her personal experiences with the various geniuses she had known that I could never have hoped to learn from books or, for that matter, from Mahler's scores.

She held my hand all through my visit, and whenever I tried to leave, she thought of something new she wanted to tell me. I didn't mind, for I was completely under her spell. Unfortunately, the enchantment was so powerful that I lost track of the time and missed my flight to Paris.

This would turn out to have rather unpleasant consequences for me. I had originally been scheduled to meet with a well-known critic, Bernard Gavoty (who wrote under the pseudonym Clarendon), as soon as I arrived in Paris. When I did not show up, for the interview, he became absolutely furious. Remember that this was at a time when I couldn't just send him an e-mail about missing my plane. We never did meet.

I pride myself on being loyal to friends and colleagues alike, as well as to the orchestras with which I worked back at the beginning of my career. Naturally there were attempts and temptations, if I may call them that, to take on new challenges. I have grown immeasurably fond of the Israel Philharmonic Orchestra and, over the years, of the orchestras in Los Angeles, New York, and Munich as well. I make it a point to guest-conduct with these ensembles whenever I can. I ventured to conduct opera at the Royal Opera House in London and in Florence in the 1970s and 1980s, and Florence in particular became increasingly important for me. Some years later the Munich Philharmonic and especially the Bavarian State Orchestra became part of my musical family as well. Families expand: they branch out, and there are offspring. It is no different with this family. Some of these new branches weren't stable enough to allow us to maintain a permanent connection. But most of them were.

I had enjoyed unexpected success in the early 1960s, when I went around conducting in the most diverse places. But of course I didn't always succeed, and not everybody was satisfied with me.

My first appearance at Milan's La Scala had a bizarre beginning. My debut was in 1962, but the first doubts about me had surfaced before I even arrived. Antonio Ghiringhelli, the general director, was upset with the artistic director, Francesco Siciliani, and wondered whom Siciliani thought he was bringing into this venerable house. The previous year a Japanese conductor, Seiji Ozawa, had made his appearance in the "sacred halls of this temple of music," which was meant exclusively for the greatest geniuses among conductors. "And now an Indian, who would probably conduct in a turban!"

It was not as bad as Ghiringhelli had feared. I did not wear a turban, and I do not think I desecrated the sacred halls either. He and I even became good friends later. At any rate, my debut in Milan was not entirely successful. Once again I had chosen to program my favorite Six Pieces for Orchestra by Webern, along with Richard Strauss's *Don Quixote*, but they did not go over well at the time. It was completely wrong to begin with Webern. A couple of times I heard doors slamming, and once there was a loud and sarcastic "Che bella musica" that sounded rather menacing.

I was much more successful as a guest conductor in Florence, where in 1964 I conducted my first opera in Europe. However, it would be some years before I returned. Since 1986 I have had a permanent position there as *direttore stabile*.

Another debut was more pleasant, though it remained largely inconsequential. At the coaxing of Helga Schmidt, who was the artistic soul of the Royal Opera House in Covent Garden, London, I took my first step toward opera in that city. I conducted *Otello* there in 1977 with Jon Vickers, a singer I admire greatly. That same year I also worked on Puccini's opera *La fanciulla del West*. Puccini himself thought this one of his best operas, and from a musical perspective I tend to agree with him, though the story is really rather silly. The score still strikes me, as it did then, as extraordinarily modern; some of it is strongly influenced by French impressionism. I am sure that Puccini, who, by the way, was a great admirer of Schoenberg, would have gone much further had he lived longer. It was first performed with Enrico Caruso and Emmy Destinn in December 1910 at the Metropolitan Opera in New York, with Toscanini conducting. The part of Minnie is vocally grueling, and even well-known sopranos give it a wide berth. Helga Schmidt convinced me that she had finally found a singer who was willing to take on this challenging role: Carol Neblett. Plácido Domingo was Dick Johnson/Ramerrez. It was a huge success. Everything about their performances was perfect, the singing as well as the acting. With Puccini, text and music are inseparable; he was a master at marrying the two.

Unfortunately, *Fanciulla* is almost never performed. Nowadays a sensible staged performance of the piece is hardly possible, but the director Piero Faggioni made the best of it with the help of Ken Adam's excellent stage sets. The recording we made with the ensemble at that time was great fun and won many prizes.

Covent Garden and I—it was not a deeply moving story. One performance that became relatively well established was the New Year's Eve performance of *Die Fledermaus* under the direction of Leopold Lindtberg in 1977–78. The cast was superb. Since Hermann Prey was Eisenstein and Kiri Te Kanawa was Rosalinde, we turned Eisenstein into a Viennese man married to an Englishwoman in order to justify a mix of English and German in the conversation. The great Viennese actor Josef Meinrad charmed everyone as Frosch, the jailer. In the second act Isaac Stern surprised the audience with a movement of Mendelssohn's Violin Concerto during the traditional party interlude, followed by Daniel Barenboim playing Liszt's *Rigoletto Paraphrase*. It was a very funny performance and at the same time vocally outstanding. The next year I conducted *Fledermaus* again, this time with Birgit Nilsson as a surprise party guest. She sang one of the all-time great Viennese songs, "Wien, Wien, nur du allein . . ." (Vienna, Vienna, just you alone). It was certainly not your average everyday performance!

I continued to conduct in London until the 1990s—Verdi, Strauss, *Tristan*, Puccini once again, and *Tosca* with Pavarotti. Twice I was asked to take over the musical direction of the house, and Sir John Tooley, Covent Garden's revered general director, even came to Los Angeles in the 1980s to negotiate with me. But it would have been impossible for me to take on another major position in addition to my job as music director of the New York Philharmonic.

In this chapter I have talked about my encounters with people primarily in the world of music—mostly my meetings with singers and soloists, or other conductors and my idols from the early days. But there are plenty of people from entirely different walks of life to whom I am drawn purely out of friendship. At this juncture I want to talk about two friends who have been loyal to me since my days in Bombay. One of them is Nusli Wadia, one of the foremost industrialists in Mumbai. His wife, Maureen, is deeply involved personally with looking after the poorest of the poor. The Wadia charities not only build homes for poor Parsis, but also provide free medical treatment for everyone at their hospital. Nusli and his sons Ness and Jeh are also involved in countless other projects, such as real-estate development, textiles, petrochemicals, food products, and—their latest venture—a budget airline within India. Another great friend is Yusuf Hamied, the chairman of Cipla Pharmaceuticals in Mumbai, whom I've known since we were babies. Apart from producing an immense portfolio of medications in India, he is known throughout the third world as the savior of thousands thanks to his seemingly unlimited supply of antiretroviral drugs to combat HIV. These he sells at cost to scores of African countries. I respect both these friends immensely and admire them for their dedication.

Zarin and I are extremely indebted to Mehroo Jeejeebhoy, a close friend who almost single-handedly administers the Mehli Mehta Music Foundation, which is dedicated to the furtherance and teaching of Western classical music—a project that my father greatly appreciated and to which he gave his blessing. My brother and I give as much advice as possible, but the main brunt of the day-to-day work falls on Mehroo and a wonderful group of volunteer friends without whom none of this organization's fine work would be possible.

Both my personal and professional life would be a disorganized mess were it not monitored diligently and daily in every aspect by my dear and invaluable assistant, Natalia Ritzkowsky. She was my assistant for eight years at the Bavarian State Opera and now works for me exclusively from her little nest on Lake Starnberg, together with her husband, Klaus, and their adorable little son, Yannick.

Having talked about these friends, colleagues, and musical idols, in the end there is nobody on this earth to whom I feel closer than my children, my grandchildren, and—last but not least—my dearest, loving, and dedicated wife, Nancy. I am indebted to her immeasurably for four decades of patience, wisdom, and above all the love she has showered on me always.

For the last fifty years I have been pursuing a career that has brought me in contact with people who are in their own way unique, extraordinary, crazy, strange, imaginative, and without parallel. Along with my musical and artistic concerns, which I have to clarify for myself and deal with on my own, I also must adapt to all kinds of people and personalities. I need to have insight into the inner feelings of my musicians and to help as much as I can. And I have to deal with doubts, to be able to justify my simple daily routine, and to struggle with one or another of life's basic vital questions.

In the wake of an increasing public perception of me as the director of an orchestra or the head of an opera, I also get to meet the so-called powerful and mighty. Politics likes to adorn itself with culture, art, and music in order to demonstrate that practical, everyday business and an interest in beauty can seem to coexist. Music is especially suited to this purpose, be it simply as background or in connection with matters that can be made clearer through music.

When I was younger I had practically no interest in political matters, either because of the ignorance of youth or because of my immaturity. But after a while I started following economic and political developments with great interest. This change has been brought about in large part by my engagement with Israel. Besides, I believe that an artist cannot withdraw into some protected space where he can devote himself exclusively to his art and to the creative opportunities available to him. I'm not like Tosca—I can't just say, "Vissi d'arte, vissi d'amore!"

Whenever I disagree with a political situation I find myself in, I speak up. I react with the means available to me, both verbal and musical. As a conductor I express myself through music. I try to help, and I also try to protest or to make people think. This is, I think, a wonderful responsibility. I protested with my music against the Vietnam War, against the dictatorship in Greece, in solidarity with the people of Bosnia, and in many other instances.

There are many "great events" for which a concert can create a marvelous context. Of course, opinions differ as to whether this constitutes a misuse of music. But for better or worse, it is a part of public life.

When the United Nations celebrated its twenty-fifth anniversary in 1970, the festival program included a concert with the Los Angeles Philharmonic that I was supposed to conduct at U.N. headquarters. This was both a very great responsibility and a very high honor. Many heads of state were going to be there, and Beethoven's Ninth Symphony, with its verses by Schiller, was supposed to create the right mood. The premiere of Krysztof Penderecki's *Cosmogony* was also planned to go along with the Beethoven. We had to work very intensively. Even though orchestras play it infrequently, Beethoven's gigantic work is so familiar to so many people that it must be carefully rehearsed. And the Penderecki premiere obviously required really thorough work.

My problem with this jubilee concert was that the General Assembly Hall was reserved for President Richard Nixon's speech before the delegates during my rehearsal time. As luck would have it, there was a banquet before the anniversary in Los Angeles. Nancy and I were there, seated at the president's table. When he brought up the topic of the concert, I grabbed the opportunity to tell him about the problems I was having with the rehearsals. I emphasized how important these rehearsals were, saying that it was absolutely essential to rehearse in the hall itself not only on account of the premiere, but also because the acoustics were not particularly good.

I got through to him. Nixon sent for his national security advisor, Henry Kissinger, and told him to reschedule the speech. Organizing the allotment of the auditoriums in the U.N. headquarters was not exactly in Kissinger's job description. But what else could he do? He had gotten his orders from none other than the chief executive.

Kissinger was beside himself with fury. At the end of the evening we ran into each other again in the elevator. "I'll get you for this!" he snarled.

I did not feel the least bit guilty. On the contrary, I thought it was nice of Nixon to take an interest in my rehearsal. Nixon's address was postponed to another day, and I could rehearse in the hall to my heart's content. But there was indeed hell to pay. Enraged by my brazen (as he saw it) intervention, Kissinger had arranged for the state reception to take place in Washington. And so, instead of letting themselves be regaled with Beethoven and Penderecki, when the evening arrived the heads of state all went to a banquet in the capital. Not one of them showed up for my concert in New York. Indira Gandhi wrote to me later that she would have loved to hear her favorite Beethoven but could not refuse the Washington invitation. So much for the idea that music allows politicians to come together in peace.

Years later Kissinger and I actually became friends, and every now and then we still have a laugh about this story.

8

NEW YORK AND FLORENCE

The Music of the Twentieth Century

At the turn of 1975–76 Carlos Moseley, managing director of the New York Philharmonic, came to Los Angeles with a question from their board of directors. They wanted to know if I would be interested in the position of music director. I was under contract in Los Angeles till 1978, by which time I would have been the conductor of the Los Angeles Philharmonic for sixteen years without a break. During that time I had personally hired about eighty-five musicians. We all knew each other very well and reacted to each other's smallest cue. On the other hand, this intense proximity over such a long time had also led to certain signs of wear; a change of conductor would no doubt be beneficial to both the orchestra and me. I had repeatedly performed, rehearsed, and studied the classical masterpieces with the musicians, and they knew the notes by heart, which is not in itself a disadvantage—but they knew them only in my interpretation. In fact, the musicians could probably have played just as well without me. When an orchestra and a conductor are so closely connected and have mutually influenced each other over the years, it can lead to sloppiness.

So I reflected seriously on whether a new beginning with a different orchestra would not be an interesting challenge. Of course, this wasn't the first time I'd asked myself this question. So far, though, I had been fully occupied, apart from my duties in Los Angeles, with the orchestral work in Israel, the concerts in Vienna and Berlin, and the occasional appearances in Florence, Milan, and London. In addition, I had been engaged regularly as a conductor at the Met in New York for six years, from 1965 to 1971.

And now the New York Philharmonic, with which I had already had a rather conflicted encounter, wanted me as its music director. There was a lot to consider. Nancy and I liked living in Los Angeles and had a beautiful home there. My parents lived close by in happy and secure circumstances. Did I really want to give all this up?

And then there was also that unpleasant event from 1967, which for a while had left me and everyone else concerned with a bad taste in our mouths. I had made a remark privately about the New York Philharmonic that a journalist had then published, leading to considerable irritation. I had said that the New York Philharmonic sometimes did not care about its conductors, that it simply ignored them, no matter how reputable they might be, and that it had become a "cemetery for conductors."

My comment did sound really harsh. At the time I was thirty-one years old and busy with a new *Carmen* production at the Met, and I was supposed to conduct the New York Philharmonic the following season. My remark caused a huge stir in the press, and I did not come off looking good at all. The planned guest-conducting engagement was postponed. Later I formally apologized for what I'd said. Even if there was a grain of truth in what I had said, the fact remained that it had been phrased clumsily, and it embarrassed me awfully. It was several years before I was invited back to New York, this time by my colleague Pierre Boulez, who asked me to guest conduct. Before I started my first rehearsal I apologized to the orchestra, telling them that it was I who in the end lost out on years of making music with them.

It was ten years after this incident when I got the offer to be the orchestra's new music director, and the furor had long since died down. In the end I accepted with pleasure and began working in New York in the 1978–79 season. The working conditions were very good and seemed easily compatible with my other obligations. The contract stipulated, in accordance with my wishes, that my presence was required for sixteen weeks.

At the beginning of my engagement in New York the press welcomed me with two kinds of responses. On the one hand, my unfortunate comment from 1967 was again fished out and bandied about with relish. On the other hand, the press also reported on the remarkable coincidence that one of my most famous predecessors in this position, Arturo Toscanini, had given his farewell concert with the New York Philharmonic on the day I was born—April 29, 1936.

For their part, the musicians evidently harbored no lingering resentment over the old story. They collaborated with me in every way, and we began our music making together with a clean slate. The contract, initially limited to three years, lasted thirteen long, fruitful years. I often made mistakes, both musically and on the human level (just as in Los Angeles), and I will be forever grateful for the musicians' boundless patience with me. I felt 100 percent loyal toward my new colleagues and was constantly in awe at the depth and understanding with which this great orchestra played. My time with them was again a real education—inspiration coupled with great camaraderie.

However, the entire time I was subjected to malicious attacks in the New York press, especially during my last years there. In the beginning the *New York Times*'s Harold Schonberg did always try to achieve some kind of balance in his criticism, but his successor constantly wrote really vicious things about me. It was so heartwarming when I returned as a guest conductor. The orchestra struck up "Hail to the Chief" as I walked onstage for my first rehearsal. All my visits to the Philharmonic since then have given me such musical satisfaction that their supremely high standard of playing is something I carry with me wherever I go in the world.

Of course it hurts to read a bad review, but the dismay and anger don't usually last longer than fifteen or twenty minutes. Even if one operates on the assumption that the musicians have read the review too, it is never actually discussed, and life goes on.

I am not at all against criticism as long as it is objective and backed by real knowledge. Very often critics make superficial, know-it-all comments that are either nonsense or even in some instances downright wrong. I would like to present two examples of this that especially impressed me—in a negative sense.

We were playing the "Gran Partita," Mozart's Serenade in B-flat Major for twelve wind instruments and double bass, in New York. Among the wind instruments Mozart specified are two basset horns, which we of course used. The basset horn was brought by Bohemian musicians to Vienna, where it was extremely popular for a short time around the end of the eighteenth century. It has a very characteristic sound, somewhere between that of a clarinet and a bass clarinet, and Mozart used it in *The Abduction from the Seraglio* and the Requiem, among other works. It is very difficult to play and requires someone who specializes in it. Of course I had suitable musicians in the orchestra. But what did I read—to my surprise— in a review of this concert? The critic claimed that the conductor was not in favor of original instruments and really had something against original texts, and this was the reason the "Gran Partita" had unfortunately been performed with two bass clarinets instead of the basset horns prescribed by Mozart. The readers must certainly have been deeply impressed by the writer's supposedly vast knowledge, but I was extremely annoyed. When one is confronted with such gross ignorance and blatant misinterpretation one cannot simply brush it off and get on with one's day. It takes a while to get over something like that.

Another example has to do with the end of the Schubert Fourth Symphony. There is an empty bar at the end, which is naturally printed in the score. Once, at the end of a concert, I beat time for this empty bar too, much to the musicians' amusement. A critic wrote that I had obviously not known the symphony was over and that even the musicians were laughing at my unbelievable ignorance. It was true that the musicians had laughed—but they had laughed at my joke.

I have colleagues who, after misunderstandings like that, get in touch with the critic responsible. I never do. One might be able to edit the written word, unlike the note played and the beat given—but to what purpose? One of many anecdotes about conductors involves the wife of my French colleague Paul Paray. During her husband's South American tour she took to task a journalist who had written a very bad review about her husband. She made sure that he was really the same journalist, and once the poor man confirmed it she slapped him right in front of the audience as they were waiting for the concert to start.

Around that time some reports kept circulating in New York accusing me of having a "Hollywood attitude" or attacking me for supposedly attending some glamorous social event night after night. This was meant to undermine the seriousness with which I pursued my profession. When something like this happens, one just has to grin and bear it. It is too ridiculous to merit a reaction.

However, one article in a magazine really bothered me because it quoted verbatim some rather unkind things said by a couple of the more than one hundred members of the New York Philharmonic. One of them complained that I pulled too many grim faces and grimaced too often; the other complained about something he could have said to me directly. As a conductor one cannot expect to be loved by all, but this kind of public complaint about internal matters really hurt me. So after the article was published I called a meeting of the orchestra and suggested discussing the quoted assertions in order to try and clear up virulent problems and to soothe inflamed tempers. This conversation was interesting and informative, and the open discussion was salutary for both sides. We explained to one another what attitudes needed to be changed and what had to be accepted as unalterable. Among other things, I was accused of grimacing. In this respect I promised to improve, because I realized that in a concert one should not reveal it when one does not like something or when something does not turn out particularly well. Naturally, I made some requests of the musicians as well. It is terrible for a conductor to see a musician who is obviously getting bored, barely concentrating on his part, who does not seem prepared to contribute his or her all. I was surprised many members of the orchestra echoed my criticism. A wind player described how unbearable it was for him to have a violinist practically dozing in front of him while he himself was going all out to do a good job.

Unfortunately, there are a couple of bored musicians in almost every orchestra. It is a mystery for me that a publicly visible expression of boredom can even exist. Why do these people practice sometimes eight hours a day in their youth if they just get bored later on? And how many people can actually claim to deal with so much beauty and perfection in their profession as musicians do?

This meeting did clear up many things, and afterward a positive work atmosphere was established between the two sides so that we could continue making music. All in all, I had a wonderful time in New York. I could see this orchestra, which had been led by the most important musicians of the twentieth century, such as Bernstein and Boulez, begin to flourish again.

I performed a lot of modern music with the New York Philharmonic, far more than I do now. In my opinion New York is the right setting for twentieth-century music. Both Bernstein and Boulez had already made some important strides in this direction, and in the thirteen years of my work there the orchestra played fifty-two premieres, of which I personally conducted thirty. While I was in New York we were awarded the prize five times from the American Society of Composers, Authors and Publishers (ASCAP), an organization founded in 1914 primarily to support American composers.

There is no way a music director, even with the best of intentions, can make any headway into organizing his daily hours without the assistance and support of the people "upstairs." The staff "upstairs" in New York was headed by Nick Webster, who had nurtured and trained the most efficient and willing group of people I could imagine. Nick himself was an invaluable help regarding all matters concerning my communications with the board of directors, the planning of future tours, the promoting and organizing of festivals of modern music, and most of all the solving of personal and human problems between the orchestra personnel and me. Frank

Milburn was my right-hand man and my musical consciousness when it came to programming; he is an invaluable walking encyclopedia of music and a wonderful friend. Karl Schiebler and his predecessor James Chambers were the ideal personnel managers, the best a music director could wish for. Both were excellent musicians who not only understood the day-to-day workings of each individual musician but also, being musicians themselves, knew exactly how to appreciate their workload and often would correct my sometimes too demanding schedule. Another invaluable help to me was the assistance and advice of Francis Little, who was the head of our Public Relations office. For thirteen years these gentlemen cleared all possible obstacles from my path to give me complete peace of mind and allow me to make music with my beloved New York Philharmonic colleagues.

At this point I also have to say that throughout my professional life I have been blessed in being able to work with the most humane and demanding friends "upstairs," who have made my life and musical ambitions so worthwhile. These include Pierre Beique in Montreal, and Jay Rubanoff and Ernest Fleischmann in Los Angeles. In Munich, I could not have survived my eight years there without the constant advice and encouragement of Sir Peter Jones and his wonderful head of operations, Ronald Adler. And in Italy it was Cesare Mazzonis and the ever faithful Gianni Tangucci, who saved me from the umpteen daily problems of that country's bureaucracy.

Obviously not all new works will catch on and become a permanent part of the repertoire, but one must be ready and willing to come to grips with them. In my opinion it is the duty of a music director to pave the way for young composers so that they may be seen and heard by the audience. This has nothing to do with some wish to be the obstetrician every time a masterpiece is born, but rather is a matter of seeing to it that developments in a composer's career or indeed in the history of music in general are followed by others.

In Los Angeles as well as in New York I had with me a composer-in-residence, a kind of in-house composer who takes over some of the director's work, such as examining the scores of new works that come in. The music director of a huge organization such as a major symphony orchestra cannot study in detail everything that is submitted. The sheer abundance of works waiting to see the light of day is simply staggering. And not everything that has been written recently should be considered new—only when it constitutes a kind of music worth studying and knowing because it incorporates a new idea or sound. One of the main composers with whom I worked from 1982 to 1986 in New York was Jacob Druckman. He is very well respected in the United States and a wonderful human being. Some of his works have premiered at the New York Philharmonic, and not only under my direction.

From 1979 to 1986 New York had a concert series called Horizons in which only contemporary music was performed. But one has to face reality: the audience did not always like what was played. Nor is this a peculiarly American phenomenon. The fact that a big orchestra is interpreting some new piece of music does not necessarily mean that it will be accepted. I have experienced some terrible things, such as the time we were performing Messiaen's ten-movement *Turangalila-Symphonie*. This massive work is a full evening's program. Messiaen was in the audience, and he was forced to witness more and more seats emptying after each movement. It was terribly embarrassing, but I learned a lesson that day. When I conducted the same piece in Chicago, Messiaen was again present, and this time I introduced him to the audience and commented upon the piece before the concert began. That broke the ice. Since then I have made a habit of delivering this sort of a prologue. I have learned that it is extremely important to lead the audience to what the composer is trying to say with his work. On the other hand, one must be careful with such introductions. People do not come to a concert to hear a lecture, as if they were in school. Most of them come because they want to experience a spiritual journey, or because they want to be transported to a different world, a world of sound and of feelings. People's reasons for attending a concert are extremely varied, but the fantasies and expectations of each one of them must be fulfilled. It should at the very least be possible to fulfill them.

My first season in New York opened with a premiere: Samuel Barber's *Third Essay for Orchestra*. Barber came for the rehearsals from the very beginning, which I generally appreciate greatly with premieres. I really love to have the composer present during rehearsals of his or her work. The composer can explain his or her vision to me and the musicians, give us suggestions, and correct us if we make a mistake or misunderstand something. Two composers in particular, Olivier Messiaen and Pierre Boulez, have given me the most invaluable insights into their works, and I have learned more from them than from any other composer.

There are also some contemporary composers who do not know their own works as well as might be expected, or who do not understand what I as the conductor need to know so that the work can be successfully interpreted in accordance with the composer's ideas. Others give us details that are simply not helpful in getting any further along with the work. In the worst case this can lead to even greater uncertainty.

It can be a big help if one can discuss a modern work with colleagues who have already had some experience with it in their own performances. Once the New York Philharmonic and I were rehearsing the extremely complicated *Symphony of Three Orchestras* by Elliot Carter, the grand old man of American music whom Aaron Copland called the most important American composer of the twentieth century. I think very highly of Carter's compositions, but they demand a lot from the musicians. All of us are used to classical rhythmic modulations. But it is quite different with modern music in general, and with Carter in particular. For example, one has to count a quintuplet and then adjust three-eighths of this quintuplet in the next tempo, a terribly difficult thing to do. Carter was there at the rehearsals, but he could not really help me. And I had huge problems of my own. Three orchestras actually sit together on the stage for this piece, but there is only one conductor.

One day when we were due to rehearse this piece, I happened to run into Lenny Bernstein, who had conducted the premiere. I pounced on him and asked him how he had solved the problem of metric modulations and the different tempi associated with them. Bernstein had a lot of experience with modern pieces, and he explained to me with an expression of great composure that I was worrying too much and that the orchestra simply had to play slower sometimes and then faster.

That was not really a satisfactory answer; at least, it did not fix my problems. At the concert the New York Philharmonic did a good job, and I think Carter was satisfied. But it was not a brilliant performance, and we certainly did not come up with a definitive interpretation.

What was amazing, though, was the press response. One critic compared my performance with the one by Bernstein on CD and claimed that my total time had been half a minute faster than Bernstein's, which for such a complicated work can hardly be a basis for comparison.

Premieres have special importance for a conductor. One is a part of a creative process and feels at one with the composer. I feel basically the same thing when I conduct a Beethoven symphony, but of course it is different when one knows that the creator of the work is present.

The musicians and conductor do everything in their power to be true to the intent of the new work and to the ideas of the composer. They also suffer a great deal when they realize that something has not worked out in the way they had hoped. Sometimes it is external circumstances that make it impossible to give a perfect rendering, such as when there is not enough time to rehearse together. An orchestra almost always plays several pieces in a concert, which means that the time devoted to each has to be carefully allocated. Since the number of rehearsals is limited, one has to decide how much to rehearse what.

It can be a great help to the conductor and the musicians if a composer works with the orchestra and is willing to give constructive advice. But it can also be counterproductive if the amount of attention given to his or her work comes at the expense of the others. This is exactly what happened to me once with a world-famous composer whom I find highly interesting. In Los Angeles I had programmed a ten-minute orchestral piece by this composer. Usually there are four rehearsals scheduled in which the orchestra goes through the entire concert program. I had set aside one and a half rehearsals exclusively for this new piece, and parts of the third and fourth rehearsals were also reserved for it. (The program also included the Bartók and Tchaikovsky violin concertos with Isaac Stern.) Unfortunately, the composer, who was present at all the rehearsals, was dissatisfied with every single one of them. It was very discouraging for both the orchestra and me. At the end of the performance I invited the composer onstage, but he refused, putting me in an extremely embarrassing situation. We never saw each other again.

My debut with the New York Philharmonic was an extraordinary event because of the huge audience. It was in Central Park at one of those famous open-air concerts that anyone can attend for free—a terrific achievement on the part of the city—and about 140,000 people came. Open-air concerts are a normal part of the music scene in the United States, unlike in Europe, where there are very few free concerts. However, one must not forget that in the United States such concerts are often a sheer necessity. The seasons there are much shorter than in Europe, and the orchestras always have to look for summer residences. The orchestra in Los Angeles plays at the famous Hollywood Bowl, which can accommodate seventeen thousand people. There is even an actual "summer season" there. Similarly, the Boston Symphony plays in Tanglewood, and the Philadelphia Orchestra plays in Saratoga, New York, and at the Mann Center in Philadelphia. The New York Philharmonic plays free concerts at the city parks of all five boroughs.

I think highly of such concerts because they contribute to musical education and give us a chance to win over a new audience. The arguments normally directed against them seem to me rather snobbish. I see no reason to object if people go to a park with a picnic basket and listen to a world-class orchestra, even if that means the music has to be somewhat more accessible. Who knows how many of those listeners, come winter, might then want to go to hear an orchestra in a concert hall? Conductors should do at least one concert a year where the normally high ticket prices the public has to pay during the year are waived.

This first season in New York was eventful in other respects too. The orchestra and I made several records together, we had various television appearances, we played the soundtrack (all George Gershwin) for Woody Allen's film *Manhattan*, and we went on our first tour, which took us to Argentina and the Dominican Republic.

New York contains every kind of contrast one can imagine, and the concerts of the New York Philharmonic are no exception. On the one hand there were the famous "opening nights." These are the gala openers of the new season. Big stars, singers and instrumentalists alike, are featured. The crowning event is a banquet attended by the city's rich and beautiful. It is well-known that American orchestras have to finance themselves in a completely different way from European orchestras. Fund-raising is absolutely crucial in the United States; one can never pay enough attention to it. Well-to-do people have to be won over, and in return possible donors are offered a special and artistically enjoyable evening. For these occasions all ticket costs as well as donations are completely tax deductible, an approach that is almost nonexistent in Europe.

It always gives me pleasure to have my friends from the world of music with me at such concerts, friends with whom I can make music for the well-being of many and the pleasure of all. In 1980 Itzhak Perlman, Pinchas Zukerman, and Isaac Stern got together on the occasion of Stern's sixtieth birthday. Stern played Bach, Mozart, and Vivaldi with his friends, as well as the Brahms Violin Concerto. On another occasion I turned the opening concert into an Indian evening: There was an Indian festival going on at the same time in New York, and we managed to arrange an unusual performance with the revered Indian sitar virtuoso Ravi Shankar. My friendship with this grand sage of music began back in the 1960s, when I met the "Heifetz of India" in Los Angeles. I was already quite familiar with his music through his recordings. Ravi had by then become a household name in all the major European and American cultural centers. The high point of our relationship was definitely *Raga Mala*: Second Concerto for Sitar and Orchestra, which he composed specifically for the New York Philharmonic. It met with enormous success in New York and, later on, in London and Paris as well. The fusion of Indian and Western styles is at best a very complicated affair, since Indian music is completely improvised whereas Western classical music is fully notated. Panditji Shankar wrote extensive passages for different soloists in the orchestra that sounded more or less improvised. The result was that what they played from concert to concert was always the same, whereas what Shankar interspersed along the way, in perfect Indian tradition, was of course improvised. This made each performance a fresh experience, to the great amazement of the musicians, who responded wholeheartedly. We even performed *Raga Mala* in India with the European Youth Symphony.

In September 1990 I gave my one thousandth concert with the New York Philharmonic, along with Mstislav Rostropovich, whom we all affectionately call Slava. But here it was only the number that was impressive. At the end of the day, I feel fulfilled only if I achieve evening after evening that to which I aspire spiritually, and if I know that I have done my best to realize the composer's intent.

There is another side to New York, one that contrasts vividly with the glamorous gala events and the big concert evenings. All over the world there are people whose concerns and needs are too great to be dismissed. Still, I am convinced that we can bring some light into their difficult lives, even if that means only that for a couple of hours, at least, something other than their daily struggle for survival comes to the fore.

After long talks and negotiations with the pastor of Abyssinian Baptist Church in Harlem, the orchestra and I decided to give concerts there from time to time. Harlem is marginalized in every sense of the word. We went there not because we were convinced that our music could undo anything, alleviate any misery, or prevent any violence, but because we felt that we could at least share some of what we had been so generously blessed with, something that touched people deeply and that our fellow men and women in Harlem almost never had a chance to hear, or at any rate not from an orchestra like the New York Philharmonic. It was ironic that the orchestra performed literally all over the world yet had never played in Harlem, just a couple of miles away. We gave our first concert in this church in April

1980. Needless to say, nobody accepted any payment for it. And as soon as Leontyne Price heard about our plans, she called up and declared that she absolutely had to be a part of this project. She had actually been married in this very church, and now she wanted to perform there with us.

The concert with Leontyne Price was a resounding success. The great soprano sang not only Verdi and Puccini arias, but also spirituals. The church's excellent choir also contributed to the evening's positive energy. In the following years many prominent artists performed at these concerts, which became an annual tradition.

The basic idea behind this concert was the same as that behind the concerts in Watts, in Los Angeles. The pastor of the church in Harlem was a very experienced man. He was also sensitive enough to know what it meant to bring together the two radically different worlds of Harlem and the New York Philharmonic. The morning after the concert, the phrase most heard among the orchestra members was, "The Philharmonic finally took the A-train"—the line that runs from Manhattan to Harlem. Unfortunately, this wonderful concert series ended rather unpleasantly some years later because the new pastor made some remarks that were not too smart politically, which led to considerable annoyance among the musicians.

I like going on tour with the orchestras I am responsible for. It is quite well-known that I am always happy to accompany any of "my" orchestras all around the world, and with the New York Philharmonic I have undertaken some remarkable journeys. In the summer of 1980, my second year with them, we went to Europe. We performed in some German cities as well as at the festival concerts in Salzburg. The year 1984 was a particularly happy one for me because we went on a big Asian tour, during which we performed in India. My mother traveled all the way from the United States just to attend our concerts in Bombay, Calcutta, and New Delhi.

Two concerts in East Germany in June 1985 made a particularly deep impression on both the orchestra and me. They were organized in Dresden and Leipzig. It was not that the audience was any different from audiences in the rest of Europe. Rather, it was the political situation in which the country and the people found themselves at the time that made some of us very thoughtful. We were paid in East (not West, as the contract had stipulated) German marks, which were not of much use outside East Germany. So we either gave the money to music students or bought sheet music in bulk.

A very funny event that grew out of a complete misunderstanding took place in Dresden. When I'm touring abroad with the New York Philharmonic I always like to perform a famous march by John Philip Sousa as an encore. Just as the Viennese might play Strauss polkas, Americans often play *Stars and Stripes Forever*.

The East German authorities were beside themselves: they thought it was the American national anthem. Backstage I was taken to task and told in no uncertain terms that I had caused extreme displeasure at the highest levels; the official post-concert dinner was even canceled. The matter could have been easily cleared up, but we couldn't make any headway with the officials.

In the summer of 1985 I brought my touring career full circle. Apart from Germany and Austria, we also performed in Italy, Spain, and Turkey, and we ended the tour in Israel. I could bring together both the orchestras with which I was so closely connected at the time. The high point of our visit was the joint concert in Tel Aviv of the Israel Philharmonic Orchestra and the New York Philharmonic. We played Berlioz's *Symphonie fantastique*, as we often do on such occasions. I am sure that having such huge performing forces—two full orchestras—for this symphony would have been a dream come true for Berlioz. For this performance I had the musicians dress differently: one orchestra was in white tie, the other in black. After the third movement everyone in each orchestra stood up and swapped places with his or her counterpart in the other orchestra, and the solo parts that in the first three movements had been played by the Israel Philharmonic were taken in the fourth and fifth movements by their colleagues in the New York Philharmonic. This is just fun, but it is fantastic, and the audience was thrilled.

Another event that made a big impression was our tour of the Soviet Union. Despite *glasnost* and *perestroika*, the Soviet Union was still a very foreign country in 1988, isolated and distant. The high point of this trip was again a concert with two orchestras: the New York Philharmonic played with the Moscow Philharmonic Orchestra in Moscow's Gorky Park. Thousands of people came out in the pouring rain to hear Berlioz and Shostakovich's Fifth Symphony. The Russian conductor Gennady Rozhdestvensky and I shared the conducting: Rozhdestvensky conducted a rousing rendition of Shostakovich's Fifth Symphony, and I took over for the Berlioz after the intermission.

Even at that time my activities were not limited to New York. I constantly had to keep up with my duties as director of the Israel Philharmonic Orchestra as well as many other commitments. Since 1961 I had regularly conducted both the Berlin Philharmonic and the Vienna Philharmonic, with which I had been closely associated since my days as a conducting student. This led the Vienna Philharmonic to appoint me an honorary member in 2001, on the occasion of the fortieth anniversary of my first appearance as a conductor. The reasons put forth at the general meeting were very flattering, and it was stated that the board of directors of the Vienna Philharmonic had demonstrated "courage and vision" when they invited me to conduct a festival concert on June 11, 1961. I hope that I can continue to come up to this orchestra's high artistic standards. At the festive ceremony Clemens Hellsberg, a member of the board of directors, made a speech that touched me deeply.

Another orchestra that is still a second home for me is the orchestra of the Maggio Musicale Fiorentino. I went to Florence for the first time in 1961, and the first European opera I conducted, *La traviata*, was performed with this orchestra in Florence's Teatro Comunale. This was followed by repertoire performances of *Tosca* in 1965. There were years in the meantime when we did not work together, but our connection was never severed.

In 1969 I was asked to take over the music direction of that year's Maggio Musicale, a commitment that was easily arranged despite my engagement in Los Angeles and my increasing work with the Israel

Philharmonic Orchestra. The Maggio Musicale Fiorentino Festival was first held in 1933, making it one of the oldest music festivals in Europe, along with those in Salzburg and Bayreuth. The orchestra takes its name from the festival, which takes place in May and June each year using musicians who perform operas and ballets in the fall season and symphony concerts from January to April.

The 1969–70 season was a real marathon, artistically. There were new productions of *Aida* (by Carlo Maestrini) and *Fidelio* (by Giorgio Strehler), and my favorite *Abduction from the Seraglio* was borrowed from Salzburg. There were also concerts with all my friends from the world of music. Arthur Rubinstein played Beethoven with the Israeli Philharmonic Orchestra under my direction; Claudio Abbado came with the London Symphony Orchestra; and Daniel Barenboim and his wife, Jacqueline du Pré, performed with the English Chamber Orchestra. It was a grand and very high-caliber musical collaboration.

The Maggio Musicale Fiorentino has a long and important history and is associated with some of the greatest names in music. Bruno Walter, Wilhelm Furtwängler, Dimitri Mitropoulos, Herbert von Karajan, and Riccardo Muti appeared there as conductors, Maria Callas had her debut there, and even contemporary composers—Bartók and Stravinsky, as well as Luigi Nono and Luciano Berio—found a platform in the Teatro Comunale where they could introduce their music themselves.

In 1978, after I had started working in New York, I was offered Wagner's *Der Ring des Nibelungen* in Florence under the direction of Luca Ronconi, with stage design by Pier Luigi Pizzi. This was certainly not my first Wagner, but it would be my baptism with the *Ring*. Finally I had an opportunity to apply myself intensively to Wagner. Each year one opera from the *Ring* cycle was performed, which meant that I did not have to learn everything at one go while trying to keep up my work in New York. Instead, I could approach it in a more relaxed fashion and work it up thoroughly. The Italians do amazingly well with Wagner, and this production of *Das Rheingold*, for which Pizzi had recommended very simple staging, was an immediate success. Even *Die Walküre* and *Götterdämmerung* worked well there, though I remember *Siegfried* as being pretty terrible. The quality of the singing was not always very high, and later I learned to insist on a higher caliber of singer. Gwyneth Jones was, however, a great Brünnhilde.

From 1978 to 1981 I went to Florence each year as a guest conductor, and the intensive collaboration on Wagner between the orchestra and me led to the development of a close bond between us. In the 1980s Riccardo Muti, who had been the music director and had raised the level of the orchestra considerably, left Florence rather suddenly. That created an artistic emergency. The orchestra committee came to Israel, where I was working at that time, and asked me to help out. I agreed and stepped in as guest conductor without asking a fee to make it clear that I was indeed just helping out.

In 1986, however, I accepted the position of music director of the orchestra in Florence. The title sounds very distinguished in Italian: "direttore principale del Teatro del Maggio Musicale Fiorentino." Florence is yet another home for me. Whenever people ask me where I feel really at home, it is always in the places where I work and where I feel connected to everything that is important in my life. I really adore working in Florence, in part because of the system there. When I do an opera in Florence we give it many times in a row, and I always have the same musicians in front of me and can count on them being there from the very first rehearsal through each and every performance. Whatever I undertake, encourage, and criticize musically remains limited to a relatively small circle. I understand completely that for various reasons this is not possible in other opera houses, such as those in Munich and other German cities. Altogether there are approximately 140 musicians in these opera houses, and the sheer number of performances necessitates a change of musicians or a rotation system. One cannot maintain a huge opera house with an enormous repertoire any other way. But this does not change the fact that it is nice to always work with the same musicians, as I do in Florence.

I conducted Mozart's Da Ponte operas (*Don Giovanni*, *The Marriage of Figaro*, and *Così fan tutte*) for the first time in Florence in productions by Jonathan Miller. Working with him was sheer delight. Jonathan has an uncanny way of getting singers, who are not always the greatest actors, to immediately grasp his sense of urgency or comedy, as demanded by Da Ponte's texts. He comes up with the most unbelievable solutions especially during the recitatives, when most of the action takes place. Another fantastic production was Mozart's *The Magic Flute*, directed by Julie Taymor. She became famous for her direction of the musical *The Lion King*, for which she has won countless awards.

I have gone on many tours with this orchestra as well. Touring was a new experience for these musicians. We went to South America, Europe, and Turkey, and also twice to India. Olivier Messiaen was present in Paris when we played his *Turangalîla-Symphonie*, a favorite of mine, and in Florence we also performed his last work, *Éclairs sur l'Au-delà*, composed in 1991 for the New York Philharmonic.

Contemporary pieces were performed in Florence. It is the duty of a music director to make sure that new works are played, even if the audience reacts initially with irritation. But when incomprehension is combined with ignorance, the level of acceptance sinks very low. I believe more and more firmly all the time that a conductor can contribute to a better understanding of the music he or she programs. Often before a contemporary work I try to prepare the audience for what it is going to hear with a little analytical explanation. But I would never dream of suddenly talking about Beethoven's Sixth Symphony, for instance, although I often feel that it could be very helpful too.

We have to find ways of bringing the younger generation to opera halls and concerts. All the statistics show that our audience is getting older, and the interest in subscriptions, which give arts organizations a way to ensure attendance at a concert, is also declining. Younger people, it seems, are more spontaneous and less willing to commit in advance to an evening of music. Music directors and managers of orchestras and opera houses, as well as concert agencies, have to think of ways to rekindle public interest so that the culture is preserved for future generations. That is why I believe we should encourage innovations and even gimmicks to entice people into the concert hall and opera house. Ceremonious solemnity alone is not sufficient to win over the younger generation. We have to come up with new ways of piquing young people's interest in the valuable musical heritage with which we have been entrusted.

How the world-famous *Turandot* performance came about in Beijing's Forbidden City is another story worth telling. The idea was born in 1996 when I was on a tour of China with the Vienna Philharmonic. As we walked through the Forbidden City, the Austrian producer Michael Ecker, who specializes in performing operas on location, began raving about how wonderful it would be to perform Puccini's last opera against the backdrop of the Ming Palace. It was a fascinating idea and a daring notion. We would need the approval of the Chinese authorities before we could make any further plans.

It was not easy to interest the Chinese in this idea. When the film director Bernardo Bertolucci shot *The Last Emperor* in the Forbidden City, many tiny architectural details were apparently destroyed. Ever since then, Chinese authorities have been unwilling to allow agents of Western culture—or whatever one might want to call us—to use this legendary venue. But we finally succeeded. I grabbed an opportunity to talk to the Chinese minister of culture during intermission at a Vienna Philharmonic concert and managed to convince him that a performance such as the one we were proposing would be spectacular and might even have a positive impact on China's international image.

At this point I have to backtrack a few years to 1995, when we were planning a new production of *Turandot* in Florence. I came up with the idea of approaching the Chinese film director Zhang Yimou, whose *Raise the Red Lantern* had made a deep impression on me.

It was very difficult to get in touch with Zhang. Despite the success of his film in the West—or perhaps because of it—the Chinese authorities at first threw up a number of obstacles in our path. We finally managed to enter into negotiations with Zhang in 1996, and after thinking it over for a little while he agreed to take the project on. It was a completely new direction for him.

Zhang's extremely imaginative staging of *Turandot* premiered in Florence. He was a complete newcomer to the field of opera, but he immersed himself in the work with the utmost seriousness. The magnificent costumes, all of them made by hand, were absolutely beautiful, and his understanding of the music grew as he worked on the opera. The result was a great success. It was at this point that Michael Ecker officially approached us about taking the production to Beijing.

However, it was no simple matter to bring the entire production from Florence to Beijing. In fact, it was impossible. Many elements had to be completely redesigned. All in all there were more than a thousand people involved in this huge project, and the logistics eclipsed anything that I had ever experienced. In Florence Zhang had learned all that there was to know about *Turandot*, so he could give clear instructions in Beijing about what had to be done. It was a challenge, but in 1998 we were finally ready, and the orchestra of the Maggio Musicale Fiorentino—about 450 people—flew to Beijing.

Of course, the audience saw a very fairytale–like Ming Dynasty China, with an unending wealth of colors and resplendent costumes all seen against the colorfully lit Ming Pavilion of the Forbidden City. We gave nine performances in as many days with three different casts before an audience of roughly four thousand each time. It was an enormous success. The production later toured Europe with performances given in soccer stadiums, though without my personal involvement.

After the performances, on September 14, 1998, I boarded a flight from Beijing to Munich in order to start my first day of work with the Bavarian State Opera as its music director.

⌒⌒

I absolutely have to mention the world-famous "Three Tenors" and the role I played in this connection. A lot of buzz was created all over the world by a number of completely over-the-top rumors, mostly about the fees. I hope

I can help clarify the actual genesis of this concert and correct some of the misunderstandings about it.

Mario Dradi, a very enterprising Italian agent, came up with the idea of organizing an unusual, never-before-seen concert during the 1990 soccer World Cup in Rome. Luciano Pavarotti, Plácido Domingo, and José Carreras were to sing together at the ancient Baths of Caracalla. It was primarily intended as a musical welcome for the convalescing Carreras, and in addition the concert would be a fund-raiser for his foundation for leukemia research, to which the evening's ticket sales were to be donated; we wanted to raise a lot of money for this worthy cause. I agreed to conduct the orchestra on only one condition: that my orchestra from Florence be allowed to play along with the orchestra of the opera in Rome. Since there are no trios for tenor voices in the operatic literature, I suggested that each singer choose his favorite hit song. We then asked the Argentinean composer Lalo Schifrin to create a medley that included the songs that were selected. And so, after an evening of innumerable operatic tenor arias, my three friends came out together and sang the medley, to the delight of one and all.

Decca was willing to record the evening and produce a CD. That sounded like a good idea, and we all agreed. We were told quite convincingly that it would be fairly difficult to make a recording and that the commercial success of the venture was completely uncertain, so it would be best if we signed an agreement renouncing all our royalties. And to show how naive we all were, that's just what we did. What we, and probably also Decca, could not possibly have guessed was that this CD would become one of the best-selling classical recordings of all time. And we didn't make a penny from it. It is nice to meet with an unexpected success, and we are all sufficiently well off so that it did not hurt us to not get a share, but all the same we feel that Decca could have at least sent us a little Christmas card thanking us for their enormous profits.

For us the concert that evening, under a luminous full moon, was primarily a bright, happy, and unique event. That this idea would later become a concept that is still with us today was something that none of us could have known back then.

Four years later, in 1994, we repeated the performance (although with a completely different repertoire) in Los Angeles with the Los Angeles Philharmonic, again on the eve of soccer's World Cup finals. By now the Three Tenors had become a household name and would draw a huge crowd. This time we were well paid. Whereas there had been about eight thousand people in the audience in Rome, this time more than sixty thousand people came to Dodger Stadium—much to the glee of the Dodgers' owner, Peter O'Malley, a devoted music lover and a great friend of mine.

I conducted only these two concerts. Later the Three Tenors toured all over the world with enormous success.

9

BRINGING MUSIC TO PEOPLE

I am not altogether sure whether one should talk about one's good deeds. For me it is natural to help other people if I can. This means that I intervene when I come across an injustice. Usually I can reach only that part of the public that is interested in music, but sometimes I can use my position to reach a wider audience. I am very gratified whenever I can use my talent to make even the smallest difference in someone's spiritual life.

It hurts me to see people in distress, be it due to war, poverty, or a natural disaster. I am always ready to direct the public's attention to suffering and to raise money for relief efforts. I am eternally grateful to the orchestras and choruses of the Bavarian State Opera and the Maggio Musicale Fiorentino for offering all their services to help deal with natural disasters in India and China, respectively. I am no more noble-minded than anyone else, but I feel a profound gratitude for all the help and love that people have offered me.

I have to thank my parents and also, later, my Nancy for almost everything I have managed to achieve spiritually in my life. Without my mother's caring concern and my father's musical proficiency and personal indefatigability, I would never have been able to pursue my professional career in the way granted to me. I hope that during their lifetimes I was able to show my parents that I was conscious of what they had done for me. Till the end their advice was important to me, as were the care and affection they lavished upon me. Nancy continues her spiritual support in all our endeavors, and I don't know where I would be today without this rock on which we have built forty years of happiness.

The Mehli Mehta Foundation School was founded in 2003 in my hometown of Mumbai. This is just a small way in which I demonstrate my gratitude to my parents. Again, without the volunteer contributions of friends like Mehroo Jeejeebhoy, Nusli Wadia, Yusuf Hamied, and, last but not least, my old school friend Ratan Tata, who helps me each time I visit India with an orchestra, it would have remained just a dream. I am unfortunately not very well organized myself, nor do I have a personal foundation to help me take care of such enterprises. The idea of having to administer large organizations and deal with management issues fills me with horror. This may be a personal failing of mine, but at this point it cannot be helped. One day Rostropovich, who deeply loved and respected my father, called up. He wanted to perform two concerts in Mumbai with me and the orchestra of the Maggio Musicale Fiorentino in order to raise funds for a music school where Western music would be taught. So far this school consists of only two apartments, but it is already in operation. I make sure that my entire family is involved in it; even my grandchildren have done their part.

Artistic talent seems to run in our family. That is why I consider it even more my family's duty to ensure through such a project that the name of Mehli Mehta lives on.

Perhaps I demand too much from my musicians when I persuade them to travel all over the world with me to encourage people, or in order to ensure that the worst and most perfidious crimes against humanity are never forgotten. I believe that it is always worthwhile to put up with some inconveniences for a good cause. I was in Chennai, formerly known as Madras, with the Bavarian State Orchestra on the first anniversary of the tsunami that hit on December 26, 2004. All the musicians had to leave for India on Christmas Day, and no doubt to some of them it must have seemed like an imposition. Catastrophes, though, are a much bigger imposition. That in this particular case I was also able to show my musicians my country of origin and give them an impression of its beauty—I wanted them to see the Taj Mahal in Agra—was a lucky by-product of this good deed. The trip was made possible thanks to the generosity of many sponsors from Germany and India.

The concert in Chennai took place in a very simple theater where European music had scarcely ever been played before. From the stage I asked for donations to help the victims of the tsunami. We also played a concert in Indira Gandhi Stadium in New Delhi, where I had played in the past with the Israel and Munich Philharmonic Orchestras, for an audience of fourteen thousand.

I am reluctant to mention here all the many concerts that might perhaps have brought some relief to people in distress or that could have been helpful even indirectly. However, two outstanding concerts in particular that I would like to mention were remarkable because of where they were held.

One of these was a concert given in the park of Tiefurt, in the city of Weimar, on August 29, 1999, before an audience of about five thousand. At the concert, which had been requested by the city of Weimar, that year's European City of Culture, the Israel Philharmonic Orchestra joined the Bavarian State Orchestra to play Mahler's Second Symphony together as one ensemble on a single stage. The concert was intended as a symbol of tolerance, dialogue, and reconciliation. Weimar reflects both aspects of German history, the beautiful as well as the terrible. The musicians were naturally very charged up emotionally, but the music eventually worked to unite them strongly.

The day before the concert I visited the Buchenwald Memorial with the members of the Israel Philharmonic Orchestra. One of the cellists, Micha Haran, played at what used to be the concentration camp's crematorium in memory of the many people who perished there.

The second concert that deserves mention because it was so unusual took place in June 1994 in a place marked by destruction, war, and, unfortunately, continued hostility as well. Once again it was Mario Dradi's idea.

He asked me to perform Mozart's Requiem in the bombed-out National Library in Sarajevo. We wanted the concert to signify mourning and, at the same time, optimism. Unfortunately, the circumstances were hardly encouraging and did not allow for much hope that there would soon be peace and calm.

I immediately agreed to the concert, and Mario persuaded the singers to participate as well—Cecilia Gasdia, the Hungarian Ildikó Komlósi, José Carreras, and Ruggero Raimondi. My wife accompanied me. We flew together in a military aircraft from Ancona, Italy, to Sarajevo. Many people attended our open rehearsals in the still-intact opera house, since there could be no audience in the ruins of the National Library. We wanted this concert to attract a lot of media attention. As it happened, it was broadcast by twenty-six television channels and even distributed on DVD. The entire proceeds went to the United Nations High Commission for Refugees.

We played with the Sarajevo Symphony Orchestra, and the musicians' distress was obvious and palpable. The string players had no strings and the clarinetists, no reeds, but they all used the supplies we had brought with us and gave it their best shot. We were living in a hotel in which all the windows had been covered with blackout paper. We could hear gunshots in the night, and shortly before the concert we heard that a little boy had been shot dead. It all brought home to us the absurdity of the war. Still, we were just there on a short visit and had to be a part of this distress and misery for only a couple of hours. It made us appreciate how peaceful and contented our lives are.

Besides all these very serious occasions, I am also always available for happy commemorations. In 1994, on the anniversary of the peace treaty concluded in 1993 between the Israelis and the Palestinians, the Norwegian organizers invited me to give a commemorative concert in Oslo's basketball stadium. I was most grateful that Harry Belafonte consented to be the master of ceremonies; it was a delight to be with this multidimensional man and to learn of his involvement with so many charitable causes. The participants in the classical part of the program were Ivo Pogorelich and my very dear friend Ivry Gitlis. Part pop, part classical—the concert straddled the line. Yassir Arafat and Shimon Peres, who shared the Nobel Peace Prize that year, were among the guests. Everybody was happy that there would soon be lasting peace in the Middle East, a feeling reflected in the general mood. Just how sure people were of a peaceful coexistence between Palestinians and Israelis in the future and how promising everything seemed was demonstrated when twenty-five Israeli, twenty-five Palestinian, and twenty-five Norwegian children struck up a song for peace. Nobody could have known that a year later all those efforts and hopes would once again be put in jeopardy by the assassination of the Israeli prime minister, Yitzhak Rabin.

10

CONDUCTING

A Labor of Love

I n his book *Crowds and Power*, Elias Canetti described a conductor as an occasional "ruler of the world." According to him, "There is no clearer expression of power than in the person of the conductor. He is omniscient. The musicians only have their own parts in front of them whereas he has the complete score in his head or on the music stand in front of him."

I see my position differently. For me it is not at all invested with any all-embracing power. It is rather a position that requires love, empathy, and sensitivity. A conductor is certainly in the privileged position of knowing all the parts, but it is not a privilege he should exploit. I think of myself much more as a coordinator, sometimes also as a supervisor, but most of all as a communicator.

At this juncture it would be worthwhile to set forth the history of conducting. The profession is actually rather young, at least in comparison to the history of the music that we hear and play, which is music from the early seventeenth century to the present. It was only in France that as early as the eighteenth century, orchestras specifically deputized one member to give the beat. Everywhere else in the world this was considered unnecessary until the late nineteenth century. In France it was the first violinist who gave the beat, and sometimes he played standing so that the orchestra could see him better.

The role of the conductor had been recognized in France since the time of Louis XIV. The conductor would stand with his back to the musicians and beat time on the floor with a stick. This was not particularly helpful for a number of reasons, but most of all because the noise of the stick hitting the ground must have really disturbed the audience's enjoyment of the music, although it did ensure that all the musicians played in the same tempo.

In the nineteenth century the conducting baton gradually caught on. Back then, its use was considered almost revolutionary. Composers such as Mendelssohn and Carl Maria von Weber prided themselves on using this new type of baton, though, which soon became indispensable, particularly for choirs. Yet the violin bow continued for a long time to be used for simple orchestral performances. It was only toward the end of the nineteenth century that the baton became an obvious component of every orchestral performance. Since then the profession of the conductor has been established without any further requirement that he or she also specialize in an instrument or as a composer.

~~~~~~~

I learned the craft of conducting from the legendary Hans Swarowsky in Vienna. Above all, he taught me discipline and faithfulness to the musical work. We young students were very surprised when we realized that these two fundamental virtues were not valued everywhere; I heard things that sounded completely different from their score. Swarowsky always set an absolutely inflexible standard, an element of our musical education that imposed extremely strict discipline upon us. Any interpretation that depended on mere inspiration he considered highly suspect; he would never tolerate it because he believed it would encourage a laissez-faire attitude in the orchestra.

Naturally, this raises a question: what exactly does this fidelity to the work imply? Think of cleaning an old painting, taking off the layers of varnish that have been applied over the years, so that as each layer is removed more of the true picture emerges. Its lines become clearer, the colors fresher, and the basic idea more lucid. In music, the varnish represents the practice by many conductors of the late nineteenth and early twentieth centuries of regularly making interventions in the music, interventions that led to new listening habits, which can be revised now only with great difficulty.

It should be mentioned that before Toscanini's time, conductors such as Wagner or even Mahler often "touched up" or embellished the old masters' orchestrations, supposedly in order to help realize a composer's true intent. This was true of Schubert's symphonies as well as those of Beethoven. Toscanini was the first conductor to insist on working only with the original score and playing only what the composer had put down on paper. He avoided all retouching, extensions, and additions.

Furtwängler often talked of the message that lay between the notes. I understood this as interpretation, but his statement also expresses the mystical aspect of our profession, which is so hard to describe. Listening to old recordings of Furtwängler's interpretation of the Adagio from Anton Bruckner's Eighth Symphony, one detects a completely mystical musical experience. One feels how Furtwängler pushes the musicians beyond their normal capacities. Josef Krips once told me that many more overtones were produced under Furtwängler's conducting than under anyone else's, and that the musicians produced more musical colors with him than with other conductors.

The art of conducting consists of inspiring, but not without the necessary discipline. One must never allow sheer pleasure to gain the upper hand. Nothing should ever be allowed to escape from one's control. Anarchy and "inspiration" of this kind can spell the death of all kinds of music.

If there is one attribute a conductor must possess, it is knowledge—knowledge of at least four hundred years of the various styles of music he is conducting, knowledge of musical forms, knowledge of the orchestra as an instrument, complete and detailed knowledge of the music he is interpreting. Once he has acquired all this, he must also develop the skill of communicating his or her knowledge to the fine musicians before whom he or she stands, at rehearsals and at the concert.

The image of the conductor as a dictator who wields absolute power seems false to me. This type of conductor, the feared and simultaneously adored chief of hundreds of musicians whose well-being depends entirely on him, undoubtedly existed in the past. However, those times are over, even if some really grotesque notions about conductors are still floating around in the media. What is simply overlooked is that the activity of a conductor consists to a large extent of plain old hard work and practice. The rehearsals with the musicians are not only time-consuming for both sides but also very strenuous. When everything works more or less according to the listeners' wishes and expectations on the evening of a concert or an opera, they notice none of the preparation—and this is just as it should be.

I always try to be available to talk with my musicians, something I hope I have always been able to let them know. The musicians need to feel certain that they can depend on me and my basic musical ideas. Obviously, this also means that everyone has to submit to some basic discipline. But if a horn player, for instance, wants to play a little rubato, I might just accede to him on the spur of the moment.

Swarowsky always preached that a conductor had to place his technique at the service of the orchestra. After simple communication is established with the orchestra, variations in the techniques of communication are always possible and are welcomed by the musicians. It is said that Richard Strauss was technically very precise and that everything always sounded absolutely correct whenever he conducted his own works; but one got to hear a lot more of Strauss's real intent when Clemens Krauss conducted, because he poured his heart and soul into the performance.

I will allow myself a not altogether serious comparison: as a conductor I see in myself a friendly cultural policeman who shows people the way and directs everything. The musicians have to reach a high level of what I call "precise organization." What they do is of course to a considerable extent notated in the score, but I, for my part, must have such command of it that all the musicians are able to play in perfect harmony. When I conduct a work that I have known for decades but that I play only every two to three years—such as Beethoven's Ninth Symphony—then I have to adjust my approach to it. This means that I discover something new in it each time, details I hadn't noticed before. Again, it's like a picture one is very familiar with: when one takes the trouble to look at it more carefully again, one discovers a new detail.

A conductor must also be the conscience of the orchestra. He or she is committed not only to discipline, but most of all to the composer's intent, which brings us once more to the topic of fidelity to the score. The musicians of an orchestra must feel free and comfortable enough with the conductor to express their doubts if they believe something is not being performed in the way that has been discussed with and rehearsed by the orchestra. I am always open to suggestions of this sort. Whether I actually accept the suggestion is a different matter, but I am always happy when the musicians ask questions.

Yet the conductor must also be something of a dictator, not in the sense of someone who bullies his subordinates, but rather in the sense of controlling the way the music is organized. The upbeat and the tempo must come from the conductor. Only a single opinion is required here; it is not open to discussion. Sixteen violinists cannot all decide for themselves the tempo of Brahms's Fourth Symphony.

One should remember that the role of the director of an orchestra is multifaceted. So far I have only talked about the musical demands of this profession. I also have to constantly keep in mind the fact that I often need to deal with very sensitive people who are using their skill and talent to produce music on their respective instruments. Unfortunately, I sometimes hurt some of my musicians unintentionally or, just as bad, offend them on a point that has nothing to do with the original reason for my anger.

I see myself as a generalist in this profession. I have to master many roles, from confessor to musical adviser. My taste in music is quite catholic. I have never wanted to specialize in any one particular kind or style. In fact, given the direction my career has taken, that would have been impossible. In Los Angeles and New York, for example, where I had to conduct regular concerts for sixteen weeks, with sixteen different programs, it would not have been possible to concentrate on any one thing in particular.

It is primarily owing to my recorded repertoire that I am considered a specialist in post-romantic music. This can be traced back to my time in the United States. There the entire orchestra has to be paid whenever a recording is made. Even if it is a piece by Mozart and only 50 musicians are required, all 110 musicians still have to be paid. Thus the music companies make a very simple calculation and prefer to record the romantic repertoire instead, in which all the members of the orchestra would be needed.

A question that is often raised is whether and how musical memory wears out, whether one can have any memory at all of music that one has performed in the past. It is true that the sound evaporates over time, disappearing or merging into the next piece.

It is hard to describe how I feel at one with the music when I am onstage. It may sound absurd, but I am convinced that I play the orchestra like an instrument. And as long as I believe that this huge instrument is mine, I can always remember how to play it or how I have played it in the past. I feel the music coming from deep within me and communicate it to the musicians. It goes without saying that I do not always have this feeling and consequently do not play the instrument well. When that happens, I can only try to learn from my failure and rectify it the next time. I can do so because I remember how the musical line should sound, and I can concentrate on a particular deviation of line that escaped me the last time.

I am always talking about what "I" can pull off successfully—a phrase, a modulation, a gap between performance and reprise, or some other trifle. What I actually mean by "I" is this huge instrument, the orchestra, with which I have been entrusted. It becomes a part of me, and I draw strength from it. It is only through our combined efforts that the correct interpretation emerges.

Sometimes while performing I can become distracted momentarily. It might be due to external circumstances, such as an auditorium with terrible acoustics, or it might be because of an emotion that is just then occupying my attention. The orchestra senses this immediately, particularly if we have known each other for a long time and are well attuned to each other. Ideally, there is then a kind of interaction between the musicians and me, and I feel the orchestra bringing me back into the musical cosmos, reintegrating me into it. This can be a very exciting game, but such an interaction can happen only with musicians whom I know very, very well and with whom I have a personal rapport.

I consider it absolutely normal and a part of human nature for there to be moments when either one of the musicians or I am not fully concentrating. On the other hand, I can also switch over in no time at all from a tense situation and concentrate instead on the music the orchestra and I are about to play. Often the eagerness with which I look forward to a piece I am about to interpret increases my alertness so that I become very agitated, so I sometimes step up onto the podium and give altogether the wrong tempo.

Although I have devoted my life exclusively to music for many decades, I still feel blessed all over again whenever I get a chance to really throw myself into studying and performing a composer's entire oeuvre. I see this as a tremendous blessing granted to us as musicians. That's why it makes me furious when I see a musician obviously playing in the most routine manner. The opportunity to re-create the work of a master should be inspiring, not boring. Of course I hope that my communication with the musicians never lacks the inspiration they so need. There are many musicians whose passion for music can be heard in every single note and for whom playing is important and fulfilling. As a conductor I want to give them whatever I can.

I can sometimes lose my focus for a moment or two in the midst of conducting a piece. And occasionally I'm not in the right mood when I walk onstage. Again, it is the musicians who, with their enthusiasm and joy, bring me back to where I should be.

There is also a sad and unpleasant side to my profession: having to tell a musician that his or her time is over. I find it ridiculous that in Europe a cellist or violinist absolutely must retire at the age of sixty-five. In many countries it is all over for a musician—often for no other reason—the day he or she reaches this age. In such cases a musician should at least be allowed to continue until the end of the season. Age does set limits for certain brass and woodwind players because they become physically weaker and can no longer produce the desired sound, though obviously there are always some exceptions to whom none of this applies. I am sometimes compelled to make radical changes in the makeup of the orchestra, even though it hurts me to do so. And of course, it is unfortunate when, for whatever reason, a particular musician does not accept the fact that it's time to go. This creates an uncomfortable atmosphere and can disturb the general peace, since we have to constantly make music with each other no matter what kind of unpleasantness might be in the air.

The most important position in an orchestra is that of the concertmaster. He is like the prime minister of the orchestra. His interpretation of a piece must be compatible with that of the conductor; otherwise irreconcilable differences can develop. Such differences can also crop up when the concertmaster's musical ego is very strongly developed and he or she thinks his or her interpretation is the only valid one. This happens sometimes if the conductor is young, because often a young conductor still has to overcome his or her own uncertainties and may need more time to convince more than a hundred seasoned players of his or her musical decisions.

Things like this demonstrate that the balancing act between yielding and leading is an art that a conductor simply has to master. I do not necessarily take it as resistance or opposition when a musician in an orchestra wants to do things his or her way rather than mine. I am ready to listen to solutions that to my ear sound new or unusual, and if it seems convincing, then I am flexible enough and willing to change my ideas regarding that particular phrase.

The section leaders of the various string groups are also extremely important in an orchestra, particularly during the rehearsals. The section leader is an indispensable assistant and guide. There are talented and highly gifted soloists among them whom one instantly respects not only because they are such fine instrumentalists but because they are also great intellects.

In the early years of my career I was fortunate to have mature and wise musicians in the orchestras I conducted. I am still grateful to them. My section leaders in both Montreal and Los Angeles were musical giants from whom I learned a great deal and who set standards that I have carried with me my entire life. The section leader must soar throughout the universe with the conductor and be capable of taking his group along with him, all without any apparent effort.

I see an orchestra basically as a string quartet expanded to immense proportions. By the same token, the musicians must be able to play as if they were playing chamber music. They must be in contact with each other while playing and able to agree with and rely on each other, all the while constantly maintaining their connection with me. To use a parliamentary metaphor again, these four are actually my most important cabinet ministers. Early Haydn and Mozart symphonies can in fact be played without a conductor if there is absolute cohesion among the string leaders. In fact, the entire body of Viennese classical music is rooted in the string quartet.

As a conductor one must never forget that the musicians of any large and prominent orchestra play with several different conductors and in the course of their careers accumulate a great deal of experience. Therefore they must be allowed to point out corrections and raise objections—and they should also have the right to protest if asked to do something that seems to them utterly illogical or weird.

There are many seemingly insignificant examples I could give to illustrate how difficult it is for a conductor to deal with musicians—and also vice versa! For example, every oboist interprets the opening solo in the funeral march of the "Eroica" Symphony in his own way, putting his own interpretation on Beethoven's instructions. In the last analysis, musicians are artists who have thought through musical questions on their own. Their playing embodies their musical convictions and must be taken seriously.

This would not prevent me from critiquing something, but I have to find a way of formulating my criticism so that the respect that the artist deserves and my sense of the correct interpretation can coexist.

This dependence on a highly regarded section leader, a soloist whom one trusts completely, can also lead to some indelible musical memories. One never forgets an encounter with an extraordinary musician, especially when one is just starting out. It is like the memory of a great lover, met once and never forgotten.

There is another reason a conductor must always be willing to grapple with new things and to listen to the suggestions of a musician or soloist: it is one of the best ways to avoid routine, which is not just dangerous but even deadly, every bit as much so as the anarchy created by lax or weak leadership. This aspect of conducting is fascinating to me.

I've already mentioned that I expect a particular sound from an orchestra, depending on the style of the music. It is my knowledge of these styles that I try to impart to the orchestra when we rehearse. I used to play recordings of the Vienna Philharmonic for the Los Angeles Philharmonic brass players to give them an idea of the sound I thought ideal for the Viennese classics. In those days I was obsessed with the idea of sharing what I had learned in Vienna. For sixteen years I tormented the musicians by expecting them to grasp the Viennese sound and reproduce it. Imagine my joy when I took them to Vienna and had them play Bruckner's Seventh Symphony! As if this was not enough, I also expected them to adapt to the sound of French music. An orchestra must be flexible enough to be able to play various sounds—Russian, French, and Viennese. This is what makes an ensemble truly world-class. It should be possible to hear two absolutely distinct types of sound in a single concert, such as when an orchestra plays Debussy's *La mer* before the intermission and a Beethoven symphony afterward.

In my opinion the music of the twentieth century, especially those of the post–World War II era, does not have a particularly striking sound of its own. The music of this century is based much more on rhythm, clarity, and intonation, as one can hear in the later works of Stravinsky or Stockhausen.

It is different with Messiaen. His sacred music in particular can be played softly and warmly, almost like Bruckner.

I firmly believe that the musical origin of the musicians has a decisive influence on the orchestra's timbre. One can see this most clearly in the Israel Philharmonic Orchestra. When I began working with them, most of the musicians came from the old Habsburg-Austrian tradition. As a young conductor influenced by Vienna, I was comfortable with them, and that soon enabled us to have a great working relationship. Today most of the members of the orchestra come from the former Soviet Union, bringing with them a completely different notion of sound. I am not trying to make any value judgments here. It is much more a matter of my own notions. Most of these violinists are to a much larger extent striving for great virtuosity, and they still have much to learn about warmth of tone— in Schubert or Brahms, for example. Naturally, there are many variables when it comes to sound production, so we have to work very precisely, and I have to be able to describe exactly what I want to achieve. It is not enough to say simply that they have to play with more love; I have to go into a great deal more detail about such things as playing technique and how to begin the note. Communication, though not easy, is managed with a little Hebrew, a little Russian, a little Yiddish, and mostly English, with a few Italian musical phrases tossed in here and there. It helps greatly that wherever possible, a new member is seated next to an older colleague, so that the new player's concept of sound is transformed almost mysteriously into our traditional sound.

For me the question of sound is also connected to the degree of familiarity one has with a composer, even if I sometimes erroneously believe that I know the composer personally. I have read extensively about the great masters and have studied their correspondence. So intimately am I connected with their work that sometimes I actually believe we must have met. This illusion has great significance for me, just like that of "playing" an orchestra. It's how I feel about Brahms, Mozart, Wagner, and Schoenberg. Since I spent my formative years in Vienna and matured there musically, it seems to me to go without saying that I feel very close to these composers, as if I know them personally.

Some of my colleagues keep an account of which pieces they have played, and how often. There are pieces that I could easily conduct every day with almost no preparation, such as Brahms's Second Symphony or Beethoven's "Eroica" Symphony, both of which I have studied so thoroughly that an hour's work before the rehearsal would suffice. Opera is a different matter. Although I have conducted Mozart's *Marriage of Figaro* and Puccini's *Tosca* umpteen times, I cannot enter the pit without completely going through the score in solitude and quiet. And even though I could conduct the "Eroica" or Mozart's Fortieth Symphony in G Minor every day of my life, I would not be able to do the same with Strauss's *Ein Heldenleben* or Rimsky-Korsakov's *Scheherazade*. I love these works, but when it comes to conducting them I simply could not be emotionally sincere in my performance or inspire my musicians that often. When I take this romantic repertoire on tour, I see to it that between performances of Richard Strauss or Mahler I can conduct Beethoven, Brahms, or Schubert. I cannot support the constant surfeit of emotion of this music and simply concentrate on its programmaticism. It can only be done time to time. I also have a problem with Schumann. Unlike Brahms, he lacks the discipline that has become emblematic of Viennese composers. I do not believe Schumann ever accepted the formal discipline that became decisive in Viennese music from Haydn onward. Although he is a phenomenal song composer and his piano works are grand fantasies of passion, his symphonies must be rehearsed very carefully because of his relatively poor command of orchestration. They simply do not play themselves. However, when a Schumann symphony works well after careful rehearsing and balancing of the inner voices, it is particularly satisfying musically. Many conductors reorchestrate Schumann: Mahler, for example, thought that was the only way to bring out what the composer really intended.

One of my favorite works from the romantic period, and one that I conduct often, is Bruckner's Eighth Symphony. I have the most beautiful memories of this music dating back to the first time I heard it in Vienna and also to the time in 1956 when I heard it played by the Concertgebouw Orchestra in Amsterdam under Eduard van Beinum.

The credit for introducing Bruckner's symphonies in the United States must be given to Mahler, when he was conducting in New York. However, I've found that it is still difficult to attract the North American public to Bruckner's music. The great American orchestras have a great affinity for it, but the audience listens only when there is a famous conductor, and not simply for the sake of the music. It is different with Mahler. One simply cannot be indifferent to him. He challenges each musician and each member of the audience, taking them from the heights of joy to the depths of despair.

Mahler was almost never happy in the fifty-one years he spent on this earth. He was constantly persecuted and hounded, and most of all he had a difficult time as a young conductor in Lvov, Budapest, and Hamburg. He probably felt much better in later years, particularly when he went to one of his favorite lakes in the summer, at one with nature and free to compose in his little country house, from which he undoubtedly drew strength. Mahler's work is always a challenge for me, and I need all my strength to deal with it. But each time I do, it is a source of deep musical fulfillment. In 2004 I rehearsed Mahler's Third Symphony thoroughly with the Bavarian State Orchestra, which played it with great under-standing and an ideal sound. I had already had a long conducting career before this symphony revealed itself to me in all its unheard variety and world-weariness. There is a famous anecdote about Mahler and Bruno Walter, who visited the composer at Lake Attersee in July 1896 while he was working on this symphony. When Walter looked up in wonder at the sheer power of the mountains of the Höllengebirge, Mahler told his famous guest, "You don't need to admire them anymore—I've already composed them away in my symphony." This also explains Mahler's own assessment of this work, namely that it was "almost not music anymore," that it was simply the "sounds of nature." Conducting this symphony is always deeply moving for me. It was with this symphony that I debuted with the Munich Philharmonic in May 1987. Playing with this orchestra, which was strongly influenced by Sergiu Celibidache, was a defining experience in my musical development. Once, when Leonard Bernstein turned up for one of my performances of this symphony with the New York Philharmonic, he and I had a long talk about it. He advised me not to shy away from Mahler's occasional vulgarities, particularly in the first movement. He thought I was too tame during some of the more bombastic moments. He liked the middle movements a lot but thought the finale too rushed at times. This kind of advice from an older colleague is most beneficial, and one must be humble enough to accept it. I really admired Lenny tremendously, and all of us at the New York Philharmonic and the Israel Philharmonic Orchestra miss him enormously.

In the fall of 2004 I conducted Mahler's Seventh Symphony with the Bavarian State Orchestra. Before that I had only conducted it once with the Los Angeles Philharmonic and once with the Israel Philharmonic Orchestra, with a long gap between the two performances. The latter concert had been part of a tour that took us to Lodz, where we played this extremely difficult work under extraordinary circumstances—in an auditorium with worn-out carpeting and music stands of different heights. It was a real nightmare for the musicians. But the music has such enormous strength and power that this concert became one of the most convincing of the entire tour.

I consider this symphony to be one of the most difficult works in the entire orchestral literature. Although Mahler actually hews to classical forms, one can see in the work great structural freedom. In the first movement there are three different themes in the introduction itself that are then cited again here and there in the reprise. The development consists of eight different sections, and before the recapitulation we hear the three themes from the introduction again. The classical and disciplined reprise is followed by a final coda. In spite of what seems to be an immense musical structure of infinite complexity, it is still the logical evolutionary product of Haydn's symphonies, written a little more than a hundred years earlier.

One cannot simply conduct this work from one measure to the next. The musicians are so busy with their own parts that they hardly know where they are within the structure. They have to concentrate very hard in order not to lose the musical line that runs through the entire symphony like a fine silken thread. In such a difficult situation one must clearly use some of the rehearsal time to explain the form of each individual movement to the musicians.

On the one hand Mahler composed paradise and heaven, and on the other, the bleakest of musical landscapes. Mahler himself once described the Seventh Symphony as "predominantly cheerful." Despite the massive sound structures, the orchestra has to be constantly aware of an ever present transparency throughout the music. One cannot afford to get anything wrong in this symphony. It is in every respect an extraordinary work that is just now starting to be accepted by the public, thanks to conductors who have made it an important part of their repertoire.

11

THE MOVE
TO MUNICH

My contract with the New York Philharmonic was up in 1991, though it was suggested that I stay on at least one more season to help celebrate the orchestra's 150th anniversary. (Incidentally, the Vienna Philharmonic is exactly the same age, making these two orchestras probably the oldest existing major orchestras in the world.) I still had my commitments in Tel Aviv and Florence, but on the whole I could now dedicate myself to new assignments when and as I pleased. I was looking forward to my new freedom.

Around this time the Lyric Opera of Chicago offered me a chance to perform the *Ring* along with August Everding as the producer. After Ardis Krainik, the general manager of the opera, assured me that the singers of my choice would be engaged, I accepted the assignment with pleasure. It was a four-year commitment. Each year one opera from the cycle would be produced anew, and the whole project would be completed by 1996. It was the first time since before World War II that the entire *Ring* was to be performed in Chicago.

Up to now I had dealt with the entire *Ring* only sporadically. I could fall back on my experience in Florence, but that had been some years ago. During my student days in Vienna I had been very hesitant in approaching Wagner, and it had taken me a long time to develop a close relationship with him. When Karajan became the music director in Vienna, the first opera I heard him conduct was *Die Walküre*.

I had conducted my first Wagner opera, *Lohengrin*, in 1974 in Vienna. Unfortunately, the performance did not go well. I was inexperienced, and to make matters worse, the tenor fell ill before the dress rehearsal. During this rehearsal a substitute sang sitting behind me in the first row. A few rows back my kindly colleague Carlos Kleiber sat chuckling, witnessing the tension I was going through with obvious schadenfreude. It was a catastrophic rehearsal, and the premiere wasn't much better. The general atmosphere at rehearsals was made even more unbearable by the attitude of an East German stage director who constantly screamed obscenities at the choir and didn't get along with the singers either. The great Christa Ludwig, who was singing Ortrud, was asked to spit on the crucifix during the wedding procession in the second act, which of course she refused to do. The young soprano, of the newer generation of Germans, was constantly fighting with the elderly bass because of his Nazi affiliations. Maybe an experienced conductor would have been able bring all forces together, but I failed miserably. Still, conducting the wonderful Vienna Philharmonic in the pit gave me my first insights into Wagnerian style at its best.

This was followed by a "half" *Ring* in Vienna. We had a good go at it; there's no other way to describe it. The director, Giuseppe Sangiust, was Luchino Visconti's stage designer and a very cultured man, but he knew little about directing. *Das Rheingold* and *Die Walküre* were complete failures from the point of view of the production. The director explained his concept brilliantly, but nothing good came out of it in the actual performance. Very few stage designers are also good directors. The two exceptions who come to mind are Franco Zeffirelli and Jean-Pierre Ponnelle. There is another reason that the premiere of *Rheingold* was a night I will never forget: it was the first time I was publicly booed. The audience's displeasure was clearly directed at me, the conductor. I could not completely understand it and became very depressed.

After the premiere we all left together. Lorin Maazel was also there, and he tried to comfort me by saying that this happened to everybody once; it was just part of the job. The next day a friend called me up. He had sat through the performance in his box with a famous conductor sitting behind him who, to my friend's great surprise, had waved to the people booing in the standing-room section. What was I supposed to do with this information? When I went back to the opera house a little later that day, one of the ushers came up to me. He belonged to the old guard and remembered me from my student days, when he used to throw me out of the standing-room section for sneaking in without a ticket. Since then he had become my biggest fan; perhaps he was proud of our shared past. He told me that the hecklers who had booed me had come into the opera house only after the end of the performance—they never even heard it. They were obviously fans of the conductor in my friend's box, who, I later found out, was most upset at not being asked to conduct the *Ring* cycle himself. Be that as it may, this ill-fated half *Ring* was closed on the advice of Lorin Maazel, who then became the general director, simply because we both agreed that the production had no real future.

I was vehemently booed on one more occasion in Vienna. It was after a performance of *Il trovatore* under the direction of the celebrated Hungarian film director István Szabó. The opera director, Ioan Holender, and I had found his concept very interesting, but the public did not approve and booed Szabó when he came up onto the stage after the performance. When I embraced him as a gesture of conciliation, the booing became even louder. My parents, who were in the audience that night along with Nancy, suffered terribly.

After this came the Chicago *Ring* cycle—one opera each year, with Everding as director. It was a pleasure working with him, because he took every word of the text very seriously. I am convinced that the *Ring* is a *Gesamtkunstwerk*, a comprehensive synthesis of the arts, just as Wagner intended. Everding had brought out the meaning of every word through his directing, and I was happy that the singers could sing the text correspondingly. I have already said elsewhere that I cannot conduct Wagner from memory because I simply cannot memorize the text. The conductor often recites the text along with the singers, kind of like a prompter. He breathes with the singers. He has to accompany the singers not only musically, but also with the words. This is an essential part of the job.

When a singer has mastered his or her part completely, musically as well as dramatically, I allow him or her a lot of freedom of expression. But still the performance must always be led by the conductor. The connection between the conductor and the singer is critical, and the intentions of each must dovetail in order to function. "Function" is really too technical a term for what happens during a performance. Something must flow between the stage and the podium, and this flow must never be interrupted.

Wagner did not want his works to be understood only musically, although he conducted concerts himself because he was always short of funds. Many people find his texts bombastic, but I enjoy them immensely. Wagner's intent is for the music to work with the unconscious so that the listener is able to digest the text. It is not enough for the music to be beautiful; one must fully grasp the total meaning of the text and music combined.

It is very difficult for non-German-speakers to sing Wagner, since they are unable to express the true spirit of the text. And if they fail to do this, Wagner will remain incomprehensible to the audience. A conductor must give singers whose native tongue is not German more time to get used to the tongue-twisting alliteration, at least if he or she maintains, as do I and many of my colleagues, that each word in the text must be understandable.

The attitude toward the question of whether a singer must sing comprehensibly has changed a lot in the last few years. Many young conductors do not attach much importance to it anymore, so when singers work with one of us veterans, we sometimes make their lives really difficult. Daniel Barenboim, for example, practices very thoroughly with the singers, and it is a pleasure to work with them afterward. The fact that the singers are scarcely intelligible has a lot to do with the routine that marks the entire music industry today. Singers run from one opera house to the next, sometimes without so much as a single piano rehearsal. At the end there is no time left to work on their diction to ensure that they do not swallow their words.

It is different when a new production is being prepared. Then the conductor can insist that the words be pronounced clearly and correctly, even in the director's rehearsals, even when they are marking (singing gently in order to preserve the voice). Everything I have said about singing Wagner, incidentally, is also true for singing Mozart and Verdi.

During my time in Chicago I received an invitation from the Munich Opera to lead a new production of *Tannhäuser* in 1994 under David Alden's direction. Sir Peter Jonas was the director of the opera house in Munich, having succeeded Wolfgang Sawallisch in 1993. I knew Jonas only slightly. He had been assistant manager of the Chicago Symphony Orchestra and later general director of the English National Opera in London.

Several years earlier, while Everding was still the general director, he had offered me a post at the Bavarian State Opera in Munich. At that time I declined because I did not feel confident enough to lead a major German opera house. My only experience with the Bavarian State Orchestra dated back to one engagement during Sawallisch's time, when I conducted a concert of Haydn, Penderecki, and Richard Strauss.

Thus, *Tannhäuser* was going to be my first opera for Munich. It would also be my first time conducting this opera. From the very first day it was a pleasure to work with the orchestra in Munich; it had a sound that was very close to that of the Vienna Philharmonic. And of course the Bavarian State Orchestra knew from generations of experience how Wagner should be played, so I could begin rehearsing at a very high level. In some places Alden's directorial concept was somewhat problematic in terms of realization, but I understood what he wanted to say. Alden had a very contemporary view of musical theater, which accorded with what Wagner wanted to represent with *Tannhäuser* as well as all his other operas.

The work on the opera fit in well with my schedule. That year I had also started to work much more with the Munich Philharmonic, which I had learned to appreciate since the concert with Mahler's Third Symphony. I am quite sure, though, that back then Sir Peter looked upon me as a rather dubious partner. I took leave twice during the festival performances of *Tannhäuser*, once to conduct a concert in Sarajevo's National Library and then once again, to his horror, to accompany the Three Tenors at the soccer World Cup in Los Angeles. I am sure that he did not take me very seriously after that. But I made a deal with him. If he released me from the summer performances, I would come in the fall instead and conduct *Tannhäuser* once more for free. He accepted.

I had been in Munich from time to time in the past. In the 1980s I had conducted the *Gurrelieder* and Bruckner's Ninth Symphony with the Bavarian Radio Symphony Orchestra. After that Celibidache invited me repeatedly to the Munich Philharmonic, and I substituted for him often when he fell ill. One such occasion was a performance of Bruckner's Fourth Symphony in Florence and Vienna, and I knew that he would have loved to conduct this symphony himself. I felt very sorry for him, and during my conducting I constantly had the feeling that Celibidache was standing behind me, spurring me on. I was so moved by the way the orchestra played in Vienna that I donated my concert fee to set up a fund supporting young musicians.

My collaboration with the Munich Philharmonic consolidated in the years leading up to 1998. I developed a good, musically very satisfactory relationship with them. We played everything together that I appreciate in the First and Second Viennese Schools, beginning with Schubert, Brahms, Bruckner, and Mahler and going all the way to Webern's Six Pieces for Orchestra, which I love so much.

In April 1997, shortly before the fiftieth anniversary of India's independence, I went on a tour of my homeland with the Munich Philharmonic, the orchestra's first guest performance on the Indian subcontinent. The tour was supported financially by the city of Munich as its contribution to the celebration of Indian independence. We performed with great success in New Delhi and Mumbai, and the young German violinist David Garrett was very well received. As always, it was quite moving for me to perform with an orchestra in India. I think such performances bridge the gap between nations, especially when there has been animosity between them.

I had assumed that I had made a dubious impression on Sir Peter. However, in early February 1995 he and the director of operations, Gerd Uecker, came to Chicago, where that year we had performed eight completely sold-out performances of *Siegfried*. Jonas offered me the post of music director of the Bavarian State Opera in Munich starting in 1998.

Until then I had never wanted to lead an opera house. I had turned down similar offers in Berlin, Munich, and Covent Garden. But now I was convinced that I was in a position to accept this challenge, and I felt confident enough to accept without hesitation. We decided to keep mum about the appointment, so my future association with the Munich Opera was not officially announced until after Easter. The five-year contract obligated me to conduct forty performances a year. In addition, I also had to give two Academy Concerts, a long-standing concert series, at the Opera House.

I was already familiar with the musical landscape in Munich and was happy finally to be leading an opera house. Over the years I had garnered a lot of experience in the field of opera, but I had never really been involved in the usual business of repertoire performances, as was customary in Munich. Until I took up my position at the Bavarian State Opera, I had actually conducted more concerts than operas. All that changed with the beginning of my association with the Bavarian State Opera as their general music director in 1998.

I soon grew fond of the orchestra. The choir was wonderful, the acoustics magnificent, and all of us worked together smoothly from the very beginning. Sir Peter always took care of administrative matters, all dealings with the ministry of culture, and the search for sponsors. He was a wonderful mediator between art, politics, and business, and he knew how to get the Bavarian authorities and audience alike on board with the new regime. He had had tons of experience with such things during his stints in Chicago and London.

Munich was also my first permanent engagement in Germany. My first repertoire performance gave me quite a few gray hairs: I was suddenly expected to conduct an opera with just one rehearsal. Although by that time I was comfortable with opera, this was nonetheless a difficult and challenging project—to learn something new again in my early sixties! The repertoire began with *La traviata*. It went fairly well, but the next performance, *The Marriage of Figaro*, did not. One always needs more rehearsals for Mozart. The cast had not changed since the premiere of this production, and they made a good team and could rely on each other. But then I arrived, and my way of doing things was different from what they were accustomed to. In the very first performance I felt that there was something missing, that I lacked the experience of this long-standing team. It is even more difficult to suddenly step into a repertoire set than to start a new production in which one is involved from the very beginning and can grow with each performance.

However, the orchestra in Munich is so experienced and musically flexible that the musicians were extremely helpful to a quasi-novice conducting his first repertoire Mozart performance. Obviously, they had not known me long enough to always know what I meant. However enthusiastic an orchestra and a conductor might be about each other, it takes a certain amount of time for a relationship to develop between them in which each little gesture is understood perfectly and a kind of blind connection can be established between them.

By the end of my time in Munich we had rehearsed and played together so often that we could even do *Die Meistersinger* without rehearsing and have it turn out beautifully. I conducted the "old" *Ring* during my first season in Munich. When this was replaced by a new production in 2002, my admiration for the orchestra grew even more. I learned a lot from the musicians and from their understanding of the correct style for Wagner.

Many of my colleagues are put off by the idea of conducting repertoire performances. For me it was just one more reason to come to Munich. Nowhere else is it possible to come to know so many different styles. Undoubtedly the business of performing repertoire has an inherent danger of becoming routine. One can avoid this danger only through self-discipline. Most of all, though, one must have the right kind of approach, a mixture of love, dedication, and discipline.

All my life I have had a steady relationship with an orchestra. I need that. It has been not only very important to me, but also a great honor to be at home in an establishment as committed to tradition as the Bavarian State Opera. Before I came it had been led by great music directors, men I could never hope to measure up to, like Bruno Walter, Clemens Krauss, Hans Knappertsbusch, and Wolfgang Sawallisch, to name just a few. However, I shared a fundamental quality with all of them: like me, none of them were specialists in one particular style. A conductor in a German repertoire theater should be at home in styles ranging from the classical era to the present day. He should not pronounce himself an expert in any particular period, era, or style.

In 1998 I opened the festival performances with Wagner's *Tristan und Isolde*, an opera I knew very well. I had conducted it for the first time in Rome in a concert performance with Birgit Nilsson. Later I also conducted it in Montreal, at the Berlin State Opera, and in Vienna, Florence, and Los Angeles. In fact, I have conducted it more often than any other Wagner opera. I particularly remember my collaboration with David Hockney and Jonathan Miller for the performance in Los Angeles. On that particular occasion the Los Angeles Philharmonic played for the Los Angeles Opera House. Miller gave it his all, even though he confessed that he was not a fan of Wagner. Hockney's imaginative stage set was stamped with his own inimitable style and yet completely true to the composer's wishes.

Peter Konwitschny's production in Munich was not completely uncontroversial, to put it mildly. However, the reviews of the singers, the orchestra, and me were unanimously favorable. I was very happy with my debut as general music director of the Bavarian State Opera.

That same season there was a very successful new production of *Der Freischütz* with Thomas Langhoff and Jürgen Rose. I could look back on my first season's work with satisfaction. The outcome had surpassed my expectations, which had been very high to begin with. None of this would have been possible without the undying support and confidence offered me by the intendant, Sir Peter Jonas. He and his excellent staff, headed by Ronald Adler, supported me 100 percent throughout my eight happy years in Munich.

The Munich Opera Festival performances have long been a firmly established institution. Surprisingly, Munich's is also the oldest opera festival in Europe. Any complaints that during the festival audiences are simply offered the normal repertoire performances but at higher prices must be countered with the argument that nowhere else can a visitor to a festival see seven different productions in seven days, neither in a repertoire performance nor in Salzburg, not to mention other festival venues. And Sir Peter was uncompromising when it came to choosing the highest caliber of singers.

I learned a lot in Munich, including a lot of new repertoire. I conducted sixteen premieres, of which *Tannhäuser* was a personal premiere as well. And I added three more operas to my Verdi repertoire. *Don Carlos*, in Jürgen Rose's production, was really special for me. I knew Rose from an earlier collaboration with him at La Scala, when we staged *Salome*. I had always been in awe of *Don Carlos*, but it was several years before I worked up the courage to attempt it in Munich. It always looked to me like a distant towering mountain that because of its immense size must be climbed very slowly and carefully. The figures in this opera are terribly complex and intense, unlike those in other Verdi operas. What I liked about this production in Munich was that the director situated the opera in a historically recognizable time and also that I could perform it in the five-act version, that is, with the "Fontainebleau" act. Happily, in Munich Verdi was accepted in the musicians' pantheon along with the established gods—Wagner, Richard Strauss, and Mozart.

I was also able to celebrate personal premieres with two Verdi operas that were new to me, *Falstaff* and *Rigoletto*. Of course, Verdi was by no means unknown to me. My affection for his music, like much else, began in

Vienna. However, because I started conducting opera relatively late in my musical career, even today there are certain works by Verdi that I have never conducted. Besides, I am not one of those conductors who want to master a composer's entire oeuvre. I never conduct Verdi's early operas—with one exception: I performed *Jérusalem*, the French adaptation of *I Lombardi alla prima crociata*, in Vienna, and in 2001, the Verdi Year, I gave a guest performance of the same production with the Vienna Philharmonic at La Scala in Milan. *Jérusalem* can only be sung in French—anything else would be absurd—which is why this opera cannot be included in a repertoire. If any of the singers were absent, it would be extremely difficult to find a replacement. Besides, the Verdi that I really want to perform someday is *Simon Boccanegra*.

Naturally, I have conducted Verdi's Requiem many times and with great enjoyment. My first time was in Montreal. Since then it has almost been a leitmotif in my fifty-year conducting career.

I had been looking forward to the new *Ring* in Herbert Wernicke's production, but after he died suddenly, David Alden took over. Hans-Peter Lehmann was kind enough to produce the semi-finished *Die Walküre* according to Wernicke's overall concept, and a year later it was produced again under David Alden's direction.

In 2004 there was finally a new production of Wagner's *Die Meistersinger von Nürnberg*. The old version had been performed for so long that it was overdue for some radical changes. With this the Munich Opera had produced eight new versions of Wagner operas within just a few years, a more than respectable achievement for everyone involved.

I am often asked about the extent of my influence on directorial concepts. I think my role in this respect is greatly overestimated. Certainly, in the beginning we discuss things, we look at various models, and the director explains what he has in mind. Models are small, and it's easy to get things to work right with them, but doing the same things with full-sized sets, props, and people is often a very different matter. I am considered rather conservative, though I don't think that's really true since I am very open to new things. But there are concepts and ideas that I do not take to very easily. At the very least, I like to ascertain that there is always some logic behind what we perform. I was very happy and satisfied with some of the productions in Munich, but there were also some with which I didn't agree at all.

I have always been a fan of Berlioz and waited all my life to do his opera *Les Troyens*. Finally I got my chance to conduct it in Munich. Peter Jonas had a lot to do with twisting my arm till I finally accepted. Before the premiere my friend Daniel Barenboim offered to let me conduct a concert performance of it in Chicago. He probably thought the practice would be good for me, and as it turned out, he was right.

Among my most beautiful memories from Munich is the premiere of Aribert Reimann's opera *Bernarda Albas Haus*. I have said again and again that I am very interested in performing contemporary music, and that includes operas. I had known Federico García Lorca's play for a long time, having seen it in London, and even before I signed the contract with Munich I knew that I wanted to conduct the premiere of this opera.

During our sessions with the score, I got to know Reimann personally and developed the greatest respect for his abilities. He is a musician through and through, and he knows his own music. This is not always the case; I have come across composers who don't even know the tempi of their own music till they consult their own markings.

I received Reimann's score six months before the premiere, which was scheduled for October 30, 2000, in Munich. I had six months to study it, which I did wherever and whenever I could. It is impossible to prepare something like this at one go, but one cannot work at it day after day either. The study of a score can only progress gradually. The musicians have to sit down together, and any difficulties in comprehension have to be resolved before one can move on. One must always recapitulate what the composer wants and where he wants to take the audience. This was the primary aim of my efforts—along with a thorough study of the text. It is of vital importance to understand how the composer has interpreted the text musically in order to grasp the new work in its entirety and eventually to present it to the audience coherently and credibly. And there are some details that can be completely understood only in rehearsal.

This score is so dissonant that I cannot hear the music in my head by simply looking at the sheet music, and I presume that nobody else can either. Occasionally I am also confronted with some puzzles that I have to solve for myself before I can work on the piece with the orchestra. Sometimes during a theoretical study one can head off in the wrong direction. Then one has to review what one thought had already been cleared.

The orchestra Reimann called for was very unusual. There were four pianos, two of which were prepared. Objects were placed between the strings to create a rather ugly sound. Paper was also placed between the strings, producing a harpsichordlike sound. Sometimes the pianist had to get up and pluck a string. And there were twelve cellos, woodwinds, brass, and percussion—but no violins, violas, or basses. The four pianists were Klaus Sallmann, Massimiliano Murrali, Donald Wages, and Nobuko Nishimura-Finkentey. Reimann, an excellent pianist himself, helped out a lot. I had many rehearsals with just the pianists or cellists before the whole orchestra played together.

It was an extremely exciting task. Reimann filled me with enthusiasm. Working with Harry Kupfer, the director, was also wonderful, and I was immediately convinced by his ideas, in particular the prisonlike main scene. The audience responded well to the premiere. Its demands didn't elicit any booing, and in any case audiences today generally do not boo the music anymore, unlike in Stravinsky's time, when they pelted the composer with tomatoes during a performance of *The Rite of Spring*.

For the last new production I was to head as the general music director of the Munich Opera House, I chose Arnold Schoenberg's *Moses und Aron*. This magnum opus, staged by David Pountney, was my and Sir Peter's farewell premiere in Munich. Schoenberg had begun to treat biblical material long before 1930, when he began working on the opera. Two years later he concluded it with the end of the second act. He planned to set the third act to music, too, but the work remained unfinished. The first staged performance took place in 1957, six years after Schoenberg's death. For me this production was yet another opportunity to thank my teacher Hans Swarowsky, who led me to Schoenberg very early in my musical career. The performance also came full circle from the Second Viennese School to Munich. It was a happy end to my tenure.

I hope that I will always have opportunities to come back to Munich. A close relationship has grown up between the Bavarian State Orchestra and me in the course of our musical collaboration, and whenever I think about eventually parting from this house and its musicians, a slight melancholy comes over me. We went on four great tours together, twice to Japan and twice through Europe. Nothing binds musicians together so well as tours like this, where people depend on each other much more than in the normal work routine. They spend a lot of time in relatively close proximity to each other. Although our last journey together, in December 2005—the trip to India—lasted only four days, we will all remember it forever, and not only because of the music. It was certainly a great strain to undertake so much in such a short time, but it forged a deep human bond between us. Nancy and I were also very happy to have offered all our musicians and colleagues a little taste of India.

My ties with Munich are many, be they with the opera house or with the Munich Philharmonic, of which I was appointed honorary conductor in 2004. It was an important mark of distinction that made me very happy. Imagine my joy when the Bavarian State Orchestra, with which I spent eight sublime years, gave Nancy and me a party at which I was made their honorary conductor and presented with a wonderful commemorative ring.

I don't know whether I should mention other honors conferred on me. It would be rather like taking stock of my career, and I don't really want to get into that here. But maybe to end the story of my tenure at the Munich Opera I should mention that in the fall of 2005 I was presented the Bavarian Distinguished Service Cross by the minister-president of Bavaria, Edmund Stoiber, and, later, the Order of Maximilian by his successor, Günther Beckstein.

I have many plans for the future. I will continue to be involved in those places that have determined the course of my life for decades: Israel, Florence, Vienna, and now Munich and Valencia. I feel nostalgic whenever I think of my departure. At the same time, even though my appointment book is completely full for the next several years, I can finally proclaim, with a feeling of gratitude, "I'm free as a bird again!"

INDEX